SOUTHERN MERCY

Empire and American Civilization in Juvenile Reform, 1890–1944

Mercy, like punishment, expresses a nation's core values: its hopes, fears, and politics of rule. *Southern Mercy* makes a case for the use of juvenile judicial discretion as a "civilizing" strategy of Southern white progressives as they sought to situate themselves within the imperial politics of American nation-building and to preserve their regional identity in a post–Civil War industrializing South. In the late nineteenth and early-to-mid twentieth centuries, New South advocates helped to secure their regional affiliation with the American empire through spectacles of mercy, variously racialized, gendered, and linked to sexuality, and keyed to the South's own subordinate status within national US politics.

In *Southern Mercy* Annette Louise Bickford uses the example of juvenile reformatories in North Carolina to examine how mercy is related to Southern modernity, and how both are related to liberal humanism. The book is organized around analyses of restricted archival records of juvenile reformatory racial policies as well as historical examples, including a show trial involving white girls who faced the electric chair for the capital crime of arson, negotiations for state funding for the sexual reformation of "wayward" Black girls, and a reformatory mandated to protect Black boys from lynch mobs. A transdisciplinary study in critical race studies, postcolonial studies, anthropology, and criminal justice history, *Southern Mercy* explores how reform efforts and shifting interpretations of civilized mercy in the New South modified punishment in ways that actually strengthened existing stereotypes and biases, and were crucial to the reinscription of white Americanism in the post-emancipation twentieth-century liberal-humanist context.

ANNETTE LOUISE BICKFORD is an assistant professor in the Department of Social Science at York University.

ANNETTE LOUISE BICKFORD

Southern Mercy

Empire and American Civilization in Juvenile Reform, 1890–1944

UNIVERSITY OF TORONTO PRESS
Toronto Buffalo London

© University of Toronto Press 2016
Toronto Buffalo London
www.utppublishing.com
Printed in the U.S.A.

ISBN 978-1-4426-4574-5 (cloth)   ISBN 978-1-4426-1398-0 (paper)

∞ Printed on acid-free, 100% post-consumer recycled paper with
vegetable-based inks.

Library and Archives Canada Cataloguing in Publication

Bickford, Annette Louise, 1964–, author
Southern mercy : empire and American civilization in
juvenile reform, 1890–1944 / Annette Louise Bickford.

Includes bibliographical references and index.
ISBN 978-1-4426-4574-5 (cloth).–ISBN 978-1-4426-1398-0 (paper)

1. Reformatories–North Carolina–History–19th century–Case
studies. 2. Reformatories–North Carolina–History–20th century–
Case studies. 3. Juvenile delinquents–Rehabilitation–North Carolina–
History–19th century–Case studies. 4. Juvenile delinquents–
Rehabilitation–North Carolina–History–20th century–Case studies.
5. Racism–North Carolina–History–19th century–Case studies.
6. Racism–North Carolina–History–20th century–Case studies.
7. North Carolina–Race relations–History–19th century–Case studies.
8. North Carolina–Race relations–History–20th century–Case studies.
I. Title.

HV9105.N9B52 2016   364.3609756   C2016-905196-X

University of Toronto Press acknowledges the financial assistance to its
publishing program of the Canada Council for the Arts and the Ontario
Arts Council, an agency of the Government of Ontario.

Canada Council   Conseil des Arts
for the Arts   du Canada

ONTARIO ARTS COUNCIL
CONSEIL DES ARTS DE L'ONTARIO
an Ontario government agency
un organisme du gouvernement de l'Ontario

Funded by the   Financé par le
Government   gouvernement
of Canada   du Canada

I am sustained by the love of my children.
This book is for Jane Scarlett and Gaelan.

Contents

Figures

Acknowledgments

The initial impetus for *Southern Mercy* came from a conversation around the table at a memorable dinner party. That evening marked the beginning of an exploration of a set of questions that intrigued me long enough to result in a book-length answer. I am grateful to Karen Anderson, dinner host and Associate Professor at York University, for her enthusiastic encouragement, her friendship, and her support of my first forays into this research.

Clear-sighted, patient, and supportive, Douglas Hildebrand, my editor at the University of Toronto Press, has been such a pleasure to work with. I pledge a debt of gratitude to my anonymous peer reviewers for their considered feedback, encouragement, and valuable suggestions. I thank managing editor Anne Laughlin, copyeditors Beth McAuley, John St. James, and Kathy Frost, and indexer Sergey Lobachev. I also wish to thank the LuEsther T. Mertz Library, New York Botanical Garden, for providing the image of what would become my book cover.

The archivists at the North Carolina State Department of Archives and History were enormously helpful, especially Earl James, Kim Andersen Cumber, Ian Dunn, Matthew Waehner, and A. Christopher Meekins. I thank Richard Rideout, Director of Youth Services, for gaining me access to restricted archival records and to the site and private archives of Samarcand Manor in Eagle Springs, North Carolina. I am grateful to Sterling E. Stevens, who generously allowed me to reprint his evocative photograph of the ruins of the Stonewall Jackson reformatory, and to Jo Huddleston, for sending me a number of photos of her grandmother, Felester Forrester, once committed to Samarcand Manor.

I am fortunate to be a faculty member of the Department of Social Science at York University, and to have colleagues who have all been wonderfully welcoming since my arrival in 2014. I am most grateful to Kean Birch, Amanda Glasbeek, Peggy Keall, Mark Peacock, Nalini Persram, Anna Pratt, Miriam Smith, Matt Tegelberg, Richard Wellen, and Kimberley White for their invaluable professional advice and support. Patricia Burke Wood, Diane Beelen Woody, Kate McPherson, and Brenda Spotton Visano have also been strong allies. I am grateful for financial support received from York University's Faculty of Liberal Arts and Professional Studies in 2016, and for a CUPE 3903 research grant in 2013.

Many have played a part in the development of this book, and I offer a preemptive apology to those I have neglected to acknowledge. I am indebted to those who so graciously allowed me to interview them, especially the late Maud Wells, and the many residents of numerous retirement homes in the Piedmont area.

I thank colleagues and friends who have supported me in my work at critical points along the way, including Himani Bannerji, Stéphane Beauroy, Gregor Bingham, John Broughton, Helene Cummins, Gordon Darroch, Tammy George, Pearl Goodman, Michael Hardt, Douglas Hay, Jan Hill, Ed Hore, Lou Kontos, Christopher Kyriakides, Neil Mclaughlin, Susan Pearson, Charlie Rathburn, Michael Redhill, Ashraf Rushdy, Kelvin Sealey, Penni Stewart, Carolyn Strange, Johanna Schoen, Victor Streib, Jane Toswell, Andrea Townsend-Nicholson, Jim Turk, Mariana Valverde, Alexander Verbeek, Perla Weinstock, Lorne Wolk. I would like to thank Michael Levin, now Associate Professor Emeritus in Anthropology at the University of Toronto, whose friendship and monthly discussions over lunch on the book's progress kept me on track. The late Jane Ryan was always there, checking in and cheering me on. With great patience and generosity, Sal Trapani, Professor at Western Connecticut State University, read chapter drafts before they were coherent. I am grateful to William Westbrook for reading and extensively commenting on early chapter drafts, and for making me laugh the hardest. Many thanks to Dipankar Gupta, Professor at Shiv Nadar University, who was there at the finish, helping me to sharpen my critique. I also thank the National Ballet of Canada's Elisabeth Leyds-Holmes for years of demanding ballet classes that let me forget everything for a while and fly.

Others contributed to the monograph in crucial ways. I am particularly grateful to Kathy Frost for so generously keeping vigil through a long night of final edits, for her always perceptive insights, her indefatigable encouragement, and her unrivalled wit. Her friendship is a treasure. Anne Russell graciously shared her archival material on Samarcand Manor, and offered valuable suggestions on chapter drafts. I am grateful to Meg Fox for her enthusiastic support of this book, her discerning editing, and for always being game for midnight swims at the lake. A quintessential academic and cherished friend, Kathryn Pauly Morgan, Professor Emeritus at the University of Toronto, has supported my career enormously. I owe her very special thanks, knowing how very fortunate I have been to have her in my life. This book is deeply indebted to her mentoring, and to her friendship.

I come last to those who come first. My parents, Jane and Sam, instilled in me deep political conviction and intellectual curiosity that I am delighted to now see in my own children. My grandfather, Allen Stainback, engendered my interest in Southern history. I am grateful to my siblings Mary, Bobby, Suzie, Richard, Arthur, John, and Christopher for their abiding encouragement. My brother Bobby, especially, has been my anchor during the writing of this book, extending wise counsel at every turn, and feeding my soul with frequent excerpts from his own profoundly beautiful writing. My beloved children, Jane Scarlett and Gaelan Ash, have supported my long preoccupation with this book with incredible patience and generosity, and I dedicate this book to them.

SOUTHERN MERCY

Empire and American Civilization in
Juvenile Reform, 1890–1944

Introduction

A mere lynching, without special tortures, is regarded down there as a lemon-ady sport for women and children.

H.L. Mencken, 1921[1]

> The quality of mercy is not strain'd,
> It droppeth as the gentle rain from heaven
> Upon the place beneath. It is twice blest:
> It blesseth him that gives and him that takes.

Shakespeare, *Merchant of Venice*

Just after midnight on 20 August 1930, two hundred masked white men stormed North Carolina's Edgecombe County Jail, seizing Oliver Moore, a twenty-nine-year-old field hand held on charges of attempted rape of two white girls – five-year-old Ethel Morgan and her seven-year-old sister Lucille. Presumably, it was their mother who had discovered both had virulent cases of gonorrhoea. In a motorcade of fifty unplated cars, the mob drove Moore six miles over the county line and lynched him. At dawn, his body was found swinging from the limb of a pine tree, riddled with bullets, his arms tied to a plough-line. The Raleigh *News and Observer* reported that "whole families came together, mothers and fathers bringing even their youngest children. It was the show of the countryside – a very popular show." Amid the raucous joking, "girls giggled as the flies fed on the blood that dripped from the Negro's nose."[2] Dr Curtis Norfleet, the physician who examined the children, may have doubted Moore's guilt, admitting that this was the first time he had ever seen such a virulent case of gonorrhoea develop in just three days' time. The preliminary trial court requested a test, but the likely guilty father who had made the initial accusation against Moore was never tested and, as it turned out, neither was Moore, until after his execution. The attending physician explained that he "just failed to get around to make an examination."[3] Governor Gardner ordered an investigation, and pathology test results on Moore's body came back negative for gonorrhoea.[4] The North Carolina press widely censured Moore's murder as a "surprise sortie against law, order and civilization," and in his recollection of the event, historian Arthur Raper would lament, "North Carolina slips back."[5]

Chivalrous lynching came to be widely regarded as a crime against the honour of the nation, and many would come to reject it for generating social disorder that jeopardized capitalism and American global ascendancy. Setting itself apart from the rest of the South, North Carolina would, in 1922, take the lead to end formal lynchings as macabre rituals of honour-based vengeance. An influential group of white New South advocates mobilized for reform through such organizations as the American Social Science Association, a network of journals like the *Nation*, and the *Chicago Tribune*. They publically denounced reactionary forces such as the Ku Klux Klan for exposing them to Northern allegations of regional inferiority and primitivity.[6] Lynching photographs, once currency of racial pride, increasingly came to signify lawlessness and mercilessness, risking the South's – and the nation's – status as civilized. The Raleigh *News and Observer* published a photo of Oliver Moore's body on 20 August 1930, and faced a storm of public criticism.[7]

The National Negro Business League implored Governor Gardner to "curb the forces of lawlessness and bring to justice the perpetrators of Moore's murder." Gardner, vacationing at the time of the lynching, denounced it for bringing disgrace to North Carolina, and offered a $400 reward for the identification of the perpetrators, who, in the end, received immunity. The three police officers on duty at the Tarboro jail the night of Moore's murder all claimed to have known nothing until it was too late. Launching its own investigation, the National Association for the Advancement of Colored People (NAACP) secured evidence of the identities of several of the members of the mob; but fearing retaliation, their witness retracted. Governor Gardner declined a bid from the Home Detective Company of Greensboro to verify the mob leaders, and in time, the state closed the investigation. Many local officials and white citizens tacitly accepted the incident as "legally awful, personally admirable." Editorials in popular daily newspapers expressed concern over outside criticism and "the State's shame" in this "reversion to the primitive in man." A county official admitted, "I hate that this thing occurred on account of the criticism it has brought."[8]

Many regarded the South as a spectacle of otherness in a stagnant region, and Southern whites, as aberrant, a "degraded Anglo-Saxon stock" in need of colonial rehabilitation. During the 1920s, eugenicists like H.H. Laughlin attributed social ills, from "feeblemindedness" to alcoholism and tuberculosis, to racial degeneracy. In 1935, attorney T.N. Jones wrote, "In the South, there is more abject poverty and illiteracy than in any other country on earth in which a high state of civilization is supposed to exist. The squalid condition of the cotton raisers of the South is a disgrace to all Southern people." In 1937 H.L. Mencken described Southern living conditions as a "ghastly spectacle." Drawing parallels with the Balkans, China, Asia Minor, and Serbia, he claimed the region "lacked American attributes and values."[9] Public intellectual George Schuyler echoed this, arguing, "There was hope at one time that the cracker might become one of the vanishing races like the Maoris and Tahitians ... I doubt that his basic nature can be changed by these heroic efforts in his behalf and at our expense."[10]

The South's place in the nation depended upon the "civilized" (lawful and merciful) salvaging of the racial "fitness" of poor whites, because fictional narratives of evolutionary ascendancy underpinned US imperialism. In keeping with C. Alexander McElway, who declared cotton mill workers to be of the "purest American stock," reformer Walter Hines Page led the North Carolina Hookworm Campaign, claiming in 1912 that pellagra was the true cause of indolence among poor whites; one could be eradicated with the other. Page wrote: "The Southern white people are of almost pure English stock. It has been hard to explain their backwardness, for they are descended from capable ancestors and inhabit a rich land ... all these wretched and a burden, not by any necessity of heredity or by any wilful defect of character, but because they are sick."[11]

Despite a longstanding Southern repudiation of Northerners as culturally base and pecuniary, many Southern whites found themselves increasingly compelled to defend their own capacity for civilization after the Civil War. C. Vann Woodward observed that the South "suffered from a prevailing sense of inferiority, and a constant need for justifying a position." Deriding the South had become a national pastime after Reconstruction, reaching its height in the first decade of the twentieth century, and lending urgency to the most intensive wave of reform from 1900 to 1914. Efforts around sectional reunion at the height of American imperialism were not coincidental.[12] The South struggled with its semi-colonial position. Well into the twentieth century, Northern public opinion frequently maligned the region as atavistic. In his popular 1920 caricature of the South, "The Sahara of the Bozart," H.L. Mencken wrote that for "all the 'progress' it babbles of, it is almost as sterile, artistically, intellectually, culturally, as the Sahara Desert … It would be impossible in all history to match so complete a drying-up of a civilization." In the 1930s, Franklin D. Roosevelt identified the South as "the nation's number one economic problem." While North Carolina prided itself on its progressivism, it shared regional economic under-development with the rest of the South. Dependent upon Northern financiers, and sensitive to Northern charges of Southern barbarism, white progressives understood that defining the South's cultural place in the nation state was linked to its economic recovery. Regional semi-colonial status drove modernist New South advocates to seek national belonging with hopes of sharing in national wealth through the rejuvenation of the region's status as "civilized."[13]

As a transdisciplinary study in critical race studies, postcolonial studies, anthropology, and criminal justice history, this book explores ways in which shifting interpretations of civilized mercy in the New South modified punishment in ways that actually strengthened the ubiquity of the racist épistème under liberal humanism. In a region with the country's highest historical national homicide rates – almost double those of New England – a disparity consistent since at least the nineteenth century, when recordkeeping began, ethnographic histories have focused on punishment. But as Carolyn Strange has noted, merciful restraint, as a technology of governmentality, is as complicated in its reasons as punishment. In keeping with Strange, and with Michel Foucault, I examine mercy as a technique involving complex political and social functions.[14]

Christian tradition emphasizes mercy, especially in the New Testament, where Jesus identifies it as a generous and gratuitous gift in the parable of the Prodigal Son (Luke 15:11–32). Biblically, it is implied that the merciful will obtain mercy (The Beatitudes, Matthew 5:7). In the strict legal sense, mercy refers to clemency from execution extended to one convicted of a capital crime. The pardon has partly functioned to strengthen the legitimacy of the social order and legal system, infusing it with virtue.[15] I use the concept much more loosely, as lawful restraint motivated by, but not synonymous with, kindness as a perceived marker of "civilization" and sympathetic civic duty, often extended to "deserving" recipients. The expansion of formal justice in the American

South focused on ethical debates about merciful civility more than legal precedent.[16] One of my arguments throughout the book is that in the late nineteenth and early-to-mid-twentieth centuries, New South advocates helped to secure their regional affiliation with the American empire through the showcasing of "civilized" mercies, variously racialized, gendered, and linked to sexuality. The American South's status within national politics and the reinscription of white Americanism in the post-emancipation twentieth century liberal-humanist context depended upon spectacles of mercy.

Working-class whites became central to concerns about racial degeneration and disability *within* constructs of whiteness. Signifying ritual pollution, disease, corruption, and "savage" libidinal energies, poor whites had presumably become "unlike [their] race." This uncertainty about their true evolutionary status invited questions about the South's place in the nation, inspiring reformers to "restore" whiteness to poor whites through eugenics and civic "uplift." Challenges to poor whites' claims to whiteness exposed the instability and inaccuracy of "race," and of colour as a racial marker.

The Southern white working class threatened the status of North Carolina's white middle class, many of whom feared the spread of degeneracy. Coming to fruition in the Progressive Era (1890–1920), the idea of the South as a retrograde space alarmed concerned Northerners who espoused, indeed, had battled for, American socio-political, and economic imperial ascendancy as a eugenically fit and unified nation. The North's main objective in the Civil War was to preserve the Union, and this directive persisted after Reconstruction. Especially under Jim Crow, the idea of an atavistic white race threatening to infect the national body politic, jeopardized American claims to imperial ascendancy, even into the era of American isolationism, when the nation's imperialism took on new forms. American empire was not a transitory, contained project. With their anti-imperialist stance, interwar isolationist progressives advocated white Americanism, promoting this national citizenship as a safeguard against African, rather than British, empire. Attended by new recognition of global issues of public health and education, nation building developed into the interwar period as a racialized project carried out through merciful, "civilized" reform.[17]

I use four historical examples of juvenile reformatories established in North Carolina between 1891 and 1923 to explore interconnections between mercy, Southern modernity, race, gender, and liberal humanism: The Stonewall Jackson Manual Training and Industrial School [for white boys] (1907), the State Industrial School at Samarcand [for white girls] (1918), the Morrison Training School [for boys of African descent] (1921), and the State Training School for Negro Girls at Efland (1926). Segregated by race and gender, these institutions represent systems of merciful discipline linked to a range of effects that cannot be accounted for by law enforcement alone. I am interested in the exercise of productive power through merciful uplift in juvenile reformatories, where the state management of bodies, inclinations, and character furnished a foundation for racialized national belonging and governance.[18] Nascent discourses of responsibilization, which blamed working-class whites for poverty and for social disorder, lead not in a straight line to, but are in the groundwater of today's neoliberal prescriptives. How did reformers, working to consolidate the regulatory state, secure white Americanism and sectional reunion through the intimate sites of sexual regulation and benevolent moral uplift? How did new forms of discipline in segregated juvenile reform institutions figure in the making of racial categories and in the development of the modern liberal state in North Carolina between 1890 and 1944? What place would the Black population and poor whites have in the American nation? As citizen-building ventures with a merciful mandate, juvenile reform institutions demonstrated North Carolina's commitment to "civilization" through lawful, benevolent discipline, especially in the case of criminalized Black boys protected from extralegal lynching. In addition, civic uplift served as a biopolitical tool of state racism, indoctrinating white working-class children into racialized Americanism as patriotic, compliant labourers. Biopolitical technologies of governance emerged with liberalism in a shift away from sovereign power. They exercised political power over human populations biologically, through bodies, and socially, through subjective selves. Foucault has argued that biopolitics manages the major life processes of populations and "deals with the population ... as political problem, as a problem that is at once scientific and political, as a biological problem and as power's problem."[19] As biopolitical tools of state racism, Jim Crow reform institutions extended liberal humanist mercy that simultaneously fed non-compassionate racialization, defining America, with implications for our current state of supposed "post-raciality."

Collective Identities

As Douglas Hay has argued, the way a nation – or region – punishes indicates much about how its citizens define themselves as a certain kind of people, their collective values, and their fears.[20] Southern spectacles of sovereign rule – the convict lease (often lethal, contracted prison labour, popular between 1865 and 1940), a history of plantation slavery (a nascent biopolitical experiment, emblematic of the state of exception), and Klan supporters' penchant for neo-medieval, honour-based lynching – conveyed white anxieties about racial "amalgamation." These practices offended Northern middle class sensibilities, jeopardizing the South's place in the nation at a time when evolutionary anthropologists perceived the world as comprising either "civilized" or "barbaric" lands.[21]

As an eighteenth-century strategy to sidestep severe penalties, the "prerogative of mercy" sometimes spared the convicted from the death penalty, while exempting juveniles. The common law defence of infancy was an effective technique justifying legal discretion protecting youth from the harshest retribution. Many celebrated the move to mercy in North Carolina as a hallmark of juvenile reform. In fact, a sentimental call to rescue white boys from the lethal convict lease inspired North Carolina's first juvenile reformatory. The Raleigh *News and Observer* reported that moral suasion was the preferred method: "And while there is splendid discipline, it is not enforced discipline, but the sort that come from the desire to do what is right because it is right and out of regard for those in authority."[22] Middle class reformers and state administrators governed with the conviction that a civilized response to minors' transgressions included extended court commitments to reform institutions for lengthy programs of normalization based on moral suasion rather than corporal punishment. Through an imagined epistemological shift in subjectivity, New South modernists believed they had the capacity to love their children more sentimentally through extended, protected childhoods. While progressive reformers rejected corporal punishment as antiquated in theory, reactionary anti-modernists openly endorsed an authoritarian approach. Like liberal progressives, they were interested in civic uplift and moral regulation. Feeling an obligation to "patrol the moral standards of the populace," they promoted moral clean-ups to strengthen national integrity. Just as progressives engaged in moral panics over "the amatory and erotic tendencies of modern degeneracy," Klan supporters complained that modern children were developing impertinent characters as a result of petting parties and suggestive fashions for girls.[23] Progressive modernists and anti-modernist Klan supporters also shared racism in common, but sought white supremacy through oppositional (legal and extra-legal) means. They differed over which methods best reflected a "civilized" polity.

Mercy and severity are, for Carolyn Strange, "incomprehensible outside their cultural and political logics." There is, she argues, no ontologically stable category of "goodness," and in fact, we can trace shifts in penal culture by examining popular meanings attributed to various rationales for punishment. In penal debates, people assess sanctions as just and civil (or not) against culturally and historically specific conventions. Different forms of punishment carry many possible meanings relative to historically specific definitions of what is "civilized" and "uncivilized."[24] Modifications in punishment as a response to humanitarian sentiment are but one element of an intricate set of concerns "ranging from commercial and administrative to the pragmatic and expedient."[25] Moral regulation studies attribute the rise of the American juvenile reformatory movement in New England to social issues arising from urban life and capitalist industrialization, but North Carolina's juvenile reform institutions emerged in the absence of a strong industrial capitalist base. While Northern progressives attributed social problems such as prostitution, poverty, disease, and labour unrest to rapid urban and industrial growth, North Carolina remained largely rural and was notable for its relatively quiescent, nonunionized labour force. Unlike their Northern counterparts, North Carolinian progressive reformers worked within a context of regional economic underdevelopment and a relative lack of industrialism, a recent history of mercantile rather than industrial capitalism, and a tradition of local republicanism that curtailed state powers. North Carolina's juvenile reformatory movement can only be effectively analysed with attention to its locally specific political and socio-economic context. While the juvenile reformatory movement in North Carolina borrowed heavily from Northern models, the biopolitical state emerged as a response to a different, locally specific set of conditions, among them, the legacy of Reconstruction.

Reconstruction

The Civil War launched a revolution that dismantled formal slavery, and, for a time, interrupted the established power of the planter class. Lincoln's Emancipation Proclamation effectively launched the largest uncompensated seizure of property in American history. In an unprecedented move, Congress challenged the Takings Clause of the Fifth Amendment (which prohibits the uncompensated public expropriation of private property), wiping out almost half the value of all Southern assets, or about $3 trillion USD (2016).[26]

White Southerners would come to occupy a distinctive positionality as both semi-colonized and colonizers. The South's economic subordination (involving a weak labour force, production of raw materials, and dependence on Northern financiers), along with its military defeat, occupation, and readjustment, resonated with the classic colonialism of the Global South. Even when it did not operate as a strictly dependent market, many perceived the South to be a racially aberrant geographical space, and its dependency on Northern infusions of capital functioned as colonial within the context of imperial modernity.[27]

The 1870s Depression debilitated the South more profoundly than other regions in the United States. With the decline of tobacco, sugar, and rice production, and the depreciation of the value of cotton by almost half between 1872 and 1877, Black and white farmers spiralled into poverty. In 1880, Southern per capita income was barely one third of the national average, and the total value of the South's agricultural and industrial output was lower than it had been a decade before. Merchants faced bankruptcy as credit dried up. While the South foundered economically, a manufacturing boom in the North enabled it to complete the nationalizing railroad network, and consolidate a capitalist industrial economy.[28]

Confederate defeat compounded economic dependency with allegations of failed nationalism and a crisis in masculinity, where nationhood stood for manly virtue and protection. Popular stories parodied the Civil War and reconciliation as a lovers' spat, the reunion of a Southern wife with her Northern captain. Confederate soldiers, disgraced by their failure to protect the South from Northern defeat, displaced their resentment of "Yankee" invasion and shame of feminization onto various groups of racialized others. This transpired in pursuits of masculine militarism, such as the rape-lynch syndrome in their own region, and through wider, national ventures, like "Indian killing," as part of popular imperialism and Westward expansion. Ian Hartman has argued that nation-wide participation in the militaristic subjugation of the Plains Indians furnished a basis for the ideological alliance of Southern white supremacy and Northern pride in the political and economic might of the Union. By 1890, the combination of industrialization and capitalist expansion with American military victories in the Mexican War,

Civil War, Indian wars, and Spanish-American War, had mobilized the Union as a formidable global power.[29]

Romanticized and minimized as "settlement" rather than conquest, this genocidal expansionism contributed to the "myth of the essential white American," in what Benedict Anderson has called the "imagined community." Here, national identity developed as a matter of racially hierarchal, rather than simply political, sovereignty.[30] Alon Confino and Benedict Anderson have shown that national identity excludes other nations, presenting an ostensibly homogeneous "deep, horizontal comradeship" of disparate groups that overshadows actual exploitation and structural inequalities based on class, race, and so on.[31] Forged through popular imperialism and displacement or genocide of indigenous peoples, then, a re-narrated white Americanism was already beginning to form in the late nineteenth century.

Free Labour

The federal government supported free labour as the foundation of its industrial economy, drawing Southern labour into alignment with capitalist Northern interests. News of Klan-based efforts to thwart free labour by rescinding Black Constitutional rights provoked Northern indignation, resulting in a period of constitutional dictatorship through federal military occupation of the South. This peaked in 1866–7, threatening the South's readmission into the Union and representation in Congress. The Freedman's Bureau oversaw enfranchisement, and in 1868, motivated, in part, by a directive to secure free labour, Congress approved the Fourteenth Amendment, a Reconstruction Amendment that addressed national citizenship rights and equal protection of the laws.[32] Officially free, but landless, Blacks had little choice but to return to the plantations to work under the tyrannical rule of former masters.[33]

Defining America

Despite the American rhetoric of "one people," narratives of national identity were in a liminal state. Discourses of reunification were socially, linguistically, and culturally disparate, and uncoordinated. A multiplicity of voices, among them, white professionals, intellectuals, merchants, railroad promoters, and bankers, freedmen and women, Black and white women's groups, indigenous groups, as well as Black and white veterans, labour organizations and Republican supporters of Reconstruction, competed to define America though issues ranging from white supremacy and the racialization of patriotism, militarism, imperialism, and regional autonomy, to social justice, including anti-imperialist, antiracist, and emancipation claims.[34]

Black political conviction, organization, and patriotism thrived during Radical Reconstruction, and between 1864 and 1867, political participation and leadership expanded through state-wide conventions held in North Carolina and throughout the South. One resolution proclaimed that America was "now our country – made emphatically so by the blood of our brethren." While most white Americans would abandon the grand narrative of emancipation, the period between Reconstruction and Jim Crow was a time when radical emancipatory discourses came to fruition. Mobilized in part by the "meteoric rise of the Union League," Black leaders further politicized the church, and education, drilling self-defence militias, and organizing labour companies in the 1870s. During Reconstruction, men of African descent exercised political power as Republican Party leaders, legislators, magistrates, justices of the peace, and jury members.[35]

Some local leagues organized trans-racial labour solidarity during Reconstruction. Before the withdrawal of federal troops in 1877, Republican Party biracial government functioned in parts of the South, despite white domination of politics. This, and local leagues' growing labour solidarity across race threatened Southern planters, Northern industrialists, and Western railroad owners, who responded by pushing for shifts in the accepted currency of debate. By the 1873 Depression, a conservative sentiment had crept even into Republican circles, and emancipation claims capitulated under persistent structural inequality. By 1877 the Republican Party had changed. Finding themselves increasingly sympathetic to conservative Democratic criticisms of Southern government, Northern Republicans widely lost interest in Reconstruction, agreeing to pull out as financiers, industrialists, and merchants mobilized to obstruct trans-racial labour solidarity. Reconstruction had become a serious threat to capitalist interests. Like their Northern counterparts, white Southern Republicans (including many social reformers) advocated wage reduction, increased discipline of labour, and union-busting. Although they had contributed to the Reconstruction acts and amendments, they now believed that the nation had done enough for Blacks, and North Carolina, along with most of the rest of the South, became increasingly unwilling to ensure Black rights. Federal troops were reassigned to strikebreaking in the North, instead of redistributing Southern property in the name of emancipation.[36]

The industrial system required free labour. As a post-bellum penal labour system that effectively renewed slavery, the brutal convict lease fell out of favour in North Carolina with the rise of corrective detention, which refocused on the body, developing it as a mercifully subjected and useful force. North Carolina juvenile reformatories employed merciful disciplinary techniques to train wayward working-class youth to be compliant, hard-working and patriotic.[37]

National Amnesia

While huge numbers of American Blacks had allied with antebellum Abolitionists to resist slavery, emancipation claims were mostly unfulfilled and undone, diluted to present-day renditions. Radicals like Charles Sumner fought for the Civil Rights Acts of 1866 and 1875, but restoration of the Union, having been the primary objective of the war effort, would take precedence over emancipation claims, which would disappear from public memory. As liberal interpretations of freedom supplanted Republican calls for positive entitlements like equal protection of the laws, white popular culture redefined emancipation in a truncated way, as simply the absence of constraint under slavery. Shifting responsibility, white leaders advised Blacks that they might some day become "worthy and respected citizens of this great nation" through their own exertion, notably, not self-directed, but always guided by "wise counsel." "The attainment of freedom," as Hartman has noted, "depended upon the efforts of the freed themselves."[38] Such discourses of responsibilization were very much in keeping with the conservativism Booker T. Washington would espouse in the post-Redemption South. Black servitude and economic self-help would be reincorporated into the emancipatory narrative of mercy, involving an interpretation of freedom as a "gift" bestowed on the weak, establishing indebtedness and moral obligation of the freed to their "benefactors."[39]

Wilmington Coup d'État

In 1883 the Supreme Court declared the Civil Rights Act of 1875 unconstitutional and in 1896 the Supreme Court would support the introduction of Jim Crow segregation. Conservative Democratic Party reactions to "Negro domination" precipitated race wars and Klan-based terror campaigns like the Wilmington Coup d'État of 1898, which exemplified precedence of "the people" over citizenship rights.

With a population of 10,000 in 1860, Wilmington, North Carolina was, by 1898, the largest city in the state, and Blacks formed the majority of its population. Wilmington's Republican Party had formed a biracial coalition, granting the franchise to emancipated men. Black residents served in the police force, the fire department, and in elected government positions.

Having lost power in North Carolina in 1894, white Democrats conspired to regain control of the government in the 1898 elections. Despite intimidation from organized terrorist militias of "Red Shirts," Republican voters elected a biracial city council and Fusionist white mayor to office in Wilmington on 8 November 1898. Two days after the election, armed white Democratic Party insurgents descended on Wilmington's city hall and overthrew the legitimately elected local government, forcing the removal of Black and white officials, running many out of town. The coup was the culmination of a race riot in which a mob of nearly 2,000 terrorized people and destroyed property in Black neighbourhoods, murdering an estimated ninety residents. They torched the offices of the *Daily Record*, North Carolina's only Black newspaper, razing the building. They took photographs of each other to mark the occasion. As the only coup d'état in US history, the Wilmington insurrection of 1898 precipitated a dramatic turn in post-Reconstruction politics in North Carolina. The event cemented white supremacist rule not just in Wilmington, but also in the region and the nation, ushering in racial segregation and Black disenfranchisement.

Forced to flee after the coup, at least 2100 residents left Wilmington permanently. The last nineteenth century Black congressperson from North Carolina was elected in 1896; a century would pass before another was elected. North Carolina Democrats passed numerous Jim Crow laws in 1899, and new voting restrictions further disenfranchised Blacks through a poll tax and literacy test, which violated the US Constitution under a veil of legality.[40] Disfranchisement of Black men in North Carolina effectively passed in 1901 through the constitutional amendment of 1900. State-sanctioned violence targeting people of African descent continues to the present day.[41]

The South's racist heritage persisted beyond slavery in the "regulatory power of a racist state obsessed with blood, sex, and procreation."[42] Imagined communities structure national political culture, partly defining national citizenship and belonging through an exclusionary focus on common memories. Developing between the Civil War and the First World War, a re-narration of the historical memory of emancipation forged a white racial alliance across class boundaries. Selective memory extinguished the legacy of emancipation, redefining America as a white republic. As Cecilia O'Leary has shown, national amnesia was already evident in turn-of-the-century official accounts of Civil War and Reconstruction history, which condemned Reconstruction for its "excesses," and downplayed emancipation. Seeking alliances through a national brotherhood, the Grand Army of the Republic turned a blind eye to the South's treasonous attack on the nation. During the First World War, and into the interwar period, white supremacist militaristic protection provided a common, racialized enemy for Northern and Southern whites, pushing aside emancipation claims for social equality. Reconciliation depended upon a regional and cross-class white alliance, because Confederate defeat had initially tied emancipation to the loss of Southern white racial control.[43]

Internal Colonialism

I situate this study within historical scholarship that contextualizes the American South within intersecting regional, national, and transnational relationships, discourses, and practices. I explore the development of liberal-humanist reform in the South as a response to Northern charges of Southern barbarism, projected against a backdrop of imperial modernity. While implications of colonial histories have been widely studied at a global level, I seek to chart locally specific ways in which North Carolina's state administrators and reformers applied elements of earlier colonial relations abroad to the intimate spaces of segregated juvenile reform institutions through internal colonialism in their own semi-colonial region.

As an analytical abstraction and metaphor, internal colonialism is about the domestic othering of racially or ethnically targeted groups within a sovereign state. Between the 1890s and the Second World War, civilizationist rhetoric extended back into the empire-state through imported colonialism, whereby moral reform linked North Carolina's emergent biopolitical state to the renewal of white Americanism. Reformers often viewed this character readjustment of wayward youth in the nation's "interior frontiers" as a microcosm of colonial instances abroad, borrowing strategies to unify the nation as a racially "fit" population. With reliance on the social sciences, the increasingly interventionist state, along with reformers who identified as missionaries, operationalized expert knowledge in public health, education, race relations, and agriculture to mercifully modernize the "rural sea" of the South to the national standard. The regulatory state, political liberalism, a corporate-capitalist economy, and global ascendancy had already been developing in the United States, and the South became an experiment in social change. Regulatory state-run juvenile reform institutions expedited North Carolina's alignment with Northern industrial capitalism through normalizing education – "teaching the task of intelligent living" – and public health initiatives.[44] Analyses of internal colonialism have typically overlooked the social-cultural effects of domination on private subjectivities. Normalizing efforts of juvenile courts and reformatories were meant to rejuvenate ostensibly depleted whiteness in poor whites. Families were sundered, their intimate bonds severed to establish new loyalties and "structures of feeling" aligned with white middle class values.[45] For instance, in 1927, the Raleigh *News and Observer*'s Susan Iden reported, "There is nothing that shows more convincingly, the change in the manners of the girls who have been at Samarcand for a few months than their humiliation at the behaviour of their relatives who come to visit them. It is also a time of siege, when the parents come determined to take their daughters home with them, and to escape the endless arguments, Miss MacNaughton has found it wise to absent herself from the institution on those occasions."[46] Samarcand's Superintendent, Agnes MacNaughton shamed young inmates and their families, calling visiting days a "nightmare." Pointing to the upholstered wicker furniture of the administration building parlour, she explained that for visits, held on the third Wednesday of each month, "We have to move out all of the furniture and bring in some of the chairs from the school building … After the first time or two that we tried to entertain the families of the girls in the parlor, we found chewing gum stuck on the chairs, pieces of cake and candy, fruit, and sandwiches beneath the cushions of the chairs and on the floor."[47] I examine what Ian Hacking has called, "making up people," and Foucault has identified as "constitution of the subject" in the racially laden classifications and treatment of young people in segregated state institutions. Juvenile reform was a critical nation building project to "build character," through the honing of new habits, accepted norms and loyalties, as a matter of patriotic duty. Exploring the intimate spaces of North Carolina history through which poor white children were reclaimed, sheds light on the usefulness of black, white, and indigenous youth in the defining of white Americanism.[48]

Civilizing Adolescence: The Role of the State

Forming a loose confederation of interest groups in North Carolinian social politics (including eugenics, interracial cooperation, mother's aid, education, child labour, and juvenile courts), progressive Black and white reformers mobilized around "the sin of the unprotected child."[49] The theme of "The [white] Child" emerged as a central focus in the early twentieth century, evidenced by the North Carolina Conference for Social Service, established in 1912 in the absence of government welfare services, as part of the Progressive reformers' sentimental concern for the welfare of children. The conference advocated prolonged childhood and the reclamation of wayward children by the state as a national resource of future citizens and workers. The conference advised the General Assembly, lobbying for the 1916 bill to establish county welfare offices.[50]

The capacity of the state to impose stricter morals policing grew exponentially in the early twentieth century, as white reformers made increasing demands for state support of reformatories and other regulatory schemes for social improvement. Scandalized by the conviction and imprisonment of young people, but wanting to root out the potential for white working-class resistance, North Carolina child-savers lobbied for legislation to establish the juvenile court and reformatories, which, discretionary by definition and mandated to "foster, nurture and cherish life," would offer a merciful, disciplinary alternative to adult justice. Finally established around the turn of the twentieth century, Southern reformatories emerged as significant penal reforms, and part of a complex apparatus aimed at youth: juvenile justice, welfare and public schools, age-of-consent laws, as well as the policing of parents' and children's conduct.[51] By the early twentieth century, the state amplified the regulatory efforts of families, communities, and churches, making unprecedented arrests for morals offences.[52]

As part of modernist social-purity campaigns, the reformatory movement in North Carolina was uniquely syncretic, reflecting both regional and national loyalties, fed by racial anxieties generated by persistent civilizationist rhetoric. Through state juvenile reformatories, North Carolina progressives invested in regional cultural capital through social engineering. Indeterminate sentences in reform institutions cost more than custodial options, but reflected positively on those who wished to present a "civilized" countenance for the nation and the world.

As part of the emergent biopolitical state, reformatory institutions managed life processes and reproductive capacities through eugenic sterilizations, and the provision of home-like environments that instilled white middle class standards of sexual propriety. This state intervention reordered the daily lives of boys and girls through new affective relationships that were neither familial nor compassionate.[53] Governing through habits and private subjectivities, with a new scientific focus on the purported causal relationship between "failed" family patterns and social disorder, reform institutions cultivated and trained racialized subjects, placing working-class white girls under particular scrutiny. Speaking to New York's state legislature in 1879, white reformer Josephine Lowell suggested, "There are two distinct and separate objects to be aimed at in dealing with these women: To reform them if possible, but if that cannot be done, at least to cut off the line of hereditary pauperism, crime and insanity, now transmitted mainly through them."[54] In her address at the National Conference for Social Work in Toronto (1924), state Commissioner of Public Welfare Kate Burr Johnson stated, "We must make people see that it is more economical and humane to give the predelinquent child such care and training as he needs than to continue to build institutions to care for delinquents ... Segregation and prevention of increase of the mentally defective is absolutely essential to the purification of our blood stream."[55] In keeping with Michel Foucault and Zygmunt Bauman, Stoler has argued that racism is not an aberrant offshoot, but an integral, formative feature of modernity, "deeply embedded in bourgeois liberalism."[56]

Defining "Civilization"

Seeking to redress its national alterity, and under the Northern gaze, Southern white modernists adopted prevailing Northern interpretations of civilization that linked humanism to constitutional law. Northern discourses of "civilization," grounded in *humanité* – merciful benevolence through a tender disposition to relieve all creatures in distress – eclipsed interpretations of civility grounded in Old South, honour-based *politesse*.[57] While Southern white anti-modernists rejected the adoption of Northern standards as threatening to their regional identity, New South advocates aligned themselves with conceptions of civilization as modern and grounded in *humanité*, with its adherence to the fairness rational objectivity promised. They encouraged lawful social stability through circumspection and self-restraint, instead of gruesome, honour-based lynchings. Show trials and other spectacles of *humanité* (including "legal lynchings") ostensibly demonstrated Southern white civilization, and its rightful place in the Union. The process was contested and uneven, as elements of politesse persisted syncretically. For instance, North Carolinian suffragettes complained that men who challenged them were unchivalrous, and many Southerners continued to dismiss Northerners as pecuniary and uncivilized for rejecting honour-based codes.[58]

This syncretic shift, of recuperation, and distillation of earlier discursive forms, hardly required fundamental changes in race rhetoric; scientific racism neatly rationalized old biases.[59] Many white reformers saw state expansion and legal justice as a way of reinscribing their Southern identities as civilized, folding *humanité* into it, while attenuating certain antimodernist parts of the chivalric code, such as extralegal vigilantism and antiquated forms of corporal punishment. The North Carolinian reformatory movement relied upon the juvenile court to apply humanitarian techniques of rational discipline within reform institutions, as a civilized practice.

Nationalist Passions

The discursive shift linking civilization and *humanité* involved the expansion of state regulatory power and a commitment to building national identity on the ideals of citizenship based on inviolable rights – ideally, culture-blind constitutional law and liberties. Citizenship-based rights, which modern polities strove to uphold, were in tension with vengeful protectionism of "the people." Modernist Republicans rejected notions of blood, soil, and the passion of the *ancien régime*, increasingly interpreting the violence of lynching as evidence of barbarism. Proponents of legal and extralegal justice vied for the power to impose their own visions of order, gradually defining themselves in opposition to each other. Noteworthy here is Giorgio Agamben's state of exception (the sovereign's ability to transcend the rule of law for the public good), which emerges when nationalist passions emphasize "the nation" and "the people in peril" over "citizens" whose liberties are ensconced in constitutional law.[60]

Moral panics over Anglo degeneration "into Africanism, Orientalism, and racial chaos" through sexual mixing and potential interracial labour solidarity persisted in the South beyond emancipation.[61] By the 1870s, national white anxiety about a permanent class of criminals and paupers also targeted "fallen" white women and girls, who many feared were endangering "the Race" and the republic with ostensibly degenerate progeny. Anti-miscegenation laws, having developed during the colonial period, increasingly expressed racism as a biopolitical state effort to protect the population's well-being against the racialized other. Well into the twentieth century, these laws affirmed North Carolina's obsession with legitimate union defined by pure blood linked to race, hygiene, and degeneration.[62]

Through training in good citizenship, the state differentially extended "mercies" to wayward adolescents as a civilizing strategy, securing its regional affiliation with American global ascendancy. Grounded in humanism, reform institutions provided Black boys state sanctuary from lynch mobs and imprisonment, while indoctrinating all adolescents into the racial order as eugenically managed, compliant labourers who would eschew interracial solidarity. Campaigns for the reclamation of disorderly North Carolina youth sentimentalized only white childhood, and reform efforts demonstrated a considerable racial investment in the moral training of working-class white, but not black, children "to attach those skills of self-discipline and the learning of civilities to the strength of the nation, to the redemption of the republic in the US and to the survival of the master race."[63] Chronological primitivism and recapitulation theory drew an analogy between the sexuality of "primitive" humans and that of the child as an archaic human form, reflecting humanity's early sexuality. G. Stanley Hall regarded white adolescence as an evolutionarily "savage stage." Growing emphasis on merciful protection in juvenile jurisprudence was commensurate with increasing, non-compassionate racialization.[64] North Carolina's juvenile reformatories contributed to a growing national cross-class white alliance through the selective "civilization" and inclusion of court-committed adolescents as a resource of compliant future citizens.

To get at the larger questions framing my research on mercy, and the persistence of racialized national belonging under liberal-humanist reform, I ask three specific questions about the application of discretionary mercy in the segregated South's legal framework. First, while reform institutions were initially non-state-sponsored responses to feared degeneracy and future criminality in working-class adolescents, the state typically took over their costly operation. How, given the current overrepresentation of women and girls of African descent in the criminal justice system, did the state rationalize its refusal to fund a reformatory for errant Black girls? Second, why did North Carolina commit Black boys to a reform institution, rather than shunting them into the adult penal system or letting them fall prey to lynch mobs?

Finally, as a category of identity, how did race operate within liberalism, and how did North Carolinian liberal-humanist reforms in the Gilded, Progressive, and New Eras work to renew racism? White Republican reformers, while opposing extra-legal Klan-based violence, effectively re-narrated earlier racisms. What might this tell us about the possibilities of deep-seated change within a non-radical, reformist framework? How does it inform a critical assessment of our current "post-race" assertions?

Racism without Racists

More than an "ideology," racism was exercised in juvenile reform institutions to safeguard national purity and "the physical well-being of future generations."[65] With a race-based strategy serving as a foundation of transregional reform goals, North Carolina followed Northern reformatory models. Still, North Carolina's biopolitical state emerged as a response to very different, locally specific historical catalysts. Acting to protect the population, the state managed sex with indirect, racist effects, thereby enabling the re-narration of white supremacist citizenship within the national imperial context, through more "civilized" mercies.

Like Giorgio Agamben, I question the claims of humanitarian liberal rights discourses, given their effective complicity with the very inequities they set out to dislodge. Legally institutionalized racial oppression may have seemed to end with emancipation, liberal individualism, and the conferral of the inalienable rights of man, but, arguably, it only became obfuscated. Alexis de Tocqueville in his *Democracy in America* (1835, 1840), and Gunnar Myrdal, in his mid-twentieth-century *An American Dilemma*, acknowledged the presence of American racism, but concluded that its incidence was anomalous to that essentially egalitarian liberal democracy. Certainly, post–civil rights era civilities denounce flagrant displays of racism and public contempt of the othered (with the exception of Muslims and the criminalized).[66] Yet, in considerations of social change and American identity, there is a danger in overstating the imperial era and its aftermath as radically different from today, leading us to incorrectly conclude that legally institutionalized racial oppression ended along with emancipation, leading to our present state of "post-raciality." For Myrdal, racism was exceptional, a deviation from America's true principles. But arguably, exclusions generated through principles of liberalism were foundational to an

Americanism coloured white in its structure and normative assumptions. Ultimately, as a critical narrative of the deep rootedness of multiculturalism, *Southern Mercy* is directed more at the present than the past. As perhaps quaint forms of past racism, exclusionary practices of historical juvenile reform in North Carolina have currency as implicated histories of the present.[67]

Structure of the Book

The format of this book follows that used by anthropologists such as Lee Baker and George W. Stocking, who offer vignettes as a method to illuminate wider relations of power. Drawn from substantial archival records, a multitude of voices range across a show trial involving white girls who faced the electric chair for the capital crime of arson; a reform institution mandated to protect Black youth from lynch mobs; reformatory racial policies; and records documenting negotiations for state funding of the moral and sexual reformation of "wayward" Black girls. These narratives show how the pastoral project of mercy was connected to North Carolina's own subordinate regional status within the nation, and to the long and complicated renewal of white Americanism after Reconstruction. They delineate "civilizing" strategies linked to regional status and national identity formation in North Carolina. They also show some of the systemic constraints under which various groups of the othered lived and the ways in which they made sense of and moved around them.

Through the Foucauldian genealogical method, I retrace negotiations of national identity formation as historical and contingent, rather than natural and inevitable.[68] Michel Foucault discerned large and small-scale shifts from those directed against the state and conceived in terms of a war for political relations, to those imagined in biological terms and involving eugenic technologies as a "condition of survival." I am interested in the transformative dynamics of social change and its limitations within liberal-humanist reform. I examine locally specific changes associated with the emergence of the biopolitical state linked to internal colonialism in interwar North Carolina, and, building upon Giorgio Agamben's work, foreground the politics of resistance, and ways in which racism was renewed under biopolitics in this historical context. The movement from lynching, the convict lease, and chain gangs to juvenile reformatories follows the kind of modernization trajectory that Michel Foucault describes in *Discipline and Punish*. While we can see clear evidence of the cultural normative shift that Foucault describes in the treatment of white boys in the growth of the reformatory movement, we must be cautious about applying this framework to the shift from lynching to reformatories for Black youth. As I will demonstrate throughout the book, and particularly in chapter 4, modernity does not herald the end of racism.

My focus is on the contribution to racialized national identity formation through the renewal of racism under liberal-humanist reform, but this book also contributes to gendered analyses of nation building, documenting the central role of Black and white women in shepherding juvenile reformatories.[69]

The accounts I have selected illustrate the kinds of knowledge generated about national belonging, as well as the contradictions, and the emancipatory possibilities, in various relations of power. My empirical focus is on North Carolina, lauded as the South's most progressive state. As a rapidly developing section of the South in the first half of the twentieth century, it offers a rich context for examining the renewal of racism in modern liberal reform.[70]

In addition to reformatories, I examine historical records of a community that state agents fictitiously named "Swamp Island," from which the state recruited white adolescents for institutionalization. I draw upon a large volume of largely uninvestigated archival material, some of it restricted, and a multitude of voices, among them, those of the socially invisible: black, white, and indigenous adolescents, institutional employees, and Southern Black reformers. My reading of this archival material has sought out what Stoler calls "discrepant tone, tacit knowledge, and stray emotions" as a way of presenting the perspectives of the typically silenced as contributors to the contested process of national identity formation.[71] In this way, I use the archival record ethnographically.

Claude Lévi-Strauss claimed that ethnology must be limited to that which has not been written, or printed. But for Stoler, archives, as "sites of the expectant and conjured," do embody a sense of the unwritten. Without seeking their "real" hidden messages, one can read archival records for things understood as unspoken rules, and things considered unwritable or undefinable. In the North Carolina archival records, I noticed shifts and negotiations in the defining of Americanism. More than just an accounting of events or documentation of whatever people recalled, these archival records convey the identity of the imagined community, people's anxieties about race, national belonging, regional alterity, and degeneracy. Stoler contends that archives register "against the sober formulaics of officialese ... the febrile movements of persons off balance – of thoughts and feelings in and out of place. In tone and temper they convey the rough interior ridges of governance and disruptions to the deceptive clarity of its mandates." In this way, archival records can be used to study cultures.[72]

Carolyn Strange and Tina Loo identify three developmental stages of the legal regulation of morality: first, the induction of formal legal structures of moral regulation, followed by a state resolution to begin shifting religiously inspired reforms to legal reforms, and, third, the extension of moral regulation through the nullification of radicalism and the development of social welfare. Because industrialization was slow, the relatively late emergence of the welfare state in North Carolina makes for an interesting case, occupying many of these stages concurrently in the decades around the turn of the twentieth century.[73]

This book follows a simple structure. Each chapter considers an instance of Southern mercy in juvenile reform connected to efforts to redefine the South's place in the nation. In chapter 1, I explore communities from which white children were recruited for merciful moral "uplift," and include interviews of relatives of former juvenile inmates. Chapter 2 documents a fascinating and little-known capital arson show trial – the Samarcand Arson Case of 1931 – involving sixteen adolescent white girls who torched the institution to which they were committed, raising questions about gendered mercy in juvenile jurisprudence. In chapter 3 I consider Black female invisibility in the founding of the North Carolina Industrial Home for Colored Girls in 1926, and examine the question of agency in the face of social structures that thwarted even nominal political opportunities for Blacks.[74] The State Training School for Negro Boys at Hoffman, an institution mandated to protect Black boys from lynch mobs, is the subject of chapter 4. Chapter 5 analyzes records from the state's first juvenile institution, Stonewall Jackson Training School [for white boys], and the contested development of the biopolitical state.

Lee Baker critically examines ways in which white American anthropologists around the turn of the twentieth century created a racial politics of culture, targeting American Indian, but not African American culture for study and ethnological preservation. Guarded disciplinary boundaries between anthropology and sociology constructed a

division of labour within American social sciences, whereby sociologists focused on examinations of immigrant and Black cultures in the
United States, while anthropologists tended to specialize in "far-away"
indigenous cultures. White Western anthropologists examined othered
cultures, overlooking any direct interrogation of traditions and colonial
histories "at home." Meanwhile, sociologists conducted their analyses
within accepted binary interpretations of assimilation/civilization and
racial uplift/evolution without attendant integration or equal rights,
contributing theoretically to desegregation. Baker notes that while anti-
African, this approach was radically pro-Black for specifically identifying poverty, racism, and slavery as damaging to formerly enslaved
Americans. Interpreted this way, anthropology and sociology shared
common assumptions of pathology, ethnic essentialism, and cultural
authenticity, and Baker calls for the troubling of these dichotomies.[75]
Animated by questions pertinent to anthropology and the historical production of culture, Southern Mercy connects various branches
of inquiry. Responding to Bruno Latour's call to "do anthropology at
home", I turn a critical eye to North American cultural practices, calling
for greater reflection on the substance and meaning of mercy.[76]

Chapter One

Swamp Island

We are all blind until we see
That in the human plan
Nothing is worth the making
If it does not make a man.
Why build the nation glorious
If the child unbuilded goes?
In vain we build the city
Unless the child also grows.[1]

Do you know, I had to look at one of those girls for two minutes before I could make her drop her eyes.[2]

In 1921, the State of North Carolina launched an investigation into a white bootlegging community, resulting in a report by the superintendent of public welfare, "Swamp Island – A Study of Conditions in an Isolated Section of North Carolina."[3] The report cited fearful and tragic conditions in a district where impassable roads hindered state surveillance. The point was "to show what isolation, ignorance, ill-health and idleness can do in a community probably not fifty miles from where you read this report."[4] With its population dependent upon begging, bootlegging, wood chopping, and subsistence farm-ing, the superintendent of public welfare identified Swamp Island as a blockade district rife with fornication. The "loose morals" of the community's many single mothers had presumably led to their rejection of legal marriage in a community that was "not straight." Ross, "an old man near 70 ... crippled by a recent accident," was the only man in a household of "three and possibly four" generations of illegitimate children. He lived with ten others, including his seventy-two-year-old second wife Molly, her forty-eight-year-old daughter Jane, and Jane's six children, all of whom officials suspected he had fathered. The eldest, nineteen-year-old Annie, had two children of her own. The superintendent expressed alarm that the women of Swamp Island performed outdoor labour, with "elderly Molly" doing most of the ploughing and heavy work, while the rest of the family chopped wood and begged. David Roediger points to national literature of the early republic – narratives like John Smith's commentary on the hard work performed by indigenous women and children – as reflective of imagined primitivity.[5]

Discouraged by the four-mile walk, Swamp Island locals did not attend the one-teacher school, and church services were offered only "once a month when a preacher [could] be had." For advice in managing the situation, the superintendent of public welfare consulted moral and legal experts – pastors, the judge of the county court, a juvenile court judge, social workers, the sheriff, local academics, the citizen elite, the Department of Public Welfare, and county superintendents of public welfare.[6] A government official took photos to document evidence of alleged immorality: "When the Welfare Officer had tried to take a Kodak picture of Jane's children, she snatched them away, and her eyes flashed fire as she took them in the house and – 'You ain't gonna take no picture o' none o' my young uns.' Pictures of all were finally taken later, however, with the aid of the good local deputies."[7] The juvenile court summoned parents from Swamp Island, and unmoved by their pleas, forced them to surrender their children to "the care of those who could train and educate them and give them a chance to become good citizens." Annie's and Jane's four toddlers were committed to the Children's Home Society of North Carolina, in Greensboro, but "were not content to leave home, and cried pitifully" when the welfare officer and deputy sheriff carried them off. Jane's fifteen-year-old daughter Mary-Eliza was sent, along with Annie, to the Samarcand state industrial training school for white girls. They too, resisted institutionalization; Annie's involved separation from her two-year-old daughter: "So trying was the experience for the Charity Organisation Society Secretary that she was unable to leave with Annie on the night train as she had planned."[8]

The Swamp Island bulletin documents court officials' concerns about the absence of fathers. Bastardy caused economic problems, where every illegitimate child was a potential drain on the public purse. In these cases, civic officials would pressure mothers to name the fathers of their children, so that they could be assessed for child support. Annie Wilkes signed an affidavit identifying the now remarried Leslie Parks as her children's father. Parks acquiesced at the trial, giving a bond to pay Wilkes one hundred dollars in child support. Having been served a warrant for fornication and adultery, Annie received a six-month suspended jail sentence, and was sent to the Salvation Army Home in Greenville, South Carolina, with her infant. Annie and Mary-Eliza stayed with a "respectable and motherly" woman who kept boarders, and other "good women" offered to escort the girls later in the week. They delivered Mary-Eliza to Samarcand, and the same deputy who had earlier taken Annie's two-year-old and the other small children to Greensboro, later escorted Annie and her infant to Greenville, South Carolina.[9]

Carolyn Strange and Douglas Hay have observed that mercy can have a wide range of qualities, from attenuated punishment and compassion to considered cruelty.[10] While North Carolina reform institutions had an instrumental purpose linked to the juvenile court, a detailed analysis of the historical, cultural, and (geo)political context is needed to understand the specific dynamics of mercy as a nation-building exercise. This chapter takes as its subject an examination of unprecedented state intervention into the private lives of potentially subversive young people as a strategy of uplift and racialized national inclusion. While brief, the Swamp Island report offers a glimpse into one community under surveillance by reformers and state administrators. Along with other records, it demonstrates a context of knowledge production and strategies of governance that were private, and micro-regulatory.

Michel Foucault traces a shift through which disciplinary strategies to produce docile bodies in reformatories, prisons, schools, and asylums were replaced under modernity by an increased emphasis on the management of the life of populations.[11] As syncretic sites of normalization and eugenics, North Carolina juvenile reformatories emerged relatively late. Foucault's account of anatomo-politics likens the human body to a machine integrated into wider economic systems, focusing on its discipline and the efficient optimization of its capabilities, its usefulness and docility.[12] This reinforces biopower – calculations and knowledge-power as agents of transformation of human life – operationalized in scientific racism.[13] This chapter provides context for subsequent chapters on individual juvenile reform institutions, offering a sense of the kinds of communities and families North Carolina targeted.

Liberal reformers proactively removed children from Swamp Island, and similar communities, shepherding them back into the national fold to prevent them from becoming either financially dependent paupers, or a formidable political threat. This played out in a wave of institution building and a legal framework to deal with preventing their full-blown "moral degradation."[14] There was an added urgency in North Carolina, where some feared regional degeneration as the reason for national alterity. Members of the white bourgeoisie regarded juvenile reform as "the moral life-saving station on the highway of North Carolina progress."[15] Reformers rejected children they deemed too insentient to uplift, or too incorrigible to rehabilitate, typically either sending them back into their communities, or institutionally warehousing them, sometimes for life.[16]

White reformer Wiley Hampton Swift argued, "The rights of the state rise above family rights in the child, and there should never be any hesitation about invading the family circle when the best interests of the child demand it."[17] As Mariana Valverde has noted, privileged with privacy, the white middle class escaped much of the surveillance and censure inflicted on poor whites. While middle class whites were trusted to regulate their own sexual conduct, legal regulation was put in place for all Blacks and poor whites. Early social workers liaised with the juvenile court to counteract imagined racial degeneration through a set of pastoral strategies directed at everyday family life. Infiltrating the private lives of poor whites, investigations "began with the kitchens, clothes, cupboards of the poor, but it did not end there: the prying gaze of philanthropy sought to penetrate the innermost selves of the poor, including their sexual desires, which were categorically conceptualised as vices involving incest, illegitimacy, and prostitution."[18] While poor whites resisted and at times returned the disciplinary gaze, embarrassing state administrators into providing better care for their children, they were at a decided legal disadvantage.[19] The affluent who limited their pregnancies may have endured criticism for committing "race suicide" and shirking their national duty, but they rarely, if ever, lost custody of their children. Reformers justified their intrusion into white communities like Swamp Island, and their coercive legal intervention as a merciful extension of protection to those incapable of protecting themselves. "It seemed like a good idea at the time," remarked interviewee Maude Wells, who transported half a dozen "bastard" new-borns – laying them down in a row across the seat of her car – across the state to adoptive parents.[20]

Defending Society against Itself

As a region surveilled and spectacularized as popular exotica by many in the Northeast, the South in the decades around the twentieth century recalled nineteenth-century human zoos, which combined anthropological studies of exoticized peoples with public exhibition.[21] The American South was a curiosity too, and Northern whites would venture there to engage in cultural tourism and explore spectacles of elsewhere. During their tours, they would draw comparisons between the tropics and Southern topography and culture, describing the South as an atmospheric, but diseased and degenerative, space.[22] One traveller remarked that she was most intrigued by Southerners' "determined resistance to the inroads of civilization."[23] Employing colonial tropes of infantilization to describe cotton mill workers while touring the South, Columbia historian Frank Tannenbaum lamented in 1924 that the South had "buried its Anglo-Saxons ... They are like children."[24]

Reformer Walter Hines Page campaigned for the merciful uplift of poor whites as "The Forgotten Man" who languished in the South, and puzzled over the ostensible racial decline of people in "the region which had given Thomas Jefferson and George Washington to the world." Insistent that the South represented the purest Anglo-Saxon strain in America, Page cited 1897 North Carolina census records and voting lists indicating that only one person in four hundred was of "foreign stock," with the vast majority bearing Scottish and English names as descendants of original settlers. He identified an antiquated political and economic structure as "the foundation of our poverty." North Carolina, like much of the South, was still ruled by a "little aristocracy," he argued, organized upon a feudal-like structure that resisted taxation and state-funded public education and social services.[25]

The Swamp Island bulletin and institutional archival records reflect the dynamics of the boomerang effect described by Michel Foucault that colonial practices had on the Occident's own legal and political structures, whereby colonial models abroad informed social regulation of the other at home. The Swamp Island report urged "that real things can be accomplished even in so apparently hopeless cases when science, common sense, and sympathy combine in an effort to solve humanity's problems." In tone, this archival document conveys a regional effort to adopt national welfare policy to defend society against the other within – something that Foucault has argued all racist empire states do. Similarly, Lauren Berlant has observed, "The fantasy of a private, protected national space is a fantasy only a non-stigmatised person, a privileged person, can realistically imagine living." Internal colonialism defined those who belonged, in contradistinction to the other, "the abject of empire: the rejected from which we cannot part." The other provided a critical platform for normalized American identity within a transnational movement of empire building, and arguably, this persisted even after the rhetoric of American imperialism ended around the First World War.[26]

As a hierarchical concept, race emerged alongside of the European Enlightenment's universalization of whiteness and reason, developing further in the Age of Empire and into the twentieth century, generating a binary system that divided the world into the "civilized" versus the "savage." Such épistèmes for Michel Foucault normalized certain practices, functioning as an unquestioned knowledge structure from which discourses emerge in a given era. Eurocentric discourses emerged from the racial épistème, increasingly rationalizing white Americanism through naturalized and normalized dichotomies of reason/ignorance, religion/superstition, and scientific knowledge/indigenous knowledge. As Anne McClintock has argued, "Imagining the degeneration into which humanity could fall was a necessary part of imagining the exaltation to which it could aspire."[27] The threat of evolutionary decline was intrinsic to theories of progress, with tension between constructions of the morally and culturally superior "good (white) citizen" and the degenerate other within the nation, imagined as a pathological internal threat to society, imagined metaphorically as a social organism. Some perceived the racially "degenerate" – envisioned as prostitutes, alcoholics, feebleminded and "deranged" people – as a moral malignancy, a worm infesting the healthy national body politic.

A mounting concern over "retrogressive" sexualities intensified in North Carolina in the decades around the turn of the century. Disorderly whites, the "degenerescence" state officials discovered at Swamp Island, signified an internal source of disease generating a national threat, not from beyond the nation's borders, but from the "great unwashed," its own, fecund, "waste matter of evolution" who survived ominously within the modern nation. Sexual deviance was imbricated with racial alterity: Swamp Islanders were white, but as Sander Gilman has argued, deviant sexuality "is the most salient marker of otherness, organically representing a racial difference." Thus, degeneration theories conflated degenerative decline with race and promiscuity, with the corollary that various groups of social abnormals came to be identified as sexual transgressors – and racialized – as part of whatever else marginalized them. Essentialist discourses associated the bodies of white prostitutes, women confined in asylums, and lesbians with sexual disease, corruption, and the libidinal energies of the "savage," and public health reform reduced them to yet another source of pollution. Degeneration theories added mental defectiveness to moral bankruptcy, resulting in the ascription of a conflated alterity, especially to white women like those from Swamp Island, presumed to drain "the Race" through rampant bearing of atavistic and illegitimate children.[28]

Regulation of sexuality through heteronormative, bourgeois marriage and procreation concretely defined national boundaries with a focus on genealogy and origin, or *Volk/nation*. Such nationalisms are exclusionary; the nation is imagined as limited to those born into membership, with a common origin. This nationalist agenda becomes one of regulating sexual reproduction and marriage to avert the threat of "contamination" of racial purity through interracial sexuality. The political, economic, and racial potency of the body politic depended upon its status as civilized, and sexual purity was intrinsic to this. In fact, the sexual purity of white women and girls, regardless of class position, became paramount to American national identity around the turn of the twentieth century, through their indirect political role as literal and metaphoric bearers of nation. In the American South, state management of reproduction intensified as Jim Crow laws criminalized interracial marriage to limit the reproduction of biracial children, feared, as Lauren Berlant has argued, for straddling and melding the racial divide.[29]

While careful not to suggest that "degenerates" were beyond rescuing, many Southern white reformers, like those in New England, harboured growing apprehension that reform projects would be no match for the vagaries of racial degeneration in America. Improving the racial stock through childrearing came to be regarded as a patriotic, imperial duty of middle class whites in the decades around the turn of the twentieth century. With support from the American Eugenics Society's Committee on Popular Education, events like Fitter Families Contests, widely held at state fairs during the 1920s and 1930s, judged "human stock" along with agricultural selective-breeding entries. Positive eugenics extended to some poor white women when the State Board of Public Welfare administered Mothers' Aid "to help worthy mothers deprived of their husbands' support to rear their children in their own homes." Mentally and morally qualified mothers were not considered charity cases, but "employees of the State whose job is to raise good citizens."[30] While debates about hereditary versus environmental causes of deviance flourished, in practice, both were addressed through regimens that combined rehabilitation through normalization with prevention through forced sterilizations (which persisted in North Carolina into the 1970s), and encouragement of rational breeding through birth control legislation. White reformers hoped eugenics would help resolve the complicated issue of ostensible, failed whiteness, protecting the nation and "the Race."

Between 1910 and 1939, the philanthropic Carnegie Corporation funded the eugenics records office in Cold Spring Harbor, New York. As agents of the emergent biopolitical state, juvenile judges and reformatory administrators exercised power through negative eugenics – sterilization – following the identification of "abnormals" through mental tests. Once North Carolina's sterilization program launched in 1929, surgeries were typically performed on girls just before their release from Samarcand, especially if they had histories of being sexually active, IQ scores below 70, or came from families deemed immoral. This accompanied constitutive efforts to develop adolescents' collusion with self-discipline, in keeping with hegemonic standards of normalcy.[31] Consent of the patient, next of kin, or legal guardians for sterilization was deemed unnecessary in the 1933 passing of North Carolina's Public Laws, chapter 224. Moreover, administrators and surgeons would not be held liable civilly or criminally except in cases of negligence in the performance of surgeries. Eugenic sterilizations justified restraints on the sexual exploits of poor whites as a necessary means of protecting the "fit" from the "unfit."[32]

Illegitimate and white, James Carpenter became an "asexualization case." Admitted in 1922 to the Epileptic Department at the Dix Hill State Hospital in Raleigh at the age of fifteen, he suffered from an average of fourteen convulsions a month. Still confined eleven years later at twenty-six, James had escaped fifty-four times. Administrators expressed concern only when James began to engage in sex with other male patients. They noted, "This patient is a sexual pervert," his advances on other male patients resulting in "extensive ... pathology ...

in the rectum following these acts." His 1934 sterilization blank identified him as an epileptic with mental deficiency. Listed effects of his surgery were unexpected: "There has been no particular change in this patient's sexual attitude since castration. He continues to molest low-grade patients when he has the opportunity. He continues to have the power of erection."[33]

Disability: "Deeds of mercy above all material things"

Eighteenth-century political discourse rationalized exclusion from democratic equality based upon "natural inferiorities," construed as disability. While the disabled have historically been assigned inferior status, disability rhetoric has also contributed to widespread oppression of positionalities based on gender, race, and ethnicity, in the conflation of these with impairment. Douglas Baynton has argued that disability played a significant role in nineteenth- and early-twentieth century citizenship debates. Medical journals invoked imagined disabilities of racialized groups, claiming a higher incidence of blindness and deafness among free Blacks than slaves. In 1896, the *North Carolina Medical Journal* inquired about "the effect of freedom upon the mental and physical health of the negroes of the South," associating emancipation with a "harvest of mental and physical degeneration." Following slavery arguments, opponents of gender equality cited white women's disabilities – physical frailty, irrationality, and hysteria – as barriers to suffrage and education. In fact, *Popular Science Monthly* argued that education would impair physiological functions. Denying their disability, in seeking equality, many marginalized groups still implicitly accepted that disability justified inequality. By 1907, the commissioner general of immigration made exclusion of the disabled central to immigration policy, and the concept of disability became conflated with race, through a rhetoric of "defective races," supposedly prone to disease and congenital disorders.[34]

Mercy played a vital role here. In his 1921 inaugural address, Governor Cameron Morrison declared, "The institutions and organizations set up by the State for the care of our defective and unfortunate people must be made adequate for the treatment, care and training of these helpless and defective ones within our borders in a manner worthy of a people who love deeds of mercy above all material things." Governor Morrison argued for the humane care of "defective and unfortunate people" unable to care for themselves.[35]

White Middle Class Alterity

Poor whites, presumed to embody racial deterioraton, were as "necessary to the self-definition of the middle class as the idea of degeneration was to the idea of progress. Various groups of middle class Americans constructed their own identities as modern and civilized in contradistinction to "savages" abroad and at home. Concerned that cultural devolution would generate racial decline among even the "most fit," middle class white progressives mobilized the state to address white poverty and the perceived breakdown in racial health. McClintock has posited that while sanitation syndromes counted as earnest efforts to stave off the "diseases of poverty," they also functioned to guard class boundaries between the "contagious" classes and the citizen elite.[36]

Ring identifies alliances of white middle class Northerners and Southerners in New York social clubs who scrutinized the South as a group. I suggest that while they shared class position, they were not on equal footing. For the Southern white middle class, "poor whiteism," along with racial segregation, was a problem that required careful containment. Imagined individual perversion indicated the potential for group perversion, which threatened the national belonging of the Southern white middle class, and potentially, the nation's position on the imperial stage. The standing of the white middle class in North Carolina was especially precarious, inflected as it was by quasi-colonial North–South relations. North Carolina white liberals struggled against their own otherness, borne of regional affiliation in the wider context of civilizationist discourses. Black and white middle classes of North Carolina directed disciplinary and regulatory mechanisms not just at the poor, as marginalized "abnormals," but also at themselves. By the twentieth century, the increasing measure of civility and racial worth by what people did in private encouraged their moral self-regulation in the affective minutiae of everyday life.[37]

Fearing the loss of their regional claim to Americanism, Southern white reformers sought to demonstrate their capacity for civilization through merciful show trials and spectacles of benevolent juvenile reform. Their stated sentimental concern for wayward children was inflected by the desire to convey a clear message of "civilization" – as "a great State of a noble and humane people." Reclamation of children within penal welfarism through merciful moral suasion demonstrated Southern civility grounded in liberal humanism, and Black, as well as white, reformers staked a claim in this.

Class divisions were dangerous, particularly in the Jim Crow South. A spectacle of Southern mercy, North Carolina's juvenile reformatory movement facilitated a white cross-class alliance that averted interracial working class solidarity with the assignment of racialized citizenship compensating poor whites for class subordination. Normalization efforts aimed for white working class compliance and agreement about the conventions of Anglo-Saxon supremacy. Many young white, and Black, inmates learned to accept white class rule as legitimate, and adopted middle class standards of moral and sexual propriety, along with a "desire to work," with no guarantee of economic security. Samarcand inmate Donita Summerlin addressed white clubwomen who had beautified the grounds, saying, "I hope to marry someday. My experiences with the lovely things you are providing has made me quite anxious to have a home of my own. I plan for it to be beautiful in simplicity and orderliness. It doesn't matter if it is a small home, for I have learned that with the proper care, a single rose can be as lovely as a bouquet of orchids."[38]

Early Social Work

The State Board of Charities and Public Welfare formed in 1868 to secure protection and care for "the unfortunate elements of the State's population." Upon recommendation of the governor, the General Assembly elected seven members to the board. Kate Burr Johnson, the board's executive officer and state commissioner of public welfare (1921–30), headed the staff of the State Board of Charities and Public Welfare. The work of the board was divided under five bureaus: county organization, institutional supervision, child welfare, mental health and hygiene, and publicity. By 1917, it supervised all of North Carolina's charitable and penal institutions promoting children's welfare, inspected state institutions, and studied the social conditions of the state, with special consideration given to mental defectiveness, to make policy recommendations to the General Assembly for legislation. The law required at least one member to be a (white) woman, and by 1924, there were three, representing both Republicans and Democrats.[39]

The emergence of state regulatory bodies was pivotal to modern state formation, but schools, religious institutions, families, and factories all exercised regulation, too. The state initially accommodated volunteering clubwomen's efforts before the process was rationalized with the emergence of professional social workers. In North Carolina, they were assigned to the training schools to consult about intake and discharge policies, to assist with individualized treatment plans, to prepare homes for returning children, to supervise and report on parole, to serve as liaisons in the courts, to prepare case histories, and to monitor children's progress.[40] Prison reform extended to an abiding concern over "wayward" children, as philanthropic groups like the North Carolina Federation of Women's Clubs intervened through "social housekeeping" – liberal-humanitarian racial uplift and reform – as the primary vehicle for their participation in public life and nation building. Strengthening their own sphere of influence both within and independently of the state, these women policed sexual prohibitions and codes of segregation. Clubwomen of African descent, who founded an institution for the moral reformation of court-committed Black girls, challenged this standard, as I will demonstrate in chapter 3.[41]

As a civilizing mission, the Swamp Island case documents the centrality of middle class white women in shaping racialized national belonging. If white men relied upon stories of chivalric protection of Southern womanhood as a defence against imagined threats of "Negro colonization" (mirroring "the black peril" in Africa, "the red peril,"

Figure 1.1. Forest picnic, North Carolina Federation of Women's Clubs. Reprinted with permission from Samarcand Manor (private archives).

in the Americas, or the "yellow peril" in Asia), liberal white women expressed their anxieties about interracial sexuality through ideals of protective motherhood and directives for proper domestic relations. Marshalling technologies of sex around fears of racial degeneration, these women mounted child-saving campaigns through the articulation of sexual discourses with a racist logic.[42]

The Swamp Island report conveys middle class white women's participation in internal colonization and the biopolitical fight against white degeneration through a preoccupation with soap and bathing. When the state seized Jane Wilkes's youngest children, members of the Women's Christian Temperance Union, the secretary to the superintendent, and "good neighbors" were all waiting in their homes with soap, scrub brushes, and contributions of fresh clothing.

> The Charity Organisation Society Secretary and her sister took them, one at a time, for their novel experience of baths ... They were the dirtiest, most ragged and uncouth little fellows imaginable. Dirt was caked on them. Never before had they experienced a real bath. The little waifs screamed like they thought they would drown. But never was there a greater change in appearance and disposition in children ... These good women fitted them out completely with fresh, clean clothing. This remarkable change made the girls happy ... They were happy and proud of their new clothes and clean bodies.[43]

By the late nineteenth century, soap had become a technology of cultural imperialism and ethnic cleansing, as Anne McClintock has shown, associated not just with domesticity, but with racial hygiene and imperial progress, signifying national and evolutionary ascendancy.[44] McClintock has argued that "the poetics of cleanliness is a poetics of social discipline" whereby purification rituals demarcated boundaries between communities. As a fetishized imperialist commodity, soap promised to wash away the stigma of class degeneration, and thereby restore racial potency to the Family of Man.[45] Soap did not attract attention at the height of imperialism, but "emerged during an era of impending crisis and social calamity, serving to preserve, through fetish ritual, the uncertain boundaries of class, gender, and race identity in a social order felt to be threatened by the fetid effluvia of the slums, the belching smoke of industry, social agitation, economic upheaval, imperial competition and anticolonial resistance."[46] Soap served as an instrument of merciful amelioration, applied to the dangerous classes of poor whites, but not

Blacks, whom white reformers believed could get so far, and no further, in the evolutionary process.[47] As subsequent chapters demonstrate, this imperialist rhetoric informed the development of North Carolina's juvenile reformatory movement.

White juvenile reform reflected wider colonial interventions including missionary work, the acculturation of immigrants, teaching mothers household management, and supervising charity recipients. It cultivated a strong work ethic in poor white children, who threatened the presumed racial imperviousness of Anglo-Saxons. In addition to fears of the loss of race, what united various interest groups of Progressive thinkers was the conviction that the failure to uplift the other "to behave in the image of the Teutonic people" increased the risk of interracial solidarity and the organization of labour. Moral regulation of working class whites shaped their private selves, and it shaped internal colonialism. Arriving in the Southern Blue Ridge in 1898, reformer W.E. Barton called attention to "fallen Anglo-Saxons," who were of the "purest British blood," yet faced destitution in America. Barton believed that this population of "sturdy American children who were fortunate enough to have been born in the 'inland empire'" must be distinguished from "the empire beyond."[48]

To obstruct interracial labour solidarity in the South, reformer Robert C. Ogden argued for "a white civilization the black man can respect." One reformer described the ideal Southern (white) boy as full of "ambition to perform great deeds of industry and progress." He was "alive and bristling with energy and horsepower," and ready to conquer "savage beasts and men," build empires, steer ships, and conduct trains.[49] Juvenile reform institutions sought to root out shiftlessness identified in communities like Swamp Island, training working-class white children in skilled manual labour to produce useful, docile bodies and compliant political beings. Institutions were largely self-sufficient, and depended upon inmates' labour, both on-site and as hired hands on local farms.

On-site agricultural and domestic work provided cheap labour, spun as a morally worthy activity that would impart a politics of purity, Christian piety, and respect for family and Americanism.[50] Samarcand had livestock, its own laundry, cold storage, crops, and an energy plant. Inmates performed almost all of the work on Samarcand's several-thousand-acre farm.[51] North Carolina adopted the model of agricultural colonies and the cottage system, through which young people derived rehabilitation through "all manner of domestic work." These

Figure 1.2. Sorting hay – farming at Samarcand Manor, c. 1930. Reprinted with permission from Samarcand Manor (private archives).

children learned to labour in institutional replications of the idealized family home, isolated from the outer world, with matrons or staff "parents," who would teach self-discipline in benevolent, if austere, surroundings that thwarted expectations.[52]

Discourses of Responsibilization, Prostitution, and the Libidinal Economy of the Nation

The Progressive Era saw a dramatic growth of juvenile jurisprudence and specialized reform institutions established to stem the moral and sexual corruption of working-class white youth. This escalated during the Great Depression with the spectre of unemployment, which heightened fears that white girls would become fallen women, and boys would "join the degenerate enemies of the state." As Ann Stoler has argued, promiscuity cast the empire in a bad light, weakening its claims of white evolutionary ascendancy, and undermining colonial authority. White prostitution undermined the perceived legitimacy and racial vitality of European and American colonizers abroad, diminishing the façade of Anglo-Saxon supremacy. This led, for instance, to the British policy forbidding the migration of single white women to the colonies, given that insolvency might lead them to prostitution. White women's sexualities threatened the "libidinal economy of the nation" into the interwar period and the era of isolationist foreign policy. Rather than presenting a minor aberration in normalcy, fallen (white) women embodied a serious threat to social decline, and they were targeted for reform efforts.[53]

In the early-to-mid-twentieth century, medical and psychiatric experts, reformers, and public officials expressed concern that an alleged rise in prostitution was jeopardizing the health of troops, and by extension, the nation's political, economic, and racial vigour. Far from a transitory exercise in puritanism, then, state management of sexuality was a response to white fears of racial decline through inter-racial sexuality and national contamination. The *Rocky Mount Telegram* mused, "No one expects Samarcand to produce the flower of woman-hood. One does expect that Samarcand will at least instil in its inmates some self-respect, some appreciation for values."[54] Nineteenth century discourses conflated imagined potential white degenerative relapse with uncontrolled sexuality attributed to lesbians, "hysterics," and the institutionalized, resulting in a moral panic. A multitude of acts, among them, walking alone at night, incest, and smoking cigarettes, raised the spectre of prostitution, which, and as Carolyn Strange and Tina Loo have noted, was inflated "into the master problem of the age – '*the* social evil.'"[55]

An incubus of transgressive sexuality, feeble-mindedness, and racial degeneracy came to be regarded as a social condition of poor whites, marking them as "invalids of civilization" and "the waste matter of adap-tation." Experts argued that poor whites' alleged reckless reproduction was the cause of crime, destitution, and disease. Rather than locating and dealing with social problems as a part of industrialization and capital-ism, reformers sought improvement through the alignment of individ-ual subjectivities through discourses of responsibilization.[56] Although some lawmakers recognized that the feminization of poverty led poor girls and women to prostitution, for instance, most treated destitution as a moral failing, indicative of individualized pathology; poverty of spirit, and intellect.[57] At the turn of the last century, American medical interest in degeneration identified adolescent deviance as a marker of perversion endangering "civilization." Subversive white children, the future of "the Race," intensified white anxiety about the South's place in the nation, and the nation's positionality within imperial modernity. In tone, the Swamp Island report conveyed reformers' concern that "the very fate of the race and the nation seemed to turn in large part on its sexual practices."[58]

Mirroring this evolutionary rhetoric, the aptly fictitious name "Swamp Island" insinuated the ominous presence of white primitivity, as remnants of the primitive archaic. For Hegel, "the swamp" represented the earliest stages of human history, marked by uncontrolled sexuality. It also alluded to the assumed progress made by Occidental "civilization" in establishing self-control and global imperial ascendancy.[59]

The Swamp Island bulletin reflects a discursive shift that developed as moral panics over "white slavery" gave way to incrimination of girls and women who got themselves in trouble. Progressive and New Era reformers increasingly rejected Victorian discourses of female passivity and victimization, insisting on the need to manage female sexual proclivities, while also protecting young women from deleterious environments and guiding them to avoid men's supposedly natural inclinations. Child study expert and psychologist G. Stanley Hall widely influenced this discursive shift, suggesting that "sexuality occupied and defined [girls'] lives to a far greater extent than it did for boys." While adolescent white girls could not be directly faulted for their home environments, reformers increasingly attributed their "illicit encounters," including rape, to bad character.

Many white girls incarcerated at the Samarcand state industrial school were actually incest survivors, and while reformatories policed white adolescents' sexuality and exploited their labour, it was a double-edged sword, because they also provided sanctuary for some, and occasionally parents sought their protection. Committed in July 1928, one adolescent recalled that "a lady told my mother about Samarcand and she thought that it was a good place for me."[60] In another case, a mother requested that the juvenile court commit her venereally infected five-year-old daughter, though the child's classification as a sexual incorrigible casts doubt on her mother's intentions. Her case prompted the *Durham Morning Herald* to urge the state to pay more attention to the morals of children. More often, the court committed girls against their parents' wishes, and even in cases of rape. William Bush has noted that the juvenile court charged many white girls with sexual delinquency, despite the fact that they were actually victims of men, often relatives, who avoided legal and moral sanction.[61]

After a day of helping her family on their farm, fourteen-year-old Mildred Watts returned home with her mother, helped prepare dinner, washed the dishes, and went to bed. Mildred was, according to her mother, a "most helpful and obedient child." "Very tired" from the day's work, she was already fast asleep by the time her mother retired. During the night, a thirty-year-old man who boarded across the street "reached into the window beside her bed and pulled her out the window, hurried her away before she had fully awakened and committed an act that is unspeakable." Bettie Watts claimed her daughter had been raped, but the court held Mildred responsible, committing her to Samarcand, while the man paid a small bond and was free to go. Watts's letter indicates much about the blame cast on mothers when the court found their children wayward. She lamented that she had not properly trained her daughter to prevent rape. At Mildred's age, she wrote, there could be "no carnal consent." She refused to marry the fourteen-year-old girl off to avoid scandal, pleading in vain that her daughter should remain in school, and, as the oldest child, be permitted to continue to live at home, where she was an indispensable help to her mother and disabled father.[62]

This focus on the responsibilization of girls is also relevant in the Swamp Island case. It is curious that the Swamp Island report of a possible criminal act of rape or sexual enslavement of a multigenerational family by seventy-year-old Lewis Ross did not result in his removal from the community. Members of the white middle class habitually accused poor whites of engaging in incest as part of their presumed depravity. But the fact that reformers suspected Ross as a sexual predator (going so far as to take photos of children as proof of alleged immorality), yet chose not to investigate the possibility of felony, indicates much about shifting interpretations of rape. Sandra Gunning has argued that transgressive white women "figured both as race traitors and as diseased bodies."[63] Juvenile reform institutions trained working-class white girls in domestic arts with a strong focus on biopolitical sexual regulation in the name of public health. It was the women of Swamp Island who faced gendered moral condemnation, and subsequently lost their children. Because they did not bear children, there was little concern over white boys' sexual behaviour, as long it followed the heteronormative standard. The aim for white boys, whatever their offence, was their development as humbled, pacific labourers.

At the turn of the last century, the nascent juvenile court, informed by medical discourses, identified adolescence as a distinctive stage and critical time of sexual awakening that was also malleable. So, while girls were increasingly held responsible for morals offences, reformers attributed character development to nature, but also environmental influences. Supposedly set in their ways, "fallen" women responded poorly to reform efforts, but institutional stints taught children self-control, normalizing their still adaptable characters through merciful care and a watchful eye.[64] Unprecedented state intervention into family life facilitated moral guidance in white middle class standards of sexual propriety. Interviewed in 1929, Superintendent of Public Welfare Bost advocated environmental explanations for wayward white girls' transgressions, pointing out that "the majority of girls are not fundamentally bad, but only ignorant or neglected and the victims of bad environments. The result is that they quickly respond to the new ideas and ideals with which they come in contact at the school and develop into women of real character and ability."[65]

Samarcand's 1931 institutional records catalogue inmates' charges or offences, their dispositions, and their diseases in the early decades of the twentieth century. Records show that some inmates as young as five years old did time for offences like suspected immorality, delinquency, incorrigibility, masturbation, stealing, lying, and unreliability. The court committed others as deserted or abused children and dependant orphans, delivering many from home environments involving neglect, incest, and rape ("lived with prostitute: older men running after her"). The juvenile court committed eleven-year-old Ruth when her mother died, and her father started dating, or as state administrators saw it, "bringing in notorious women." Judges sent girls over ten years of age to Samarcand mostly for victimless public-order offences like "waywardness," stubbornness, vagrancy, petty larceny and "habitual drunkenness," or if they suspected home environments to be detrimental to physical and mental welfare. Most girls entered Samarcand for sexual misconduct, which included a whole range of transgressions: "running wild," "wayward and under a bad influence," "incorrigible: left home for several months," "crimes against nature," being "boy crazy," flirtation, masturbation, and walking alone at night, all interpreted as permutations of prostitution – an umbrella term.[66] White working-class girls' behaviour often transgressed accepted middle class gender standards, enabling the criminal justice system to cast a wide net.

The statutory provisions of the Public Laws introduced the longterm incarceration of children for ill-defined, non-criminal status offences only vaguely related to their actual behaviours. The original statutory provisions of chapter 254 of the Public Laws of 1917 establishing Samarcand Manor set forth the criminalized behaviour under which females under eighteen (many of whom were under ten years of age), if convicted, could be committed to Samarcand: "fornication and adultery, keeping a house of ill-fame, or a bawdy house, or a disorderly house, or violating the laws of this State as to chastity." Vagrancy was

Figure 1.3. Lake scene at Samarcand, c. 1925. Reprinted with permission from Samarcand Manor (private archives).

added in 1919. The statutes qualified underlying concerns, specifying: "Provided, nothing herein shall be construed to give to any judge of any court the right to commit to such reformatory or home for fallen women any virtuous female."[67]

Normalized Self-regulation

Responding to fears of racial degeneration, and connected to the development of the biopolitical state, North Carolina juvenile reformatories engaged in merciful character building, alongside eugenic sterilizations. State administrators removed children from working-class parents they believed to be ignorant and morally lax, corrupting innocent children in deficient home environments.[68] Direct and personal therapeutic intervention aimed to reset adolescents' intimate ties, and their loyalties:

A girl who had a very vile tongue and hot temper when she came, who had worked in a cotton mill since she was small (being only fourteen when she came to us) remarked the other day that she didn't think of saying or doing what she did when she came here, and felt as though she wanted to laugh the whole time, which she does … Another girl writes pathetically to her mother to attend a clinic "cause I know what is the matter with you." This same girl fifteen years old had been taken by her mother from camp to camp, the mother soliciting soldiers for her own child. She is an example of the younger girls who is an innocent victim as many of these are. When one sees her playing with her doll it is hard to realise that she knows so much about the "underworld."[69]

As a mechanism of productive power, normalizing discipline involved the architectural organization of space, and time supervised through strict schedules and bells. Military discipline administered through drills, formations, and marches became part of daily life, instilling respect for authority, discipline, and patriotism. In a 1920 letter home, a Samarcand inmate wrote, "Oh, I forgot to tell you, I am taking military training. My, you ought to see me drill, you woulden believe it was that 'slow poky' Beulah that ust to be around home. Realy sister I have adopted so many nicer habits, in fact I have refrained and dismiss all the old rude habits I ever had. And its wonderful to overcometh, don't you think so?"[70]

Shirley Steinberg has argued, "The viability and functionality of power relations are intrinsically tied to disciplinary power and the regulation, or self-regulation, of the oppressed. Simply put, the insidious

Figure 1.4. Drills at Samarcand Manor, c. 1925. Reprinted with permission from Samarcand Manor (private archives).

nature of oppression manifests itself in the ability to implicate the oppressed in the maintenance of their own oppression."[71] Foucault posits that normalization involves an intricate web of processes that function to construct cultural norms of rationality and self-discipline in ways that respectively mark the other as abnormal. Through expert benevolence, the state refashioned the private subjectivities of those who endangered it, as a matter of internal colonialism and in the name of public health (defending society against itself).[72]

Nikolas Rose has argued that free citizens in liberal states are managed through personal regimes of reflexive self-discipline that align identities with wider national agendas, but are assumed to be private, and voluntary. In this way, self-regulation in juvenile reformatories theoretically surpassed the need for dictatorial techniques of social control, through "coerced voluntarism," because as liberal regimes, they were paradoxically regulated by liberal freedom. These state reformatories governed the soul.[73] Samarcand girls collaborated in their own learning of social place, affiliating their desires with the class- and race-based order of things. Censored mail at Samarcand Manor reflects this: "I have done dirty but that is no reason i can not make a lady out off myself every lady hase had failures and have had mine but it will come out all right some sweet day and I know I can bee sum lady and I am a goying to ..."[74]

Northeastern and Southern white reformers worked within very different historical political contexts, and class status alone did not allow them to cast off racial and regional distinctions. The juvenile reformatory movement in the Northeast responded to social issues associated with rapid industrial capitalist growth and life in urban slums. North Carolina, notable for its regional underdevelopment and suppressed labour force, remained largely rural. Liberal reformers there endeavoured to centralize state mechanisms within a context of a recent history of mercantile capitalism, as well as a long history of local republicanism that curtailed state powers. Additionally, honour-based cultures found throughout the South traditionally defined civilization in terms of *politesse* rather than Enlightenment *humanité*, complicating the emergence of the biopolitical state. Lacking the standard structural and cultural conditions, the reformatory movement in North Carolina borrowed heavily from the Northeast. Northern liberals advocated development in the South, transplanting there "the higher civilization of the North." The civilizing project of mercy was keyed to the South's own subordinate status within national politics, and to to the complicated remaking of white Americanism in the twentieth century.[75]

Discretionary by definition, the juvenile court offered a humanist alternative to retributive adult justice. While punishment and mercy were theoretically intended to reduce crime, their application was mediated by political and economic objectives as well as the prevalent social and political identity through which the populace defined itself as a certain kind of people, for instance, modern, civilized, law-abiding, and patriotic. Seeking to disassociate themselves from the reputed atavism of the South, the emergent white middle class, self-proclaimed "new men of the New South," regarded themselves as an epistemologically new kind of people, set apart from dissolute ancestral aristocrats and from poor whites, despite the racial alliance they sought to forge across class boundaries. As industrialists, reformers, and "forward thinking" citizens, these "best" people defined themselves during the Gilded, Progressive, and New Eras in opposition to anti-modernists who hoped to salvage the wreck of the Old South through the Lost Cause movement. The new Black and white middle classes sought to demonstrate their own capacity for civilization by aligning themselves to Northern interpretations of it – through lawfulness and the adoption of liberal-humanist values that called for the protection of children.

The New South movement brought together coalitions of Progressive and New Era experts who sought to develop the defeated South through expansion in business, railways, and industrial, rather than mercantile, capitalism. In keeping with Max Weber's *The Protestant Work Ethic and the Spirit of Capitalism*, manuals like "The Law of Success," printed by the Southern Methodist Publishing House in 1885, instructed Southern whites in the appropriate new morals and manners. A New England writer noted in 1890, "Now, like a mighty apparition across the Southern horizon, has risen this hope or portent of the South, – The Third Estate – to challenge the authority of the ruling class." By the 1880s, business values had gained credence with the hope they would bring the South into step with "the most highly civilised States."[76]

Reformatories and Industrial Schools

The terms "reformatory" and "industrial school" are often used interchangeably in the North Carolina archives, though "training school" is more common by the turn of the last century. Unlike reformatories, which housed young offenders, industrial schools were generally intended for children who had not yet committed any serious crime, but

North Carolina interpreted these classifications loosely, broadening the institutions' catchments. Children transported to these institutions had been charged with infractions ranging from status offences to larceny and store breaking, attempted rape, and "assault and battery with a deadly weapon." William Bush has noted that in the case of Black boys, institutions throughout the South tended to perpetuate assumptions of the earlier reformatory era, of children as inmates rather than students. More often, he contends, these adolescents endured hard labour, rigid discipline, and the employment of guards, as opposed to parental mentors. My findings suggest that North Carolina was more syncretic in its approach, referring to all committed children as inmates at least some of the time, and requiring all to identify as labourers. Gender policing featured hegemonic masculinity for white boys, and sexual regulation, reproductive management, and domestic training for white girls.[77]

George Mosse has argued that moral codes came to be associated with nationalism, and Valverde has noted that through everyday customs, post-religious moral discourses normalized certain ways of being, while marginalizing alternatives. The state's task, according to Gramsci, was to educate, and to legitimate "civilized" self-government. Samarcand's Superintendent MacNaughton wrote, "We hope to raise the moral standard of each girl so that a gradual growth of moral sense within her may create the desire to live right, and thus enable her to take her place once more in society."[78] Merciful uplift played out as a domestic civilizing mission within internal colonialism, where industrial training and state policies of public health operated through microstructures that mirrored global colonial patterns of dominance.[79]

"Rescued" by the juvenile court, wayward white children faced a range of treatments designed to benevolently ameliorate environmental and hereditary causes of "racial degeneration." The sentimental concern for wayward children within penal welfarism also reflected positively on those who advocated scientifically informed agricultural and industrial education, and merciful moral suasion over retributive punishment. State administrators routinized internal colonialism through the banal (but classed, raced and gendered) everyday normalization of habits, comportment, and character building.[80] As penal and pedagogic institutions, industrial schools offered micro-environments to expedite internal colonialism through the manipulation of inmates' private subjectivities as a preventative technology. Describing a juvenile reformatory for white girls, Nina Bernstein observes, "They were at times allowed to talk to each other in 'a low, pleasant voice,' but only under the eyes of the supervisor. Even unhappiness was cause for reproof. A complicated point scale was used to grade inmate behaviour, backed by a system of surveillance, denunciation, and self-confession for such small faults as tilting a chair or sitting on a bed."[81]

The General Assembly of 1917 established the State Industrial School (for white girls) at Samarcand, at the urging of moral reformers. Desiring "a positive influence for upbuilding rather than a mere reformatory with some flavor of the prison about it," Samarcand Manor became the informal title, while its official title was the State Industrial School at Samarcand.[82] Despite this compassionate presentation, many young inmates resisted incarceration, and some would escape, only to be tracked down by bloodhounds.[83] When three men pinned a note to the hog pen offering to help girls escape, teachers, wearing inmates' bloomer suits, went out to meet them in the forest with guns. "The men ran towards them with outstretched arms until within about a hundred and fifty feet of them, when realizing that they were not inmates they turned and fled as men never fled before while the teachers pursued them firing shots which only served to quicken their pace."[84]

Columnist Nell Battle Lewis noted the irony of keeping the name "Samarcand Manor" from its former estate, writing that Samarkand, "a Moslem city in Central Asia," evoked "harems, Turkish delights and loose luxury ... hardly the kind of thing to be associated with the erring adolescent.[85] One reporter argued, "The girls who find their way to Samarcand via the Juvenile Courts are children with problems – not necessarily 'Problem Children.' It is our aim to help them solve their problems ... We are endeavouring to have the public look on Samarcand as a school, and not as a place for punishment."[86] In keeping with biopolitical concerns, by the 1920s, many white working-class North Carolinians regarded Samarcand as mirroring child expert G. Stanley Hall's appeal to white bourgeois mothers to pay special attention to their daughters' sex education so that "the girl will be anchored betimes to what is really the essential thing, *viz.*, reproduction and the carrying beneath her heart and then bearing children which are the hope of the world."[87] Sometimes frustrated parents would commit white girls to Samarcand when discipline at home failed to keep them in check. Others misconstrued reformatories as boarding schools, and actively sought institutionalization for their children, especially during the Depression, with hopes that it would at least provide a steady diet; but most often, children were forcibly removed from failed parents by the merciful courts.[88] In 1923 The *Public Welfare Progress* assured its

Figure 1.5. Swimming at Samarcand under the gaze of visitors, c. 1925.
Reprinted with permission from Samarcand Manor (private archives).

readers that contrary to popular perception, the 255 inmates at Samarcand Manor were not sexually depraved, fallen women. "They are girls
whose days out in the pine woods of Moore County are filled with
normal work and study and play. It is rather disconcerting to the visi-
tor prepared to sentimentalize over the widely-advertised delinquent
to have a pleasant-faced, rosy-cheeked little girl of twelve … give you a
first-class lesson in good manners."[89]

Status Offences, Indeterminate Sentences, Social Stigma, and the Merciful Juvenile Court

As the Swamp Island bulletin demonstrates, unprecedented state intrusion into the lives of poor white families involved the dissolution of
ostensibly unfit homes "in which [children] had been accustomed from
their earliest infancy to drunkenness, immorality, obscene and vulgar language, filthy and degraded conditions of living."[90] Sometimes,
early social workers and parole officers appeared as angels of mercy.
Ninety-six-year-old Maud Wells, a Depression era "police-woman"

I interviewed, reminisced about delivering food from her own pantry to a destitute white family. When she arrived at their home, they were burning an old battery in the woodstove, for lack of wood.[91] Like benevolent social workers, the juvenile court in North Carolina, as in New England and Canada, presented itself as a kind of helpful family clinic. Juvenile courts tried young people separately and differently under the 1908 Juvenile Delinquents Act under the premise of paternalistically caring for, and not just punishing, young offenders. The Juvenile Court held hearings, not trials, and made orders instead of passing sentences. Unlike criminal courts, juvenile courts tried to move beyond determinations of guilt or innocence to make assessments of conditions leading to a child's waywardness. Authorities brought white families to court with the expressed intention of aiding them, protecting their children from moral degeneracy through rehabilitative education in good citizenship. Yet the court remained part of the criminal justice system, and the threat of incarceration through repressive state intervention was ever present.[92] Allegedly benevolent interventions played out as punitive, and ever-present threats of long-term incarceration kept white girls of all classes in line.[93] One interviewee recalled her mother's frequent warning during the 1930s: "You behave yourself young lady, or I'll send you to Samarcand!" The merciful protection underlying reform could also manifest as legally backed coercion.[94]

Perhaps inadvertently, in sparing them from the full force of the rule of law, courts denied young status offenders the criminal procedural safeguards of due process extended to adult offenders.[95] Once committed to Samarcand, inmates served indeterminate sentences, their release formally granted by a board of managers upon recommendation of the staff. As Bernstein has observed, girls convicted of prostitution or vagrancy might have been subjected in the past to terms of ten days to six months in a county jail, but now faced lengthy sentences. A girl committed for alleged vagrancy, typically carrying a maximum of thirty days, could be held for up to three years in a North Carolina juvenile reform institution, or until she reached the age of majority. A 1921 revision of the original 1917 statute stipulated that the board of trustees "had the sole right and authority to keep, restrain and control her until she is twenty one years old."[96]

At the turn of the last century, the juvenile court emerged because errant children could not be dealt with as fully rational agents. Adopted into American jurisprudence in 1838 to commit children to houses of refuge, *parens patriae* would expand during the Progressive

Era to justify the forcible removal of young offenders and unsupervised children from "unfit" parents. The scope of juvenile court powers afforded a protective discretionary tone and flexibility in the law, such that "the care and custody and discipline of a juvenile delinquent shall approximate as nearly as may be that which should be given by its parents."[97] Under *parens patriae*, the state assumed "the privileges that parents enjoy, exercising the wholesome restraint which a parent exercises over his child … No constitutional right is violated but one of the most important duties which organized society owes to its helpless members is performed" – co-opting the state in its expanded role as merciful parent.[98] This legal doctrine mobilized the coercive authority of the state to act *in loco parentis* under the premise that not intervening on behalf of young "social victims" would amount to mercilessness, rendering parents' legal challenges mostly futile. These parents lost custody, contact, and, often, their children's respect when young sons and daughters entered into long commitments as wards of the state.[99]

North Carolina's dramatic growth of juvenile jurisprudence, expanded court authority, and scope of welfare reforms at the end of the nineteenth century can be partly attributed to the status jurisdiction.[100] Carolyn Strange and Tina Loo have noted that definitions of sexual offences were broadened to protect children as the most vulnerable members of society, but some of these laws ultimately stigmatised them through long-term incarceration, especially when allegations of sexual deviance attended their commitment.[101] Status offences, dependent upon one's identity rather than one's actions, marked young people a priori as transgressors. If perpetrated by adults or even class privileged white children, status offences would never be criminalized. Southern white working-class children found themselves vulnerable to moral reformers' definitions of offences, which the state then acted upon.[102] Thus, while reformers argued that Samarcand was not a home for "fallen women," and that commitment would simply "prevent them from progressing in ignorant or unbecoming ways if left to their own unprivileged situations," it disgraced them, nonetheless.[103] The nephew of Samarcand inmate Margaret Pridgen, whom we will encounter again in chapter 2, recalled in a recent interview that the family, humiliated by Margaret's incarceration, "drew a curtain around her life as it touched upon their lives."[104] Public shame typically attended commitment, as Felester Forrester's story demonstrates.

Felester Forrester's Secret[105]

Jo Huddleston, a hobbyist exploring her family tree in the state archives, stumbled upon information pertaining to her grandmother Felester Forrester's court commitment to Samarcand Manor from 1922 to 1925.[106] In 1922, the *Durham Morning Herald* reported, "Juvenile court was in session this week for the purpose of taking up the case of Ruthie Forrester and Lucy Forrester who were arraigned before Recorder P.C. Graham yesterday on a charge of running a disorderly house."[107] The state seized fourteen-year-old Felester Forrester, and her twelve-year-old brother Wesley, committing them to state industrial schools. Older brothers Bill and Monroe had been charged before for carrying guns and knives, and the court deemed the family home too violent for the children. The *Durham Morning Herald* reported, "It was alleged by witnesses that the quartet, who reside in the Bragtown section, occasionally engage in family rows in which various forms of weapons are utilized and the out-of-doors used in which to carry out their warfare."[108] The children's father had died in the 1919 flu epidemic, leaving Ruth as the sole parent. The family lived in an isolated rural area, and relatives would later speculate that the complainant was a local store proprietor who retaliated by contacting the sheriff when the Forrester family refused to sell her their property. Whatever the merciful intentions of the court, the stigma of commitment ran so deep that Felester would keep her experience at Samarcand a secret from even her future husband and children. Jo Huddleston remembered, "My grandmother was an excellent swimmer; I remember her knowing a lot of swim and dive moves. I had sometimes wondered where she learned all of that, growing up on an isolated farm in Durham County, NC, which only had a creek on the property, but no lakes nearby, and certainly no public swimming pools." Felester would tell her family that she had learned to swim in Pinehurst, where she spent summers with an uncle. But her granddaughter said, "I've spent years researching our family genealogy, and I can tell you there was no uncle in Pinehurst, no relatives there at all."[109] She added:

> My aunt remembers that she set the table every night for dinner, very nicely with napkins and a tablecloth and silverware and china, and had the kids take a bath before their father came home. She seemed to know all kinds of things that she couldn't have picked up in a one-room schoolhouse near the farm; one time in New Jersey she had some ladies over for a cookware party and gave a talk about proper nutrition. I suspect she didn't pick up any of this growing up on a very rural farm.[110]

Figure 1.6. Felester Forester, Durham, NC, engagement photo, 1928. Courtesy of her granddaughter, Jo Huddleston, Whitsett, NC.

Prohibiting her return to her family upon her parole after a three-year
sentence, the state placed Felester with white middle class guardians
in Durham, where she briefly attended high school. After spending
the required year with this family, Felester changed residences, found
work in a hosiery mill, and relocated to a boarding house for women.
She then met Avery, and married him in 1929. Active in the labour
movement during the Allen A. Hosiery dispute of 1928–9, Avery vol-
unteered in "flying squadrons" that would drive in on short notice from
all around the country to aid in labour demonstrations. A photo shows
Avery standing beside a car with a sign affixed to the rear bumper,
"Allen A. Hosiery is unfair to organized labor; it is made by unskilled
workers." Felester bore two children. Jo Huddleston surmised, "She
[must have been] at the school before the sterilizations started, or else
my family wouldn't be here." Felester used her vocational training in
millinery and dressmaking skills attained at Samarcand to support
herself and the children by working in hat and dress shops after her
divorce.[111]

The Red Letter Day

The *Charlotte News and Observer* ran a story, "Samarcand Girls Given
Chance to Prove Worth to Society," accompanied by a photo of an adolescent girl gathered up in her father's arms upon her parole from the
institution. "The red letter day is, naturally, the day when girls are told
they can go home again. Here, Marie Tate, who has been at the school
for eighteen months, greets her father who is ready to take her back
to their hometown. Marie's face darkened, however, when she told
her friends good-by." Martha Azer, staff writer for the *Charlotte News*,
found the atmosphere of enthusiasm and excitement surrounding the
girls participating in the graduation and May Day and exercises effer-
vescent.

> The girls were dressed in white, flowers in their hair, broad smiles on
> their faces. And they were talking among themselves – "Do you think
> mother will come today? ... I do hope she brings brother ..." The pro-
> cessional was the same, as for any other graduating class ... One of
> the unusual things about Samarcand is the happy attitude of the girls
> who were sent there. Somehow, they have a school pride and a spirit.
> Almost without exception, they'll tell you, "I like it here. They're good
> to me."[112]

Tucked among archival documents applauding the benevolence of this nationally recognized state institution, a letter written anonymously in October 1936 by a "citizen of High Point, N.C." seems alarmist. "Mr Gill, Dear Sir will you please investigate what they call the jail at *Samarcand Manor*, Eagle Springs N.C. where they keep these girls locked up in this hot weather and see if they have beds to sleep on at night. Please investigate at once."[113] As we will see, other records indicate that Samarcand could indeed extend harsh qualities of mercy.

In Samarcand's parole report, Superintendent MacNaughton explained, "A girl upon becoming twenty-one years of age automatically passes from the care of the institution, although she is observed from time to time … An effort is made to place the girl in the best possible surroundings, and in the wisest care. Because of the very special training given them along certain lines, many good places are found for them."[114] Seventeen-year-old Bernice Kidd, who had undergone an oophorectomy in February 1930, was, by February 1934, working in a hosiery mill. The Eugenics Record Office at Cold Spring Harbor, in Long Island, New York, noted that she had been sterilized just before being paroled, and "is more tractable, less given to temper tantrums and works regularly. With one lapse when she apparently became infatuated with a married man, she has behaved well."[115] Administrators typically found placements for newly paroled inmates, returning them to the bottom rungs of the socio-economic ladder as apprentices and domestics, where their moral training and surveillance continued indefinitely.[116] Samarcand inmate Margaret Pridgen lived with her parents upon release, and at twenty-four worked as a public restroom attendant in downtown Wilmington. She would die of renal failure at the age of sixty-three in a North Carolina nursing home.[117] While no record of Margaret's surgery survives, it is probable that she, like so many working-class white adolescents, had been sterilized while at Samarcand. Margaret would marry upon release, but was never able to become pregnant following her incarceration. Her relatives suspect that her youngest sister, Eunice, may have actually been her child, newly born the month before Margaret's father, Strange Pridgen, had her committed to Samarcand. Eunice was five when she first met Margaret, and remembered:

> I was glad I had another sister, and I was excited to meet her. I heard about her. I used to ask my parents, "Why is she not here with us?" and they said when I was a baby she would take all my brothers and sisters to the park

without permission, so they decided she needed to be put in this school so they could tend to the rest of us. When I got older, I went to stay with her and her husband who was a truck driver. She was about eighteen years old when she married him, and I saw him abuse her so bad … Margaret wanted a child so bad, but she couldn't seem to get pregnant. One time she bought some baby clothes in the hope she would have a child of her own. She loved my five children, so I told her I had children for her, too.[118]

In 1959, Margaret was identified as bipolar. She said she felt "mean," and doctors hospitalized her in Raleigh for eighteen months. Her nephew David Pridgen remarked that he found her strangely docile after her discharge, "in the manner of people who have been lobotomized."[119]

Chapter Two

The Samarcand Arson Case

Please give me liberty or death.[1]

As the Pridgen girl, scantily clad, told of her part in the affair, a cigarette rolled out on the floor from the bed on which she was sitting.[2]

For months in the spring of 1931 North Carolinians followed sensational newspaper accounts of a capital arson case involving the possible death penalty for sixteen white female juvenile reformatory inmates, ranging in age from twelve to seventeen years. The fire occurred at dusk on 12 March 1931 at the Samarcand Manor State Industrial Training School for Girls. Situated in an isolated section of rural Moore County, twenty miles from the nearest fire department in Carthage, the institution was doomed to burn; by the time fire trucks arrived, it was too late to save two residence halls, already engulfed in flames. While there were no fatalities, damage was considerable, having been conservatively estimated by the *New York Times* at $100,000, which would be approximately $1.5 million USD in 2016.[3]

On Thursday, 12 March 1931, residents of the Chamberlain cottage dining room heard that the Bickett Hall residence was on fire. The girls razed Bickett Hall without difficulty, and then set fire to the Chamberlain Discipline Hall attic. The first attempt failed. That section of the attic had been constructed with oak planking rather than heart pine, and was difficult to ignite.[4] Staff members detected the fire and extinguished it. But around nine o'clock that night, as girls were turning down their beds, sixteen-year-old Estelle Wilson stole upstairs with matches to another girl's room. She would later confess, "I lit a paper dress hanging in a closet. I didn't want to stay in Chamberlain. I wanted to go to an honor cottage, but they wouldn't send me. I was looking for a whipping the next day anyway. I thought they would send me home ... [I] shut the closet door and stood there to see that the fire burned."[5] The room was ablaze in no time. At ten past nine, inmates "began hollering 'Fire!'" Fifteen girls trapped in solitary confinement in the discipline cottage struggled to get free as the fire raged. One girl attempted to free them, picking the locks with a spoon. Fleeing the burning building, a staff member hesitated, and tossed her the keys.

That night, Sheriff McDonald placed sixteen girls under arrest, fifteen of whom were inmates of the discipline cottage. Between ten o'clock and midnight, Superintendent MacNaughton and Sheriff McDonald interrogated them without assistance of counsel. Six girls went to the Moore County jail, and ten more followed to the Montgomery County jail the next afternoon. The warrant charged that the girls "did feloniously set fire to Chamberlain Hall, of Samarcand Manor, which was occupied by several inmates in the night time." The "Samarcand Sixteen," having been charged with the destruction of two state buildings, faced charges of first-degree arson, one of North Carolina's four capital crimes. According to Criminal Statute # 4238, "Arson at common law is the willful [sic] and malicious burning of the dwelling house of another. To Constitute the crime (a) There must be some burning, though it may be slight. (b) It must be of a dwelling house, or an outhouse used in connection therewith. (c) The house must belong to another, at least as occupant. (d) The burning must be caused maliciously." The statute additionally specified, "Any person convicted according to course of law of the crime of arson shall suffer death." That night, the sheriff arrested Pearl Stiles, age fifteen, Marian Mercer (15), Margaret Abernethy (16), Chloe Stillwell (16), Edna Clark (17), Thelma Council (16), Ollie Harding (17), Bertha Hall (16), Estelle Wilson (16), Josephine French (15), Virginia Hayes (16), Dolores Seawell (15), Mary Lee Bronson (16), Wilma Owens (16), Margaret Pridgen (15), and Rosa Mull (12).[6]

At a hearing on 16 March, North Carolina filed preliminary charges of first-degree arson and attempts to commit arson against the "Samarcand Sixteen," each of whom had allegedly "naively confessed [to] taking part in the burning of the buildings" four days earlier. Fifteen-year-old Marian Mercer would confess to appointed counsel Nell Battle Lewis, "I hated Samarcand ... Me and another girl (Margaret Abernethy) set Chamberlain on fire the first time. Me and her went back in the kitchen and got some matches, and we lit a stocking in the attic ... I thought that would get me home." Virginia Hayes explained, "Ollie

Figure 2.1. Samarcand Manor. Photo taken from the biennial report of the board of directors and superintendent of the State Home and Industrial School for Girls, Samarcand Manor, Samarcand, NC, for the Two Years Ended 30 June 1938. Courtesy of the State Archives of North Carolina.

Harding went to get the matches, but she didn't get them. I got them. Marian Mercer and I went into the attic, and I held a stocking and Mary Lee lit it and we put it in a hole … I thought that if I set it on fire they would send me out, and I was tired of that place – I had been there twenty nine months."[7]

Along with the girls' statements about the fires, Lewis gathered information about their sexual histories and families: Marian had been committed to Samarcand for promiscuity in October 1928. Her twice-married mother allegedly operated a brothel. Her father John, a sailor, had drowned. Eva Godley testified against Chloe Stillwell, informing authorities that Chloe had said, "We set it on fire." Eva added that Chloe was very nervous and "walked the floor all night."[8] Chloe denied her involvement. Bertha Hall would testify, "I was washing towels when

Chamberlain caught the second time. Miss Stott said I passed matches, but I didn't ... The second time that Chamberlain caught fire I was getting ready to go to bed, and I opened my door and saw smoke, and Margaret Pridgen had set fire to a paper dress in my closet."[9] Margaret Abernethy initially admitted to setting fires, but later retracted. "I told them I done it to get out of Samarcand ... I was locked in my room – I was sick – when I looked out and saw that Bickett was burning." Ollie Harding also denied her involvement. "I heard some of the girls say that Virginia Hayes said that she was going to set it on fire. I was getting in bed."[10]

Bound over to the county superior court, the girls remained in custody without bail for sixty-seven days awaiting the 19 May "trial for [their] lives."[11] After almost a month of confinement, scandal intensified when some of the girls set more fires. The group held at the Carthage jail went on a spree, igniting their bunks, kicking out windows, and allegedly attacked a fire fighter with his own knife. Six of those being held at the Robeson County jail in Lumberton rioted too, ripping out electric light fixtures, tearing up their bunks, and setting more fires. Newspapers reported that some of the girls turned on the jailer, cutting his finger and face with shards from broken windows. Within two weeks of their transfer to the Moore County jail, these girls secured more matches and started more fires. The media had a field day. Some accounts described girls who, upon release from their cells, stormed the building, running naked through the corridors and torching whatever they could until the town sheriff ordered a fire hose turned on them. Reporting on the defendants awaiting trial in jail, the *News and Observer* observed, "The girls are almost minus clothing, but the modesty of most of them seems not affected. As the Pridgen girl, scantily clad, told of her part in the affair, a cigarette rolled out on the floor from the bed on which she was sitting."[12]

The ways communities punish reflect their collective values and fears, and the way they self-identify culturally, as a people.[13] In this chapter I examine the Samarcand judgment as a locally specific negotiation of white collective identity in Depression era North Carolina. Over months, the Samarcand arson case of 1931 became a sensational media event mounted in a show trial. I am interested in changes in public perceptions and opinion that gradually shifted from condemnation of the "Samarcand Sixteen" as wanton slatterns who threatened national integrity to widespread public support of the girls as innocent victims sending "smoke signals from Samarcand Manor."[14] Infused

with nationalist scripts, the case became a spectacle of mercy, "civilization," and national belonging. This fascinating and little-known trial
raised the unprecedented legal consideration of how North Carolina
should respond to adolescent white girls who had committed a capital
crime, arson, on state property. Like any proceeding, this case raised
questions of whether to bring the full force of the law to bear against the
defendants, how much discretion to extend, and how to find a balance
between justice and mercy as a matter of liberal-humanist civilization.

"Civility" was integral to modernists' self-definition. These
eighteenth-century discursive changes, which Norbert Elias identifies
as concerned with *humanité* and the fairness promised by objectivity,
are believed to have initiated the earlier reconfiguration of penology
in England.[15] In early twentieth century North Carolina, the criminal
justice system upheld Enlightenment discourses of certainty of punishment over severity as a "civilized" alternative to both vigilante and
pre-penitentiary rule. As one North Carolina planter argued, "Whip a
dog every time he enters your parlour and kitchen and you will soon
be unable to coax him to put his nose inside the door. But if he is sometimes allowed to lie by the fire and sometimes severely lashed, he will
take ten thousand stripes and be a house dog in spite of them."[16] Discretion reinforced respect for secular law in its adherence to Enlightenment reason and its commitment to neutrality. Nevertheless, executing
white adolescent girls would have been disadvantageous to a region
wishing to present a mercifully law-abiding countenance for the nation
and the world at large.

One hundred and fifty years earlier, in 1777, Thomas Jefferson had
introduced a bill in Virginia's House of Delegates to abolish the death
penalty except in cases of treason and murder. While the bill was
defeated, it reflected a shift that reduced offences classified as capital
crimes. By the nineteenth century, many states regularly substituted
imprisonment for execution. Lagging behind, North Carolina maintained "the bloodiest code of laws of any state in the Union," with
twenty-eight capital crimes in 1817, and still twelve in 1855.[17] Late
nineteenth century judges did extend mercy to young capital offenders, extending pardons to imprisoned white minors who became ill.
Those incarcerated in North Carolina's state penitentiary were sometimes pardoned before their sentences were up. For instance, with public support, county officials and the judge recommended the pardon
of a fourteen-year-old boy, "a weak-minded idiot," convicted of arson
in North Carolina in 1869. The judge concluded, "His extreme youth

suggests a doubt whether our civilization and the more humane feelings of the age would permit his execution." North Carolina also pardoned an eleven-year-old white boy convicted of larceny in 1877, and a ten-year-old boy charged with capital arson for setting fire to a house. The ten-year-old's brother had torched a jail in another North Carolina county, and while the judge expressed concern about heredity leading to a long line of arsonists, he issued a pardon. The child's health was failing after having been confined in jail for many months, and the judge elected to send him to a reformatory "of some State fortunate enough to possess such an institution." Sometimes citizens would come forward to urge the pardoning of children. In 1896 the trial judge, chairperson, other members of the board of county commissioners, county officers, and several hundred citizens, called for the pardoning of Ester McGuire, a white boy convicted of homicide. His 1897 exoneration rested on the agreement that the incident had been accidental. Public opinion would also influence the outcome of the 1931 Samarcand arson case.[18]

Legal Executions of Women and Children in the United States from 1632 to 1984

While mercy was sometimes extended, the United States was not historically averse to executing women and children. Between 1632, when legal executions were first recorded, and 1984, there were 398 legal executions of female offenders in the United States, and 282 documented cases of legal executions of juveniles. Of these, ten were girls, and all but one were of either African or Aboriginal descent.[19] In 1787, New London sent twelve-year-old Hannah Occuish (a girl of Pequot descent) to the gallows for the murder of a six-year-old white girl, Eunice Bolles, in a dispute over strawberries. Deemed a cunning liar and thief with a malicious disposition, Occuish transgressed both racial boundaries, and normalized gender scripts, as did her mother, allegedly "much addicted to the vice of drunkenness." Legal executions in the United States reached an all-time high in the 1930s, and twentieth century executions of women happened mostly during the 1930s and 1940s. As recently as 1944, in South Carolina, fourteen-year-old George Stinney would be the youngest person in the twentieth century to die in the electric chair. Accused of murdering two white girls, Stinney was convicted, the sole evidence being his signed confession, quickly obtained by two white police officers behind closed doors.[20]

In 1928, one hundred and forty years after Hannah Occuish's execution, but sixteen years before George Stinney's, Ruth Snyder, a thirty-three-year-old white woman, was electrocuted in Sing Sing Prison along with her lover, a corset peddler, Henry Judd Gray, for the murder of her husband. Sexual policing attended legal regulation, such that women's sex crimes were, in the interwar period, "as subversive of American domesticity as the anarchism of Nicola Sacco and Bartolomeo Vanzetti was of the American political and economic order." But this was nothing new. Following English common law, eighteenth-century colonial lawmakers had defined mate slaying by a wife as a capital crime of petit treason, given the husband's position as "lord" of his wife. Rising up against husbands threatened disruption of social power, and was punishable by burning at the stake.

As an adulterous "mate slayer" in 1928, Ruth Snyder received no legal chivalry. When her attorney made a plea for mercy, the courtroom responded with mirth. A *Post* reporter wrote, "He was a knight fighting a battle of terrific odds for a golden damozel disguised as a blonde, fattish and ice-hard housewife." As Ann Jones has argued, "The newspaper-reading public, which doubted Ruth Snyder and condemned her, eagerly supported her right to die in the electric chair. Even before the trial began, the *Mirror* quoted a female social worker who claimed, "Any woman who commits a man's crime should be given a man's punishment." State senator William Lathrop Lave of Brooklyn urged "equal 'rights' for Women Criminals ... If a woman enters the competition with men she has a chance to gain the same ends, and I see no reason why she should not suffer the same penalties." Ann Jones has shown that for offences traditionally viewed as masculine, women have tended to receive harsher punishments. Having exercised sexual prerogatives reserved for men, Ruth Snyder was tried for murder and adultery in 1928.

Before Ruth Snyder, Martha Place died in the electric chair in 1899 at Sing Sing Prison for throwing acid at and asphyxiating her stepdaughter. Defying gender norms, Martha represented the antithesis of self-sacrificing, altruistic maternalism associated with idealized American womanhood. Governor Theodore Roosevelt denied her clemency, stating, "In the commission of a crime, a woman is deserving of the same blame as a man in a similar case. I would deal with the woman as with the man – no whit differently." A *New York Times* editorial stated, "Equal suffrage has put women in a new position. If they are equal with men before the law, they must pay the same penalties as men for transgressing it."

Women had been subject to equal treatment by the criminal law in mid-seventeenth-century New England, too. By the time of the American Revolution, one third of the thirty-five to fifty thousand convicts transported to America were women. They were pilloried and set in the stocks alongside men, publicly whipped, burned at the stake, forcibly held under water, maimed, branded, and dragged through the streets. In 1731 in Delaware, a white woman, Catherine Bevan, was burned at the stake, falling into the flames alive, in a grisly spectacle. In 1737, 1745, and 1769, Black women servants and slaves were also burned alive for murder convictions. In seventeenth- and eighteenth-century Europe, the public regularly indulged in festive hangings of women. At the turn of the eighteenth century in the United States, "Four or Five Thousand People at least" gathered to see Esther Rogers hanged in Massachusetts. Katherine Garret was hanged in New London, Connecticut, in 1738, and ten thousand gathered to watch Sarah Bramble hang in New London in 1753. At the mid-eighteenth century, women's status was in decline because, among other reasons, they were no longer a scarce resource in America. Moreover, with industrialization, cottage industries gave way to factories and the increased separation of men and women into essentialized spheres. Increasingly defined as inferior, women found themselves barred from certain occupations, paid less, deprived of voting rights, and removed from state offices. They also lost the rights they had enjoyed under marital-equity law. One of the informal privileges they gained in lieu of all they relinquished was the exemption from corporal punishment; but this effectively applied only to upper class white women.[21]

Change was uneven, but the tempering influence of Enlightenment thinkers made corporal punishment and public capital punishments like burning increasingly distasteful to the citizen elite. In 1699, no man would assume the task of whipping white women offenders in Hartford, Connecticut. While fifteen American women were convicted of capital crimes after 1718, ten were pardoned. Catherine Bevan's horrendous execution in 1731 had a lasting impact on public sensibilities because she had fallen into the fire alive. When Mrs Thompson, a white woman, killed her sleeping husband with an axe in 1769, the judge pronounced her "deranged," and incarcerated her to avoid burning her at the stake. Burning of women of African descent eventually stopped, too. In Orange County, a judge acquitted an enslaved woman, Letty, charged with poisoning a Black man and a white man. The judge acquitted her because the "horrible scene so recently enacted at the burning of Eve" was too abhorrent to repeat. Massachusetts changed the penalty for petit treason from burning to hanging in 1777. By the mid-eighteenth century, most of New England discontinued whipping women for petty offences, though not for adultery and repeated bastardy.[22]

Old-style penal practices, especially for white children, became a mark of inhumanity. American judges grew increasingly reluctant to execute minors, and by the turn of the twentieth century, North Carolinian jurisprudence regularly practised discretionary sentencing, particularly for white youth, extending individualized sanctions as a more effective response to their transgressions. Artfully manoeuvring the 1931 Samarcand arson case towards a merciful verdict, the defendants' lawyer, Nell Battle Lewis, made a point of presenting the "Samarcand Sixteen" as harmless children, downplaying their same-sex relationships within the institution, and their chequered histories prior to commitment. Replacing strict applications of punishment came to be seen as a political gesture meant to counter authoritarian anti-modernist punishment, demonstrating a merciful interest in children's welfare.[23] Perceptions of the young defendants mattered to the iconography of the New South within the broader context of American national discourses and global politics. While poor Blacks and whites suffered execution more often than did propertied whites, the legal execution of even poor white girls for arson involving no fatalities would have made North Carolina's criminal justice system seem exceptionally cruel by the national mores of the time. Merciful dismissal of the charges would signify a regression from twentieth century law, then, but strict application of the law would require North Carolina to try the girls for their lives, sentencing them to the electric chair if the grand jury returned an indictment of arson. In the Samarcand arson case, even lawful execution would have cast North Carolina as backward and barbaric. It would have also threatened the status of the state institution, lauded as a model of its kind, for failing in its role as *parens patriae*. And so it was that in spite of the defendants' confessions to setting fire to Samarcand, a considered ruling of partial mercy spared the girls' lives, exhibiting North Carolinian modernity through a show trial.[24]

Complicated Mercy

Historians Susan Cahn and John Wertheimer have also examined the Samarcand arson case in their analyses of gender and punishment in the interwar American South. Cahn argues that female offenders have been doubly punished historically, by gender and poverty, noting systematic misogyny inherent in legal regulation that has resulted in harsher punishment for behaviour in women deemed unremarkable in men. While the sexual desires of middle class white girls were increasingly channelled into heteronormative marriages, those of the working-class threatened social disorder, and national degeneracy through racial decline. Cahn argues that "the State's actions spoke to an abiding distrust and even revulsion" for working-class girls, who, through their ostensibly transgressive sexuality, had the power to "honey-comb the foundations of a state." These girls often perceived their court experiences and rehabilitative treatment as "an unfairly harsh and undeserved punishment," rooted in gender and class inequities.[25] John Wertheimer has also addressed gendered juridical bias within the Samarcand proceedings, making a case for legal chivalry, and claiming that women, as women, have routinely enjoyed special leniency affording them unfair advantage in a paternalistic legal system. Wertheimer denounces the defendants' "unladylike" conduct while in custody awaiting their trial, observing that their "trashing [of] state facilities ... confounded the legal system." He adds, "North Carolina chose not to prosecute any of the Samarcand women for any of the crimes they committed during their two jailhouse riots."[26] According to Cahn, solicitor Lewis's defence strategy failed and the young defendants received adult sentences because they were female and poor; but Wertheimer maintains that the defendants took full advantage of gender bias, soliciting lenient sentences for their crimes. Days before her trial, fifteen-year-old defendant Pearl Stiles wrote to the governor,

Dearest. Governor. Gardner. Will You please help us 9 girls in this case of trouble? ... Mr Gardner the way we were treated is terrible. We were locked, beat, and fed on bread and water most of the time. Please give me liberty or death. we girls in Robeson County Jail, is just as innocent of this crime. they hold against us as a little child which has never known anything. Please pardon us ... If you will only help us out of this trouble we will be happy. Mr. Gardner this is Pearl Stiles writing and I am always trying to be good I didn't have one thing to do with that old fire. Well all the girls said to give you their love for them Will close with good heart. From Miss Pearl Stiles to Mr. Gardner. Lumberton NC. answer at once.[27]

Noting that Stiles's letter closes "with a distinctively feminine flourish ... appealing humbly to the protective reflexes of a powerful

Southern man," Wertheimer claims that Judge Schenck mercifully rescued the young appellants. As "criminal defendants," he argues, these
"women became beneficiaries of the state's legal chivalry," getting
away with arson, and avoiding just punishment in the electric chair. In
using a defence strategy that emphasized corporal punishment within
the institution, Wertheimer contends, solicitor Lewis actually "hoped
to evoke the sympathies of a paternalistic court."[28]

While eliciting sympathy may have been part of Lewis's strategy, she
actually focused on *parens patriae*, and the state's failure to intervene
in loco parentis on behalf of young "social victims," in keeping with
liberal-humanist and "civilized" Americanism. Lewis challenged North
Carolina's claim to civilization in its toleration of extreme corporal punishment of children, given that floggings had long been outlawed in the
state prison and convict camps. Juvenile reformatories were entrusted
with a merciful mandate of moral suasion and non-violent protection
of white children, and as the sensational case developed, it expanded
public debates about punishment and identity.[29]

During the trial, Lewis quoted celebrated attorney and civil lib-
ertarian Clarence Darrow, who in a Chicago courtroom in 1924 challenged the death penalty for the young Leopold and Loeb, murderers
of fourteen-year-old Bobby Franks. Darrow linked juridical mercy to
evolutionary ascendancy, arguing, "[It might] be merciful if you tied
a rope around their necks and let them die; merciful to them, but not
merciful to civilization." Linking the death penalty to savagery, Darrow suggested it "roots back to the beast and the jungle. It is not part
of man."[30] During the Samarcand trial seven years later, Lewis would
argue, "If the law was administered without any feeling of sympathy
or humanity or kindliness, we would begin our long, slow journey back
to the jungle that was formerly our home."[31] Mobilizing racist imagery
against itself, Nell Battle Lewis argued for a common past that must be
transcended through the extension of judicial discretion to the young
offenders. Darrow's connection to evolution, coupled with the South's
preoccupation with the past, made this statement evocative and politically resonant.

Ann Jones has argued that if legal chivalry ever existed, it has
long been dead. Moreover, it has rarely been something extended to
working-class white women, indigenous women, or women of African descent. The very notion of legal chivalry carries a presumption of
guilt, of defendants as having "gotten away with something." When
sentences are shortened or suspended, she writes, it should be for legal,

not chivalric reasons. With a narrow focus on gender, Wertheimer has argued for equal opportunity in punishment, overlooking the reality that interest groups cannot participate in equivalent ways, depending upon their social location and differing bases of power within a hierarchical social structure. That the Samarcand arson case was not handled in juvenile court but taken directly to adult court indicates its gravity, contrary to John Wertheimer's claim. Governor O. Max Gardner had the power to pardon the girls, yet chose not to. Judge Michael Schenck's ruling resulted in adult sentences and years of confinement in the state penitentiary for twelve people who were not yet adults. A truly chivalrous outcome would have brought a complete dismissal of charges.

Susan Cahn has offered a more convincing argument of the threat transgressive rural working-class white girls posed during the interwar period in North Carolina, reflected in the harsher treatment they could typically expect from reformers and court officials. In focusing upon the Samarcand defendants as victims of the legal system, however, Cahn has overlooked the merciful plea bargain that Lewis negotiated on their behalf. The girls may not have avoided punishment, but they decidedly benefited from a discretionary outcome. John Wertheimer's essay elucidates a social complexity that accommodates gender-based discrimination that can sometimes work to the benefit of some women and girls. However, as part of a larger system of race and class politics, legal chivalry is not a policy that operates consistently in favour of women, as Ann Jones has shown. While Wertheimer has correctly identified biases within the juridical system, his conflation of anti-modernist chivalry with judicial discretion obscures the importance of this case within its wider national context. His analysis stops short in its implication that the judgment was a matter of what historian Carolyn Strange has referred to as "uncomplicated benevolence," and it is this that I take issue with.[32]

To get beyond assumptions of mercy as uncomplicated benevolence, it must be additionally analysed as integral to political and economic considerations that extend nationally and transnationally, as "imperial concerns from 'above.'"[33] Stuart Hall has observed that nationalism "creates, reflects and reproduces structures of cultural power."[34] Thus, it is important to consider the merciful judgment as a complex political act informed by the culture of the time, rather than as a simple attenuation of punishment. Uncomplicated humanitarian sentiment has historically been just one facet of a complex of issues "ranging from commercial and administrative to the pragmatic and expedient."[35]

Carolyn Strange has argued that while punishment is altered for various reasons, "officially sanctioned mercy, like severity, ultimately expresses the politics of rule." The Samarcand ruling spared the lives of girls who embodied national danger in their reputed capacity to "honeycomb the state," and yet they received adult prison sentences. This can be most fruitfully analysed as a complex set of negotiations related to national identity, and narratives about "civilization" within racialized and gendered imperial modernity.[36]

Nell Battle Lewis

By the time of my fieldwork, all of the Samarcand defendants had died. There is no surviving transcript of the trial because Moore County burned the entirety of the records except for the official handwritten sentences. My analysis relies on newspaper clippings recording eyewitness accounts of the trial, scrapbooks from Samarcand's private archives kept at the institution before it closed in 2011, and the personal papers of Nell Battle Lewis, housed at the North Carolina State Archives in Raleigh. These surviving records document the voices of the socially invisible, including adolescent reformatory inmates and low-level institutional employees. We are most fortunate to have Nell Battle Lewis's largely uninvestigated personal notebook documenting the unfolding of the case with detailed personal notes, and, significantly, testimony taken from the young defendants.[37] Historical voices of young people reflecting upon their experiences of reformatory incarceration in the United States are a rare find.

Having received her licence to practise law only twelve days before the burning of Samarcand, journalist Nell Battle Lewis, one of North Carolina's most prominent socialites, entered the case at the age of thirty-eight as counsel for defendant Virginia Hayes. Male lawyers were reluctant to get involved, and the court-appointed public defender "neglected to mount a serious defence." Not only an inexperienced barrister, Lewis was also one of a very few women in North Carolina practising law in 1931; and yet many, including colleagues from the North Carolina Women's Movement, supported her. Reverend H.L. Canfield wrote, "It may seem a thankless task you have undertaken; for an intelligent and just course of procedure requires a finer technique than existing penal codes and precedents in court modes can provide. Perhaps this case may be instrumental in pointing the way to a saner method of dealing with society's recalcitrant members." The case appealed to

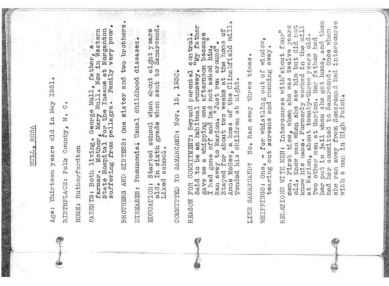

MULL, ROSA

Age: Thirteen years old in May 1931.

BIRTHPLACE: Polk County, N. C.

HOME: Rutherfordton

PARENTS: Both living. George Mull, father, a farmer. Mother, Mary Mull. Now in Western State Hospital for the Insane at Morganton suffering from pellagra. Family very poor.

BROTHERS AND SISTERS: One sister and two brothers.

DISEASES: Pneumonia. Usual childhood diseases.

EDUCATION: Started school when about eight years old. In sixth grade when sent to Samarcand. Liked school.

COMMITTED TO SAMARCAND: Nov. 15, 1930.

REASON FOR COMMITMENT: Beyond parental control. Said to be an habitual runaway. "My father gave me a whipping one afternoon because I had gone off and had not asked him." Ran away to Marion. "Just ran around." Stayed for about two weeks at the home of Amos McGee, a boss of the Clinofield mill. Tended his children at night.

LIKE SAMARCAND? No. Ran away three times.

WHIPPINGS: One. - for whistling out of window, tearing out screens and running away.

RELATIONS WITH MEN: Intercourse with "about four" men. First time, when she was twelve years old. Knew man when she saw him but did not know his name. Formerly worked in the mill at Marion, about twenty-three years old. Two other men at Marion. Her father had her put in jail when she got home, and then had her committed to Samarcand. Once When she ran away from Samarcand had intercourse with a man in High Point.

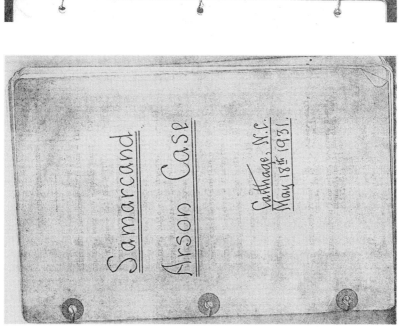

Figure 2.2. Pages from solicitor Nell Battle Lewis's notebook, Samarcand Arson Case, Carthage, NC, 18 May 1931. Nell Battle Lewis Papers, Private collection 255, box 162. Courtesy of State Archives of North Carolina.

Lewis, who had a long-standing interest in prison reform, and in women's rights, best advanced by "a few parades, some heckling, a smashed window or two and a little arson." To a friend she wrote, "This is exactly the sort of thing I want to do in my practice of the law. These children have been greatly handicapped by society. The whole problem of crime and delinquency interests me tremendously. I hope to make it my specialty – not theoretically in an office, but practically in the courts." This would be Lewis's first and only case. She effectively represented all sixteen defendants, assisted by George W. McNeill and W.R. Clegg, court-appointed to represent all but Virginia Hayes. While jailed at the Lumberton and Carthage jails, Virginia Hayes and Thelma Council both underwent surgery, ostensibly for appendicitis, but more likely for eugenic sterilization, at Moore County Hospital. Dubbed "Mississippi appendectomies," eugenic sterilizations without the patient's knowledge or consent were common in much of the South. Many girls and women led to believe that they were undergoing appendectomies were actually scheduled for hysterectomies.[38]

A North Carolinian bluestocking and suffragist active in several organizations, including the Legislative Council, a clearinghouse for seven major women's organizations that lobbied for passage of laws, "Battling Nell" advocated education, social justice, and reform. At the age of twenty-five she ran unsuccessfully for the North Carolina House of Representatives and served as a member in the organization of Southern Women Against Lynching. In 1921, she began her career as a respected public intellectual and columnist for Raleigh's *News and Observer*. In her 1935 piece "Our Official Slaughter Record," Lewis denounced capital punishment.[39]

Forgetting through Discursive Shifts

The shifting public perception of the "Samarcand Sixteen" propelled a merciful judgment that additionally identified North Carolinian whites as part of mercifully "civilized" white Americanism. Despite the advent of the sexually emancipated, independent New Woman, many still worried about reputations and marriageability. Surveillance and criminalization of working-class white girls increased through unprecedented commitments for status offences, widely interpreted as sexual transgressions. Then as now, criminalization of women and girls reflected the fundamental concern of the criminal justice system to police their gender performance. Nineteenth and early twentieth century expert discourses attributed moral corruption, and racial degeneration to transgressive white women, comparing them to "Hottentots." White women and girls who violated "natural law" defied hegemonic gender scripts, and suffered disadvantages in suffered more severe punishments. Eminent scientist E.D. Cope believed the "masculinization of women" threatened America's survival.[40] Sandra Gunning has observed that just as white popular culture marked emancipated Black men as hypersexual "fiends," "white women who asserted identities beyond the domestic space were figured both as race traitors and as diseased bodies ... [threatening] to transform the site of white domesticity into the very definition of instability."[41] White men risked only "racial contamination" through sexual contact with darker, "less civilized people"; but white women played a pivotal role in nation building as vessels of "the Race."[42] Victor Streib's observation that female offenders who have been legally executed in America since 1632 have fallen outside of popular interpretations of "the gentler sex" is significant, because the Samarcand defendants clearly fit this description (at least, at the outset). The North Carolina public initially vilified the girls, thinking they were prostitutes. Early newspaper accounts characterized them as "hedonistic and remorseless libertines." The *Daily Advance* reported: "Sex perversion or sodomy is practised in each cottage ... All inmates are paired off as 'sweethearts' – one being a boy and one a girl, and ... they 'love each other' in that relationship." "One of the defendants is a murderess," the *Moore County News* warned, adding, "They looked like morons. One or two of them had pretty faces, in a way, but most of them looked emaciated and as if they had seen too much of the sordid side of life."[43]

To some extent, solicitor Nell Battle Lewis saw the girls differently. She noted that Mary Lee Bronson was a "pretty, attractive blond, apparently of good intelligence. Pleasant and courteous manners. Tall and slender. Looks as if she might well be at St. Mary's" (a prestigious private school in Raleigh). Strategically focusing on the institutional failure to prevent corporal punishment, Lewis argued that "the treatment and the atmosphere of the institution was such as to further rebellion." Journalistic commentary and public opinion gradually turned and gained momentum. Portrayals of the girls between the arson and the trial date changed markedly. As the case unfolded, reporters and the white public increasingly downplayed the "sordid" pasts that had brought the girls to Samarcand. The "firebugs," as they came to be affectionately called, had become the darlings of the press, and enjoyed

Figure 2.3. Inmates working in the peach orchard at Samarcand, c. 1930.
Reprinted with permission from Samarcand Manor (private archives).

widespread public affection as if preparations were under way for a wedding rather than a capital trial. Levity swelled the public mood; there was banter between solicitor Lewis and Judge Schenck. When Lewis asked Schenck what he would do with orphaned sixteen-year-old defendant Wilma Owens whose case was *nol-prossed* (dropped), he responded, "I am going to place her in your custody." "But Judge," Lewis protested, "I don't know what to do with her." "Multiply your problem by sixteen and you will have a conception of my dilemma," Schenck replied.[44]

A month after the Samarcand fire, the *Daily Advance* reported that the defendants were children needing rescue from poor home environments and the inspiration to redeem themselves. "Perhaps her home simply isn't and can't be made a fit place for her to grow up in. She is given a new chance at Samarcand ... Such an institution ... would help to reduce the criminal class and add to the State's quota of good citizens."[45] Within five weeks of the initial damning accounts, the *News and Observer* reported, "[They] were fresh and bright ... dressed in clean, brightly colored print dresses, stockings rolled to the ankles ... overflowing with energy, all trying to talk at once, hesitating, and then beginning again ... They were unanimous in their opinion that they 'wouldn't have mother see my picture in the paper for anything.' The press let the girls set the record straight on the jailhouse rampages, which they insisted had been reported "all wrong." Josephine French explained, "We were in the room [cell] and asked the jailor's wife to let us out for awhile ... There's a Victrola upstairs and we can go and play it sometimes and dance ... She didn't come back so we set fire to one bunk – to bring somebody up to let us out. We supposed they had forgotten." The defendants "shrieked in girlish astonishment" at the allegation that they had stabbed a fire fighter with his own knife, explaining that in fact, "he got cut jumping out the window. There were only two girls had knives and they wouldn't cut. We didn't try to fight anybody ... [and] we didn't break half of what was broken. The men did it."[46] A supportive Kate Ford Peele of the *Daily Advance* wrote, "Girls outside of institutions do foolish things in the springtime, too ... They are thoughtless, foolish, just like girls the world over."[47]

Writing retrospectively in 1953, Lewis echoed this, arguing, "If conditions at St. Mary's had been parallel to those at Samarcand then, there would have been a corresponding outbreak of violence at that genteel school ... Student[s] couldn't tell from one day to the next what the rules were, and if a girl who broke the rules could be laid on the floor, held down by teachers, and lashed with a leather strap two inches wide,

the St. Mary's gals almost certainly, would have busted loose."[48] As for
the sexual danger Samarcand girls posed, the *Daily Advance* explained
that "Yes, some girls who are sent to Samarcand are immoral, some
are wayward, and many are merely underprivileged and neglected.
Most of the worst ones haven't done a thing that they couldn't get by
with gracefully and easily were they in high society."[49] The changing
perceptions of the defendants from depraved and racially degenerate,
to guileless children, influenced the outcome of the case. Public sentiment and the press now overwhelmingly supported the girls as local
heroines. In a letter to the editor of the *Fayetteville Observer*, someone
wrote, "We love our wayward unfortunate girls even though they may
have fallen or strayed from the straight and narrow way." The *Moore
County News* reported that the defendants had the sympathy of court
officials and the public, given their unfortunate histories and the egregious treatment they endured at the state institution. "The community,
it was generally felt, was to an extent responsible for the crime in that
it denied the girls a square deal, and [prevailing opinion] is that Judge
Michael Schenck in his decision tomorrow will be inclined sharply
toward leniency."[50] The public generally applauded Lewis's justification of the girls' actions as defensive rather than defiant, overwhelmingly supporting her as she went to trial.[51]

Please Give Me Liberty or Death

On 19 May the defendants were tried for first-degree arson before
Judge Michael Schenck at the Moore County Superior Court. But they
did not go on trial for their lives; this was a capital case without a capital result. Instead of each case being tried out, North Carolina held a
single trial, during which, a plea bargain spared the young defendants'
lives. Solicitor Don Phillips for the State of North Carolina dropped the
first-degree arson charges that carried the death penalty in exchange
for guilty pleas to the lesser charge of attempted arson, which carried
the penalty of imprisonment from four months to ten years. North Carolinian judges exercised considerable discretionary power during the
1930s, even to the point of exonerating convicted murderers through
probation. This led to a wide range in sentencing, depending upon the
judges' political inclinations. Judge Schenck attended "strictly to business when on the bench, [while] retaining the human element which
is often considered lacking in many judges." In the day-long "drama
packed trial" held on 19 May 1931, he sat as jury as well as judge.

Figure 2.4. Arson defendants and their counsel heading into court, 21 May 1931. Nell Battle Lewis papers, PC 255.29. Reprinted with permission from *The News & Observer*, Raleigh, NC.

Samarcand's Superintendent Agnes MacNaughton did not take the witness stand. The state presented its case during the morning, and the defence through the afternoon, with speeches by solicitors Lewis and Phillips concluding the day's proceedings. Phillips defended Samarcand, "praising its operation and the way the girls were handled." Formally representing only Virginia Hayes, Lewis assumed the brunt of the defence in a dramatic appeal that moved the crowded courtroom behind the prisoners' seats, and reduced to tears the same girls who had sung all the way to the courthouse, smoking cigarettes and hurling insults at photographers as they disembarked from the bus.[52]

Criminal Responsibility: State Negligence

Defence counsel Nell Battle Lewis framed her appeal around three central points: first, the defendants could not be convicted on the basis of failed home environments beyond their individual control. Second, their feeblemindedness relieved them of criminal responsibility, and, most importantly, the state and Samarcand had failed to protect them. In her first line of defence, Lewis sought to recast the defendants' reputations, assuaging public fears of the girls as innately depraved, and garnering support for them as children victimized by corrupt home environments. Shortly after Lewis's first visit with the imprisoned defendants awaiting their trial, newspaper reports began to frame the girls' offences in relation to their family case histories. In her personal notes, Lewis described Margaret Abernethy as a "Small thin blonde, bad complexion. Seems timid. Very pathetic. Seems to be frail." Her father, a plumber, was serving a two-year term in the state penitentiary for raping her several times a week from the age of ten to thirteen. He had taken four-year-old Margaret away from her mother, telling the child her mother was dead. He drank, though not during episodes of incest. In her statement, Margaret Abernethy remembered, "It was against my will. He kept me scared ... I never ran around with boys; he wouldn't let me ... My step-mother had just had a baby and he slipped down to my room and she caught him there that night. After she found out, my daddy told me he was going to kill me, and I ran away."[53] Upon her father's conviction, Margaret became a Samarcand inmate. The intake sheet classified her as "bad."

While Marian Mercer denied "running around," the juvenile court committed her to Samarcand for promiscuity in October 1928. Hearing impaired, Marian's intelligence quotient score of seventy-seven marked her as "borderline normal." Her regular school attendance did nothing to temper the reputation of her mother Rosetta Clark, "ruined" for having married twice. She allegedly ran a brothel. Seized by the juvenile court, Marian entered the County Home at the age of four.

Josephine French's father had abandoned the family when she was just two years old, and her mother worked in a silk hosiery mill. Josephine would, at the tender age of thirteen, refuse to live with her husband and cousin Luther. Within a couple of years, he had her committed to Samarcand, and her infant son was placed with his family. This was in May 1929, two years before the Samarcand fire. Lewis suspected that the "real reason [for commitment was a] charge of prostitution in Norfolk," where Josephine had worked in a café. Josephine stood firm in her position that it was her husband, not she, who had been unfaithful, and that he had her committed to punish her for leaving him.

Bertha Hall's father had died of tuberculosis when she was only a year old, and her mother later died of cancer. Ollie Harding's mother had died of cancer, and father was paralytic and unemployed.

Lewis argued that the defendants bore no criminal responsibility, because they were not inherently bad, but at the mercy of deleterious home environments. Ultimately, this argument would strengthen support for Samarcand, exonerating the State of North Carolina, while shielding the institution from public censure and closure.

Lewis's second argument focused on the defendants' documented "feeblemindedness," which negated a rationally informed motivation for arson, establishing diminished criminal responsibility. Predictably, the defendants' mental test scores were subnormal. Dr Harry W. Crane, University of North Carolina faculty, and director of the Bureau of Mental Health and Hygiene of the State Board of Charities and Public Welfare testified that "with such mental development [the girls] would not realise the difference between right and wrong, but would only know that certain things had been indicated to them as right and wrong." While it is possible that Lewis coached her, defendant Pearl Stiles's letter to Governor Gardner indicates a clear understanding of the legal issues, highlighting the three main points that Lewis would base her appeal on: *doli incapax* (incapacity of forming the intent to commit a crime), Samarcand's failed *parens patriae*, and inadequate home environments. Sentenced to the state prison four days before her sixteenth birthday, Pearl Stiles held the most demerits of all the Samarcand defendants.

Figure 2.5. Samarcand inmates, c. 1930. Reprinted with permission from Samarcand Manor (private archives).

Figure 2.6 Samarcand inmates, c. 1930. Reprinted with permission from Samarcand Manor (private archives).

Her devastating IQ score of 61 classified her as "feebleminded," with a mental age of nine years and nine months. Pearl had begun school at "about nine," and despite irregular attendance, reached the fifth grade by the age of fourteen.[54]

Lewis contended that while the girls were wards of the state at Samarcand, the state had "failed in its duty as guardian to the 'problem of incorrigible children.'" "Forward-thinking" citizens who advocated psychiatric treatment over the strap denounced the exercise of corporal punishment at Samarcand as a serious indictment of North Carolina's correctional system. During the trial, Lewis brought attention to the unbearable conditions at Samarcand – as much as the court permitted her to. "[Virginia Hayes] says," remarked Lewis, "she had rather be in jail than in Samarcand." Bertha Hall denied her involvement in the fire, but declared that "if they took me back there would be a fire." Estelle Wilson added, "They would lock me up every time I turned around."[55]

The pivotal element of Lewis's defence rested on the testimony of defendants' experiences of severe floggings at Samarcand Manor, to the embarrassment of the state Department of Public Welfare. Its infliction on children exposed the unsettling persistence of violence in a modern sanctuary for the nation's future citizens. Lewis argued, "Young girls cannot be beaten with sticks and straps, placed in rooms where sleep is difficult because of roaches and be made to believe that the state, that the school or that the officials of the school have even so much as a remote interest in them." Margaret was whipped once "for running away and carrying desert [sic] to a discipline girl locked in her room." She recalled, "They lay you down on a rug and ... some hold their heads and others their feet ... while the other teachers ... take straps or switches. If you run away they cut your hair." Dolores Seawell stated that the superintendent, Miss Agnes MacNaughton, was "good to me except when she beat me."[56]

Lewis had also collected statements from many former employees, many of whom responded with harrowing accounts of life at Samarcand Manor. What surfaced was an exposé of the institution's techniques of punishment, scandalizing Samarcand officials. Highly respected medical personnel and former employees who had agreed to testify spoke passionately of the institution's violent practices. The resident nurse, Viola Sistare, expressed concern about the youngest inmates, children from six to ten years old, who were housed with older girls "to learn, all sorts of things which should come later, if at all." She testified, "I could show you reports of girls who have

Figure 2.7. Agnes B. MacNaughton (1872–1938), first Samarcand superintendent, 1918–33. Reprinted with permission from Samarcand Manor (private archives).

come to Samarcand clean with negative reports for syphilis and gonorrhoea whose Wassermann tests have been positive after having been incarcerated there for a time." She also expressed concern that when several of girls had come to her with dog bites from the superintendent's collie, she was ordered to omit these incidents from her reports.[57] Superintendent MacNaughton additionally forbade Nurse Sistare to treat girls with dog bites, poison oak hives, or burns from cooking or furnace work. "They deserved to suffer," MacNaughton allegedly remarked.

And suffer, they did. Refused bedding, many girls slept in window-less rooms. Employees testified that teachers addressed the girls as "little gutter rats," and "scum of the earth."[58] Lottie Mitchem, former principal of Samarcand's high school, described the locking discipline for girls of the manor who "needed a very grave measure of discipline." They were locked in a small room with "a poor feeble-minded crea-ture who has gonorrhoea and syphilis. She has such a virulent form of halitosis and a very terrible body odour that it is impossible to stay in her direction long at a time. She practices all forms of masturbation upon herself and other children – teaching them practices they have never known of."[59] Lottie Mitchem remembered, "the children were ... bawled out, told how low down they were and where they came from and what they had done on the outside and then dog stories were read to them and the dog (a school mascot) was held up by someone and the girls were asked if they did not wish they were as good as [the dog]." She recounted the time a teacher confiscated a girl's scarf, held it up and burned it. Mitchem testified, "Miss Ludie Draughn [was wearing a scarf] when she should not have been. But no instructions had been given girl previously that wearing of scarf was an infringement of rules and scarf was gift of girl's dead mother." This act, Mitchem suggested, must have incited the girls to torch Samarcand by example.[60]

In a retrospective 1945 article for "Incidentally," Lewis would compare the conditions at Samarcand to the Nazi concentration camp Bergen-Belsen, calling staff members "sadists." She recalled a child who, sick with diphthe-ria, was sent outside to play. Punishments of healthy girls included locking them in a room with her. Some inmates were reportedly held in solitary confinement for as long as three months in a discipline hall infested with vermin and placed on a restricted diet of milk, bread, and beans. In a let-ter to the editor of the *Fayetteville Observer*, 4 May 1931, Bettie Watts, the mother of the girl who had been pulled out of her bedroom window and raped, complained, "The girls ... [have had] their bodies sucked by the blood thirsty vermin. Thousands upon thousands crawled up and down the walls to their helpless victims. I am sorry this building is destroyed with the bugs but am sure there are witnesses enough left who will be glad to prove that this is true."[61] Sworn testimony from the former foods teacher, Georgia Piland, attested to routine brutality at Samarcand. "I heard screams and was told by the girls in my kitchen that they were whipping one of the girls. One would judge the whips to be either black gum or hickory, and they looked to be from five to six feet in length. It was not two or three whips, but a great bundle of them ... The entrance to Chamberlain could be easily seen from our kitchen window."[62] Viola Sistare witnessed floggings, too. She recalled that the superintendent's secretary "would come to me for "something to make a girl quiet" after caning her. One night, a student government head came to Nurse Sistare with instructions to accompany her to Chamberlain Hall with a sedative. "On our arrival a bundle of hickory switches was produced, the girl laid on the bare floor with just a cotton gown on – and held by six other girls. As they began to beat the girl – I went into another room; but I could plainly hear her cry. After an interval ... she was released and I was told to give her the pill.[63]

Nurse Sistare also related an incident of a child unable to sit, and having difficulty walking because "her buttocks and upper limbs very badly bruised, black and blue and with large welts." Sistare treated the child and sent her back to her cottage. "On the way she stopped at another cottage and some of the teachers, my sister included, asked to see the marks. The child showed them and one teacher fainted." Another time, one of the younger children had come to the clinic, asking to see Sistare alone after a whipping.[64] There were deep cuts with dried blood about her legs and buttocks.

> I did not wish to interfere with the discipline – but knowing that region is very easily infected I cleaned and bathed the child and applied ungentine because she could not sit down. I sent her to the ward to stay ... The next day Miss MacNaughton came to the hospital and in no uncertain terms laid me low for having treated the child and also accused me of having spread the report of the child's condition all over the institution ... She dragged the child out of bed and put her in her automobile ... The child was locked and threatened with dire consequences should she ever do such a thing again.[65]

Judge Schenck disallowed Lewis's request to present the extensive testimony she had gathered from former Samarcand employees at the trial because it did not refer specifically to the defendants. On a cross-examination, Lewis was only able to establish that there were no rules of punishment.

The Outcome

Lewis made a plea to Judge Schenck "for mercy for the children who were the products of their environment, of forces beyond their control or comprehension."[66] She argued that as wards of the state, the children had a right to expect sympathetic discipline. "The State had said they were not getting the proper discipline at home, and North Carolina undertook to stand in the place of their parents. The State which recognised they were problem children is now asking punishment for them." While conceding that discipline was necessary, Lewis insisted that "half-grown girls should not be laid on a whipping carpet, when flogging has been abolished in chain gangs. These children are all young with their eyes to the future, and I think the state whose wards they were when the crime was committed should give them as great a chance as possible."[67] Her appeal succeeded to the extent that Schenck reduced the charges from a felony of arson to an attempt to burn a building. In private correspondence, Lewis reflected on the proceedings, explaining, "I did all I could for these poor girls, but it was not enough to save twelve of them from the Penitentiary, out of which they will come at the experiation [sic] of their sentences even more bitter enemies of society than they are now." A few days after the trial, her friend Katherine Boyd wrote, "I can't help but thrill to the courage that burns down Samarcand and jails and raised the devil. It's tragic to think what's going to happen to those girls – contrasted with what might have happened if they had had a halfway fair start.[68]

Lewis arrived at the Wednesday morning sentencing to a packed courtroom reverberating with anticipation. Schenck addressed the defendants: "Some of the doctors think you haven't sense enough to know what I'm saying, but I rather think you have." He continued, "Upon the pleas of the defendants given through their counsel, the Court finds as a fact and concludes as a matter of law, that each and all of the twelve defendants are, in fact, guilty.[69] Schenck sentenced Josephine French, Virginia Hayes, Marian Mercer, Margaret Abernethy, Delores Seawell, Thelma Council, Ollie Harding, Bertha Hall, Chloe Stillwell, Estelle Wilson, Edna Clark, and Pearl Stiles to the state penitentiary for a term of not less than eighteen months, not more than five years. He stated that they could not be controlled at home, and "after the State had done the best it could for them at Samarcand they were still unruly and rebellious."[70] Gazing upon the defendants, he emphasized the authority of the law and the partial mercy extended them:

You have said you would rather go to jail than be in Samarcand. You are going to have your choice. You could have been tried for your lives and sent to the electric chair. The state did not want to send you to the electric chair … Your stay in the penitentiary depends entirely upon you. If you want to stay there five years, just go down there and set something on fire. If you want to behave yourself, you can get out in two years. That is the force that is going to be used on you and the options of the choice you make. The state is strong enough to hold you.[71]

The convicted girls left the courtroom for the state prison, where they occupied cells in the only fireproof wing of the prison, directly above death row. Of the remaining four defendants, Margaret Pridgen and Rosa Mull received suspended sentences conditional upon sustained good behaviour.[72]

Public outrage echoed Lewis's disappointment. A day after the trial, the *Rocky Mount Telegram* reported, "North Carolina Fails," arguing that if the former employees' reports were even partially true, the board of trustees and school officials were guilty of gross neglect: "The girls sent yesterday to the state's prison are only children. When they have completed their sentences in state's prison, they will have been completely broken … The ironic challenge of a judge telling them to make good citizens of themselves is wasted breath."[73] The *High Point Enterprise* echoed these sentiments, suggesting, "The girls, hard as they have proved themselves to be, succeeded in raising a question as to the social extent of the loss were Samarcand to be given entirely to the flames."[74] The public widely opposed the death penalty and even prison sentences for the defendants, especially given their traumatic experiences at Samarcand Manor, and the viciousness of penitentiary existence. "'Them girls have already been punished twice over for everything they've done. They've been punished ever since they were born,' was part of the comment which went along with the service of filling a gasoline tank and radiator." Of course, some people disagreed, arguing that given the mass destruction of state property and the girls' immorality, "drastic measures should be taken." Outside the courthouse, one person told a reporter, "I would have locked 'em up for the full ten years."[75] When considered in relation to the political culture of the South in that historical moment, the partial mercy extended to the Samarcand defendants suggests a concern to demonstrate Southern civilization. As a political gesture, the discretionary ruling exercised humanitarian concern for the Samarcand defendants, while also refusing them absolution, demonstrating North Carolina's "civilized" commitment to lawfulness.

The Investigation

The case drew unwanted attention to Samarcand. While the defendants had been awaiting arraignment in the aftermath of the fires, the board of managers requested a "complete and thorough" investigation of Samarcand to be made by the Department of Public Welfare before the trial. Roy Eugene Brown, director of the Division of Institutions for the State Board of Public Welfare, launched an official investigation of conditions at Samarcand.[76] Nell Battle Lewis wrote to Commissioner Kate Burr Johnson, about the upcoming investigation, confiding, "I entered this case very favorably disposed to Samarcand. As you know, I have myself written flattering stories about the place. But I am convinced now beyond a doubt that something is seriously wrong at that institution ... Of course, everything will be beautifully whitewashed." She added that the State Board of Public Welfare had interpreted her defence of the girls as an attack on welfare work, "which, of course, makes me laugh."[77] The trial concluded before the state welfare department submitted its eighty-five-page investigative report. As part of the inquiry, officials conducted a nation-wide survey on disciplinary methods used in juvenile reformatories, the results indicating a widespread and increasing rejection of corporal punishment for children. In a four-day visit to Samarcand, officials gathered data from records on file, and interviewed staffers and selected inmates. Their report included evidence from the witness stand at the Samarcand trial in Carthage, together with interviews conducted at the institution.

Former teachers raised the issue of worker dissatisfaction, and Dr C.W. Durham's earlier letter to Lewis corroborated this. He wrote, "When I left, the second nurse left along with two or three others – about four weeks ago three high school teachers were fired on about one hour's notice."[78] Staffer Georgia Piland stated that employment at Samarcand felt precarious. "We each had the feeling that at any minute we might offend [Miss MacNaughton] by the least act, never intending to, and be ordered to leave the institution in fifteen minutes." Employees described Superintendent MacNaughton as dismissive and disrespectful. Georgia Piland remembered, "When I reached the institution on Monday P.M. and was introduced to her while she sat on her car on the campus she did not recognise me, but said, 'Yes, I'm trying to get this burr from my dog's mouth.' We waited for further response, but received none, then drove on."[79] Former teacher Lottie Mitchem brought charges against Samarcand, sharing her letter of resignation, submitted just before the fire. She had written, "I am, indeed, sorry to leave the girls under such care."[80] To the girls she wrote, "Dear Girls, It nearly breaks my heart to leave you! Surely you all know that I love you and have done my best for you! Just because I am away does not change me a bit. I still love you – one and all. I am going to be so lonely without you."[81] The personnel turnover rate at Samarcand was 114 per cent per year for the period from 1 January 1929 to 1 April 1931 – or ninety-eight changes.[82]

Many employees still on staff defended Superintendent MacNaughton, dismissing former co-workers as "disrupting, harmful influences." Student government counsellor Lillian Crenshaw alleged that the former nurse, Viola Sistare, had a bad temper, was a nuisance, and had no principles, having advised the girls to burn Samarcand down. She once left the campus at night with another teacher without permission. Staffer Sophia McCrary agreed, suggesting that "Sistare should not have been here at all." Not only did she "swear like a sailor," but she rolled her hose and wore too little clothing.[83] Former employee Nora Phillips called the allegation that teachers and girls feared to approach Miss MacNaughton "absurd." She also stated that while MacNaughton disapproved of corporal punishment, she had to resort to it as a "treatment measure" when dealing with "a certain type of psychopathic individual." Instances were few, she said, and whippings were administered only after everything else failed: "Patience, kindness, affection, placing the girl in this cottage or that class, trying to arouse her interest, understand her, and see her side, and still after months of exhausting every resource she persisted in screaming, cursing, kicking, and smashing, no matter how sorry one felt for her as a poor upset individual for the sake of a very suggestible group something had to be done."[84]

Estelle Stott, secretary to Agnes MacNaughton, testified that "only three girls had been whipped and this was not done unmercifully ... Sometimes a switch and sometimes a strap is used in administering punishment to the girls and that ten to fifteen licks are given."[85] In response to the investigative report, others came to the defence of Samarcand officials, explaining that they must have been too exhausted, nervous, and spent to keep records of the merciful whippings they administered. "How they must have fought back the tears when there was nothing else to do except administer a spanking, ever so gentle and tender it might be."[86]

However, nurse Bessie Bishop's earlier sworn testimony contested this, recalling an incident of a girl showing her "great black and blue bruises." Nurse Bishop asked the girl if she had fallen, and the child began "crying and said Miss MacNaughton beat me most to death." On another occasion she was asked to carry a girl to Chamberlain Hall.

The child "was made to lie on the bare floor, on face, hands over head, was beaten with a leather strap unmercifully. You could hear her cries a great distance off and this is what they termed as getting a spank but I rather think it was being beaten instead."[87] *The Pilot* reported that Mrs W.T. Bost, commissioner of public welfare, had "declined to express her views as to the State's permitting floggings in its correctional institution for girls while floggings are banned in the State's prison and prison farms." Other newspapers reported that the evidence of mistreatment had been exaggerated, and that any public sympathy for the girls had been "grossly misplaced."[88] Lewis remained unconvinced. In 1945 she would write: "In working up the case of course I found out all I could about conditions at Samarcand that might have given the girls a motive. And I found plenty. The wonder was that, instead of burning down just two buildings, they hadn't burned the whole place down."[89] Nell Battle Lewis predicted that everything would be whitewashed, and indeed the post-trial report categorically supported the continued value of Samarcand as a reform institution. Investigators minimized whippings, and concluded that former employees' charges were based on hearsay evidence. They pointed to interviewed inmates' statements that whippings were actually not so severe, additionally citing interviews of three girls who all denied having been locked in a room with an inmate sick with diphtheria.[90]

"We Have Struck at the Root of the Trouble at Samarcand"[91]

Investigators commended the Samarcand board of managers' offer to abolish corporal punishment as a matter of institutional policy, advising that records of punishment be kept in future. They also suggested the provision of "thinking rooms" in the new fireproof building, where difficult inmates could be isolated and placed on a restricted diet supervised by the physician in charge. Dr E. Delia Dixon Carroll, chair of the board of trustees for Samarcand stated that the institution's "record of reclamation of wayward girls was higher than that of similar institutions for the country."[92] Downplaying required organizational and policy changes, she maintained that "the efforts of those in charge ... have yielded rich returns in the remaking and the reclamation of the lives of many young women who have had the benefit of the training received there, which after all is the only practical and final test to be applied." She exonerated Samarcand Manor and endorsed the state's investment.[93] Reform institutions benefited the nation and "the Race."[94] Lauded nationally as a model institution, Samarcand's role as a normalizing "station on the highway of North Carolina progress" contributed to discourses of North Carolina's merciful "civilization" and national belonging.

In absolving the institution, state administrators would come to blame the problems leading to the arson on individual employees – chiefly Superintendent Agnes McNaughton. Soon after the report emerged, Commissioner Johnson confided to Commissioner Bost, "I wonder if Miss MacNaughton is not slipping. She is not as young as she used to be and has been there so long." Bost replied, "Perhaps we might look to the time when it might be best to make Miss MacNaughton Superintendent Emeritus, thus honoring her for the fine pioneering work she has done for Samarcand." When Director of the Division of Institutions for the State Board of Public Welfare Roy Brown conducted a follow-up inspection of Samarcand, he expressed disappointment, explaining that most of the state board's 1931 recommendations adopted by the Samarcand board in 1932 were not put into effect. He wrote, "The institution needs to be thoroughly reorganized with a person of ability and experience at the head." Superintendent MacNaughton departed Samarcand shortly thereafter, in December 1933, apparently suffering from a nervous condition. Commissioner Bost would later write, "Miss Agnes MacNaughton, former Superintendent, as you know, had a breakdown and is now, according to my understanding, at the State Hospital in Morganton." Agnes MacNaughton would become a residential patient at Moore County's Pine Bluff Sanatorium, where she would die in 1938 at the age of sixty-six after a four-year illness. The board dedicated a memorial garden to her in 1940.[95]

Samarcand had not succeeded in abolishing corporal punishment, but this was typical of so many juvenile reform institutions. Wolf Wolfensberger would observe forty years later that few of the hoped-for aims were ever approximated, and the major rationales advanced for institution building were "perverted eventually."[96] Through recurring scandals, white reformers would eventually be compelled to recognize institutional failings, but for a long time, they believed the system was worthwhile, blaming problems on inadequate funding, administrators' incompetence, or the failings of individual superintendents. Discretionary goals remained popular until the 1940s, when the tide turned, and North Carolina began to reinstate harsher but less expensive custodial forms of juvenile corrections, the first being a penal institution for girls of African descent.

The Samarcand ruling reinforced the legitimacy of law, in keeping with Douglas Hay's observation that mercy would instil popular faith in the fiction that law was compassionate.[97] But as Strange reminds us, "It is jejune to assume that mercy is inspired by compassion, even though sovereigns and politicians typically adorn their decisions in the language of pity and forgiveness."[98] In examining the unfolding of the Samarcand arson case in relation to its wider sociopolitical context, what emerges is a judgment inflected by gender, class, and race discourses in North Carolina, informing a complex, nuanced set of reasons related to negotiations of national identity. This sensational case brought deep contradictions to the fore, and while it cannot by itself be said to have changed the perceptions of North Carolinians in relation to the nation, its outcome clearly exemplifies the presence of discursive shifts. Citing Modris Ekstein's observation that nations at war tend to reveal their core values, Carolyn Strange observes that "executives, faced with the unpalatable decision whether to execute or commute, articulate the central tenets of their polity."[99] North Carolinians were no longer at war, but they became involved in a crisis-generated spectacle marked by nationalist discourses. The spectacular discursive process that resulted in a judgment of partial mercy in this case indicates much about how white liberal proponents of New South ideology construed national life and sought to construct a "civilized" collective identity. The case became a show trial, a spectacle of white protection that confirmed North Carolina's national belonging through civilizationist metaphors. The legal system in North Carolina and the entire South was developing in opposition to vigilantism, not as a matter of antiracist epiphany so much as to gain legitimacy within the nation.

As for the "Samarcand Sixteen," North Carolinians demonstrated collective mercy towards the defendants, bringing them into the fold of white Americanism just long enough to declare opposition to the infliction of institutionalized violence, and the death penalty. They extended this inclusion temporarily and with ambivalence; the defendants never really shed their alterity. The girls served as pawns in a trial that was subsumed by a public negotiation and spectacle of North Carolinians' sense of national belonging. Two decades after the trial, in her newspaper column "Incidentally," Lewis wrote, "I know the fate of only one of the sixteen, one of the four who got off. She killed herself. Hurrah for North Carolina!"[100] Wilma Owens was motherless, and had been raped when she was eleven. Two years before the fires she had been hospitalized for an officially authorized "operation," likely a hysterectomy. As a patient, she "did so well" helping the nurses in the wards, that Haywood County's W.G. Byers recommended her for nurses' training. But two years after the trial, although she was *nol-prossed* with leave, Wilma Owens took her own life by drinking Lysol.[101]

Rosa Mull, having just turned thirteen at the time of trial, received a suspended sentence, contingent upon good behaviour. Her mother had recently died, and when she was to be sent home to Rutherfordton, her townspeople wired a protest declaring, "[W]e don't want her back here." Three months later, her community succeeded in having her sent back to prison, where she began serving a two-year term in September 1931. Rutherfordton residents expressed "dread of her influence," which amounted to little more than "her habit of keeping late hours and not wishing to live with her father in a motherless home."[102] Like the harsh punishments that were effectively glossed over, public support for the Samarcand girls dissipated once the spectacle was over. Twelve of the young defendants spent the rest of their teen years languishing, forgotten, in the state penitentiary. The fates of most of the Samarcand Sixteen remain a mystery.

Chapter Three

The Energy of Despair[1]

Since the population is nothing more than what the state takes care of for its own sake, of course the state is entitled to slaughter it, if necessary. So the reverse of biopolitics is thanatopolitics.

Michel Foucault[2]

From 1 July 1919 to 30 June 1939, 3839 girls of African descent under sixteen appeared in North Carolina juvenile courts. Juvenile court judges often complained about having no choice but to either release these girls back into their communities or send them to county jails or the penitentiary.[3] Winston-Salem's superintendent of public welfare A.W. Cline wrote to Commissioner Bost, "No one realises the need of such an institution more than the officials of the Juvenile Court. Hardly a week passes that we are not forced to turn loose on the community one or more negro girls, who should be confined for a period of time in a correctional institution." Presuming congenital depravity, he added, "The jail is no place to confine a girl of Juvenile Court age to force compulsory treatment for venereal diseases. If we wanted to use the jails for this purpose, it would take only a few weeks to fill them to overflowing."[4]

In an intrepid move, educator, suffragist, and president of the North Carolina Federation of Colored Women's Clubs Dr Charlotte Hawkins Brown, led the founding of the North Carolina Industrial Home for Colored Girls at Efland, Orange County. Established in 1919, after eight years of arduous negotiation, the Efland home opened its doors in September 1923. Federation members proposed this reformatory in accordance with national Anglophilic social hygiene campaigns, and in keeping with other North Carolina juvenile reformatories: Samarcand

What We Have Accomplished

1. In 1921—purchased 140 acres of land within two miles of Efland post office.

2. Paid $750 on purchase price of $7,150.

3. Women of state cancelled this indebtedness in five years.

4. Built cottage, installed light, heat, water system and equipment at cost of about $15,000.

5. Only indebtedness of $2,000 remains on this property.

6. Cared for 40 girls during this period — 20 already paroled, most of whom have returned to society, able to earn a living and to become useful members of their communities.

7. A farm has been cultivated: potatoes, corn, wheat, vegetables for canning, etc., have been raised in sufficient quantities to meet a great part of the needs of the boarding department.

8. We employ three workers—Superintendent, Teacher, Farm Director. Classes are held half day for eight months; other half day is spent in practical household work, etc.

9. Girls of Home sent creditable exhibit to the last meeting of State Federation, finding sale for many articles.

Our Aim

They Deserve Your Interest

To save the young Negro girl who is on the verge of wasting her life, and to give her a second chance.

Only girls under sixteen years of age will be taken, and these will be given a practical knowledge of the household arts that they may go out equipped to earn a living.

In His name we are launching this effort to save Negro womanhood, and we hope to surround these girls with the spirit of Jesus whose m e m o r a b l e words were, "Go in peace and sin no more."

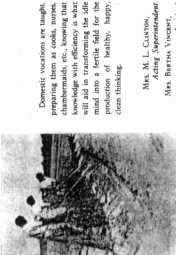

Domestic vocations are taught, preparing them as cooks, nurses, chambermaids, etc., knowing that knowledge with efficiency is what will aid in transforming the idle mind into a fertile field for the production of healthy, happy, clean thinking.

Mrs. M. L. CLINTON,
Acting Superintendent.
Mrs. BERTHA VINCENT,
Assistant.

Helping themselves while others help them

Financial Statement

RECEIPTS

Brought forward (balance 1929-30)	$ 51.42
From State Department (quarterly)	2,000.00
From North Carolina Federation of Clubs	1,196.30
From Juvenile Court (Charlotte)	20.00
From private donations	532.00
Total	$3,799.72

EXPENDITURES

Salaries	$1,453.00
Repairs	281.00
Groceries	1,204.21
Traveling expenses	42.00
Miscellaneous	278.72
Insurance	78.57
Payments and interest on mortgage	960.00
Indebtedness on groceries	497.78
Total	$4,297.50 $4,297.50

Figure 3.1. From the Efland home's pamphlet "Save Our Girls" (c. 1923). North Carolina Industrial Home for Colored Girls, Efland, Orange County, NC. State Board of Public Welfare, box 163, North Carolina Training School for Delinquent Girls, file 1939–41. Courtesy of the State Archives of North Carolina.

Manor, the State Training School for Negro Boys at Hoffman, and Stonewall Jackson Training School for [White] Boys. Having founded the Efland home in 1919 through private philanthropy, the North Carolina Federation of Colored Women's Clubs took two more years to raise $1000 "in nickels and dimes and dollars" from community members to invest in institutional property.[5] The federation worked largely with private donations, shepherding the "little institution" at Efland for more than two decades, and through the Great Depression.

By 1920, founders of privately established public welfare institutions in North Carolina could expect the state to assume fiscal responsibility for the operation of these facilities; indeed, the state appropriations committee had generously funded all other start-up institutions premised on the merciful reclamation of young status offenders. Efland's pamphlet "Save Our Girls" entreated potential supporters, appealing to Christian mercy, childhood innocence, and widespread fears of prostitution. Seeking to make Efland a proper state institution, Brown urged the importance of taking initiative in providing means of saving adolescent girls who were "easy prey of evil seekers." She further explained, "There is no better opportunity given to our women for self-expression than through this medium which strikes at the very roots of a great social evil, namely, the wasting of the womanhood of the race."[6] Using rhetoric typically reserved for white girls, Brown expressed concern that "young girls in their teens frequenting questionable places cannot long withstand the vice that stands with open arms to greet them."[7] Brown petitioned a hesitant R.F. Beasley, commissioner of the State Board of Public Welfare, who, in response to her proposal for a reformatory, disparaged the clubwomen's initiative in having already found a location, suggesting this was the wrong way to proceed if they expected to ask the state for funding. He advised, "I will be prepared to ask the State to help the right kind of institution but not the wrong kind. I would suggest that you confine your efforts to securing subscriptions and a general propaganda for the needs of such an institution and leave it with the legislature to select a location and begin the institution."[8] Five months later, Brown would again approach the commissioner:

> You perhaps recall having said that it would probably be sometime before the State could provide for the girls … [We] have our eyes on a piece of property near Efland, N.C. and hope we may call on you very soon to go out and inspect this place before any purchase is made. As mothers and sisters we want to save the young colored girls who are going astray. We

are afraid to wait but we want to move along lines that your board will suggest. We want to make no mistake for we do not want to have you do this work over.[9]

The federation attempted to exercise political power without political rights. Before suffrage, white women could at least claim a restricted citizenship that, while lacking direct political representation and power, allowed metaphoric representation as the National Symbolic (the feminine personification of corruptible racial purity and national boundaries). White women held limited representation through their association with "republican motherhood," and as "stewards and guardians" of their husbands' property. With the vote, white women effectively mobilized "women's interests" and social housekeeping within welfare discourses in ways that were often meaningless to those who confronted Jim Crow segregation: a lack of services, the sharecropping system, and a heightened racism that dismantled Reconstruction's legislatively enacted civil rights agenda.[10] With ratification of the Nineteenth Amendment, Brown had helped expedite the registration of thousands of Southern Black women, but whites defeated Black access to the polls, impeding their leverage with the legislative assembly. While by the1920s enfranchised white women were lobbying members of Congress, Black clubwomen could not. "The Negro woman," Brown chided, "has endured ignominy and insult and shame as she almost stood at the back door of legislative halls."[11] This is the legal context within which Brown, and other African American reformers fought for public health, education, and social welfare.

Their efforts circumscribed, Black reformers could only resort to old dependency strategies of persuading white leaders of the merits of their reform endeavours, and forging alliances with white women, most of whom never questioned their own, or anyone else's, racism. White reformers tended to be ill-informed about what Black communities actually needed, rarely saw racial justice as a goal, and attached galling expectations to their philanthropic donations.[12] When, in 1925, Charlotte Hawkins Brown requested that counties sending court committed girls to contribute to their upkeep at the Efland home – standard practice at other juvenile reformatories – Commissioner Kate Burr Johnson replied, "I think there will be no doubt about the counties being willing to give some financial aid to the institution eventually, but before I pressed them to this I would prove the worth of the institution to the public."[13] Lacking funds complicated institutional progress. Southern

Figure 3.2. Dr Charlotte Hawkins Brown, c. 1918, founder and president of North Carolina Federation of Negro Women's Clubs. Courtesy of the State Archives of North Carolina.

Black reformers privately funded juvenile reform institutions, as well as schools, old age homes, and medical services with events like bake sales and church dinners. Fundraising efforts sapped reformers' political energy such that Cleveland activist Jane Hunter wrote, "This money getting business destroys so much of one's real self, that we cannot do our best."[14] At the very beginning, then, Brown appointed a legislative committee to "contact the Federation of White Women's Clubs … in an effort to properly present to the North Carolina Assembly the need for establishing Efland" as a state institution. Brown involved white philanthropists strategically, inviting them to serve on the executive board of Efland as respected leaders experienced in social reform.[15] Seeking legislative support for the proposed reformatory, she asked the new chair of Efland's board "to select a group of [white] women interested in the colored people in the state who would serve with her."[16] In July 1921, Brown also implored Commissioner Johnson to write letters on behalf of the federation, writing, "I want to ask you to write to Hampton for us ... I know the Hampton folks, but as in anything, a letter going from your office would arouse greater interest. I do not wish to burden you, but if you will help us in the organisation of this whole thing, you will be doing us a great service."[17] White clubwomen readily complied, having a vested interest in Southern Black women's political reform work, involvement which facilitated their own advancement in a humanist milieu. Ellen Winston, for one, had worked with the president of the State Federation of Negro Women's Clubs, and would become commissioner of public welfare.

The Efland story indicates the presence of complex relationships, and ambiguity, in Southern Black reform. Some whites seem to have been better allies than others. The Legislative Council of North Carolina Women, an alliance of white women's state-wide organizations, included support for Efland among the five bills they introduced in 1925. In 1927, a white activist explained, "In advocating state support for the [Efland] institution ... the white women realized that the aspersions cast in this region upon the morality of the Negro woman, and the Negro girl are, certainly to a large extent, a racial prejudice fostered by white men for their own convenience." Some politically active white women disagreed with conventional views held by many Southern white men, though they never demanded substantial change to the racial épistème.[18]

Throughout the tenure of the Efland home, clubwomen would continue in vain to secure adequate state funding through legislative bills. From 1925 to 1939, Efland operated on a shoestring budget while the North Carolina state appropriations committee, which met every two years, made empty promises to "look into the matter" in the coming session. Yet, in session after session, the state stalled over funding. The appropriation it finally granted was not enough to cover the costs of running the institution, much less allow for its expansion. In 1927, the appropriations committee granted a sum of $2000 per biennium to Efland, and $72,000 for the 1927–9 biennium to Samarcand Manor. Samarcand's biennial appropriation for 1941–3 was as high as $133,258 with per capita costs of $348 for the 1942–3budget year. Efland received arbitrary annual state support of $1400 to $2000 between 1927 and 1938. While an exponential rise in apprehension and relocation of juvenile status offenders to state institutions characterized the first decades of the twentieth century, the Efland home, circumscribed, would only ever be equipped to house a maximum of fifteen inmates at a time.[19]

Relative to other facilities, and to the historical overrepresentation of Black women in prisons to the present day, this number indicates much about the gendered and racial politics of mercy in the founding and operation of North Carolina juvenile reformatories. In her survey of Southern Black female reform institutions, Susan Cahn has observed that their collective history is ultimately one of dereliction. When state governments did establish parallel reform institutions, "they left a record of financial and human neglect that speaks volumes about the low official value placed on the moral condition of and social welfare of black teenage girls in the South."[20] State officials, along with white popular culture, saw few commonalities between Black and white girls' "waywardness," especially with regard to causation, treatment, and ultimately, national relevance.

In a last-ditch effort to persuade government officials to assume fiscal responsibility for the Efland home, the leaders of the North Carolina Federation of Colored Women's Clubs met with Governor O. Max Gardner in 1931 to present him with the deed to the entire property of Efland as a gift to the state of North Carolina, its 147 acres and its buildings valued at $22,500, less $1,500 outstanding on the mortgage. In a newsclipping dubiously entitled "A Seductive Offer," the reporter deliberated whether "sufficient funds can be found with which to go through with it on the large scale that such delinquency in the State would call for."[21] The state responded with lower grants, while continuing its surveillance of the Efland home. As the Great Depression wore on, private funding within the Black community dwindled, and the "little institution" foundered. In a 1934 report of investigation of the institution field agent Wm. R. Johnson advised,

> They have no wagon or car at place. Mr. Lassiter [the farmer/matron's husband] made a Hoover cart – they have one mule. Tools with which to work on farm are not there. It is a mystery how the farm has been operated. Last week there were probably five bushels of green lima beans or more ready for picking and canning … It is understood that the Home owes Forrest store $610.00 for groceries … With no facilities for travel,

in an emergency it is hard ... There are more than thirty girls on waiting list ... At present school received $1400.00 Annually from State as grant. Women's Federation raised about $700.00. Some other small gifts were made ... This amount is far too inadequate for a school of this type.[22]

In 1935, W.C. Ezell, field agent for the State Board of Public Welfare, again reported on the desperate situation at Efland, writing that the sheriff's office had been alerted about escapees. "One of the girls said an aged white man by name of McCauley had harboured some of the girls and helped them escape. Also reported that same McCauley had paid some of the girls for sexual relations with him."[23] Ezell added that the program at the school had been abandoned.

The Board of Public Welfare took issue with the lack of separate accommodations for inmates with contagious venereal diseases, and in fact, all residents shared a single bathtub and one toilet. In 1939 the State Board of Charities and Public Welfare deemed the Efland home "substandard and wholly inadequate," ordering its immediate closure "by mutual agreement" with the Federation of Colored Women's Clubs for the merciful protection of its inmates, who would have been "better fed in jails and county workhouses."[24] The federation consented to the closing of Efland "in order to arouse the conscience of our legislators to a sense of their duty and obligation to the Negro citizens of North Carolina in making some provisions for caring for delinquent Negro girls."[25] Shifting blame onto Black clubwomen, the *Winston-Salem Journal* reported that while the state had contributed to the Efland home, the facility had failed.[26]

White insistence on Black incompetence had deep roots. During Reconstruction, the Freedman's Bureau perceived Blacks as dependent upon government handouts, despite all evidence to the contrary. In many localities, bureau aid went mostly to white recipients. Wherever possible, the Black community independently cared for orphans, the elderly, and the destitute. Ironically, Blacks were often forced into a state of dependency on whites for access to and leverage in government, since they were barred from lobbying autonomously. In a spirit of collective self-improvement following emancipation, clubwomen, Masonic lodges, and other voluntary associations had initiated a wave of educational institution building during Reconstruction. The Freedman's Bureau, Northern benevolent societies, and, after 1868, state governments, funded most Black education during Reconstruction, in support of schools already initiated by them. Without outside aid,

Southern Blacks had expended over $1 million on education by 1870 ($18.2 million in 2016 currency).[27]

Many state administrators regarded the closing of Efland as an act of mercy, but in the federation's view, the state appropriations committee had effectively besieged the reformatory. Durham's Black newspaper, *The Carolina Times*, suggested that support for the institution had been "grossly neglected by the state, which means it has an uphill fight to keep its doors open."[28] Neither education nor health – priorities in Black reform – could be properly attended to at Efland during the years of its decline.[29]

Reformer Minnie Pearson anguished over Efland's failure, despite many years of conciliation made by Black clubwomen to white public welfare officials, juvenile judges, the governor, members of the state legislature and white philanthropic clubwomen.[30] In an open letter to the people of North Carolina (November 1938), Brown announced that the federation had raised over $35,000 for the institution, which she had hoped the state would take over "and vouchsafe to the Negro girls, in part at least, the training fitting them for better citizenship offered to similar groups in the white race." She applauded the North Carolina Federation of Negro Women's Clubs, and white allies who had supported the institution for twenty years, but reproached the state legislature: "We feel that an appropriation of $2000 a year is not only a mere pittance but a positive disgrace to the social welfare program in North Carolina for the care of delinquency of Negro girls who, with proper supervision and training, could be directed into channels of industry and Christian character."[31] She warned that degeneration was contagious, and degraded members of both races would find each other.

In the interwar period, despite sentimental concern for children, Southern whites widely regarded moral regulation of "innately impure" Black and Native American girls a wasted effort. In response to the intensive lobbying in the late 1930s by Black clubwomen and their white allies, the *Charlotte Observer* explained the white public's reluctance to support the Efland home with state funds: presumably, "such a large proportion of the Negro girls might fall within the scope of such a correctional institution that the state would simply be overrun with inmates – the job is too stupendous to talk about except wistfully."[32] Former white North Carolinian caseworker Maud Wells, who was ninety-six when I interviewed her, suggested "an umbrella over the entire state" would have been required to cope with Black female promiscuity.[33] Reflecting on the 1938 failure of the Efland home, she rationalized white reformers' involvement with the Efland home as a paternalistic effort to "at least do something" to remedy the situation.[34] On 15 March 1939, as Efland closed its doors, an embittered Minnie Pearson recalled how members of the state legislature had responded "with derision and scepticism as to the moral possibilities of this most neglected class." In session, they had "howled with laughter at the prospect of uplifting Negro womanhood."[35]

"Until I forgot the noon prayers"

In June of 1935, Girls' Commissioner Corinne Cannady wrote to Mrs W.T. Bost, state commissioner of public welfare, concerned about the conditions at the North Carolina Industrial Home for Colored Girls at Efland. The reformatory had deteriorated, she thought, since the matron, Mrs Lassiter, had left. Some years earlier, on an unannounced visit, officials from the Department of Public Welfare found girls playing in the yard unchaperoned. Lassiter assured them there was no trouble with girls running away; actually, they had just picked flowers for their rooms from the nearby woods.[36] But girls did flee when a new, authoritarian matron arrived at Efland. Young escapees complained of severe abuse. A state official noted "a contrast in the atmosphere of the home and the attitude of the girls" since the former matron had left. The new matron allegedly whipped inmates with a board, and locked them in a room for days at a time with only bread and water. On a 1935 visit to the institution, Cannady reported, "When the matron came to the door she reprimanded [several girls in the yard] ... and engaged in conversation with them before she even so much as spoke to me ... It was quite evident that she had very little feeling and interest for the girls and it was equally as evident that the girls had no respect for her."[37]

Field Agent William R. Johnson reiterated this in his follow-up inspection two years later. He noted that while the farm showed prospects of good yields, "the cow walked away about three weeks ago and no trace of her has been found." Inmates had been wandering off, too, leaving of the institution without permission for days at a time. Expressing concern over the situation there, Johnson reported, "Shortly before my arrival, one girl had snatched a whip from the matron and tossed it across the room. According to the matron's own story, 'I choked and beat her until she foamed at the mouth! I tried my best to kill her. I beat her so much until I forgot the noon prayers.' This information was unsought and told in a boasting manner." Johnson implored state administrators to attend to the matron's pernicious influence, which rendered the whole project a waste of money in its failure to aid the state in "solving one of its most important problems."[38] Similar stories from Samarcand Manor just six years before had incited a show trial, an official inquest, and subsequent ban on corporal punishment as part of a whitewashing campaign to protect the state institution. However, the revelation of such abuses at the North Carolina Industrial Home for Colored Girls at Efland only strengthened the state's resolve for its peremptory closure.

Ten months later, on 11 April 1938, George Lawrence, director of field work for the Division of Public Welfare and Social Work, stopped by the "little institution." Alarmed he wrote an urgent letter to the head of corrections, describing "the total absence of just about everything essential toward the conduct of an institution for delinquent negro girls." He claimed to have "no confidence at all in the ability of the present personnel to in any respect handle the situation adequately," and while he had long thought that the institution should either be closed or greatly strengthened, he now believed that "the conditions at Efland are a disgrace to all of us interested in the Public Welfare program." "The place is worse than useless," he wrote. "At least in the county jail a girl would be assured of enough to eat … It might be possible to get further with the program by not having any institution at all than by perpetuating such a farce as I believe this place to be."[39] The General Assembly of North Carolina ordered an investigation, which confirmed that the home was poorly planned and inefficiently run. Rather than increase funding, the state closed the Efland home, in what many considered an act of mercy.

The Jim Crow tenet of separate but equal presented a dilemma explicitly debated in the Southern juvenile reformatory movement, defining the configurations of the conferral of American identity. Records of the Efland home, the only reformatory institution for Black girls, indicate systematic Black female invisibility within civic uplift. While disproportionate imprisonment of indigenous and Black women and girls has been the case in historical and current contexts of custodial containment and punishment, this was not the case under expensive regimens of merciful juvenile reform.[40]

Samarcand's Racial Policy

With the closure of the Efland home, having nowhere else to send Lumbee tribal members Bessie Locklear and Gertie Mae Oxendine, a

Robeson County juvenile court judge recommended they be committed to Samarcand Manor. The Lumbee, one of eight indigenous tribes of North Carolina, are mainly located in Robeson County, approximately 130 kilometres southeast of Samarcand. On record as a self-identified "Indian," fourteen-year-old Gertie Mae Oxendine found herself incarcerated at the Lumberton jail following her foster father's report that she had been caught having sex with a Black boy "for a week." She denied it, explaining that while she had resided with the boy and his mother, he was rarely at home and they were never alone together. Director, Division of Institutions and Corrections, J. Wallace Nygard encouraged Superintendent Grace Robson to at least accept Bessie Locklear (identified as Indian), if not Gertie Mae, "with the same conditional acceptance as for white girls." Nygard added that while the State School for the Blind and Deaf rejected indigenous peoples based on Criminal Statute 5384, Jackson Training School for white boys "has a separate cottage for Indians in which there are at present two Indian boys."[41] W.A. Stanbury of the Central Methodist Church took the position that "if occasion should arise, we should look with favor upon admitting girls of the Indian race." While guarded, other board members did not oppose Stanbury. Myrtle Page did. She argued, "I don't believe [the school] was intended for Indian girls. In Robeson County the Whites and Indians have different schools. I am opposed to it. I think it will be the beginning of a great deal of trouble – and, I think, expense. For, of course, the White girls and the Indian girls cannot use the same quarters."[42] In the end, Samarcand's board refused to admit both Bessie and Gertie Mae, citing the financial impracticality of building separate quarters for them. Director J. Wallace Nygard supported the board's decision, stating that Gertie Mae Oxendine "is described as having curly hair, a broad nose and being of dark color. Her foster mother is purported to have called her in a slurring manner 'a nigger.'"[43] Nygard agreed that the children at Samarcand would not accept her socially.

Officials classified Bessie as "Indian" and Gertie Mae Oxendine as "mulatta." They suspected her having "Black blood," though she self-identified as a member of the Lumbee people. The social caseworker refused to comment upon the girl's race. When pressed for a statement, she said, "I would be mobbed if I said." Another official, identifying only as "X" for security reasons, remarked that although Gertie Mae Oxendine identified as Indian, she looked like a "Negro and kept company with a Negro boy ... Whatever the race of this girl may actually be, she would not be accepted by the girls at Samarcand, nor by White people in general, as anything but a Negro."[44] White officials noted that all Gertie Mae's family members were lighter than she was. Her father had straight black hair and a light complexion and one sister had sandy hair. Gertie on the other hand, had a broad nose and curly hair. According to government officials, community leaders had claimed that Gertie Mae's foster parents, "nervous and unstable" members of the Holiness Church movement, neglected her. She had attended an Indian school, and scored just 65 on an IQ test administered there. The Indian caseworker concluded, "Since the girl is mentally deficient and persistent in delinquency, she should be sterilised." "X" suggested post-sterilization placement with "capable people of Gertie Mae's color" who might take her in to train her as a domestic: "This child is attractive enough of feature that, if she had proper training, she would be placed in service in some home." Authorities agreed that this was the next best thing to being housed with relatives.[45]

Racial classifications at the time focused on phenotype and blood quantum, which defined people through equations of blood proportions and racial ancestry identified by anthropometric tests and genealogical charts. Government officials failed to look beyond physical traits to recognize the Lumbee's existence as a political community. The Lumbee self-identified as a People marked by experiential kinship identity defined by shared history and place. Their schools generally accepted children whom the educational committees regarded as Indian according to kinship and settlement affiliation. Hair texture and skin colour held little significance.[46]

White officials, however, struggled with Gertie Mae's biracial status because she visibly blurred racial boundaries. Lauren Berlant has argued that many whites have feared "mulattas," as the most abstract of embodied citizens, exceptions to the American rule of racial binarism.[47] Cheryl Harris has demonstrated that an oppositional definition of Black as other facilitated the melding of numerous European ethnicities into a monolithic American identity. "Fundamentally," Berlant contends, "the question was not so much 'who is white,' but 'who may be considered white.'" Ann Stoler has noted that nineteenth century colonial anxieties revolved around "mestizos, Eurasians and Indos" who, "mixed by blood," threatened the racial status of the nation state as those "who were the same but not quite."[48]

Dobb's Farm

Soon after Efland's closure, in 1942, reporters could think of no special service institutions the state needed more urgently than a state training school for "delinquent Negro girls." The state's sudden support seemed like a victory to the jubilant federation. By 1943, five years after Efland closed down, Governor Clyde R. Hoey urged "immediate action" in establishing a "real first-class modern home fully supported out of state funds." That same year the General Assembly authorized the founding of the State Training School for Negro Girls, granting a biennial appropriation of $25,000 for operating expenses. The mood was effervescent; the public lauded North Carolina for the merciful generosity it extended to these girls. White public welfare officers explained to the press that they had been trying to establish such an institution all along. Elated clubwomen believed their prayers had finally been answered. The federation sold the property at Efland, donating the entire proceeds to the new venture, declaring they would find ways of "helping to rescue perishing girls and indeed of helping the state to snatch them in pity from sin and the grave." Having worked closely with the clubwomen to press the General Assembly for action throughout Efland's tenure, Commissioner Bost embraced the idea of the new institution, declaring, "This makes a four-square program for North Carolina in the care of delinquents."[49] The wider Black community echoed these sentiments, as Pinehurst resident Edna B. Taylor's correspondence suggests: "Dear Mr. Johnson – When I read yesterday that our governor had approved a plan for a Home for delinquent Negro Girls, I was so deeply touched with joy and thanks that I could hardly keep back the tears. It has been my daily prayer, my talk, my song that God would touch somebody's heart that they might help us save our wayward girls."[50] The struggle around the Efland reformatory would generate new public interpretations of what constituted gendered mercy as a cornerstone of juvenile jurisprudence and a "civilized" Americanism.

Merciful juvenile reformatories were expensive to run, because indeterminate sentences involving intensive moral training typically lasted for the duration of minority. Socially invisible and lacking state investment, girls of African descent mostly missed out on the juvenile reformatory movement, and in some respects may have actually benefitted from this. As Michel Foucault has noted, "The new practices for training bodies, behavior, and abilities open up the problem of those who escape a system of norms."[51] The founding of the new State Training School for Negro Girls was no victory. Reform grounded in benevolent moral suasion would have been preferable to the custodial, retributive "justice" that was now coming to fruition.

In 1939, the *Charlotte Observer* suggested that most taxpayers would probably react with hostility to any initiative involving allocation of public funds to a Black girls' institution, but by 1942, the proposal gained immediate and uncontested state support, and the public applauded the expenditure as generous and merciful. The politics of punishment has swung historically between reform and retribution. The move from expensive reform to custodial retribution in North Carolina juvenile justice marked a historical juncture, with mercy, as a hallmark of liberalism, persisting in a re-narrated form.[52] By the end of the Second World War, moral suasion and the expensive reformatory model fell out of fashion with the rise of the custodial model coupled with psychiatric methodology. While coded as merciful, retributive "justice" was relatively harsh. Many whites supported state funding for the removal and containment of "dangerous" and "insentient" Black girls.[53]

Welfare officials publicized statistics indicating that delinquency had risen since the beginning of the Second World War, and newspapers such as the *Winston-Salem Journal* urged the state to remove "the Negro girl" under twenty-one from community life to prevent the development of other delinquents. In contrast with calls for the protection of childhood innocence in juvenile reformatories, demands for tougher, "law and order" measures reflect public perceptions of young offenders as fully responsible, dangerous felons. Superintendent of Public Welfare A.W. Cline warned the commissioner of public welfare about the supposed threat, citing the example of a girl put on probation by the Forsythe County Juvenile Court: "It was not very long," he wrote, "until one morning the newspapers carried a story about a murder and the girl that I have just mentioned was the murderer." Female sexual danger is a recurrent theme in religion, and also in criminological theory. Western criminal justice systems are plagued by institutional racism, and heterosexism. Legal regulation of women and girls has historically pivoted around gender policing, regardless of the transgression. It marks women who fail to meet heteropatriarchal standards of white femininity as more dangerous, and these women more readily receive the death penalty. The closer women approximate ideals of femininity, the more shocking the public find their transgressions.[54]

When a white national youth administration camp was abandoned at Rocky Mount, North Carolina, the new State Training School for Negro Girls moved in, opening its doors in 1944. Susan Cahn has noted that training facilities for Black girls established in the mid-1940s throughout the South were underfunded, and conditions were abysmal. This institution was no exception, with its roofless buildings, absence of desks, and chairs borrowed from a local funeral home. The site had served as a treatment facility for white women with venereal diseases, but the new Black inmates received no treatment. The act authorizing its establishment carried with it a biennial appropriation of $25,000 authorized by the 1943 General Assembly for operating expenses, stipulating no expenditure allowances for building improvements or new construction. One writer objected, "The Legislature and the Governor have handed the correctional institution board a big job – to establish a training school without anything to establish it with." In September 1944 the State Training School for Negro Girls in Rocky Mount admitted its first inmate. Three years later, when the state moved the North Carolina Industrial Farm Colony for [white] Women (Dobbs Farm) to a brand new, state-of-the-art facility, it permanently reassigned their old housing to criminalized Black girls.[55]

Reverse Discourse as Resistance

How can we make sense of reformer Charlotte Hawkins Brown's long struggle for a reformatory for wayward Black girls in the context of the racist empire state? Why was merciful civic uplift and sexual regulation for Black girls problematic for most whites, and how did the very idea of the Efland home challenge gendered nationalist scripts? How was internal colonialism enacted through these institutions and disciplines? Finally, how effectively did Charlotte Hawkins Brown and her allies challenge dominant race discourses, local power relations, and dominant social structures?

In his 1944 study *An American Dilemma*, Gunnar Myrdal gives scant attention to Black resistance through collective action, focusing instead upon the harm inflicted by Jim Crow. Highlighting passive victimization leads to assumptions that historians like Glenda Gilmore have sought to dispel, arguing instead, that despite racist structural constraints, North Carolina became a hotbed of Black women's political activism during the Progressive Era. Institutions such as the Palmer Institute and the North Carolina Industrial Home for Colored Girls attest to this. Nevertheless, they did confront formidable limitations acknowledged and protected by American law, and their enforced dependence upon whites infantilized them, constantly hindering their efforts.[56] While it is important to acknowledge and celebrate the positive contributions of Black reformers and their band of white allies, then, to frame their advances as dependent upon individuals' sheer will and perseverance against all odds is consistent with current neoliberal calls for individual voluntarism over collective action. We must not discount the shaping of political opportunities by existing social structures.[57]

While ultimately unsuccessful, the Efland project exemplifies subversion through what Michel Foucault has (not uncritically) termed "reverse discourse." Brown reclaimed the Christian narrative of mercy in the Magdalene parable, extending it to the moral reformation of wayward Black girls as a citizen-building effort. Her willing adoption of bourgeois white standards of sexual propriety constituted a radical proposition at a time when judges might not bother to indict Black girls on morals charges, deeming their sexual transgressions instinctive. Brown's reform project challenged Black female invisibility, calling for national inclusion, and her vehicle was conformity to white values. Taken to its logical conclusion, this would have dealt a massive blow to the racial épistème.

Reverse discourses for Foucault involve the gaining of legitimacy using the same categories and vocabulary by which a thing was initially disqualified. He uses the example of the interpellation by nineteenth century sexologists of "homosexual" as a category, with an attendant "strong advance of social controls into this area of perversity." But this also made possible a reverse discourse where "homosexuality began to speak on its own behalf," to demand its legitimacy be acknowledged, using the same terms. This involved attempts to redeploy the knowledge and rhetoric of homosexuality to appeal for its decriminalization in the late nineteenth century. Identity politics comes into play, whereby those who are constructed as deviants may find a common dissenting voice that converts their otherness into positions of strength. Foucault critiques his own idea of "reverse discourse" for the reductionist binary opposition it assumes, acknowledging that various and contradictory discourses can coexist within the same strategy. Nevertheless, as something fluid, discourses can mutate, becoming points of resistance.[58]

Modelled after early twentieth century Black settlement houses, or "missions," the Efland home incorporated religious rhetoric into political activism. Eric Foner has noted that during Reconstruction, African American communities often elected preachers for legislative seats, and churches served as "Ecclesiastical Court Houses," offering civic uplift, and adjudicating family disputes. Such religiosity is evident in Efland's brochure, which mobilized Christian rhetoric, appealing to the parable of the alleged prostitute Mary Magdalene, whose story exemplified the worthiness of the "lowest of the low" through her friendship with Jesus. "In His name we are launching this effort to save Negro womanhood," it read, "and we shall hope to surround these girls with the spirit of Jesus whose memorable words were, "Go in peace and sin no more."[59] While aligning their Efland campaign with dominant white standards of sexual propriety, reformers couched it in scriptural images of a penitent Magdalene and calls for mercy, re-narrating it to overturn claims that naturalized Black female hypersexuality and insentience. Charlotte Hawkins Brown's reinterpretation of the Christian Magdalene narrative for emancipatory ends is a variant of Foucault's "reverse discourse," a reappropriation of the same discursive elements for alternative, effectively subversive ends.

In analyses of power and resistance, it is well to remember that resistance is not necessarily just reactive, "forming with respect to the basic domination an underside that is in the end always passive, doomed to perpetual defeat." Foucault has argued that the effects of domination are always tenuous, and various kinds of resistance include those "that are possible, necessary, improbable, others that are spontaneous, savage, solitary, concerted, rampant, or violent; still others that are quick to compromise, interested, or sacrificial." The Efland case shows a complicated "plurality of resistances," troubling the paradigm of dichotomous opposition between oppressors and oppressed.[60]

In developing social service agencies and educational programs for girls lacking skills, finances, and education many Southern Black training school founders shared Brown's strategy of reform that cooperated with the white status quo.[61] As Darlene Clark Hine has observed:

Couched in the rhetoric of religious piousness, their efforts to do good deeds on behalf of black people, to save black women from lives of poverty and induced prostitution, appear on the surface to reflect a conservative embrace of American moral values and of the status quo. Yet each black girl and boy saved from the streets, educated to be productive and self-respecting citizens, restored to good health, and trained for a skilled job represented a resounding blow to the edifice of Jim Crow, patriarchy, and white privilege.[62]

Hine has noted that those reclaimed would often become politicized, joining in the collective struggle for change.[63]

Resistance can also manifest through silence. Deborah Gray White has noted a paucity of archival collections of Black women.[64] I additionally noticed an overall tone, in the Efland records, at least, of considered restraint. Much seemed left unsaid. Black reformers used a cautious tone in their correspondence with state administrators, and the record lacks the miscellany found in corresponding white records. Michel Foucault has suggested, "Silence itself – the thing one declines to say, or is forbidden to name, the discretion that is required between different speakers – is less the absolute limit of discourse … than an element that functions alongside the things said, with them and in relation to them within overall strategies.[65] Aliyyah Abdur-Rahman has noted that silence can constitute a form of resistance when used as a defence against those whose dominance is legitimized through language as authorized discourse.[66] Silence can also offer an alternative way of communicating through inference.[67] It is still important to be mindful that Charlotte Hawkins Brown and the federation were working against formidable racist social and legal structures.

Anatomo-politics

White reformers and state administrators remained interested in anatomo-politics (physical discipline and optimization of capabilities for integration into economic systems) because they wanted reliable domestic workers. In 1941, two years after Efland's closure, Forsyth County's superintendent of public welfare, A.W. Cline, advocated the training of girls of African descent, explaining, "These girls might go into an institution and be trained principally along the lines of domestic work, which would fit them for better servants in our home."[68] In the rural South around the turn of the last century, and during Efland's tenure, the majority of Southern Black women worked as waged sharecroppers, or as domestic servants and laundresses in white homes. Some 40 to 65 per cent of Black married women worked in wage labour, in contrast to white wives, 98 per cent of whom remained financially dependent upon husbands as homemakers.[69] Brown assured the commissioner of public welfare that the training of "such class of students" at Efland would not involve academic training; they would not become teachers, but "farmers, mechanics, house girls and all other forms of industry in which they may learn to take pride and contribute back to the state what we expect the state to spend in developing this kind of useful citizenship."[70]

It is difficult to ascertain Charlotte Hawkins Brown's political positionality. While she advocated industrial training for Efland's charges, she also filed numerous lawsuits "whenever insulted in a train or forced to leave a pullman coach and enter the Jim Crow car," as a matter of social justice, refusing occasional small settlements.[71] Perhaps she shared reformer Nannie Burroughs's perspective that with little opportunity beyond domestic or agricultural work, at least training to do such work well would put the girls in good stead.[72] Nevertheless, while deeply important, the issue of vocational versus academic education is less at issue here than the question of national inclusion of girls of African descent. Brown's appeal "for help to save all the youth by providing adequate care and proper treatment for Negro girls who have been made the victims of circumstances over which they have no control" declared Black female "sex delinquency" environmentally rather than biologically determined, and therefore reformable.[73] This was a radical statement.

The juvenile reformatory movement meant to stem degeneracy, restoring racial purity to the national polity for imperial ascendancy. The political action of the North Carolina Federation of Negro Women's Clubs must be considered in the context of a racist épistème sustained by social workers, state administrators, experts, and institutions though popular patriotic, imperialist discourses. In its very conformity to white middle class codes of sexual propriety, an institution mandated to reform Black girls engaging in prostitution (even loosely defined) posed a potentially devastating challenge to the race/nation apparatus in America and the ideal of sexual "purity" at its heart. The federation's call – during a period of open Klan-based terrorism, no less – to "snatch [wayward girls] in pity from sin and the grave" radically challenged panoptic nation-building movements that were sweeping aside emancipation claims, and defining America as white through both legal and extra-legal means.

Brown's successful recruitment of respected white socialites and reformers as Efland's board helped to legitimize her challenge to Black female invisibility within the nation. These political allies expedited Black access to the state government. With state acknowledgment, this claim to "civilized" status would have had the potential to radically overturn powerful scripts of Black female hypersexuality with far-reaching implications for national inclusion. At a time of nation-wide denial of emancipation claims, Brown and the federation mobilized the hegemonic imperative that Black womanhood be included in nationalist narratives of civic duty and womanhood – and the National Symbolic.

Sexual Regulation, Collusion, Subversion

The Federation of Colored Women's Clubs continued to campaign for the reformation of wayward girls. In 1940, a governor-appointed committee recommended that the Palmer Memorial Institute, a North Carolina professional school that Charlotte Hawkins Brown had also founded, be reassigned as a penal institution for delinquent Black girls. Brown disagreed: "We have upon our walls costly paintings and sculpture and furnishings ... What they would break up and smash up in the first four or five years would forever destroy the foundation of material cultural accumulations which my race will have greater appreciation for as the years go by.[74] She implored the state to develop the Palmer Institute as a women's college, to preserve its New England prestige.

Brown separated herself from the "immoral alley girls" she sought to reform, insofar as she refused to turn over the Palmer Institute for their accommodation. But the middle class status of Black clubwomen, many only a generation removed from slavery, was tenuous. Jim Crow laws reduced the spatial distance between the middle and lower classes living together in segregated neighbourhoods, and the federation's motto "Lifting as we climb" suggests closer affective ties than many white reformers shared with recipients of their moral uplift. Black and white clubwomen commonly prioritized childhood protection and social hygiene, sharing the conviction that the poor needed reforming along the lines of sexual morality and "the A B C's of living."[75] However, while white reformers typically blamed labourers for their children's delinquency, Black reformers accommodated a gender framework that valued women's wage work.[76]

Black women and girls also faced constant allegations of being "unrapable" with the corollary that rape was "never against [their] will."[77] For whites who idealized suicidal gestures portrayed in films like *Birth of a Nation*, surviving rape only confirmed the imagined spiritual inferiority of Black rape victims.[78] Whites typically minimized sexual assaults on African American women, instead, marking them as sexual predators. In the antebellum period, many Southern whites regarded enslaved women as seductresses who preyed on white masters. According to Southern writer Myrta Lockett Avary (1906), "The heaviest part of the white racial burden was the African woman, of strong sexual instincts and devoid of a sexual conscience, at the white man's door, in the white man's dwelling."[79] Many white Southerners assumed that from the post-bellum era, Black women "were doing to black men after slavery what they had done to white men during slavery," supposedly inciting Black on white rape. Around the turn of the last century, whites often held Black women accountable for the rape-lynch syndrome, suggesting that their imagined debauchery precluded any understanding of sexual violation in Black men. Lynching additionally reinforced the edict that Black women should expect no sexual protection from men, Black or white.[80] Consequently, before demonstrating against lynching, Ida B. Wells and other activists in the late nineteenth to mid-twentieth century felt compelled to clear up assumptions of their own complicity before they could proceed.[81] The National Association of Colored Women (1895) formed partly to counter popular fictions that naturalized promiscuity in Black women.[82] In 1893 Fannie Barrier Williams wrote, "This moral regeneration of a whole race of women is no idle sentiment – it is a serious business; and everywhere there is witnessed a feverish anxiety to be free from the mean suspicions that have so long underestimated the character strength of our women."[83]

The tenacity Brown and the federation demonstrated in their long struggle for the Efland home reflects the critical importance of sexual purity to the status of Black women. Middle class Black women upheld and exemplified a standard of sexual propriety in Southern communities. According to Susan Cahn, the spectre of promiscuity amongst those of the working-class threatened the collective positionality of all, providing incentive to early twentieth century campaigns for benevolent, state-run, juvenile reformatories.[84]

"Good breeding" was (and still is) implicitly raced in America. Despite an historical American patrilineal kinship structure, racial descent has historically run through the maternal line. Fining "interracial fornicators" in 1662, and outlawing interracial marriages in 1691, the Maryland laws represent the first unequivocal instance of statutory racial discrimination in the United States. Reversing the usual common-law status of children ensuing from the father, the 1662 Virginia colonial assembly decreed that "children got by an Englishman upon a Negro woman shall be bond or free according to the [legal] condition of the mother." In the same period, laws were passed to ensure that white colonial women's offspring were freeborn.[85] Two hundred years later, during Reconstruction, while some states repealed their miscegenation laws, North Carolina clamped down, making its own miscegenation law more rigorous than ever, in 1868.[86] This historical context shaped the sexual regulation efforts of Black women and girls, whose managed or unmanaged sexuality was of little consequence to the racist body politic. Black social-purity activists' adoption of strict personal codes of sexual propriety was an effort to include themselves in evolving definitions of Americanism.[87]

Cheryl Harris has argued that American whiteness "was not a merely descriptive or ascriptive characteristic – it was property of colossal value."[88] The modern biopolitical agenda of "making them grow, and ordering them," never included children of African descent, who failed to embody white ideals of childhood innocence to white satisfaction. Any money allocated to Black girls' moral uplift would have been considered a merciful, but ineffective gesture.[89] Charlotte Hawkins Brown and the Federation of Colored Women's Clubs challenged this.

Western science and white popular culture have historically devalued the bodies and sexualities of Black women in relation to those of white women, and this is essential to understanding what Charlotte Hawkins Brown and other members of the North Carolina Federation of Colored Women's Clubs confronted when they tried to garner support for the Efland home. Eugenically, Black women's bodies held value for their contribution to the labour force from the seventeenth century, when they were legally cited and enumerated as "stock ... like other female animals." The slavocracy classified women of childbearing age as "breeders," and their children as "increase" and "issue." Rape of enslaved women increased slaveholders' assets, making rape "part of the architecture of early American racial and gender hierarchies."[90] A Black congressional representative tellingly declared in 1874, "We want more protection from the whites invading our homes and destroying the virtue of our women than they from us."[91] Normative standards of Black femininity thus stood apart from mainstream and white feminist interpretations, incorporating a gender system that valued women's sexual propriety and marriage as well as responsibility for children – arguing that slavery had destroyed the sanctity of marriage, home ties, and the "instincts of motherhood."[92] Reclamation of these was important, because familial ties under slavery were antithetical to the commodity market, and slave codes failed to recognize Black marriages and parental rights.

Civilizing discourses measured cultural superiority not by women's rights, but by their treatment, and as the "fair sex" white women enjoyed sexual protection as a white privilege. Popularized in industrializing North America between 1820 and the Civil War, the Cult of True Womanhood exhorted essentialist traits of deference, religiosity, domesticity, and sexual purity involving the denial of sexual desire.[93] In time, "womanhood" would come to signify whiteness and sexual purity, while hypersexualized Black women simply figured as abject. Just as the indictment of the feminized "Indian savage" evoked oppositional images of masculine white colonists, degeneration theorists' ordering of Black women at the nadir of human evolution served to glorify white womanhood. Serving as a foil to the cult of true womanhood, Black women fell outside of the idealized roles white women played as bastions of moral virtue and angels of the Victorian household.[94] In 1906, the comment "I cannot imagine such a creature as a virtuous black woman" would have seemed unremarkable in white circles.[95]

The struggle for a positive identity of American Black womanhood was a struggle against national otherness.[96] Brown and the federation recognized the need both to deracinate negative Eurocentric depictions of Black women and to reinscribe the term "Southern womanhood." This involved reformers' own sexual restraint, as a matter of self-regulation under governmentality, and the sexual reformation of sexually active girls in their communities.[97] Despite the threat wayward Black girls may have posed to middle class Black women's reputations, their sexual regulation demonstrated agency in contesting supposedly innate depravity. This strategy was very much in keeping with that launched by the NAACP to challenge miscegenation laws. Between 1913 and 1927 the NAACP did this (without endorsing interracial marriage) by combining objections to innate Black inferiority with gender-conservative calls for the protection of women.[98]

Challenging Colonial Tropes of Animalization

The growth of empire projected moral traits along with anthropological hierarchies onto racial difference, contributing to expanded racialization. Victorian evolutionism informed the gaze, and evolutionary anthropology identified racialized others as morally and culturally atavistic.[99] Carolus Linnaeus was the first racial scientist to mix character with anatomy in a taxonomic interpretation of humanity.[100] The American concept of "race" was developed around visible phenotypic markers that signified epistemological alterity, whereby the body became the focus of representation and meaning. Robyn Wiegman has shown that in Euro-American race discourses, it was this corporeal binary that historically inscribed insentience onto people of African descent, rather than economic factors associated with the slave trade.[101] Advocating polygenist degeneration theory, philosopher David Hume insisted that people of African descent constituted a distinct and inferior species. Black women experienced racialization and sex/gendering as a composite, with one attending the other.[102] David Roediger has noted that just as European elite women were idealized as white long before their male counterparts, colonial racism ascribed animality to Black women more emphatically and fetishistically than it did Black men.[103] The iconographic "Hottentot Venus" signified primitive promiscuity antithetical to "civilization." White European scientists positioned South African, "female Khoisan" taxonomically at the depth of human degeneration, "just before the species left off its human form and turned bestial."[104] Preceding this, seventeenth-century British colonial administrator and historian Edward Long wrote, "Ludicrous as the opinion may seem, I do not think that an oran-outang [sic] husband would be any dishonour to a Hottentot female."[105]

Eighteenth-century Western sexual discourses associating Black women with Jezebel (the allegedly promiscuous and abject biblical wife of King Ahab) still held currency in the nineteenth century, informing scientific degeneration theories.[106] Exhibited as one of at least two famous "Hottentot Venuses," Saartjie Baartman, a young Khoikhoi woman, toured London and Paris between 1810 and 1815 as a human zoo exhibit and spectacle of the missing link. In his notorious study of Baartman's remains Georges Cuvier sought a connection between "the African" and apes, highlighting blackness as "incomplete humanity," marked by ostensibly atavistic sexual anatomy (represented by elongated labia and large buttocks, or steatopygia). The 1819 *Dictionnaire des sciences médicales* claimed that Black female "sexual organs" exemplified by Saartjie Baartman were "much more developed than those of whites," ostensibly implying primitivity.[107] According to Wiegman, the spectacle obsession with "the Hottentot" as the missing link attended the late seventeenth century renaissance of the Great Chain theory. Baartman died in 1815 at the age of twenty-five, and the Museé de l'homme preserved and stored her dissected pelvis.

Twentieth century eugenicists and reformers, and before them, nineteenth century degeneration theorists, regarded Black women as "inherently atavistic, living archive of the primitive archaic."[108] "In the development of her brain and skull," Wiegman has argued, "comparative science locates evidence for both the African (-American) male's masculine inferiorities and the white female's gendered priority; in the hyperextension of her sexual organs, 'blackness' is saturated ontologically with animality and sexuality, thereby inscribing both black and female as deviant corporealities while forging sexual hierarchies among women."[109] The Jezebel stereotype persisted into the twentieth century, marking Black women and girls as antithetical to true womanhood.[110]

Employed by US government agencies, early twentieth century experts on race openly strategized to "preserve the racial purity of American society," setting scientific priorities and developing social policy accordingly.[111] The concept of whiteness came to signify Anglo-Saxon supremacy, legally supported through mechanisms like the "one drop rule," which identified Black blood as polluting to racial purity. Cheryl Harris has observed that,

> just as whiteness as [status] property embraced the right to exclude, white-ness as a theoretical construct evolved for the very purpose of racial exclu-sion. Thus, the concept of whiteness is built on both exclusion and racial subjugation ... The assigned political, economic, and social inferiority of Blacks necessarily shaped white identity ... The right to exclude was the central principle, too, of whiteness as identity, for mainly whiteness has been characterized, not by an inherent unifying characteristic, but by the exclusion of others deemed to be "not white."[112]

Late nineteenth and early twentieth century juvenile jurisprudence in North Carolina reflected this through scientific racism that deemed Blacks as insentient, and therefore unreachable through merciful moral suasion. The Efland home was radical in its mandate to morally uplift girls deemed inherently depraved.

By the nineteenth century, Black women's bodies became the rudi-ment against which other social identities were established. As Robyn Wiegman has argued,

> [She] becomes the material ground for defining and ascertaining other social positions: Without the masculine characteristics underwriting the dis-corporation of the public sphere, without the racial supremacy ideal-ized by nationalist narratives of civic duty and true womanhood, the Afri-can (-American) woman provides the framework for, but fails to signify as a corporeal or symbolic presence in the contestations for political power figured by "blacks and women."[113]

This equation positions feminized Black men in relation to white women, while Black women become socially invisible.[114] Efland's empirical record shows not the insidious failure of Black womanhood to signify culturally, but the importance of Black female invisibility as a function of marginality to the "normal" white standard in interwar definitions of Americanism. Within the lexicon of bourgeois civility,

Black female invisibility was constitutive of white identity, and the Efland home posed too much of a threat through its very alignment with Anglophilic social-hygiene campaigns.

Imagined hypersexuality and colonial tropes of animalization developed alongside popular interpretations of Black women as maternally unfit, resulting in their active discouragement from having children of their own. Writing about "the poor home life" of Black families, twentieth century scholars like Howard W. Odum argued that it was the "sexual and domestic laxity of black mothers" that led their families into depravity.[115] Dorothy Roberts has shown how, since the end of surveillance under formal slavery, racist popular culture has depicted Black mothers as devolving into animalistic ignorance, and failing to nurture their children. It continues to brand them dangerously fecund Black matriarchs, transgressors of domestic femininity, and transmitters of racial degeneracy into the present.

Small Mercies

Affective sexual prescriptions served to secure and delineate "authentic" citizens of the American nation. Black female invisibility, expressed through state refusal of a reformatory based upon moral suasion, demonstrated unequivocal refusal of the state to extend Southern womanhood and national inclusion to women and girls of African descent. The theme of the fecund and promiscuous Black woman, consolidated during colonialism and slavery – where forced concubinage and prostitution were common – resonated in the clubwomen's negotiations for the Efland home. Through collusion with white bourgeois standards of sexual propriety, Charlotte Hawkins Brown exposed and challenged Black female invisibility, making a claim for national belonging within post-Emancipation re-narrations of white Americanism.[116] The current social order is not inevitable, but historical, contingent, and open to transformation. Still, the outcome of the Efland story left whites to overtly "control, manage, postpone, and if necessary, thwart change," demonstrating the inadequacies inherent in individual, isolated struggles against dominant power structures.[117]

White reformers who became involved in the Efland project oscillated between identification and difference, acknowledgment and obfuscation of their common participation and belonging in the nation.[118] Their ambivalence speaks to the depth of Efland's challenge to fundamental structures of gendered racism in North Carolina, and the American

South. Substantial state support of the Efland home would be counter-productive to the national fantasy of Anglo-Saxon supremacy, but outright refusal of state funding would have exposed the contradictions in liberal humanism. In the end, the state appropriations committee granted a paltry sum.

While largely ineffective, this gesture kept up the fiction of separate but equal, and legitimized the state as indulgent and merciful, given prevailing scientific claims of innate Black incorrigibility that made reform pointless. This strategy shielded North Carolina from difficult questions about separate but equal under Jim Crow, while reinforcing gendered white Americanism. It effectively placed the Efland home under siege, forcing its disbandment, and exonerating the state from responsibility when the project unravelled.

As a show of merciful humanism the state's token funding within overarching neglect and abandonment demonstrates how the formal advocacy of equal opportunity can operate to deepen inequity. State neglect of the Efland home, projected onto the presumed ineptitude of Black reformers, exposes a fundamental liberal commitment to white supremacy, betraying, despite appearances, white resistance to anti-racism or bringing women and girls of African descent into the fold of American national belonging.

The state besieged and dismantled the Efland reformatory because white identity depended upon the positionality of Black women as irretrievably abject. The shift in juvenile penology away from the benevolent reformatory model to custodial imprisonment still presented within a rhetoric of state service for all. The public widely lauded a custodial facility based on repressive penal control as an act of mercy, which raises new questions about racialized interpretations of mercy as a facet of juvenile jurisprudence.

Chapter Four

The Merciful Executioner

It is almost impossible to reach the Negro by means applied to the white convicts. We waste time in trying to make a Negro think he needs reformation.[1]

> The woman South in her rivers laving
> That body whiter than new-blown cotton
> And savage and sweet as wild-orange-blossom,
> The dark hair streams on the barbarous bosom,
> If there ever has been a land worth saving –
> In Dixie Land, I'll take my stand,
> And live and die for Dixie ...[2]

The limits of political emancipation appear at once in the fact that the state can liberate itself from constraint without man himself being really liberated; that a state may be a free state without man himself being a free man.

Karl Marx, On the Jewish Question[3]

A distraught Georgia Cannady wrote to Governor Clyde Hoey on 29 May 1940, to inform him of the alleged murder of her son Albert at the hands of staff at the Morrison Training School for Negro Boys at Hoffman, North Carolina:

> They sent My Boy down there and then let him Be Beat to dealth and I would like for you to investigate it if there is any way possible. I don't think it is write to take peoples Children to a place like that and then let them be killed. My Boys name was Albert Cannady they Clame that he was drowned. But his head was beat up and he had Been drug on his face

it was all Brused so you Could not hardly tell who he was and one arm
was limber like it was Broke so you know a drowned person is not like
that ...[4]

Officials at Morrison Training School had reported Albert Cannady's
death as a drowning accident in a lake on the grounds. The lake had been
constructed by damming an old stream. Allegedly floating on his back
in shallow water, William Brown Hoover, a non-swimmer, panicked
when he drifted into deep water. Albert, also a non-swimmer, reportedly jumped in to rescue William, who pulled him under in his distress.
Neither boy resurfaced. Teachers and other boys dove in to recover
them, without success. They managed to get hold of the boys two or
three times, but could not pull them up. Teachers found some planks
and tried to move the boys' bodies into shallower water, and after about
an hour, when all else failed, they broke the dam to let the water out.
The flood apparently carried the corpses 150 to 200 yards downstream,
where they came to rest, entangled in vines and small trees.

That neither Albert nor William could swim raises questions about
William's ability to dive in to rescue him, especially given the presence
of two teachers, and a large group of boys, many of whom were strong
swimmers. Nevertheless, in his response to Georgia Cannady, W.C.
Ezell, director, Division of Institutions and Corrections, explained that
after visiting the school and the lake, he saw no reason to doubt that
Albert drowned on the Sunday afternoon of 26 May. Coroner W.W.
King saw no need for an inquest or further hearing.[5] However, when
fellow inmates Sylus Roberson and John Colquit escaped from Morrison, they passed word that Albert had not drowned, but was killed.
Georgia Cannady learned from Roberson and Colquit that her son
had attempted escape on a Saturday, was caught, beaten by a "police
patrol" of five or six older boys under staffer Mr Glass's supervision,
and died the next afternoon, Sunday 26 May. Glass allegedly ordered
Albert's body moved to the woods, and the lake opened up to stage a
drowning accident. After four months and no direct response from the
governor, Cannady again wrote to the North Carolina State Board of
Corrections:

I am writing you again inregards of my son that was killed in Morrison
training school last year. Do you remember that you was supose to go out
there and investagate Albert Cannadys delth [sic] you said you was sure
it was accident Well I have found out that he was killed just like I told you

Before and if you don't do something about it I am going to put in a sute for my Childs life you know that they don't kill men that is in the pen like that and nothing done about it ... They have what they coll a police petroal down there the Big Boys and when some of the others try to run of or do eny thing they are Beat by 5 or 6 and then Mr glass Beat them you know them Boys cant tell what go on down if they do they are killed ... I am going to see to the Murder of My Child Being Brought to Justice or his life be paid for.[6]

It would come to light that many boys, finding the conditions unbearable, fled the Morrison Training School. From 1 July 1929 to 30 June 1930, thirty-nine boys escaped. From 1933 to 1934, forty-nine ran away, and from 1934 to 1935, another seventy-seven. Home counties returned only one-quarter to half of them, not wanting to incur the expense of their transportation.

North Carolina heralded the training school as a benevolent place to prevent the "full-blown adult criminality" among Black youth that many whites still believed incited mob violence. The institution would additionally develop reliable labourers who would eschew "anti-social" dissidence. With a mandate to provide Black juvenile offenders with merciful refuge from lynch mobs, North Carolina established the Morrison Training School for Negro Boys in 1917 on three hundred acres of semi-arable land. Any juvenile, state, or other court having jurisdiction could commit boys under sixteen.[7]

In this chapter I examine the national exclusion of Black adolescent boys in the context of merciful juvenile reform in interwar North Carolina. I am interested in the question of how one explains the administrative application of discretionary mercy, and of regulatory modes of punishment and normalization, in the segregated South's legal framework. What was the quality of mercy at this institution? As discussed in chapter 3, the state showed little interest in extending expensive reformatory treatment to wayward girls of African descent; and yet the state appropriations committee saw reason to fund a reform institution for court-committed Black youths. As Carolyn Strange has argued, "The bodies saved were the ones power-holders chose to save."[8] In 1938 juvenile court judge Owen Gudger wrote to W.C. Ezell, explaining, "Four weeks ago today I sent a colored boy, age 14 years, named Edward Chavis, who had been in detention six weeks awaiting acceptance to Morrison Training School. This boy had attempted rape on a twelve-year-old white girl and it would have been dangerous to have turned the boy loose in this community ... You can see what our problem is in handling negro boys."[9] Why did North Carolina's criminal justice administrators develop a discourse of mercy advocating benevolent restraint in corrections that by 1917 envisioned Black boys as candidates for rehabilitation in a juvenile reform institution, rather than shunting them into the adult penal system or letting them fall prey to rampant lynch mobs? What political and cultural ends did this liberal jurisprudence, and its racialized logics aim to serve? Reflecting on the archival record of the Morrison Training School, I explore how shifting interpretations of civilization and mercy modified punishment in a way that strengthened the ubiquity of the racist épistème under liberal humanism.

North Carolina's move away from lynching to the convict lease, chain gangs, and merciful reform institutions roughly follows Foucault's projection of an extensive reorganization of the economy of punishment. Evident in early juvenile reform discourses pertaining to white boys, the intention of legal punishment moved from the body to the will and inclinations, incorporating suspended rights and loss of freedom.[10] By the Progressive and New Eras in North Carolina, the consequentialist paradigm of corrections prioritizing rehabilitation had come to fruition, at least in theory, abandoning corporal punishment as merciless. This gave rise to a wave of institution building, drawing on the expertise of social workers and psychiatrists, who would advance discretionary juvenile justice through moral regulation, probation, and indeterminate sentencing. Inmate classifications resulted in the permanent transfer to long-term custodial institutions of boys "so defective mentally or psychopathic that they cannot possibly get along in the community ... who cannot stand up under the strain and stress of modern civilization."[11]

The legal discretion manifested in the founding of the Morrison Training School for Negro Boys might seem to indicate antiracist sentiment among the white middle class because it provided sanctuary, and because it formally advocated moral suasion, implying the acknowledgment of Black children's sentience. However, the archival record tells a story of spectacle underpinned by underfunding, ironhanded violence, and severe neglect. Modernity renarrated racism, and degeneration theories, popular at the time, marked children of African descent as insentient by nature, rendering benevolent reformation impossible. Reclaiming these children, bringing them into the fold of national belonging, was not a state priority, as we will see. To assess the qualities of mercy at Morrison Training School, we must first consider the history of lynching in North Carolina.

1. Cover Stories: Evolution of Lynching Discourses

Edward Ayers has noted that post-bellum whites often associated emancipation with contagion, represented by criminalized Black men and boys. The *Greensboro Herald and Journal* warned people of African descent: "No decent, well-behaved colored man is in any danger of being lynched … but a Black rapist should know that he would be lynched incontinently."[12] By 1864, newspaper editorials were generating a moral panic over the "uproarious" presence of Blacks, it being "almost impossible to walk the streets without meeting some negro with a segar [*sic*] stuck in his mouth, puffing its smoke in the faces of persons passing."[13] Stereotypes of the harmless Sambo shifted in the post-Emancipation South with the increasing popularization of Zip Coon, the imaginary, menacing buffoon sporting a straight razor.

With roots in the American Revolution, arguments over popular versus state sovereignty framed evolving narratives around lynching. Lynching rationales overlapped temporally and substantively, structured by widely accepted reference points. Tracing the historical stages of frontier lynching, Ashraf Rushdy has demonstrated that the practice, while stable, has expanded upon earlier lynching rationales, while adopting new ideologies.[14] Rushdy notes four general trends in the development of lynching discourses in American frontier societies. Perpetrators initially rationalized it through the democratic rhetoric of Revolution. The second trend justified lynching to punish homicide and protect manly honour, sometimes in the absence of a judicial body. The third shift brought capitalist employment of vigilante gunfighters, invoking popular white supremacy. In the fourth phase, lynching became a strategy of white terrorism for the control of racial and class mobility.[15]

The Fourth Phase: Racist Terrorism

During the antebellum period, planters governed the enslaved through legally sanctioned violence. Always fearful of insurrection, predatory planters' slave patrols crushed real and imagined insurrections. In the wake of Nat Turner's revolt (a Virginia slave rebellion also known as the Southampton Insurrection of 1831), for instance, North Carolina mobs killed more than forty slaves and free Black bystanders. By the beginning of the post-bellum era, then, the threat of mob violence was already familiar.[16] Michael Pfeifer recounts the incident of a planter who told his former slaves that, as slaves, as chattel, he never would have killed them, "even on great provocation ... But now ... you are nobody's property and damn you 'Look out.'"[17] In response to emancipation claims, mob rule would supplement and supplant the elastic legal apparatus that had undergirded the slave patrol to reinscribe white popular sovereignty.

Antebellum planters in North Carolina and throughout the South re-enacted earlier claims of popular sovereignty through their resistance to the development of strong local governments that would challenge their authority, supporting only a bare-bones legal apparatus. In keeping with this, white North Carolinians argued long over the inception of the penitentiary. Issues of popular sovereignty and national alterity inflected by questions of racial equality complicated the relatively late emergence (1846) of North Carolina's penitentiary, compared to the rest of the South. Opponents who wished to keep power more localized through local republicanism argued with those who hoped to "show the world that the slave South was not the barbaric land its detractors claimed." Proponents claimed that the South's place in the nation depended upon this "black flower," which represented "one of the distinct lines of separation between a barbarous and an enlightened age." Penitence and moral reform initially guided the early penitentiary, along with the instillation of respect for authority and labour, as connected to manufactories under industrial capitalism and a strong centralized state.[18]

Throughout the post-Emancipation South, new statutes enlarged the discretionary power of local judges and juries without direct mention of race, but the spectrum of possible punishments for vagrancy, rape, arson, and burglary – crimes often associated with Blacks – expanded.[19] The first person committed to an American penitentiary was "a light-skinned Negro in excellent health," but the penitentiary was expensive, and actually intended for whites.[20] As rates of African American incarceration soared with emancipation, administrators protested that their presence in prison would only inflate Black self-worth and breed insolence, while destroying white pride. Proponents of the white supremacist Organic Law of the Land claimed that legal justice could do nothing to solve the "great problem of the destiny of the negro upon this continent." Wishing to interact only with "quiescent and pacific"

Blacks, such groups feared that political equality would generate inflated assertions of self-importance and further demands for social equality, "with its train of evils which no one can understand or fully appreciate who has not lived in the midst of these unfortunate derelicts of Fate and Nature." More than any other group, Black youths, raised outside of the confines of what apologist Booker T. Washington called the "school of American slavery" represented a pivotal site of contention between proponents of juridical process and extralegal lynch law.

In the late nineteenth century, many white Southerners regarded a trial under secular law as too merciful for Blacks, whom they suspected would only enjoy the pomp and ceremony of a formal trial before a judge. Courts responded by shunting much of the burgeoning influx of young Black offenders into the profitable industrial convict lease system, and later, when this came under scrutiny as uncivilized, into chain gangs.[21]

Two rationalizations for frontier justice, evident in rudimentary form during the Revolutionary War, would resonate in this fourth phase: first, the claim about the inefficiency of the law as an institutional mechanism of enforcement, and second, the question of popular sovereignty, whereby the people consented or not to the making and enforcement of law. In late nineteenth century debates over due-process law, opponents of local republicanism argued that it fostered mob violence. "The cause of lynching is that we are the only Government on earth that has set up several thousand little bitty, small, weak, distinctive governments ... These tiny kingdoms can kill their subjects like dogs if they want to, and under State rights they know that there is no law on earth to prosecute them but their own law; no judge ever prosecutes himself." Drawing on earlier frontier-justice rationales, proponents of early twentieth century lynch law complained that the legal apparatus failed to resolve honour-based transgressions in a swift and retributive manner. Theoretically at least, due-process law took time to weigh all evidence with systematic impartiality. An 1884 newspaper editorial suggested making it "*obligatory* on the judge of the court to having jurisdiction, to convene his court, as soon as possible after the commission of the crime, in special session to try the accused and upon conviction let the criminal be executed *instantly* ... Then will the people be spared the temptation – the almost necessity – of staining their hands in extra-judicial, though most foul blood."[22] The most popular suggestion for the prevention of lynching was the increased efficiency of the formal justice system, which would thereby substitute merciful, orderly procedure for uncivilized vengeance.

Cover Stories in the Fourth Phase

From Reconstruction on, lynching emerged as a form of white terrorism, variously rationalized to suit prevailing conditions. Ida B. Wells identified three such "cover stories" for lynching in the fourth phase, which Rushdy, following Joel Williamson, has called the "age of lynching." In the first phase, from 1865 to 1872, as Radical Reconstruction supplanted antebellum white authority over political offices and courts, counter-Reconstruction conservatives claimed that lynchings were imperative to control Black labour and mobility, and to crush Black resistance to white supremacy. Forming violent paramilitary organizations in 1868, white Democrats used lynching as a means of overturning the revolutionary resistance of Blacks and white Republican Unionists.[23] In the immediate post-bellum period, a small group of aristocratic Confederate veterans established the first wave of the chivalric Ku Klux Klan organization in Tennessee as the mystical wing of the Lost Cause movement. In North Carolina, the Constitutional Union Guard formed as an affiliate of the Klan. Republicans often spoke out against Klan-based terrorism, while Democrats more typically rationalized, minimalized, and justified it. Some Democrats denied the Klan's very existence, dismissing reports of violence as "electoral propaganda from a Republican slander mill."[24]

In 1870, North Carolina's Governor William W. Holden's entire administration foundered when he dispatched white militia units to Alamance and Caswell counties, arresting 100 vigilantes. He suspended local Klan-controlled courts, and ordered a military commission to try the prisoners. Forced to release the perpetrators by the federal courts after Democrats had appealed to them under the 1867 Habeas Corpus Act (that expanded federal courts' jurisdiction, originally, in order to protect white Unionists and freedpeople), Holden's campaign against the Klan collapsed. Shortly thereafter, Democrats crushed his administration in the 1870 legislative elections. After the 1887 lynching of Benjamin White, R.S. Taylor, editor of the *Edgecombe Watchman*, demanded identification of mob members in a public hearing, but fled when threatened with his own lynching. Drawing on earlier frontier discourses, lynching advocates pointed to a fragile emergent state that could not be relied upon to deliver legal fairness. In 1893, North Carolina required sheriffs to secure their jails, and passed a law classifying lynching as a felony. Local law enforcement officials (many of whom were former Confederate soldiers) refused to arrest their associates.[25]

Between 1865 and 1941, lynch mobs murdered 168 North Carolinian Blacks, but this figure is grossly misleading because North Carolina law defined lynching narrowly, as carried out by a mob of three or more, or involving forcible removal from jails or from the custody of law enforcement. North Carolina officially ranked ninth highest in lynching deaths, appearing relatively exemplary compared to the Deep South. But 1918 figures indicate that there were 2754 murders in North Carolina that year, giving it the notorious distinction of having the highest homicide rate in the nation.[26] Representing the Second Congressional District of North Carolina, George White introduced the first bill in Congress on 20 January 1900 that proposed to make lynching a treasonable, federal offence to be prosecuted by federal courts; but the bill, opposed by southern white Democrats, died in committee. Democratic Party justices rarely punished lynchers. Communal support and massive mob participation characterized spectacle lynchings, which civic leaders, politicians, women, and children attended. These spanned five decades, from the end of Reconstruction until the mid-1920s, when changing social, geopolitical, and economic conditions discouraged open support of lynching.[27]

The second cover story prevailed during Reconstruction and after the Fifteenth Amendment's passage (1869 in North Carolina), when Democrats argued that the prevention of "Negro domination" associated with political power necessitated lynching. Once Black men were effectively barred from voting in state and national elections, additional rationalizations to avenge imagined assaults upon "white womanhood" enabled both the chivalric manipulation of white women, and the violent control of Black men and boys.[28] The Fourteenth (1868) and Fifteenth (1870) Amendments recognized African American men as citizens with a constitutional right to vote and to participate in government. But many whites believed the vote made the Black man "feel his manhood, which in the eyes of the white man, is asking too much."[29] I have argued elsewhere that what had begun in the 1860s and 1870s as a political struggle became popularly reinterpreted as a symbolic Black violation of the nation, projected onto white women as the "snow-white citadel" of the South. As the National Symbolic, white women represented the land, and rape charges veiled fears of violated political and social space.[30]

The lynching-for-rape discourse became the dominant interpretation of what lynching meant in the 1870s and 1880s, and has persisted, resonating in current racist police violence against Black men and boys.[31] Alterity is typically sexualized and racialized. Some whites claimed that the Confederate defeat effectively unshackled Black men to lust after "the Paradise tree of the forbidden fruit – the white women beyond their reach."[32] Lynching was actually a common Southern white response to "border violations" of political participation, labour disputes, or petty crime by men of African descent, but mobs, preoccupied with fears of national violation, increasingly justified lynching as vengeance for putative sexual attacks on white virgins. A Maryland lynch mob member exemplified this in his declaration "Before God we believe in the existence of a higher code than that which is dignified by the great seal of a Commonwealth and that the high and holy time to exercise it is when the chastity of our women is tarnished by the foul breath of an imp from hell and the sanctity of our homes invaded by a demon."[33] Pro-lynching advocates, including editors, intellectuals, and politicians, claimed that lynching protected white women's honour, despite the fact that the probability of a white woman being raped by a man of African descent in the post-Emancipation era "was much less," Wilbur Cash has noted, "than the chance that she would be struck by lightning."[34] White fears of "the Black Peril" have predictably attended threats to national cohesion, and reassertions of racial difference have historically generated white nationalistic rhetoric. Establishing racial classifications within state constitutions, the Black Codes criminalized interracial sexual liaisons and social association.[35]

Built in 1886 as the first national icon, the Statue of Liberty was strategically placed as a threshold marker, in the harbour where immigrants would see it.[36] With no direct national agency, women serve as metaphoric bearers of nation. Historically construed as either sexually dangerous or virginal, women have made apt representatives, because, as McClintock has observed, national margins figure as dangerous spaces, most vulnerable along their edges. The iconic white virgin is widely presented throughout imperial Western discourses and symbolism: Liberty in America, Dixie in the American South, Germania in Germany, Queen Luise of Prussia, and Britannia, were all akin, whether they signified mothers or daughters of the Empire, motherland or virgin land.[37] National iconography of the white virgin is also found in the story of the first white woman to die in the Civil War. Playing the role of National Symbolic in a pro-secessionist fund play in 1861, fourteen-year-old Laura Alfriend stood behind a curtain on a stage as a symbol of the emergent Southern nation. The candle footlights ignited her flowing robes and the "horrified audience saw the flames flare up and envelop her and saw the Confederate flag burn in her outstretched hand." Some said the political allegory of her death proved to be truer than anyone imagined at the outset of the Civil War.[38]

So persuasive was the hegemonic lynching-for-rape script, it gave pause to even the most astute critics of white supremacy, many of whom believed the rumours of rape might be true. Making it difficult to identify the problem as one of racist terrorism and not actual rape, this rationale thwarted the anti-lynching movement for half a century.[39] Jane Addams denounced lynching as an act that degraded the perpetrators in their disregard for legitimate institutions of law. She decried "[the] peculiar class of crime committed by one race against another," and maintained that "the bestial in man, that which leads him to pillage and rape, can never be controlled by public cruelty and dramatic punishment, which too often cover fury and revenge."[40] The Women's Christian Temperance Union's Francis Willard, a major representative of progressive ideology at the time, echoed Addams's sentiments, arguing that "no crime however heinous can by any possibility excuse the commission of any act of cruelty or the taking of any human life without due course of law."[41] Never did the liberal members of the Southern white women's anti-lynching movement challenge the myth of the black rapist. In their quest for legal protection they rejected only the "chivalry that has been pressed like a crown of thorn on our heads."[42]

White reformers' rejection of retributive violence animated juvenile justice, as did their adherence to Social Darwinism. Racism persisted beyond slavery in the "regulatory power of a racist state obsessed with blood, sex, and procreation." Biopower, or Foucault's "dispositif of security," constructs binaries between "us" and "them," the normal and the abnormal, civilized and barbaric, all of which informed national belonging or expendable, racialized otherness in early twentieth century North Carolina.[43] Given this, liberal-humanist white women's Progressive Era anti-lynching campaigns, for instance, would not necessarily have laid the groundwork for the civil rights movement that would come decades later, because Southern mercy actually renewed white supremacist discourses.

The Integrative Forces of the Market

The rapid decline of mob lynching after 1922 set North Carolina apart from the rest of the South. Until then, lynching was a normalized part of everyday life throughout the region, and so North Carolina was exceptional for this shift in the particularly violent period following the First World War. Although the decline of mob rule was an important shift, it is naive to regard it as a harbinger of an antiracist épistème. As Rushdy has observed, historical change involved historical continuity, and in the absence of a deeper transformation, lynching would persist in different forms.[44] Nevertheless, its formal decline, led nationally by North Carolina, proceeded through the culmination of social, geopolitical, and economic conditions.

North Carolina's fin-de-siècle one-party political culture imposed prohibitive constraints on progressive reform efforts as the nation gradually reunited along racial lines, and white Southerners increasingly projected their counter-Reconstruction resentment towards Union forces onto people of African descent. From 1900 to 1922 race riots, and a renewed reign of negrophobic terrorism, erupted across North Carolina.[45]

There were two periods of Republican rule in North Carolina, the first from 1868 to 1870, and the second from 1896 to 1898. Freedoms won during Radical Reconstruction were rescinded in the late 1890s and effective disfranchisement followed infantilizing depictions of Black men as children, casting an "ignorant vote." Louis Agassiz declared, "No man has a right to what he is unfit to use."[46] By 1920, men of African descent had disappeared from juries and public office. Governor Charles Aycock's 1898 Democratic Party white supremacy campaign scripted Black men as unfit for public office, and crushed the Republican Party, accusing its white members of supporting "Negro rule" in North Carolina. In a speech following a recent murder of an adolescent white girl, Aycock supported lynchers, stating, "In the east we have negro juries to interpose between the vicious of their race and the meeting of justice … Why you white men of Cabarrus don't even wait for the law when negroes have dishonored your helpless innocent women." This contributed to the instigation of the Wilmington Insurrection, heralding a virulently racist administration. Following the election, the Democratic Party introduced a bill to rescind the Black vote by requiring a literacy test and a poll tax. To protect poor whites, the bill included a clause releasing those whose grandfathers had voted before 7 January 1867. Through this inclusion, the Democrats inadvertently launched a set of events that would contribute to the formal decline of mob lynchings in North Carolina.

Poor whites grew leery of the bill. Its grandfather clause, and the earmarking of state funds for public education did little to reassure them.

Democratic Party officials, worried that poor whites might break ranks, as many did in 1891 to join the leftist Populist movement, called for the expansion of the textile industry to boost white employment. This required funding, and North Carolina, having earlier defaulted on a series of bonds and unable to raise the capital, had to turn to Northern financiers, who bankrolled the state on condition of social and political stability. Lynching disrupted the social order, and the flow of capital. By 1922, market forces led the growing bourgeoisie to coalesce against the nefarious practice for the sake of economic and industrial development. As the New South, and particularly North Carolina, gradually joined the industrial economy, the new white middle class favoured modernist sensibilities of caution and circumspection (embodied in legal process) over impetuosity and heated passion (exemplified by lynching). They regarded this as a matter of civilizing the South, assimilating it into the modern, globally powerful American nation. "Nothing is so calculated to keep investors from the state as these cowardly lynchings." As lynching became a liability to economic growth, rape imagery grew increasingly ineffective, and formal lynching would become passé.[47]

The initially romantic vision of vigilantes as dispossessed aristocratic protectors fell into decline as the vengeance associated with lynching rituals became a gauge of regional primitivism. The "rite that 'concluded the crime'" became also undesirably associated with it.[48] During the 1880s, middle class whites did not abandon lynching en masse, but many increasingly attributed it to a "pigheaded and brutish criminality" of rural working-class whites practising rough justice. Eric Foner has observed that Klan-based leadership in 1870 included ministers, merchants, and planters. Membership, while mostly made up of farmers and labourers, also included lawyers and physicians. The 1920s Ku Klux Klan resurgence accompanied the end-of-lynching discourse. While white Southern reformers of this period often portrayed lynch mobs as just gangs of "working class rowdies," many middle class whites supported and participated in them, too. According to Nancy Maclean, the 1920s Ku Klux Klan was largely a middle class organization, deeply entrenched in Democratic Party politics.[49] Nevertheless, lynching came to be increasingly defined as a disorganizing principle that threatened national integrity.

Shifting class-based definitions of "civilization" also contributed to lynching's decline. In Britain, in the decades around the turn of the twentieth century, modifications of punishment followed emerging bourgeois sensibilities that condemned carnivalesque executions as

antithetical to "the values of the civilized world" and, therefore, deleterious to England's national strength.[50] John Stuart Mill observed in 1836,
"One of the effects of civilization … is that the spectacle, and even the
very idea of pain, is kept more and more out of the sight of those classes
who enjoy in their fullness the benefits of civilization … It is in avoiding
the presence not only of actual pain, but whatever suggests offensive or
disagreeable ideas, that a great part of refinement consists." By the late
nineteenth century legal executions there moved behind closed doors,
and by 1908 England abolished capital punishment for children under
sixteen.[51] State representatives would increasingly call for minimal contact with the body of the criminal – the electric chair was designed to
make death quick and as painless as possible.[52]

As part of North Carolina's efforts to curb mob violence in the
early 1920s, a state committee awarded medals for distinguished service to county sheriffs who successfully resisted mobs. The governor
dispatched troops to prevent erupting violence, while court officials
increased their efforts to prosecute lynchers and secure convictions. But
change was contested and uneven. Police not only colluded with lynch
mobs, but also privately harmed adolescent Black boys in their custody.
In 1937, for instance, Commissioner Bost wrote to R. Eugene Brown,
director, Division of Institutions, to inform him of the police abuse of
a number of boys before their arrival at Morrison. Commissioner Bost
interviewed inmate James Perry at length, and faculty members at
Morrison Training School stated that all the boys coming from Charlotte had made similar reports. Bost wrote:

> He stated that he was beaten "with something plaited on a wire that had
> ends sticking out." "They hit me on the head with a pistol and cut my
> head open." "They kicked me." "They threw water at me." "They told
> me that they had an electric chair and would kill me in it. When they put
> me in that, I told them I stole what they said I did. Then they took me out
> and asked me where I put it. I didn't steal and I could not tell them" … It
> was noticed that Frank Clark limped as he walked when admitted. Asked
> why, he said that he had pain in and about his sex organs. When he was
> questioned further he said, "The police put on gloves and pulled on my
> privates and hurt me."[53]

Boundaries between legal and extralegal policing were often blurred.
Between 1926 and 1947 North Carolina whites lynched six men, and
there were ten more incidences of mob violence, yet only one case –

the 1941 Roxboro race riot – would bring a conviction and prison sentences. In the 1942 kidnapping case of alleged rapist Godwin Bush, state officials arrested suspects and took them to trial, but the grand jury would not indict them. Governor Cherry rejected the jury's findings and called for a second investigation and retrial, which bore the same results. Nevertheless, North Carolina avoided national condemnation (unlike other Southern states), having demonstrated some willingness to prosecute lynchers.[54]

North Carolina garnered Northern approval too, for taking the national lead in establishing the Division of Work among Negroes in 1925, and perhaps it is not coincidental that the state had founded the Morrison Training School in 1922. Through the division, white state administrators organized Black civic leaders "so that through their ability they may aid the poor, the unfortunate, and the orphans of their race, thus protecting both the individual, and the group or society."[55] Of course, Black civic leaders needed no help organizing, having managed this without help from whites since Reconstruction, and during slavery, as Foner has demonstrated. White administrators launched this project in an effort to secure interracial stability to attract northeastern financial investment in the state's industry. With Northern funding, North Carolina could discourage a return to Populist solidarity through the provision of jobs for poor whites. By 1960, North Carolina would become the nation's largest textile manufacturer.[56]

Southern Alterity and National Belonging: The Impact of Antilynching Activists

In addition to economic imperatives, anti-lynching activists' efforts contributed to the discursive shift that resulted in Northern pressure to end lynching in the South. From the 1890s through the first decade of the twentieth century, Ida B. Wells and a small group of white allies campaigned against lynching, urging the white public to rethink its tolerance for it. Wells disseminated her own research, supported by the *Chicago Tribune*'s statistical evidence, to national and international audiences, contradicting Southern white claims of lynching as a response to Black criminality, and exposing their thwarting of Black success and mobility through terrorism.

Wells, the white Association of Southern Women for the Prevention of Lynching (ASWPL), and, later, the NAACP, including W.E.B. Du Bois as the NAACP's executive committee chair in charge of publicity, all contributed to lynching counter-discourses in a rapidly nationalizing culture. Du Bois, Walter White, and J.W. Johnson published articles, gave speeches, wrote letters, and organized petition drives. In 1909, the NAACP organized to defeat lynching through legislation. While assisting in litigation against sheriffs who colluded with lynchers, they campaigned heavily for a federal law against lynching. The NAACP did finally achieve its objective of federal intervention when the Department of Justice agreed to use existing laws against lynchers, but Congress declined to pass anti-lynching legislation. Almost a century later, in 2005, the US Senate finally issued a formal apology for this refusal.[57]

Early Northern white tolerance of lynching rested partly upon uninformed rationales of cultural relativism. Like Wells, White strove to disseminate news of lynching nationally. In 1918, passing as white, he investigated lynchings undercover. His reports generated much publicity, garnering support for the NAACP as it lobbied Congress to pass a federal law against lynching. In an effort to mobilize authoritative urban newspapers with wide readership, White persuaded the *New York World* editors to investigate the Klan in South Carolina. Their subsequent articles circulated nationally, with shocking revelations of police collusion with lynch mobs in the South.[58]

Wells inspired many white Northerners to take action against lynching. In a brilliant turn of colonial rhetoric, she also struck a nerve in England, persuading British reformers that they must assume responsibility for civilizing America. British activists organized anti-lynching societies in response to Wells's 1894 lectures in Bristol, sending missionaries over to investigate the atrocities "committed by fellow Anglo Saxons."[59] Americans, they declared, were "horrifying the whole of the civilized world ... when one reflects that [such things] still happen while we in this country are sending missions to the South Sea Islands and other places, they strike to our hearts much more forcibly, and we turn over in our minds whether it were not better to leave the heathen alone for a time and send the gospel of common humanity across the Atlantic."[60] Wells's efforts to dismantle the lynching-for-rape discourse infuriated many white Southerners. Assessing a lynching case in 1892, she noted that the implicated white woman had willingly agreed to a liaison. A mob razed the offices of anti-segregation newspaper *The Free Speech and Headlight*, when Wells was visiting Philadelphia. She fled to Chicago when Memphis mobs called for her lynching.[61]

North Carolina's lynchings of Plummer Bullock and Alfred Williams, and the resulting extradition case of Matthew Bullock in 1921 brought international condemnation, discouraging Northern investment in the state. Wells's earlier work resonated in the case, when the editors of England's *Pall Mall Gazette* fumed, "All extradition law is based upon the assumption that the country in which the accused is handed over can guarantee a fair trial. Assurances should certainly be required that the man will not be thrown to the mercy of white barbarism in the Southern States."[62] Regional reputation was a powerful motivator for many white Southerners. Mob lynchings fell into decline by the twentieth century with the white bourgeoisie's emergent distaste for vengeful spectacles, increasingly regarded as barbaric. In keeping with the shift to modernity Foucault describes, lynching declined at least in part because it had come to be too closely associated with the "savagery" of the criminalized. Modern, "civilized" whites regarded punishment as an unpleasant if necessary task that must eschew vengeance while seeking a "higher" aim through lawful means.[63]

In the aftermath of the Civil War, national identity reformation was as pressing as economic reconstruction, and the emergent New South middle class sought to demonstrate worthiness of their regional affiliation with the nation. The *Cleveland Leader* commented in 1894 that "acts of barbarism have been committed in this country within the last 20 years by people claiming to be civilised which would scarcely have been credited to the cruellest and most bloodthirsty savages in Africa."[64] By 1894 many argued that lynching hurt America in the eyes of the "civilized world." The *Christian World* imagined that lynching "would disgrace a nation of cannibals."[65] It reported, "The American citizen in the South is at heart more a barbarian than the negro whom he regards as a savage ... Lynch law is fiendishly resorted to as a sort of sport on every possible opportunity, and the negroes are butchered to make a Yankee holiday ... Either they mistrust their legal institutions or they murder in wantonness and for mere lust of blood."[66] Wells further challenged the lynching narrative in arguments that mob violence endangered not just its victims, but also the nation's integrity, given the persistence of rampant exploitation, racism, and barbarity. The North Carolina Conference for Social Service program of the Fifth Annual Session (1922), remarked:

> Lynching occurs nowhere else, not even among the savages whom we are seeking to Christianise ... This crime of crimes, which is not only a complete subversion of law, but a stroke at the very life of law itself, has discredited our nation in the eyes of other civilised nations ... Stories of American mobs burning human beings at the stake and exulting in their torture are

regularly published throughout Europe, in Latin America, in the Orient, and even in Africa. The effect in mission lands can easily be imagined.[67]

Southern whites increasingly reframed chivalric lynching as a crime of barbarity, a "savage threat to American civilization." The anti-lynching campaign sought to portray the animalized and criminalized Black male body as the "body of the entire nation," victimized by "a crime against law, order, the nation and civilization." Many hoped the rejection of lynching would bring about "the saving of black America's bodies, and white America's soul." They argued that lynching increasingly signified "a rape of justice, liberty, civil rights, equal rights, human lives, and the Constitution itself." Wells claimed that it was not Black communities, but "white man's civilization and white man's government which are on trial."[68]

Spectacles of Mercy: End of Lynching Discourse

In a 1936 article, "A Lofty Spirit," the *Mobile Press Register* argued that the doctrine of an eye for an eye was merciless, and undermined "civilized" society: "It was a noble and ennobling act, that of the Alabama mother who saved from immanent mob violence the Negro who had brought tragedy and horror into the life of her seven-year-old daughter. [She] put the prerogatives of the law before the emotions which she very probably had to resist … It is women such as this who are the true representatives and guardians of our civilisation."[69] Emphasizing a humanitarian approach through due-process law, the modernist Southern white bourgeoisie constructed a legal order that eschewed ritualistic mob lynchings while channelling racism into frequent capital punishment. Due process accompanied rapid convictions, expedited in cases aggravated by white public outrage. As a modern mechanism of retributive justice, the death penalty applied scientific techniques and principles efficiently and behind closed doors, reconciling the popular demand for retribution with modernist preferences for regularity and predictability.[70] But mercy for Blacks often meant a formal trial and what Jessie Daniel Ames called "legal lynchings." These Southern spectacles of "civilization" provided visible demonstrations of white Southerners' willing lawfulness. But, as Ames noted, juries could not render fair and impartial verdicts, "knowing that the shouts of gratified passion greeting each sentence of death [would] be turned into snarls of rage against them if they interpret the evidence contrary to the verdict of the mob."[71]

While Foucault has charted the disappearance of punishment as spectacle under modernity, theatrical elements persisted even as public executions and lynchings in the South became reframed as legal executions. Southern spectacles of death through extralegal lynchings did not formally end for fear that white mobs might regard their tortured victims as objects of pity and admiration. Instead, legal corrections supplanted vigilante terrorism as a show of the South's capacity for mercy, and the racialized theatre of alterity survived. Blacks continued to be vanished literally and metaphorically under white Americanism.[72] A case in point is that of young George Stinney, just finishing seventh grade at the time of his arrest, and only fourteen (or possibly thirteen) at the time of his execution. Convicted of the attempted rape and murder of two white girls, Stinney held the notorious distinction of being the youngest person legally executed in America during the twentieth century. With no physical evidence or eyewitness testimony linking the boy to the crime, his "confession" was successfully presented in court as the sole piece of evidence. In a spectacular trial attended by a crowd of 1500, an all-white jury found Stinney guilty after less than ten minutes' deliberation. Denied the right to appeal, Stinney would die on 16 June 1944 – just eighty-one days after his arrest – in a botched electrocution. At 90 pounds and 5'1" tall, he was too small to be properly strapped into the electric chair. The adult-sized facemask slipped off with the first jolt of electricity, exposing the boy's convulsing, terrified face to witnesses.[73] Yet many whites would argue that this was a spectacle of mercy that demonstrated a "civilized" respect for legal process.

By 1922, North Carolinians would increasingly pride themselves on "securing the orderly processes of the law." Walter Adams, editor of the *Ashville Citizen*, wrote, "North Carolina has striven hard to avoid lynching. There is no state in the South which has a better record."[74] Increasingly identifying as civilized humanist-liberals, many North Carolina whites distinguished themselves as dutifully willing to "foster nurture and cherish life" – even the lives of alleged murderers and "Black rapists."[75] It was within this context that the Morrison Training School opened its doors as a place of refuge.

2. The Morrison Training School

At a North Carolina barbershop in the late nineteenth century, Thad L. Tate, a barber and Black civic leader from Charlotte, persuaded his white client Cameron Morrison, a candidate for governor of North Carolina, to consider the possibility of a reformatory for Black juvenile offenders. Such an institution would ideally provide these boys with trades apprenticeships, while rehabilitating them. By 1920, many white reformers, including the League of Women Voters of North Carolina, juvenile court judges, social workers, and state administrators expressed deep interest in a "reformatory for youthful negro criminals."[76] The North Carolina legislature passed an act in 1911 to establish a state institution, but declined to grant an initial appropriation, leaving the purchase of the tract of land to "the Colored people of the state." Hoping to obtain funding, the State Board of Charities and Public Welfare decided that "the institution should be provided for at once and that it can be done without great expense. Good farm land, preferably 200 acres, with farm buildings already thereon, should be secured. Then, as soon as the staff is secured, they can begin to take boys who can then be used from the beginning on enlarging the facilities."[77] In 1919, white reformer A.M. Moore wrote to Public Welfare Commissioner Beasley suggesting, "I think it proper that the Colored people should underwrite your program rather than have you underwrite theirs."[78] Commissioner Beasley noted that members of a Black church in Kinston, NC, offered to support local juvenile court work with strong interest and "helpful intelligence." Black civic leaders requested an appropriation of $30,000 at the 1919 session of the General Assembly for the building and maintenance of the state institution. They assured officials that Morrison would offer manual, not academic training, and that while the superintendent and officers would be men of African descent, the board of trustees would include four white and two "colored" people.[79]

Several reform institutions in other Southern states predated the 1922 Morrison Training School and served as comparisons: the Virginia Manual Labor School for Colored Boys, state-funded since 1902, was apparently well managed, but poorly equipped; the Georgia State Reformatory, a self-supporting county institution, trained boys in farming; the South Carolina Reformatory for Negro Boys, and the Alabama Reform School for Juvenile Negro Law Breakers, both established in 1911, limped along on "very meagre equipment and very small revenues." Commissioner Johnson advised Trustee W.N. Everett to visit the Jenkins Reformatory in South Carolina, "to see how not to run an Institution of the kind North Carolina is proposing ... This a miserable place."[80]

In November 1921, the legislature passed a bill appropriating funds for the establishment of the Morrison Training School. Governor

Morrison appointed a commission under resolution of the Special
Session of the Legislature to consider "measures for the benefit of the
negro race in North Carolina." These members would later form Morrison's board of trustees. The board purchased eighty-six acres of land
south of Charlotte, but by 1922 the school still could not open, having
received no state funding.[81] Expressing concern, Commissioner Johnson, wrote, "The organization of such an institution is an act of justice
to the Colored people of the State, and will be very helpful to us in
our work. Hardly a day passes that we do not get a letter from some
superintendent of public welfare saying that he has a Colored boy in
jail because there is nothing else to do with him, and these boys are
frequently around twelve and thirteen years of age.[82] Wishing to sell
the existing land in 1922 in order to purchase a tract more accessible to
Raleigh and state administrators, Morrison's board of trustees placed
ads in local newspapers, inquiring about possible real estate. Receiving
no response from any counties, they concluded that residents did not
want to host a correctional institution in their communities. In October
1922, an exasperated Samuel Leonard, superintendent of public welfare in Wilson County, reminded Commissioner Johnson that a location had still not been decided upon by the appointed board, despite
an active community of Black reformers. "What we have been trying to
find out is just what the board wants and this we have never learned."[83]
Again, things stalled as white interest flagged.

But the tone of public sentiment would shift. By March 1923, the inte-
grative forces of the market compelled the state to demonstrate a concerted effort to quell the social instability generated by supposed Black
criminality, mob lynchings, and race riots. The 1923 General Assembly
would finally grant an appropriation $50,000 "for the establishment of
a reformatory for delinquent Negro boys."[84] Pleased, N.C. Newbold,
director of the Division of Negro Education of the Department of Public
Instruction, called it "one of the most important movements started for
the benefit of the Colored race in North Carolina." By December 1923,
state administrators had purchased 400 acres in Richmond County near
the town of Hoffman.

Morrison's official mandate stated, "All boys committed to the school
shall be instructed in useful trades and manual labor and shall, if possible, be taught the precepts of the Holy Bible, good moral conduct,
how to work and to be industrious."[85] Boys might be committed for
sex offences or automobile theft; burglary or unlawful entry, robbery;
truancy, running away; being ungovernable, acts of carelessness or

mischief; traffic violations, delinquent behaviour, violating probation, or injury to a person.[86] The board's president, Black civic leader Thad L. Tate, declared the Reform and Manual Training School for Colored Youths "humane," adding, "I know the great need for it in the State and the great benefit it will be to the colored youths in their uplift and making them better citizens."[87] While Johnson referenced "law-abiding citizens," and Tate wrote about moral uplift and citizen building, there is no mention of citizenship or citizen building in the official institutional mandate. In his extensive 1933 publication, *Negro Child Welfare in North Carolina*, Wiley B. Sanders makes no reference to the building of Black boys as future constitutional citizens.[88] More than any call to national membership, the decision to found the Morrison Training School was a show of merciful, legal discipline that replaced lynching.

In 1903, W.E.B. Du Bois rejected Booker T. Washington's advocacy of manual industrial education as the best means of the "uplifting and civilization of Black men in America," arguing that the policy of industrial education was "indicative of a tendency born of slavery and quickened and renewed to life by the crazy imperialism of the day, to regard human beings as among the material resources of a land to be trained with an eye single to future dividends." Du Bois's pedagogical vision recalled the schools established during Reconstruction that sought to mobilize republicanism through Black political organization, suffrage, equality before the law, and self-reliance through moral uplift. Education represented the greatest success of the Freedmen's Bureau in the post-Emancipation South. The disengagement of schooling from ideals of equal citizenship manifested after Reconstruction ended, under the auspices of white "Redeemers." Booker T. Washington supported this separation, promoting the pedagogical philosophy of industrial education.[89]

Superintendent Reverend L.L. Boyd

With the 1923 appropriation in hand, Commissioner Johnson sought applications for the job of the reformatory's superintendent. She advised the board, "He must be a negro who has the proper attitude toward the white people in his community, and with whom he could work satisfactorily." Of all the candidates, the board favoured Baptist pastor Rev. L.L. Boyd, despite his reputed arrogance, because he had been educated under Booker T. Washington's model of cooperative apartheid at Alabama's Tuskegee Institute.[90] In his follow-up letter to civic leader Thad Tate, Boyd wrote:

Since leaving you on last Sunday, I have been gripped as never before with the idea of the Reform School and its many possibilities ... It appears to me, that the greatest aim of the work should be the "making of a man" of each boy who finds shelter in this home provided by the State ... If I am appointed to the Superintendency of the school, the following are some of the things I should like to stress from the very beginning: 1) Training in Agriculture and practical farming: That is to say, specialize in growing of corn, potatoes, vegetables, hog raising, and dairying, and a year-round garden for the school and market, and not long, the school could raise fully 20,000 pounds of pork a year ... It would be a blessing to the school and a medium for cash ... 2) An auditorium for daily devotion, where every boy would find opportunity for training in religious principles, singing, development in the higher ideals of life.[91]

Impressed, board members Thad Tate and Professor Atkins recommended Rev. Boyd to Commissioner Johnson. Initially hesitant, she replied, "I am sure you know that the success of an institution depends upon the personality of the superintendent." A year later, and anxious to get the reformatory up and running, Johnson consented to Boyd's hiring, stating, "If he satisfies the Executive Committee ... I shall not object ... We have a number of young negro boys who are being held [illegally] in jail awaiting the opening of the institution. This, of course, [being illegal] is very bad."[92] A month later, Rev. Boyd wrote to Commissioner Johnson, explaining that with eighteen years of teaching experience and nine as an industrial teacher in two Tuskegee Institute branch schools, "I feel that no applicant is better fitted by nature and training for such a task than I ... Having received my education at Tuskegee, most certainly fits me for this work in a peculiar way."[93] Morrison's white board of trustees invited Boyd and his wife to meet with them, hiring him immediately.[94] Soon after, the board elected to place the entire management and responsibility of the institution under Boyd's direction, supervised by the board of trustees and representatives of Commissioner Johnson's office. Senator L.R. Varner opposed initial recommendations that "a white man business manager" would work with Superintendent Boyd, claiming this would fail because a white man would never accept a subordinate position. "All of these assistants," Newbold advised, "should be Negroes."[95] William Bush has argued that superintendents of reform institutions in this era enjoyed the level of public respect given to juvenile court judges, and "wielded near-total institutional authority." According to a US

Children's Bureau assessment of American training schools, superintendents made "decisions on all subjects, issue[d] all orders, supervise[d] all departments, [and] passe[d] on all questions of standards and scientific work," including all parole and release decisions.[96]

On 1 January 1925, the training school opened on a large farm. The law stated: "Delinquent negro boys under sixteen years of age may be committed to the institution by any juvenile, State, or other court having jurisdiction over such boys," but permission had to be secured first from the superintendent of the school.

"Very little progress is noted other than an outside show"

The 1926–7 state appropriations of $11,000 would contribute to the cost of 106 committed inmates and five staff members. The farm was run with two mules and one wagon. While the boys received "much less than ½ pint" of milk each day and lived in crowded conditions with "less than 2 sq. ft. of ventilation and light space" each, provisions were made for baseball, basketball, army drills, and other physical exercise as part of the curriculum.[97] White board member C.C. Spaulding wrote a glowing review of Superintendent Boyd's work in 1926, making a bid for increased state funding, which he presented as an investment:

> All boys seem happy and well satisfied and when we took up the matter of paroling fifteen of them, only three have yet agreed to leave the school. I recommended to the board that it might be a good idea to have the state make additional appropriation next year for the school so we can house two or three hundred boys. When they are ready for parole they can be hired out and a three or four hundred acre farm can be cleared up and it will really be a paying proposition for the state.[98]

A few months later, Rev. S.N. Griffith accompanied a boy to Morrison from Edenton County and wrote the commissioner to thank her for establishing "such a haven." Of the superintendent he wrote, "We feel proud of this institution and the way in which they are being taken care of by the most worthy superintendent the Rev. Mr. Boyd. He not only impresses me as a superintendent, but he seems to be 'A BIG BROTHER' in whom the boys may be justly proud. This school is truly a boon to the boys of my race, who otherwise would be sent to the road despite their tender age."[99] Commissioner Johnson replied, lauding the institution: "I am very proud of that institution as I helped to write the bill and get it through the Legislature. I have watched its development under Rev. L. L. Boyd with much pride and interest. I hope that eventually it will be sufficiently large to care for a great many more boys."

In 1929, Commissioner Johnson wrote a letter of recommendation to support Boyd's fundraising campaign for band instruments and a touring bus, declaring that the training school benefitted North Carolina by preventing future criminality through correcting delinquency. She informed Boyd that given the recent financial losses suffered from the Wall Street crash, the timing was bad for such a campaign. But pressured by inadequate state appropriations, Boyd had little choice. His 1930 campaign included a plea for contributions of $6000 for equipment. The newly completed six-room trades building constructed by the state, while impressive on the outside, completely lacked equipment. The building was presented as a general shop for instruction in woodworking repairs, auto mechanics, light metal work, barbering, shoe repair, and printing. Commissioner Johnson, Superintendent Boyd, and Director N.C. Newbold also applied for a Julius Rosenwald grant to fund equipment. They provided a report by Edward Boshart of the School of Education of the North Carolina College, who noted how impressed he was with the efforts made on behalf of the boys without any suitable equipment. The fund administrators replied that they would only accept a report provided by the Child Welfare League, and even with that, could give no assurance that they would interest themselves in the school. Boyd finally gave up.

Perhaps in a bid to inspire state interest, Boyd decided to dedicate the new school buildings in the autumn of 1928. The commissioner informed him that this would have to be postponed until the spring, as the fall was the busiest time of year for state officials, and the governor would be unable to attend the dedicating service. With a budget taxed to the limit, Boyd requested in 1929 that counties help defray the cost of housing boys by providing clothing ("unionalls," pants, shirts, shoes, and underwear) along with a $40 lump-sum contribution to expenses. Counties were additionally asked to pay any inmate hospital bills. The counties refused, while demanding admission of boys when the institution was already beyond capacity. Director Eugene Brown suggested to (white) county superintendents that in the past, many counties had elected to build cottages at Jackson Training School, and in so doing, provided training for large numbers of their boys. Superintendent Boyd supported this idea, confirming that plenty of land was available for building residence cottages as large as counties desired; but

Figure 4.1. The Rev. L.L. Boyd, with boys' glee club members, "there to entertain appropriations committee members in a plea for funds." C. 1930. Reprinted with permission from *The News & Observer*, Raleigh, NC.

counties never made this investment at Morrison Training School. In August 1935, Martha Taylor, Granville County superintendent of public welfare, complained about the expense of sending boys to Morrison with the required set of new clothes.[100]

In his 1932 correspondence with Director Brown, Superintendent Boyd wrote, "My dear Mr. Brown, if ever I have needed you it is now." Boyd requested $4,500 to provide adequate sleeping quarters for the women teachers who were housed in a boys' dormitory "where every semblance of privacy is denied ... They are the object of gaze of every boy who desires to become a "peeping Tom." In 1932 Boyd also requested a congregate dining hall with a kitchen, refrigeration, storerooms, and a bakery. Boyd offered to have his staff construct the new buildings to save on costs. Brown sympathized, agreeing to endorse Boyd's request in the coming legislative session. The state appropriations committee would promise funds for this purpose, but then put them off until the next session, time and again.[101]

Boyd applied for funding from the Civil Works Administration, and Commissioner Bost wrote to the Budget Bureau in December 1933, urging them to at least fund a new kitchen and dining room, given the dilapidated, unsanitary, and dangerous state of the existing wooden kitchen structure. Ezell's April 1934 report on the institution confirmed that available equipment at the school was so limited as to seriously impede training. "Actually, there are scarcely enough pencils for the students to use."[102] Repairs in the way of plumbing and paint were also needed. He concluded, "It is apparent that the school is suffering from lack of funds to carry on the work as Supt. Boyd would like, and to do the best possible work for the boys."[103] In 1935, the state Welfare Department reported that while there were three trade vocational teachers at the school, no vocational educational objectives had been defined. Education was a low priority, and no attention was given to boys' scholastic standing. There were no library books, and no textbooks. The teachers ran classes without instructional supplies. While instructors were qualified in their fields, none had received pedagogical training to prepare them for work with "delinquent" boys, and there were no professional magazines or books on site for them to consult. Morale failed. Staff meetings were no longer held. Low salaries, no spousal housing, and scarcely any vacation time resulted in a high employee turnover rate. One young teacher with a newborn baby was allowed only six days off to visit his wife and child in Virginia. It is unclear whether Field Agent William Johnson was referring to the state or to the training school administrators when he noted, "Very little progress is noted other than an outside show."[104]

Itinerant teacher-trainer S. B. Simmons reported that little attention was given to the boys' scholastic standing; actually, academic work was given as an appreciation course and was recommended dropped as impractical. "Teachers are often busy with repair jobs and construction work. Neither shop-space nor equipment was made available to the auto-mechanics instructor."[105] The institution completely lacked books for academic subjects or for industrial ones.

In 1935, two members of the North Carolina Federation of Negro Women's Clubs, Hattie Hughes and Anna Hauser, visited the reformatory to assess how much of a redemptive role the institution played, and if it was actually carrying out its celebrated merciful mandate as professed by the North Carolina legislature. They wondered if the

boys were receiving guidance, psychiatric treatment, and care to produce good citizenship, or if the place operated merely as a detention
camp, isolating criminalized Black youth from their communities. They
hoped to find a place that offered decent quarters, library facilities,
shop equipment, and playgrounds. What they found, instead, inspired
them to send a report to Commissioner Bost, expressing grave concern:

> Boys were lounging on the steps, sitting in windows … The lack of any
> plan for recreation was apparent … No classes were in session during the
> hours of our visit. So we saw no teachers. We tried to see the library, but it
> was locked and the office secretary did not know where to find the key. We
> could not go into the hospital building, for it also was locked. In one of the
> dormitories we saw one little sick boy, pale and puny, lying in his bed strug-
> gling vainly to fight the flies that swarmed through the numerous holes in
> the dilapidated screens and annoyed him. No one seemed to be giving the
> boy any attention. We tried to overlook the holes in the screens in even the
> principal's office, but we had to look a long time indeed, with unforgiving
> eyes at the several large holes in the kitchen screens that admitted an army
> of flies much to the annoyance of a woman in one corner of the kitchen
> who was cleaning a large supply of chitterlings … Our visit to the dining
> room was our most disheartening experience …The word "dirty" does not
> adequately describe the ragged things covering the tables.[106]

This stands in stark contrast to the celebrated National Negro Health
Week Observance at the institution a year later, from 3 to 12 April 1936.
Under the direction of caseworker Ruth Stevenson, the institution's
population was divided into small groups or "committees" that "took
responsibility" for developing projects, in keeping with popular white
assumptions that Blacks' material circumstances resulted from their
own moral failing. This included a range of projects from cleaning dormitories to making flower pots from tin cans for the dining room. A
posture clinic was held, and a small group conducted a workshop on
tending to personal appearance through hair combing, polishing shoes,
and washing clothes. Fred Jacobs, a young student, gave a presentation
entitled "Booker T. Washington, an Ideal." Forty health posters were
made by the students, five of which would be entered in the National
Poster Contest. A group of boys constructed a miniature health centre
and recreation centre diorama (one they would never experience) that
"included a playground with a tennis court, a swimming pool, swings,
a seesaw and ball field; also a hospital building with bed equipment,

a club house and a log cabin representing the birthplace of Booker T. Washington." An inspection just before this event concluded, "the food is fairly adequate and plentiful most of the time but there are times when meals were rather 'slim.' The boys get too little milk, no eggs, and at times, too few green vegetables." So it is especially poignant that "the Home Economics Department ... sponsored a food exhibit ... A table was set for breakfast and dinner with a balanced menu. Vegetables were displayed."[107]

In 1937, the schedules of the 150 inmates at Morrison were supposed to be divided between academic work and manual labour; but most work involved manual labour to maintain the institution. Two years earlier, 215 boys were in residence, but there were only 144 single beds available with decrepit mattresses and dirty sheets. While the superintendent had recently bought 64 dozen new sheets, laundry facilities were "totally lacking." In 1935 state administrators expressed concern about the lack of beds, and wondered if this had been presented to the Budget Bureau, because Morrison was appropriated "practically every penny that was requested ... Personally, I do not see that this is the fault of the State." They did acknowledge, however, that the appropriation to the school had not been in proportion to the number of boys committed there. In a 1936 budget questionnaire, Superintendent Boyd stated that operating costs had been kept to the very minimum, with no institution able to boast as low a per capita expenditure of $150.00 (compared to an average of $299.00 in the Southern states, and $450.25 nationally). Boyd reminded the budget committee that the purpose of the institution was to salvage discarded lives, transforming them into self-supporting citizens. Institutional needs, such as shop equipment, more teachers, and an increased food allowance would enhance the environment, key to the social, moral, and mental transformation of the inmates.

In 1936, women teachers still lived in a cramped wing of the Varser Building. There was one poorly functioning toilet, and one shower for the entire building. Bedrooms large enough for only one person, and no common area made socializing difficult. Most of the male teachers still lived in a farm cottage without lighting or bathing facilities. Toilet facilities existed only in the dormitories, not in the school buildings or shops. There was no isolation ward for sick boys. Moreover, the lack of a telephone presented a serious problem for the institution, given the necessity of driving three miles into town to call a physician in case of illness or emergency. The 1936 recommendations by state administrators included provision of a telephone, dairy cows, and additional blankets. They also requested laundry equipment, to be set up in the auto mechanics building, given that the state appropriations committee would likely not grant funds for the construction of a laundry building. The committee also recommended that boys who had been institutionalized for over two years be released to make room for incoming inmates.[108]

There Is Much Unsaid

In an apparent effort to boost morale and establish his authority, Superintendent Boyd delivered a 1933–4 schedule and scheme of operation to his staff, soliciting their support for the benefit of the inmates and the State of North Carolina:

> My dear Co-workers:
>
>   With us here, there are no big folk and little folk ... I am very anxious that each of you develop day by day the broader, sympathetic, helpful spirit towards each and all ... There will be no such thing as the proverbial "big shot." This does not mean that excellency in service will not be recognized ... It is our plan to banish from the program of activity and life of the institution the disintegrating poison of individualism and enthrone forever the spirit of collectivism. This is what all should conceive to be the true attitude of workers in a school of correction. You are a spoke in the wheel of social service; play your part well. Hold firm. Don't warble. Let us make this school a great human laboratory for the turning out of fine citizens to grace our State.[109]

Yet shortly thereafter, county superintendents of public welfare complained to the commissioner that Boyd was not advising them about escapees. They only found out about them through neighbours, or when these boys were arrested for some new charge. When asked about this, Boyd responded that the boys had fled the institution to escape a disciplinarian's brutality, and that he had just fired that staff member.[110] All the while, boys were escaping, Boyd said, often without his knowledge (recall that in 1926 boys were reluctant to leave when the question of their parole came up). "Finally I called upon my older boys to take a hand in putting a stop to these escapes and this was done," Boyd wrote. This supports Georgia Cannady's statement that "they have what they coll a police petroal down there the Big Boys and when some of the others try to run of or do eny thing they are Beat by 5 or 6." [111]

By 1935, staff members anonymously complained to the superintendent of public welfare (Bost) about the conditions at the institution:

> As a means of punishment boys are put in an ill ventilated, ill lighted and no heated dungeon. Health conditions are vile. No means of taking a bath, no lavatory, no beds. Three boys were found guilty of stealing food about five days ago and these boys were kept in this place without food for four days. Don't take our word, drive down and see. Just a glance will prove to you that every boy who has been out here as much a [sic] 1 year can be called undernourished. Staff members are entirely under subjection to this "Mighty Monarch" and no considerations are given them about real necessities or Rights ... The men are less than slaves and the women are prospective prostitutes ... Nine boys escaped within the last two days. In my opinion, if those boys had not been hungry they would now be here and in bed ... If there is any hope of ever having another superintendent here at the Morrison Training School, we will fight openly. There is much unsaid.[112]

Director, Division of Institutions and Corrections R. Eugene Brown immediately responded with an investigation, reporting that it did not "warrant definite conclusions although there are indications that the diet is not well balanced." In addition, he observed that the staff seemed overworked, there being provision for "only a day or two off once in a few months ... Staff members do not feel secure in their positions, and most of them would be glad to leave if other suitable employment could be found." Policy changes would be made such that, by 1936, employees were entitled to fifteen vacation days annually.

Following his investigation, Brown sent a letter to Superintendent Boyd, securing his promise to abandon the use of the dark cell in the Varser Building attic. The only light and ventilation came from a five-by-twelve-inch window in a solid wood door. The cell was eight by twelve feet, furnished with filthy mattresses and a bucket. At the time of its discovery, the cell housed eight boys, one of whom had been locked there for fifteen days. "You come back in a week and you will find that the cell has been torn out," Boyd assured him. In a follow-up visit to the institution three weeks later, investigators found the confinement cell still in use, a boy being locked there just the day before the visit.[113] As was often the case when government officials called, Boyd happened to be away from the institution.

Eight months later, young inmate James Page ran away, and the Columbus County superintendent of public welfare reported to

R. Eugene Brown that the boy's mother discovered body lice in his clothes when he returned home. James complained of "dirty food" and harsh treatment from one faculty member and the older boys. An employee wrote, "I wish you could have seen James before he left. He was whipped as if he was a dog. His back was cut in gashes. They treat him so cruel, he says he will never stay there." In April 1936, within weeks of this incident, Morrison officers sent another boy, Clifton Perkins, home. In the final stage of tuberculosis, he died and was buried two days later. A physician had identified the boy as a hospital case, but little was done about it. Superintendent Boyd apparently said nothing until the superintendent of public welfare in Greenville wrote to say the boy was dead. Brown remarked that "his condition should have been discovered early enough for proper treatment" because he was a source of infection upon his arrival at the institution. After a subsequent visit to the institution, public welfare officials reported "several boys with scars about the head and face that might easily develop to serious proportions," and urged the provision of a full-time nurse in the absence of a physician.[114]

By October 1937 the state would hire a caseworker to work with the superintendent as an assistant. W.C. Ezell reported: "It has seemed to us that the Superintendent has felt an insecurity in himself and the Worker has been able to help him to become more confident. This ... has expressed itself in less tension between the Superintendent and members of his staff."[115] The case worker also advised in individual cases, and "scientifically" gathered information on admitted children's home environments and "whole background," thereby enabling the framing of a well-rounded training program for each child before admission, improving the application of corrective principles and increasing the efficacy of rehabilitation so that the duration of residence could be reduced from forty-two months to eighteen months. The caseworker performed much of the administrative work: the submission of full applications in a timely manner, and the placement and parole of boys. Additionally, she organized regular staff meetings and training, compiled case summaries, periodically met with boys to prevent unrest, and monitored them all individually, noting their "personality development."

In October 1937, an eleven-year-old boy had been illegally confined in the Nash County jail for over a month for robbing houses because Superintendent Boyd refused to accept the typed copy of the required entrance form. In March 1940 a superior court judge ordered Boyd to admit a boy convicted "of a crime against nature." Boyd refused to admit the child, citing his mandated authority to accept or reject applications. Moreover, he argued, the school was already overcrowded, Mecklenburg County already had exceeded its institutional quota, and the boy, who would turn sixteen the following February, would receive little benefit from only one year of training. But the boy had already spent two months in jail after sentencing, and the judge issued a bench order for Boyd to appear "and explain why he showed 'a contemptuous disregard' for the judgment of the superior court of North Carolina." He ordered Boyd to immediately admit the child.[116] Four days later the *Charlotte Observer* suggested that the judge had acted impetuously in this contempt hearing, reporting that with adequate conference and consultation, "the negro superintendent might have been spared the obvious humiliation he suffered for no greater crime than having, he thought, done his duty and carried out the legal instructions of the state welfare board ... Boyd, a former negro preacher of this city is a man of discretion, and of dignified bearing in the presence of his superiors."[117] Superintendent Boyd explained that the wide heterogeneity of the population impeded proper training, making it difficult to find common ground on which all could meet. "There are boys committed to us whose eligibility ranges from modern high school to an asylum for the insane."[118]

Relations with state officials continued to deteriorate. Superintendent Boyd increasingly avoided communication with white country superintendents of public welfare. Ezell reported information gleaned from a caseworker in 1939, individualizing the problem and attributing it to Boyd's supposed psychological maladjustment:

> The Superintendent, who is a Negro, has some awareness of racial difference. The Worker has told me of occasions where the Superintendent had avoided conferences with some county workers ... who had made the Superintendent feel he was a Negro. The Superintendent has never been rude to such persons. The Worker has consciously attempted to make the Superintendent aware that his reactions are influenced by this feeling on his part and has thus helped him toward working through these feelings.[119]

"On several occasions," Boyd allegedly returned money to the state, ostensibly "with the hope of boosting his own stock with the state officials." But in his biennial report for 1940–1 to 1941–2, he stated that "human salvage was accomplished 'in spite' of the meagre opportunities offered by this institution," and more could have been done if "adequate financial provisions been made during the earlier years of this institution." On 12 February 1944, the *Carolina Times* decried the state for providing insufficient funding, arguing that reports on the deplorable state of affairs at the Morrison Training School "make us shudder and wonder why the great state of North Carolina has not taken definite action to correct a situation that is a menace to the health of not only inmates of the institution but those who have to do with its operation."[120] Instead of adjusting the budget to deliver much-needed funds, monies that white institutions obtained with relative ease, the state focused on the superintendent as the problem.

In 1944 the State Auditor's Office filed a report with the State Board of Correction and Training, listing $1220 ($16,507 in 2016 currency) as unaccounted for by Boyd over a three-year period, from July 1940 to October 1943. This included insufficient invoices and personal items on the drug bill, such as *Bromo-Seltzer*, toothbrushes, toothpaste, *Vitalis*, and toilet water. The invoices "did not add up to the exact amount of the reimbursement check in any one month. Usually the invoice amounted to less than the reimbursement check."[121] By 1944, state officials individualized the problems of the reformatory, vilifying the superintendent and holding him fully and personally responsible for its decline. The *Carolina Times* descended on Boyd: "It is a dark hour in any man's life when he sets out to build his own fame and fortune at the expense of his fellowman. It is the darkest hour in his life when he attempts to do so at the expense of those who are weak and unprotected ... [He] will have to pay the price of his dirty deeds. Rev. Boyd has never impressed us as being able to do anything well but talk loud."[122] Effective 1 March 1944, Rev. Boyd resigned from his post, to be replaced by Paul R. Brown, former principal of a high school in Moore County, appointed by the Negro Advisory Committee working under the Board of Correction and Training in supervising Black correctional institutions.[123]

Rev. Boyd seemed initially willing, and up for the job of working with the boys at Morrison Training School. The archival record suggests that while the state had launched the institution with much fanfare, impressive-looking trades buildings had no equipment, and staff wages were abysmal. While some white state administrators appear to have been supportive, the state appropriations committee remained indifferent. Underfunding circumscribed all efforts to run the institution. Arguably, like Efland's founders and managers, Superintendent Boyd had become disilllusioned. His lack of cooperation with state officials was not unusual for white superintendents of juvenile reform institutions in North Carolina at the time.

Boyd's violent methods of punishment may well have resulted in Albert Cannady's and other boys' deaths. The irony of firing him over the alleged misspending of petty cash while ignoring his possible role in the death of Albert Cannady and others is a profound indication that the entire reformatory project was little more than a spectacle of mercy that served to renew white supremacist discourses.

Southern Mercy and Exclusion

In light of the fact that state welfare policies and resource allocation were racially biased, and given the persistence of civilizationist rhetoric into the twentieth century, it is noteworthy that the state developed a discourse of mercy that readily incorporated young Black male offenders into North Carolina's juvenile reformatory movement. If, as Michel Foucault has claimed, "racism is the condition that makes it acceptable to put certain people to death in a society of normalization," then why did North Carolina reformers and criminal justice administrators include boys of African descent in their rhetoric and policies of merciful reform?[124] Why were these adolescents committed by the juvenile court only to be neglected within the institution, their occasionally mysterious deaths covered up?

Racism in America has been expressed through a wide range of mechanisms and forms of governmentality. This has included economic exploitation, the pathologization of racial difference through scientific race discourses, and presumptions of sexual and national danger. Mary Douglas has argued for a universal cultural propensity to protect "the normal" through ritual isolation of othered transgressors. As part of historical social hygiene campaigns, sanitation drives to eradicate diseases of poverty also served to police boundaries between the ruling elite and the "contagious" classes. In Progressive and New Era North Carolina, abject persons identified by the courts and in the superintendent of public welfare's reports were exiled to the edges of society, into "heavily surveilled threshold zones," anomalous spaces like Swamp Island, slums, asylums, and reform institutions.[125]

As merciful training grounds for the grooming of citizenship, isolated training and industrial schools intended to root out criminal tendencies and reclaim youth through normalizing realignment of their characters. This rested on two premises: first, the juvenile reformatory movement, based upon Victorian tenets of the malleability of moral identities, attributed white adolescent transgressions to poor environment. Second, the move to merciful moral suasion away from techniques of corporal punishment required the sentience of children, deemed essentially innocent and rational enough to respond to moral suasion instead of physical coercion. Entrusted with the protection of young people, juvenile reformatories emerged because of an ostensibly sentimental concern for children deemed sentient. As Foucault has posited, sets of normative judgments concerning the offender would become ensconced in criminal justice. At issue was not just the act, or what law punished it, but evaluations of heredity and environment, the intent of the transgressor, maladjustments, and family histories, all informed by scientific discourses and techniques. The juvenile court passed judgment on all things that contextualized the offence. It did "what a good and wise parent should do for his own child," but this collided with racialized expectations of who should be protected from whom. Modern whites seeking to demonstrate "civilization" required a "primitive" other to distinguish themselves from. Some white judges, hostile to the juvenile court movement in general, particularly for boys of African descent, argued that juvenile reform was "letting the youthful criminal go free." Most whites did not entertain the possibility of merciful moral reformation of Black youth scripted as innately and irretrievably degenerate, evidenced by the state's refusal to adequately fund Black reformatories.[126]

In his study *Negro Child Welfare in North Carolina*, conducted from 1919 to 1929, Wiley B. Sanders found this to be a common attitude among whites in North Carolina, but reasoned that the racial attitudes expressed by white officials in thirty-seven counties, though enlightening, would "serve no useful purpose to publish," because it might lead to "misunderstanding and criticism."[127] Some juvenile court judges sentenced children to jail even though it was technically illegal to do so. Reports made between 1929 and 1934 to the North Carolina State Board of Charities and Public Welfare on jail inspections attest to this. "*County A*. The county jail in the rear of the court house. At time of visit two Negro boys N___C___, 9 years old, and V___H___, 11 years old, were confined in the same cell block and were freely associating with about a dozen adult Negro men prisoners." Some of the men with whom the boys were confined were infected with venereal disease.[128]

As I will discuss in chapter 5, reformers established juvenile reformatories in late nineteenth and early twentieth century North Carolina to rescue white, but not Black, youth from the vagaries of chain gangs, a vestige of the convict lease. To repeat, the convict lease was a notoriously harsh and exploitative penal labour system that provided prisoner labour to private enterprises. It effectively renewed slavery as "a system in which armies of free men, guilty of no crimes and entitled by law to freedom, were compelled to labor without compensation, were repeatedly bought and sold, and were forced to do the bidding of white masters through the regular application of extraordinary physical coercion."[129] Judges imprisoned children along with adults in the early days of North Carolina's state penitentiary (established in 1846), where they were exploited as cheap labour. "I am told, reported a traveler, that the people most often convicted and sent to the chain gang are the undisciplined young negroes who have grown up since the days of slavery." A warden noted that they seldom got an old "Cuffee" who had grown up under slavery. Rather, it was young preachers, teachers, politicians, and boys as young as ten years old. In 1890 the South had more than 27,000 convict labourers, who were younger than their Northern counterparts. Two-thirds to over three-quarters of them were between ten and twenty years old. The convict lease was lethal, with a mortality rate of 17 to 25 per cent, excluding those pardoned to die at home. It came under increasing criticism in the Northern press for its brutality.

Under pressure from lobbyists, North Carolina abolished the convict lease, sending prisoners to the roads in marginally more humane prison chain gangs.[130] The Morrison reformatory was both a show of Southern mercy and a space for national exclusion, given the dismal conditions of prison labour and the notorious nature of Klan-based terrorism.

Reclamation and Neglect: "To Make Live and Let Die"

The racism of modernists and anti-modernists had a fluidity enabling it to operate at different levels, often moving between different projects and reworking earlier racial discourses for new political ends.[131] Thus, the shift from lynching spectacles (as a form of sovereign right to kill) and other forms of punishment, to spectacles of Southern mercy, was uneven.[132] The modern state recuperated elements of the sovereign right to kill, re-narrating them as part of national uplift and biological maintenance of the "better adapted" race.[133] Reclaiming or eliminating the othered through internal colonialism would, many hoped, breathe new life into the national polity. The emergent biopolitical state only reclaimed certain groups of children, cultivating their uplift under the rubric of self-improvement through the repressive instrumentality of the state.

Foucault does not mark critical differences between state formations that discursively threaten expulsion and extinction and those that carry it out. If we accept that threatening expulsion may include dominant discourses that excluded the other from national belonging, and not just literal elimination through executions and eugenic sterilizations, then we can make this distinction. A white, cross-class alliance threatened to exclude the othered from national belonging. As George Fredrickson has observed, "If the blacks were a degenerating race with no future, the problem ceased to be one of how to prepare them for citizenship [but] rather the need to segregate or quarantine a race liable to be a source of contamination and social danger to the white community, as it sank ever deeper into the slough of disease, vice and criminality."[134]

Like other juvenile reform institutions in North Carolina, the Morrison Training School was a site of internal colonialism, informed by civilizationist rhetoric and evolutionary themes. It offered a visibly merciful means of protection from lynch mobs, retraining boys to prevent the development of their "full-blown" criminality, which ostensibly incited mob murders and social unrest. White reformers' conception of modern childhood evidently did not extend to North Carolina boys of African descent. A 1923 federal census of institutionalized children found that half of all Black charges were housed in prison-like settings compared to only 20 per cent of their white counterparts.[135] Errant Black children sequestered away at the isolated Morrison Training School suffered figurative national expulsion. At best, they endured neglect, which occasionally led to their deaths, and at worst, they suffered fatal beatings. Racism under imperial modernity introduces a division between those selected to live and those allowed to die.[136]

In North Carolina, the modern statization of biology involved a refolding, a carrying over of the old sovereign right "to kill and let live" (faire mourir et laisser vivre) to the right "to make live and let die" (faire vivre et laisser mourir), a turn supported by the central bourgeois project of normalizing moral uplift as part of self-cultivation.[137] The sovereign right to excise "enemies" within the nation, to safeguard the nation's natality, persisted within juvenile reformatories as a new political technology of biopower with the targeted elimination of the othered.[138] From this perspective, interpretations of racism as a scapegoat reaction to economic crises, or an accidental repercussion – as a matter of personal disdain based on perceived differences, or as an offshoot of state formation – are unconvincing.[139] Étienne Balibar suggests that modern racism emerged from excessive nationalism, but Foucault sees it as an excess of biopower in its role as biological protector of national racial purity. In this interpretation racism is actually *integral* to liberal-humanism and the empire state, but presents as protective and life-giving, ensuring the well-being of the whole population through the elimination of some.[140] As Foucault has argued:

> It will become the discourse of a combat to be carried out not between two races, but between a race placed as the true and only one (that holds power and defines the norm) and one which constitutes various dangers for the biological patrimony. At this point, all those biologico-racist discourses on degeneration will appear as will all the institutions which function internal to the social body as principles of segregation, elimination and normalization of society.[141]

A reform institution for children whom many whites reviled, served the political agenda of eliminating a dissident element in a spectacle of mercy, through the exercise of power that was lauded for its law-abiding civilization. Ostensibly merciful treatment of young offenders had a doubly beneficial effect in that it motivated their obedience to the white legal system, legitimized as compassionate, and garnered Northern approval of the state's formal opposition to lynching. Like poor George Stinney's show trial, this reformatory served an important function as a spectacle of mercy, demonstrating just how "civilized" law-abiding white Southerners could be in protecting boys from lynch mobs. The actual experiences of boys committed to the Morrison Training School suggest, however, that their well-being was, for the state appropriations committee at least, beside the point. Arguably, they were pawns in a larger political struggle between advocates of lynching and proponents of law, each vying for legitimacy to rule. More than any other group, Black youth represented the quintessential site of contention between proponents of juridical process and extralegal lynch law.

Chapter Five

The Prodigal Son

And now I cry to You as the Prodigal:
I have sinned before You, O merciful Father;
Receive me as a penitent and make me as one of Your hired servants.[1]

The intellectually cultivated Christian mechanic
is the best safeguard of our nation,
and his moral worth is the very salt
and leaven of civil society.[2]

Thirteen-year-old Hubert Smith stole sixty cents in 1889. For this, the Superior Court of Cabarrus County sentenced him to three years and six months on the road for petty larceny, "clad in stripes, wearing chains and a ball, and working side by side with hardened criminals."[3] Thirty years later, many recognized his case as the event that mobilized North Carolina's first juvenile reformatory. J.P. Cook, editor of the institution's 1920 biennial report, would recall, "The court devoured him. The judge finished his case, in the name of the state and justice and civilization. He appeared not to see the child before him – just the criminal. He asked no questions. The birth, the home, the environment, the opportunity … this was the treatment meted out to a child in a North Carolina Superior Court of 1890."[4] The judge had defended his decision, pleading, "I do not know what to do with the boy, but the law must take its course."[5] Yet in the late nineteenth century, North Carolina courts typically either turned white boys loose or sentenced them to hard labour.[6]

With a focus on race, *Concord Standard* editor Cook effectively generated public debate through his editorial. The "strong arm of law

grapple[d]" the [white] boy, depositing him in the county jail with fifteen prisoners, "all colored." Such a scene would still seem merciless to
some white reformers thirty years later in 1921: "But the boy, why, he
was chained to a Negro. The only white person in the group, and chains
and lock around his ankles, keeping step with a hardened criminal without a hope, or the hope of a hope, building roads for civilization – that
was a queer way of punishing a boy – a miscarriage of reformation."[7]
This sight of Hubert Smith marched through the streets of Concord in
1891 stirred Cook's racist heart. He denounced the law and the courts
for imprisoning white and Black boys together, and called for the racial
separation of convicts as an act of mercy. He wrote, "One of our distinguished State officers described to me a scene which he witnessed on one
of our railroads, where two fair-faced and amiable looking boys were
chained, each of them to repulsive, degraded looking convicts, typical
house-breakers, in appearance, and were being conveyed with them to
the penitentiary." Imploring the General Assembly, he continued, "What
hope for reformation is there with such associates for these young persons? Humanity, to say nothing of Christianity, demands that arrangements be made whereby these unfortunates shall be kept separate."[8]

Townsperson W.G. Means delivered a warning to Cook "in the small
hours of the night" to publically retract his statement or he would be
charged with contempt of court. Cook refused, generating a storm of
controversy. Newspapers across North Carolina reprinted his editorial, declaring it "far ahead of the times." The *Statesville Landmark*'s
editor Joseph P. Caldwell supported Cook, assuring him, "Your position is correct; the treatment of certain youthful offenders is a crime
against civilization; there is a need for just such an institution you suggest; but the old state is so conservative that she won't listen to you
now."[9] Considerable public debate ensued, culminating in widespread
endorsement of the founding of the first juvenile state reformatory, one
mandated to rescue errant white boys from the chain gang, a vestige of
the old convict lease.[10]

Surviving reformatory records shed some light on the production
and working of the merciful, liberal-humanist épistème through the
operation of the state's first juvenile reformatory. In any given historical context, an understanding of how épistèmes are produced, and how
they work and circulate is critical to analyses of the exercise of power
within the social body. Various overlapping épistèmes defined the conditions of emergent discourses of mercy.[11] The archival record demonstrates diverse, overlapping value systems from which reformers and

government officials developed these discourses for the national reclamation of errant white boys.

Evident in this record is the contested, convoluted workings of power behind closed doors, and the rocky rise of juvenile reform as part of North Carolina's emergent biopolitical state. Internal discord over the operation of the institution contrasted with a publicly united front of state support for the Stonewall Jackson Reformatory, even in the face of well-founded allegations of abuse, including the severe beating of a thirteen-year-old child.

While Michel Foucault discerned large- and small-scale shifts (from those directed against the state and conceived in terms of a war for political relations, to those imagined in biological terms as a "condition of survival"), he did not broach their transformative dynamics – the continuity of certain elements and obsolescence of others.[12] I examine locally specific dynamics associated with the contested emergence of the biopolitical North Carolina state from 1890 to 1943. As North Carolina's first priority in juvenile reform, the Stonewall Jackson Training School set the standard, its historical records providing insight into what the state was able and willing to furnish for the children it prioritized. North Carolina's commitment to the reclamation of white boys is evidenced by the generous funds awarded to the institution. While white boys were othered by class and subjected to brutal practices, the appropriations dispensed for their institution far surpassed any the state granted to other reformatories, particularly those for boys and girls of African descent.

Homo docilis

As a dynamic political act, mercy is expressed with wide variability, affected by its gendered and racialized historical context. Through the Gilded, Progressive, and New Eras, philanthropic work rested on patriotic nation building. The Southern white middle class advocated penal reform, and lobbied against child labour, premised upon a stated sentimental concern for children. Within the late nineteenth and early twentieth century imperialist context, nation signified race, generating an increased interest in white children as a national resource.

Émile Durkheim argued that the lifting of severe, sacrificial penalties of sovereign rule would attend the modernization of societies.[13] Foucault contended that while such shifts have tempered severity, compassion and forgiveness have not necessarily been intrinsic to this trend.

New methods have instead involved increasingly precise, and more efficient control. Middle class modernists lobbied to increase state officials' authority within "a more highly socialized democracy." Reformers urged the state to "civilize" disorderly adolescent white boys through segregated management, and ultimately, national reclamation.[14]

White reformers expected state intervention to be merciful and non-adversarial: "individual welfare coincided with the well-being of the state," with prosperity following the eradication of subversion and dependency.[15] In North Carolina this manifested in an unprecedented, exponential rise in state intervention into family life around the turn of the last century, through therapeutic social reform projects geared to groom white adolescents for future citizenship. Teaching individual self-control would breed "useful citizens of a Christian republic" who wanted "to be something and to do something."[16] In this way, internal colonialism operated in the personal and intimate spaces of reformatory and industrial-school cottages, where young people learned self-discipline.[17]

Wayward youth entered geographically isolated institutions for indeterminate sentences in which they learned to monitor their private selves "in the most minute and inconsequential aspects of social life."[18] Reformers expected state intervention to be merciful and supportive: "individual welfare coincided with the well-being of the state," with prosperity following the eradication of subversion and dependency.[19]

North Carolina reform institutions followed northeastern examples. While planning the Stonewall Jackson Training School, Cook spent a month studying a Pennsylvania reformatory "practically as an inmate" before agreeing that the cottage model, with its elimination of prison features, was "the most successful of its kind in the country."[20] Spatially separated discipline and honour cottages served to prevent solidarity detrimental to order.[21] This rehabilitation was meant to literally re-form characters, affective ties, and loyalties in architecturally distinct cottages meant to resemble home-like environments. However, while intimate, these cottages were neither familial nor compassionate.[22] Achille Mbembe notes that instrumental and administrative rationality produced similar effects in factories, schools, the bureaucracy, prisons, and armies. This development informed the management of juvenile reformatory inmates.[23] Theoretically, the cottage system enabled the positive exercise of power, engaging discipline without physical coercion to constitute an efficient, obedient population of future citizens and workers under the new industrial capitalist order in North Carolina.[24]

Michel Foucault saw juvenile reform in the French village of Mettrey in 1840 as having an agenda of constitutive power in the production of the pacific individual (*homo docilis*), "supervising the internal nature of the criminal individual in order to neutralize anti-social tendencies and eliminate dissident difference."[25] He has described docile bodies as those that "may be subjected, used, transformed and improved,"[26] where "discipline increases the forces of the body (in economic terms of utility) and diminishes these same forces (in political terms of obedience)."[27] The start of a "new era" in the normalization of power in the nineteenth century Mettrey reformatory depended upon children to be mentally accessible beings, able to respond to normalizing efforts.[28]

Stonewall Jackson Training School's superintendent, Charles Boger, expressed hope that within the institution incorrigible boys, "steadied upon their feet" and inspired "with new ideals in life," would come to join "the great army of workers who forge and build the progress of the State."[29] North Carolina mandated the Stonewall Jackson Training School to mercifully develop patriotic loyalty among working-class white children, distrusted by many as patricides in the making, who might grow up "to join the degenerate enemies of the state."[30] In northeastern city slums, the threat of mass insurrection accompanied increased industrialization, immigrant ghettoization, almshouses, and tuberculosis. In the South, reformers sought to cultivate an industrial work ethic in wayward white boys, preventing their affiliation with, and ostensible corruption by, "hardened criminals" on the chain gang.[31]

In March 1867, just twenty-two years prior to Hubert Smith's conviction, newly enfranchised freedmen formed Union Leagues, electing their own integrated legislatures and holding state offices, redefining state governing apparatuses across the South.[32] As discussed in chapter 5, a grandfather clause would later permit many uneducated whites to vote while effectively disenfranchising Southern Black men. A public education campaign for poor whites responded to concerns that the white working and workless poor vote potentially threatened national integrity, for, as Southern University's President Andrew Sledd noted, "The South is the most ignorant section in the Union."[33] By the turn of the twentieth century, the Reconstruction focus on African Americans shifted to reflect a concern for whites' education and good citizenship. By 1927, average annual appropriations per child of school age reflected an enduring disparity, with Black children receiving $7.52 and white children receiving $25.51 in North Carolina. Children of African descent attended school for shorter terms, in deficient facilities. Black teachers earned inequitable salaries.[34]

This concern for poor whites would intensify during the Great Depression, when catastrophic unemployment signalled revolution.[35] Cook's central concern, that "the people composing [the boy's] family were white – pure Anglo Saxon" would resonate in North Carolina at a time when many working and workless poor whites were flocking to the newly formed, left-leaning Populist Party, which would gain state-wide office during the 1890s. This political insurgency of small farmers built political, though not antiracist, solidarity between African Americans and whites, as Populists joined Republicans to exercise revolutionary politics and oppose conservative Democrats for four years. Just seven years after Cook's editorial, white violence would undermine the Republican-Populist coalition, culminating in the Wilmington race riot of 1898. Democrats campaigned against Republican "Negro Rule" in North Carolina, and North Carolina followed other Southern states with the defeat of the Populist ticket, entering into an era of systematic disenfranchisement and Jim Crow segregation.[36]

The Stonewall Jackson Manual Training and Industrial School

By 1892, Hubert Smith, now fifteen, had completed almost two years of his sentence on the road, and the Board of County Commissioners signed a petition imploring Governor Holt to extend mercy to the boy's "aged mother," who was "almost helpless [with] an idiotic son to care for and without means." Governor Holt stood firm in his refusal to grant a pardon, so Hubert Smith solicited intervention from Cook, underscoring the negative influence of his fellow (Black) inmates. "Mr. Cook this is a hard place. It tries a boy. I hear nothing but cursing and vulgar talk … Sometimes the boys cuss and fight. Mr Cook, it is hard and it is sad, for I am trying to live a better life, but this yoke is a hard yoke for HS to work to, or any other boy that has human feelings … Oh keeping of bad company has brought me to this pass."[37] Disturbed by "the vision of the boy in chains [that] was always with [him]" and infuriated by the "horrible manhood-crushing chain gangs," Cook envisioned a large institution "under the protecting care of our state," where "underprivileged, incorrigible boys" from homes that had failed could be "mothered and educated."[38] He continued to lobby for the merciful institution, arguing, "There are youths in the penitentiary that should be elsewhere, a place far removed from the set and graduated careers of criminality to a place of wholesome, moral and educational surroundings, that they may have an opportunity to be brought back into the fold."[39] At Cook's request, Governor Fowle urged passage of the Reformatory Bill in the 1891 state legislature, declaring that the state should not act out of retribution, but to prevent further lawbreaking and build good citizens of young offenders. He urged, "As a great State of a noble and humane people, efforts should be made to reform the many youths who have gone astray, and make of them useful and upright citizens. Let it be done! The cost may be heavy at the beginning … For the sake of some mother's dissipated child, let the Legislature provide a Reformatory."[40] North Carolina's General Assembly remained unmoved.

Cook persevered in advocating for a sanctuary for "forgotten boys," attending every session of the General Assembly for twenty years. His wife could recall no discussion of planning for children of their own – "He just put his whole life in the school."[41] White clubwomen implored legislative committees to fund a state institution, lobbying for their own involvement in it, and citing their superior qualifications for moral uplift.[42] With the help of the King's Daughters, Cook gained support from influential members of the state legislature, and the state legislative sessions of 1903 and 1905 reintroduced bills for the juvenile reformatory.[43]

North Carolina's legislature continued to turn down requests for an institution until 1907, when State Representative Penn Wood of High Point counselled Cook that the coming session promised a high attendance of Civil War veterans. He advised, "If you'll name that school of yours for Stonewall Jackson, they can't refuse to approve." Cook held a caucus and garnered tremendous support from the veterans when he announced the name would be The Stonewall Jackson Manual Training and Industrial School.

Presented to the assembly bearing Stonewall Jackson's name, the bill was passed in both houses. The legislature generously appropriated $10,000 as a start-up sum, and moved to "incorporate the school under the name of the Confederate's great chieftain." The 1907 bill provided that "delinquent and incorrigible white boys" must be committed by the juvenile courts, though the governor could "transfer any person under the age of sixteen from any jail, chain gang, or penitentiary … to the reformatory."[44] The legal commitment requirements stipulated a merciful approach, noting, "Committing a child to this institution is not imprisonment as a punishment for crime."[45] The bill empowered trustees to establish a specialized institution "for the training and moral and industrial development of the criminally delinquent children of the state ... The board of trustees shall select a suitable place outside and away from any city, town or village, for the location of such school."[46] The "people of Carbarrus County" would offer the state a farm, free of debt or cost, naming Cook as the institution's director. Inspired, Cook "went to work hammer – and – tongs and finally success crowned his tireless efforts."[47] The mood was effervescent. Commissioner R.F. Beasley beamed, anticipating that "it ought to be possible to get most anything necessary from the next legislature."[48] A 1920 special session of the assembly passed a measure enabling individuals, cities, and counties to erect cottages and other buildings at Jackson, given the widespread public support for expanding the institution. With an impressive capacity of a five hundred inmates, the Stonewall Jackson Training School accepted white boys between the ages of twelve and sixteen state-wide, and by 1940 it accepted ten-year-olds by special permission of the State Department of Public Welfare. The average age in 1940 was fourteen years.[49] Once boys were admitted, the welfare departments of the various counties would approve their discharges. Unlike the Morrison Training School policy, home counties did not have to pay for inmates' transportation or clothing.[50]

Valued at approximately $279,000 in 1920, the Stonewall Jackson reformatory's holdings included 298 acres and 12 buildings housing 188 inmates.[51] By 1924 institutional land increased to 423 acres, accommodating a plant worth $750,000 and, fourteen cottages, each accommodating thirty boys and a "house mother and father" to "take place of their real parents." Mrs J.W. Cannon donated $50,000 for an administration building as a memorial to her husband. Holdings additionally included a school building, a stone chapel gifted by the state King's Daughters, a printing house, industrial building, laundry, a bakery, a woodworking shop, a shoe shop, dairy barn and milk house, "forty head of good milkers," an ice plant, and barns for horses and cows. A model of modernity, the institution featured heating, electricity, and even its own water and sewage system.[52]

By 1946, the Jackson Training School would expand its lands to almost 1000 acres, with 550 acres under cultivation, 300 acres of pasture lands, and 75 acres occupied by the campus. The administration building housed offices and apartments. The trades building furnished a print shop; barbershop; tin, carpenter, machine, and shoe shops; plus sewing and band rooms. The school building had an 800-person-capacity auditorium, a library, ten classrooms, an infirmary with twenty-five beds, a cannery, and seventeen cottages, which now included one for

Figure 5.1. Present-day (2015) ruins of Stonewall Jackson reformatory (King's Daughters' Cottage). Reprinted with permission of Sterling E. Stevens (http://sestevens.com).

"Indians," and a receiving cottage. There were also two granaries; horse, dairy, and calf barns; a milk house; a garage with sixteen bays; a gymnasium and swimming pool; a new cattle barn with a capacity for a 100-head herd; storage sheds for farm and lumber equipment; nine poultry houses; a chapel; a textile plant; a grandstand; two baseball and three softball diamonds; two dwelling houses; laundry and bakery buildings; an ice plant and refrigeration building; piggeries; and two straw and hay sheds. Farm equipment was extensive, including two tractors, ten wagons, a threshing machine, a combine, and four trucks. Farm animals included 132 hogs, 80 cows, a herd of 119 dairy cows, 10 teams of horses and mules, and about two thousand chickens. There were also 1200 peach trees, 600 apple trees, and 400 grapevines.[53]

Supported primarily by the state, Stonewall Jackson reformatory inmates learned woodworking, metal work, electrical work, mechanical drawing, gardening, poultry raising, agricultural and dairy farming, cooking, sewing, and auto mechanics, enabling both vocational training "for the work for which one is fitted" and the maintenance of the institution. The practice of the boys sewing their own overalls and shirts elicited notice from a Bureau of Public Welfare officer, who noted, "This is rather unusual for boys but the work is well done."[54] Each cottage accommodated a man, who served as disciplinarian, and his wife, who supervised the cooking and cleaning at a much-reduced rate of pay.[55] Academics went through the eighth grade. By 1931, institutional jobs included office-boy work, shoe repair, laundering, and carpentry. In 1925 there were 399 boys in the institution; in 1930 there were 512, despite a stated capacity of 470; and in 1935 Jackson housed 464 inmates.[56]

"Mothered and Educated": The Nature vs. Nurture Debate

The Stonewall Jackson reformatory sought to reclaim adolescent white boys "who had defected the influences of home, public and religious schools and society." Juvenile court judges committed white boys to the institution mostly for larceny and store breaking, but also for trespass, breaking into freight cars, vagrancy, smoking cigarettes, violating prohibition law, keeping bad company and late hours, laziness, assault with a deadly weapon, and manslaughter (one eleven-year-old killed another boy in the woods).[57]

A former Jackson employee recalled that Cook's "entire life was devoted to education and to the uplift of the less fortunate, his reward being in the fact that he was developing twisted minds into straight grooves and making men of our incorrigible boys."[58] As Cook would reflect in 1925, "The hope and faith of the originators of this institution have been verified in the large number of men – once the dropped stitches of a vanished hand – who today are elegant and useful citizens of the state, and who, I verily believe, would have been confirmed criminals had they not enjoyed the privileges and benefits of the Jackson Training School at a critical period in their young lives."[59] He insisted that every boy who passed through the Jackson Training School learned the rudiments of a trade, and went on to live "the correct life."

The recognition of a "divine spark that appeals to our best effort to reclaim" marked the exercise of state powers on subjectivity and conduct in juvenile reformatories. These sought to achieve the "gentle way of punishment," as Michel Foucault has called it, through "a mechanism that coerced by means of observation," involving classification by the legal system, physicians and psychiatrists. Adolescents' internalization of "good character" constituted the coercive mechanism "through which the social body was traversed by power."[60] For reformers, white children's eventual capacity to be self-governing indicated the proper internalization of a shared social ethic. Jackson Training School officials showcased a letter sent to the superintendent in 1930 by a former inmate as evidence of success:

> As I look back on my life I often wonder if I would have ever have amounted to anything in this life without the training I received at the Jackson Training School ... I entered the school when I was a very young boy. I was very mean before entering the school. I would not go to school, would not mind my parents, would steal anything I could get my hands on, smoked cigarettes, drank liquor, was always in bad company, only went half-dressed, always dirty, and at that time was twelve years of age. If I had kept up I guess I would have been a big racketeer. But instead I am manager of the largest store here. My salary is $8000. per year. I work a force of fifty sales girls and ten men. I am now a good church worker and am highly respected by everyone in the city, and young as well as the old. I am married and have a little son seven years of age, and I own my own home here.[61]

Judge Zeb V. Nettles would have objected to this. He claimed that he had never seen a boy committed who seemed "to come away a better boy. The school just doesn't seem to help them much." Superintendent Boger's written warning to a paroled boy (copied to his welfare officer) supports this claim:

> How anxious you were to get away to start working ... They tell me you are lazy and will not work, while there is plenty to do. No one, not even a father wants someone lying around, expecting to eat at his table and sleep in his bed when the father is out working and the parasite son stays at the house and reads ... If you do not make a quick change of attitude and begin to work gladly and interestingly, you will be back before you know it. Then, you will not mind work and you will not be asked what you want or like to do.[62]

Normalization efforts had varying results.

Rather than simply determining guilt or innocence as adult criminal courts typically did, the juvenile court made assessments of deficient environmental conditions leading to delinquency. Thus, working-class white boys' reclamation involved the additional surveillance and regulation of their parents, with the expectation that morally lax, ignorant mothers corrupted their young through an assumed failure to provide wholesome homes.[63] Director of institutions and corrections Wade Cashion sent Gastonia's county superintendent of public welfare, Agnes Thomas, a referral for a ten-year-old boy whose mother worked nights in a textile mill. Attributing her son's disobedience to maternal absenteeism and neglect, Cashion wrote, "I think we might naturally expect any child to become delinquent who does not have the guidance of a parent from the middle of the afternoon until after bedtime. It might be possible for Mrs X to change her working hours in the textile mill [or] secure another type of work which would enable her to be home at night." Cashion scheduled appointments for the boy with a psychiatrist at the Mental Hygiene Clinic in Charlotte for evaluation.[64]

Michel Foucault has examined the modernist shift from the infliction of pain and death to discipline, pastoral benevolence, and the augmentation of life.[65] For Foucault, this "inward turn" involved the scrutiny of human "depth" for indications of social dissent. Southern reformers interpreted class conflict as caused by character defects more than political and economic inequality. By the twentieth century, discourses shifted away from earlier convictions of unconscious forces underlying conscious rationality, to a notion of reality as directly and empirically observable, and scientifically manageable. Evolutionary trajectories placed the modern self at the apex of a unified chronology that emerged in a single narrative from instinctive habit to reflexivity. A trustworthy citizenry of individuals having accessible identities and essential selves could be governed through normalizing discourses and self-regulation without brute force.[66] "Mental defectives," incapable of responding to training, and beyond being "able to contribute anything worthwhile to the state so far as citizenship is concerned" did not enter into the reformatory system.[67]

Modern statization of biology in North Carolina at the turn of the last century encouraged moral uplift as part of self-cultivation. Claims of not just hereditary but also environmentally caused degeneracy fuelled more state intervention.[68] Reform discourses reframed interpretations of these white children as vulnerable to moral, physical, and intellectual degradation, but also as responsive to reformation through rational reflection.[69] As one reformer mused, "I am interested in the delinquent boy, both for his own sake and for the sake of the state to which he is returned. Most of them have had no chance either by inheritance or environment ... Some – yes, many – might be reclaimed."[70] Bruno Latour argues that modernists used biological and environmental explanations inconsistently to justify contradictory statements whenever it suited them. At one moment they might uphold the idea of social constructedness, then follow with avowals that nature cannot be transcended, with the corollary that biology drives the social, even as they also argued for environmental causation.[71] Latour states the problem thus:

> The exclusive transcendence of a Nature that is not our doing, and the exclusive immanence (inherence) of a Society that we create through and through, would nevertheless paralyse the moderns, who would appear too impotent in the face of things and too powerful within society. What an enormous advantage to be able to reverse the principles without even the appearance of a contradiction! The critical power of the moderns lives in this double language: they can mobilise Nature at the heart of social relationships, even as they leave Nature infinitely remote from human beings; they are free to make and unmake their society, even as they render its laws ineluctable, necessary and absolute.[72]

Moderns treated elements of nature, culture, society, and being as mutually exclusive and oppositional, rather than interdependent.

By the early twentieth century Southern juvenile justice had adopted environmental perspectives of deviance, but biological mechanisms of power – eugenic sterilizations and encouragement of rational breeding through birth-control legislation – persisted in conjunction with normalizing efforts, as "needed treatment to follow the Training School experience." Through behavioural and biological tampering, the state attempted to reverse poverty and imagined racial degeneration.[73] In 1919, Superintendent of Health for Haywood County Dr J.R. McCracken (an ear, nose, and throat specialist), requested castration for two boys:

> We have in, our County home, two boys, Oliver and John Sisk, brothers, who are mentally defective. There are also some mentally defective girls there, and the Supt. has lately caught Oliver and one of these girls in the act of sexual intercourse – several times. John has been giving the girls quite a little bit of attention and the Supt. thinks he is up to the same tricks. Oliver is fifteen and John thirteen years of age ... Our County Commissioners and County Board of Health have decided that the best solution of the problem is castration, especially for Oliver, and probably for both. I am writing to ask that you give your consent.

Officials did not seek parental consent for sterilizations. Fifteen years later, in 1934, the state ordered the castration of a Stonewall Jackson Training School inmate who suffered from epileptic fits. A state official advised Superintendent Boger to seek financing for the operation from the boy's home county, explaining, "If he should go to a strange community where he is not known he is, of course, likely to marry and bring on much more trouble and expense for the community."[74]

Adolescent "Savagery"

Nineteenth century scientific racism advanced two pre-evolutionary styles of racial ranking: polygenism and monogenism. Polygenists (the "American school" of anthropology) classified people of African descent as a separate and inferior species, descended from a different Adam, and without rightful claim to the "equality of man." Reluctant to renounce the scriptural position of all people's derivation from a single Adam and Eve, monogenists argued that races had degenerated at varying rates from Eden's perfection. Some monogenists believed reversibility was possible, and that Blacks might become white with time spent in Northern climates. Other monogenist degenerationists maintained that any improvement would be too gradual to have any impact on human history.[75]

Early medical research on sexual degeneracy identified masturbation and the corruption of children as indicative of the potential for perversion reflecting the biblical fall from grace. German zoologist and evolutionist Ernst Haeckel suggested that ontogeny, a species's pattern of development, recapitulates phylogeny, the evolutionary history of a species.[76] Employing colonial tropes of infantilization and animalization, his recapitulation theory classified the "darker races" as embodying a primitive stage in human development. Haeckel's followers wrote about the "everlasting infancy of the non-perfectible races," comparing adult Black men to white male children. Recapitulation theorists disagreed with the monogenist theory of degeneration, but never questioned the Caucasian standard of civilization.[77]

Eurocentric discourses have historically interpreted Africa as evolutionarily deficient (hypersexual, corporeal, childlike, and incapable of abstract thought) while upholding Europe as the imagined acme of civilization. Degeneration theories treated white children's sexuality and potential reproductivity as simultaneously dangerous and endangered, drawing an analogy between the "child as savage" and the "savage as child."[78] Explanations of their waywardness pointed to poor environment, suggesting they should be protected from the influences of their ostensibly unwholesome families, from the "savage" sexuality of the racialized other, and from their own unrestrained sexuality awakened during adolescence. In a 1976 interview Foucault explained:

> At the beginning of the eighteenth century enormous importance was suddenly accorded to childhood masturbation, which was persecuted everywhere as a sudden terrible epidemic threatening to compromise the whole human race ... At the crossroads of body and soul, of health and morality, of education and training, children's sexuality became at the same time a target and an instrument of power. A specific "children's sexuality" was established: it was precarious, dangerous, to be watched over constantly.[79]

The Stonewall Jackson Training School's 1943 employee handbook, *Instructions Regarding Training and Discipline* stated, "The well-regulated cottages will offer wholesome recreation, sympathetic friendship and other features of a good home." Wholesome recreation included "directed reading periods, wholesome indoor games, listening to radios and working picture puzzles."[80] The superintendent added, "It is a serious mistake to ever have the boys in bed before nine o'clock. To do so invites and promotes bedroom troubles of various kinds. This means that they should not be expected to prepare for going to bed until 8:30 or later."[81] Ten years earlier, an observer had noted, "The big rough boys and the small boys were housed together. The tough older ones taught their meanness to the little fellows, even to mistreating them morally."[82]

The state mandated the Stonewall Jackson Training School to "keep, restrain and control [the boy] during his minority or until such time as they shall deem proper for his discharge," typically, twenty-two months. The institution's intake sheet detailed information about inmates' families, including disclosures about parental occupations, characters, habits, and marital status. In compiling case histories, administrators made additional inquiries about each boy's neighbourhood influences, associates, grades and school attendance, Sunday School attendance, YMCA membership, mentality, and general conduct. The final section of the intake sheet, devoted to "Habits, etc." included: "Uses tobacco, cigarettes, Picture Show Fiend, Lazy, Drinks, Pool room, streets, Late

hours, Industrious, truthful, ambitious, good natured, stubborn, slov-
enly or neat." The final set of queries included questions such as: "Has
the boy been known to beat trains [hobo terminology for hopping
freight trains without being caught or killed]? Did he ever run away
from home? Where does he usually go when away? Give any other
details you know concerning the boy's former life." Poverty signified
more than deprivation caused by economic circumstances. Destitution
indicated moral failing and bad character manifested in slovenliness,
laxity, alcoholism, and idleness.[83]

The state required paroled inmates to commit to self-discipline. The
parole agreement required parolees to lead "a sober and industrious
life" using no intoxicating drinks in any form, nor tobacco, for a specified number of years. Discharge policy obliged paroled boys to report
to the Stonewall Jackson Training School's superintendent each month
with a "true account of [his] work and conduct." Living "an upright
Christian life" involved regular attendance at religious services and
Sunday School.[84] Justifying probation officers' intervention, a juvenile court judge explained, "With the great right arm and force of the
law, the probation officer ... becomes practically a member of the family and teaches them lessons of cleanliness and decency, of truth and
integrity ... and transforms the entire family into individuals which the
state need never again hesitate to own as citizens.[85] Probation departments and welfare administrators exercised discretion in decisions of
what was in the best interests of children. Reformatory administrators
sometimes sent boys to labour on farms, for low wages – "a trifle in
comparison to what the farmers would have to pay for hired help on
the farm." The commissioner of corrections expressed concern over the
placement of fourteen white adolescent boys on a tobacco farm within
an eight-week period in 1947, with "no supervision by the Welfare
Department."[86]

Corporal Punishment

Modernist white reformers strove to demonstrate their "civilization"
and "rightful" place in national visions of Anglo-Saxon ascendancy.
Consumed by moral panics over "the amatory and erotic tendencies of modern degeneracy," they governed through rational methods, including parole, mental tests, family case studies, and eugenic
sterilizations, framed by the increasing rejection of coercive corporal
punishment as antiquated. Like these modernists, conservative whites

regarded adolescents as dangerous, but they preferred strict authoritarianism, arguing that "the old-fashioned boy worked more than the modern boy ... because of the hickory stick that lay in state above the kitchen door."[87]

Institutional records demonstrate some points of convergence between modernist and anti-modernist interpretations of mercy at the turn of the last century. The antimodernist Ku Klux Klan sought to prevent what it regarded as the degeneration of Southern society into racial equality.[88] Cook envisioned a sanctuary where white boys could be "mothered and educated," yet in the early 1920s, officers and teachers of the Jackson Training School could whip boys at their own discretion, the superintendent only occasionally stepping in. But corporal punishment would come to be a state embarrassment. Emergent white middle class childrearing practices aimed to replace physical force with rational persuasion, demonstrating merciful protection of white children as an index of civilized, phylogenetic development.

Wiley B. Sanders, field agent and social work faculty member at the University of North Carolina Chapel Hill, visited one of the Stonewall Jackson Training School cottages at dinner in 1923, and alarmed, reported the abuse of boys in who failed to obey the cottage officer's [Mr Stebbins] commandment to remain silent. "Mr. Stebbins thereupon went to their table and gave one of the boys the hardest slapping I have ever heard." Sanders added that Stebbins's "experience in the negro reformatory in New York State, where, according to his accounts, the boys were treated with extreme cruelty, is but poor preparation to my way of thinking for his present responsible position over Southern white boys"[89] Superintendent Boger assured Sanders that harsh cruelty was wholly contrary to the spirit of the institution. "I'm glad that he was a new man on the job," he said. "'Tis mighty hard to get a fellow broken in at the work of the school. If he does not break out at one point, he will at another. One thing is sure, that such conduct will not and has not been permitted at the school."[90] In 1924, disciplinary methods included withdrawing boys' privileges, and sometimes making them wear dresses, presumably as a shaming device. They "always appeal to the manhood of the boy by talking to him," a government official reported.[91]

Six years later, in October 1929, the boys' treatment horrified visiting reformer Mrs M.E. Braswell, who feared for the safety of her young informant, whom she knew would face severe repercussions should his identity be discovered. She explained, "I know children need punishment sometimes, but they should not be beaten with sticks, and they should have plenty to eat, and the proper food. If they are not hardened criminals now, they will be made such."[92] She noted that food was insufficient, though the children were sometimes permitted "to eat what is left from their officer's table." Boys went hungry and were "beaten for the most trivial offense." One boy was beaten "for not working when he told the officer he was sick … After he was beaten, the paper on which he sat was bloodstained."[93] She felt certain the children were timid and too afraid to answer her questions. Commissioner Johnson privately battled with the superintendent and trustees of the institution, but presented a united front, assuring Braswell that while an official would look into this, she felt "sure that things have been exaggerated."[94]

On 15 January 1930, R. Eugene Brown, director of the Division of Institutions, visited the institution to investigate the complaint and reported, "Corporal punishment is used in the institution and some of the boys do appear to be timid about talking. It is difficult to get at the truth of such a situation when the inmates of an institution have been thoroughly intimidated."[95] Commissioner Johnson later reported that another investigation had been done in February when the weather was cold. Blankets were found to be plentiful, and the boys were well fed. "Corporal punishment is freely used at the Jackson Training School. From my knowledge of Mr. Boger I do not feel that he would countenance excessive punishment or unkindness of any kind … I think you have been unnecessarily worried."[96] These archives speak to a tension between intentions to eliminate corporal punishment, and an attendant reluctance to admit its systematic persistence, which would cast an unfavourable reflection upon reformatories as a modern mechanism of merciful juvenile jurisprudence. Such an admission would also suggest that mercy was an achieved state rather than an essential quality of liberal-humanist New South advocates.[97]

Resistance to Biopolitical State Expansion through Parole

The emergence of the biopolitical state in North Carolina was uneven and contested. The Southern Division of the Red Cross assigned New York–based Dr Philip Klein to work with North Carolina county systems of public welfare in 1919 to offer suggestions for improving coordination.[98] Commissioner Johnson worried that boys, discharged under no system of parole, were being "dumped back into the community" by the institution. But Klein disagreed with Superintendent Boger's policy of keeping inmates institutionalized for three or four years, advising that it was much too long. A boy should be let out while "still a little wild," and before becoming too dependent upon institutionalization, he suggested. Still, Klein and Johnson agreed that the reformatory should follow the exemplary parole system of the New York House of Refuge. Klein also proposed more methodical record keeping, including case histories, and annual reports documenting a boy's progress. Such records should be sent back to the county superintendents, who would parole and reintegrate the boy back into his home community.[99]

Vexed at the spotty record keeping at the Stonewall Jackson Training School, Commissioner Johnson urged Superintendent Boger to complete and organize case records. She also recommended the services of a statistical clerk to help align Boger's accounting with that of the superintendent at Mattewan, NY, whose work was so well done that all *he* had to do at annual meetings was to simply refer to his records. Boger insisted that his own record system worked perfectly well. Moreover, he saw no need for case histories, given that "it does not take the officials in charge long to get as much knowledge as they need regarding an individual." Commissioner Johnson chided Superintendent Boger's refusal to cooperate with welfare departments, which could better respond when kept informed about boys' progress. "Indeed, he thinks that information sent them is often discarded."[100] Like Boger, Cook, by then, president of the board of trustees, continually ignored correspondence from state officials. Boger agreed to look into getting a parole officer, but never did. Exasperated, Commissioner Johnson confided in a fellow official, "Nothing has been done and nothing will be done until we explode some kind of a bomb under him … Mr. Cook makes me perfectly indignant."[101] She challenged Cook's reappointment, arguing that while he was governor-appointed, there was no recent record in the governor's office of Cook's reappointment; he simply succeeded himself for years.[102] Commissioner Johnson continued, "This man is utterly unfit in temperament and character to be Chairman of the Board of Trustees of that institution. Unfortunately, I presume, he will remain in his present position until he dies. He is appointed by the Kings Daughters, and not by the Governor."[103]

Cook would occasionally rant in *The Uplift*, a publication printed by apprenticed inmates. "Perfectly furious" in 1922, he criticized the legislature's decision to finance the founding of the East Carolina (Caswell) Training School, a state institution for "mental defectives." Cook claimed he had arranged for Commissioner R.F. Beasley to do parole work, but Commissioner Johnson challenged the verity of his claim:

> In the summer of 1920 on my own initiative I wrote to Mr. Boger, before the boys were sent out in July, that if he would send me their names I would undertake, with the help of the superintendents of public welfare to see what could be done in the way of assisting the boys ... Practically every home was investigated; in one instance a new home was gotten for a certain boy; a number of the boys were met at the train by the superintendent of public welfare, assisted in getting jobs, etc. Since that time we have never had the name of a boy to be paroled sent to us from Jackson Training School ... Parole work can not be done this way.[104]

As an alternative or supplement to incarceration, probation widened the net of state disciplinary power, monitoring boys who might previously have been dismissed. But David Rothman argues that probation generally failed, because poorly trained supervisory officers, overloaded with cases, and limited by the fiscal conservatism of the state, could not adequately manage it.[105] In 1922 Commissioner Johnson remarked that while reformatory superintendents did not always agree with state recommendations, all but the Jackson superintendent discussed reports in a perfectly cordial and frank manner.[106]

Internal discord between institutional administrators and the state is perhaps unsurprising, but these records identify an unexpected tension inflected by gender. Child Welfare Services sent Miss Reeder, a young caseworker and consultant, to Jackson in 1922. Upon her arrival Reeder asked Superintendent Boger's wife to introduce her to the board members. When Boger joined them, he greeted Reeder as the "person that comes from the State Department of Public Welfare to check up on [us]." Board members politely ignored her presentation on the need for boys' placement and supervision after release. Boger advised her that the board would not approve a caseworker on staff, uncomfortable as they were with a person working there who was not entirely responsible to the superintendent.[107]

The commissioner followed up with an urgent recommendation for a parole system. Addressing Cook and Superintendent Boger, she wrote, "You will see from [Reeder's] report that it is absolutely essential that the institution have a parole officer, and I do not think the matter should be deferred for any length of time."[108] Just as Boger and his board had brushed Reeder off, they neglected her registered correspondence, later claiming they had never received it. Cook finally sent a reply, referring Commissioner Johnson to an enclosed copy of the institution's weekly publication, *The Uplift*, highlighting his own sneering commentary therein:

> Some months ago a pretty little Yankee girl, wearing her dress on a level with her knees, assuming a superiority of authority and a commission from a higher source, monkeyed about the premises for a period, then went off with her eyes skinned for "defects" and closed to the things that loomed large and important and even remarkable for an effort of just thirteen years. The tragedy of the thing lies in the fact that the pretty little Yankee girl knows no more about the science and prevailing methods concerning the handling of delinquent than a jay-bird knows about evolution.[109]

Cook informed Commissioner Johnson that he had no confidence in the investigation carried out by "the little Yankee girl" sent to the institution to promote an efficient parole system. He regarded her work as superfluous, a result of a "spectacular ... increase of offices and the sinful waste of money." She allegedly showed "every evidence of incompetency for the responsible work," resulting in incorrect, damaging conclusions.[110] Commissioner Johnson replied that Cook's statement was spurious and an insult to an accredited representative of the State Board of Charities and Public Welfare. Moreover, she pointed out, Mr Cook was making use of a state-funded magazine (edited at a state institution) to discredit the work of a state department. Defending Caseworker Reeder, Commissioner Johnson added: "I do not understand how you got the impression that she had no training experience. This seems especially strange as I was told that you had offered her a position at the Jackson Training School ... At the time Miss Reeder came to us she was serving as Assistant Superintendent of the New York Orphanage at Hastings on the Hudson, which is probably the best institution of its kind in the whole country." In fact, Reeder was a graduate of Smith's College, held an additional degree from Columbia University, and had worked several years with the New York State Charities Aid, investigating placed-out children. She also had engaged in special welfare work that resulted in the passage of new social policy.[111] Commiserating with another state official, she fretted, "Mr. Cook is not only absolutely unreliable, but is vicious with it ... This matter has been hanging on for the last two years, and we have been able to get nowhere."[112]

Superintendent Boger additionally resisted state surveillance, and the new regulatory "statization" of biological population management, where information about reformatory inmates' medical exams and mental tests, demography, and pedagogical methods had become a secular, state concern.[113] Boger withheld information, and kept disorganized and incomplete records. The institution had opened in 1909, but the official registration of cases, recording the status of parents, date of birth, town, offence, church, parental occupation, and date of parole or escape did not begin until 1927, and even then, reports were sporadic and incomplete.[114] Commissioner Johnson assured Caswell Training School's superintendent, Dr C. Banks McNairy that Brother Cook's "days are numbered and his years are few."[115]

In response to a 1922 query concerning the inadequate diet at Jackson, Boger wrote to Wayne County's superintendent of public welfare, Mrs A.E. Howell, addressing her, "Dear Sir": "We claim, and we think justly, that our 200 boys are about the healthiest, hardiest aggregation of youngsters in the state. They may not look like Fatty Arbuckle, but considering what they were when they came, there is no reason for alarm. To overcome such propaganda as this, we have taken the precaution to weigh every boy on entrance and therefore we *know* what we *know*."[116] Commissioner Johnson explained to County Superintendent of Public Welfare Blanche Carr Stern, "My sole object is to work with the board of trustees to build the school up to what it may be, and to shield it from public criticism. Social workers in North Carolina are being educated up to what good social work is and things that we could put over on the public a few years ago are no longer accepted."[117] Four years later, Commissioner Kate Burr Johnson sent the governor a copy of another parental complaint delivered to the Board of Public Welfare regarding his son's weight. She urged that careful records should be kept of boys' weight, and a trained nurse should be employed to care for their physical condition, so that a record could be immediately shown in cases where charges – "outside interference" – presumably, by concerned parents, were brought.[118]

In 1930 R. Eugene Brown, Director of the Division of Institutions, also expressed his frustration over Boger's persistent failure to produce accurate records and lists.[119] When questioned about his failure to keep a waiting list in 1930, the superintendent replied, "We take the most pressing case when room is available. When room is not available we write them to take matter up later."[120]

While the 1933 Public Laws of North Carolina (chap. 490) had provided for a $10,000 appropriation for the commitment of indigenous boys and girls at the Stonewall Jackson Training School, Superintendent

Boger refused "to care for Indians." By 1940, the institution would finally admit a small number of indigenous boys, constituting less than 10 per cent of the inmate population. Administrators housed them together in a segregated cottage, but failed to perform physicals for sexually transmitted diseases, and did not quarantine them for two weeks, as was customary. Their 1944 files were incomplete, with missing health certificates and non-existent Wassermann reports for eighteen of thirty-two boys. Superintendent Boger had ordered expensive Wasserman tests for all of the white inmates, however, despite the known low incidence of venereal disease for this population.[121]

Record keeping would be an ongoing problem for state officials who, well into the 1930s, were still requesting statements from Superintendent Boger on institutional policies, monthly reports on population movements, and the number of inmates engaged in performing institutional jobs. In 1931, Director R. Eugene Brown informed Boger that in order to carry out obligations to the state and to the juvenile reform institutions, sufficient information about the institution's daily operations must be routinely available. As a start, he expected monthly reports and statements of institutional admission and discharge policies. He concluded, "In short, we are asking your cooperation in building closer and more satisfactory relationships between the State institutions, the State Board, and county superintendents of public welfare."[122] Brown would persist in vain.

Government officials decided that biennial reports of uniform statistical data of all state penal, correctional, and charitable institutions should be combined in one volume for study and comparison by the Advisory Budget Commission, the governor, and the General Assembly.[123] A 1934 state report on reorganization of the Jackson Training School described a "lack of coordination of efforts toward one end – the training and rehabilitation of the boy." Coordination between the state institution, the county superintendents of public welfare, and the State Board was impaired by too few trained personnel and a lack of confidence in Superintendent Boger. In 1937, the State Board further submitted a plan to the US Children's Bureau to assign social workers to the training schools in order to make an intensive study of intake and discharge, to make parole supervision more effective, and to increase communication with agencies involved in the commitment of children. Social workers would work in each county, assessing casework methods and identifying problems such as the lack of social services in juvenile courts, faulty procedures, and community conditions generating delinquency. Promotion of institutions within local communities would be done through field social-service supervisors, and child welfare consultants, who would also help obtain more adequate case records, making better use of information in treating individual children. They would keep the referring agency abreast of the child's relative progress and adjustment, both during institutionalization and once paroled.[124]

Government official Ethel Speas noted, "If it were possible to get psychological services for Jackson, it would not be accepted at present." She concluded that it would be some time before individualized treatment plans for inmates could be made."[125] In 1939 Director Ezell notified Superintendent Boger that a child psychiatrist employed by Child Welfare Services would be visiting the institution for a couple of days. Ezell played down the psychiatrist's connection with the Division of Institutions and Corrections, presenting him as a consultant who simply wished to "acquaint himself with the programs and procedures so that he may fit his work into the general program of the training schools and the Public Welfare Departments."[126]

Archival records indicate that the rise of the biopolitical state was a contested, and by no means automatic, process in North Carolina. Superintendent Boger and his administration continued to defy the authority of Superintendent of Public Welfare, E.M. Land, in 1933, when a lawyer successfully released a boy from the institution without the knowledge or consent of the committing officer, who had just informed the boy's family that she did not recommend the boy's parole.[127] Boger released a number of youths in 1933 despite Superintendent Land's warning that the boys were being returned to deleterious home environments.[128] An incensed Commissioner Johnson wrote, "We have tried doing some parole work with the institution and gotten so little cooperation that it was impossible for us to continue to do the work."[129] Like record keeping, the parole of discharged boys was an ongoing issue, because state officials could not secure the superintendent's and board's cooperation. It would take the publicized severe beating of thirteen-year-old inmate George White Goodman at Jackson Training School to finally secure Superintendent Boger's cooperation with state requests for parole.

"Investigation of Treatment of George White Goodman"

The file on the investigation of George Goodman's July 1934 beating is not currently accessible to researchers, but the incident is obliquely referenced in open files.[130] In the 1930 census, George White Goodman was listed as nine years and six months old, and an inmate at the Stonewall Jackson Training School. The 16 July 1934 State Board's report of its investigation of his beating noted that before the whipping, Goodman, while small for his age, weighing only fifty-seven pounds, was in good health. Judge G.W. Watson had committed George Goodman and his brother in 1929 for "store breaking" and larceny. Administrators characterized the character of their father, a steelworker, as simply "bad." While they identified the boys' mother's character as "good," conditions at home were listed as "very bad." Housed with thirty other boys, Goodman's assigned tasks at Jackson, included housecleaning and the preparation, cooking, and serving of food. House head Mr Carriker testified that George was whipped on 2 July for carelessness, after allegedly bringing food to the table with cockroaches in it. Moreover, he had been rude to Mrs Carriker, and failed to carry out her instructions. Mr Carriker described the switch he used to be "about the size of a lead pencil and that he did not whip the boy unusually hard, although he may have struck him as many as thirty times." Superintendent Boger stated that he was unaware of the whipping until minutes before the boy's scheduled release from the institution on 3 July.[131]

Two inmates later admitted to overhearing the flogging that morning, being in the kitchen over the basement where Mr Carriker administered it. They mentioned that while Mrs Carriker did not beat them, she "knocked them around," and was "too hard to please." Mr Carriker admitted to having whipped George and other boys "several times (he had no idea how many) during his stay at the institution." Twelve years earlier, in 1921, another boy's mother had remarked, "There were scales on his back from his shoulders to his heels where they beat him – but I guess they had to do it … They made a man out of him."[132] But George Goodman's mother evidently complained to the local paper, and George's parole officer responded to the publicity, visiting the family a week later, on 10 July. The boy's mother showed him the "numerous purple marks" still visible on George's shoulders, back, and legs. George explained that he had been flogged the nights of Saturday 30 June and Monday 2 July, and the morning of Tuesday 3 July. Investigators concluded that it was possible that boys' criticisms of the Carrikers reflected that they had been "required to do cottage duty too long." They suggested that government funding of the institution was too limited, resulting in an inadequate program, and increased disciplinary measures.[133]

A field agent gathered information on personnel, noting inadequate training, a lack of cooperation between them, and a failure on the part of the superintendent to properly organize and supervise staff responsibilities.[134] Superintendent Boger readily agreed to have employees start filling out forms on daily disciplinary cases and "stated that assistance in working out a more adequate program would be welcome."[135] A few months after the incident, Boger requested parole officers, suggesting that they would be a "wonderful help."[136] Changing the whipping policy at the Stonewall Jackson Training School gave state officials hope for the leverage they needed to enforce parole and other biopolitical state management of the institution. Administrator Minnie Brown remarked, "The recent happening gives a grand opening for a wholesale clean up I think."[137] Commissioner Bost concurred: "Mr. Boger, I think, was right badly frightened and is naturally in a receptive mood so far as recommendations for the Department are concerned. We have realized for a long time that changes were needed in this institution and the publicity incident to the Goodman whipping has helped to open the way."[138] In addition to keeping records of whippings, recommendations included the setting up of individual case conferences to be conducted by the superintendent every two weeks, and to emphasize "the positive character of institutionalized treatment rather than the negative." Positive reinforcement should be given for boys' constructive efforts in work, study, and play.[139]

Yet the problem of corporal punishment persisted. In 1935, just seven months after George Goodman's whipping, a young inmate secretly mailed the following letter directly to Governor Ehringhaus:

Mr. Ehringhaus:

I'm a boy at Jackson Training School writing you ... I'm not caring about myself, but I feel sorry for the little boys here ... They beat them with grape vines, sticks, electric wires and straps. Some of them beat them until they are black and bloodshoten. Then they make them take a hot water bath. They give them medicine to make them sick ... When some of them beat a little boy they make him lie down, he will lie there and just ray and hollow and scream, and will beat them over the head and back of the neck to make them hush hollering. They get mad and curse the boys and abuse them lots of ways. But its allway's the two sides to any-thing the boys has just got to be punished but the way they [are] treated it does them more harm than good. Some of them run off ... They don't like to stay here and see the boys treated so mean ... It's been about 30 boys run in the last 6 weeks and it costs the state a lot of money to run them down ... [The officers] stick together and say they don't get enough stick ... when boy's people come they are afraid to tell it.[140]

Alarmed, Governor Ehringhaus immediately directed Commissioner Bost to investigate the "true condition" of the school, urging, "If the boy is telling the truth something should be done at once."[141] Director Ezell met with Superintendent Boger, as well as Jackson's assistant superintendent and bookkeeper, leaving a copy of the boy's letter with Superintendent Boger. Boger assured him that no abuse could have happened, and that floggings were only ever administered with a lightweight leather strop, not with grapevines and wires. He added that even this boy's parents would never believe his story, having had "too much experience" with him before his commitment.[142]

By 1943, the Jackson Training School manual prioritized discipline as something of "very great and grave importance," specifically rejecting corporal punishment as a "senseless, brutal and barbaric" disciplinary method "found in the underprivileged and disrupted home ... we must not continue with the boys in our hands the very methods of control which have always failed in their homes." The new 1943 staff manual discouraged boxing and pulling boys' ears, slapping boys on the head, or in the face, condoning instead, constructive leadership and individual counselling. Superintendent Boger claimed this "represented no radical departure from former policies," and could not agree more with Governor J. Melville Broughton's assertion that "there can be no value on the correctional institutions of the state in using brutality, harsh words, and cursing."[143] While the well-being of the young inmates was a consideration, the forms of punishment used reflected on the institution and the state, and North Carolina could ill afford any association with vengeful forms of punishment.

The archival record offers a glimpse into the actual development and operation of the emergent biopolitical state's involvement in juvenile moral reform. What emerges is a sense of how scientific, gender, and racial épistèmes functioned and circulated in overlapping ways, and how they defined the conditions of emergent discourses of mercy and the exercise of power. These records show locally specific, transformative dynamics in the continuity of punishment despite a decline in official acceptance of its practice. Evident too, is the uneven, contested development of the biopolitical state in North Carolina, at least as this pertained to the juvenile reformatory movement.

These records also document the central role of middle class white women, their roles as government officials, negotiating the management of the reformatory as an affective space that normalized and naturalized national belonging as a racialized privilege. The record shows the workings of locally specific dynamics of overlapping racial and gender épistèmes as the openly racist founder and director Cook, along with Jackson's other administrators, thwarted state officials' efforts at every turn. The internal contestations happened only behind closed doors, dissolving in the light of the public gaze, even in the face of well-founded allegations of abuse, including the merciless beating of a thirteen-year-old boy.

Epilogue

What I am afraid of about humanism is that it presents a certain form of our ethics as a universal model for any kind of freedom. I think that there are more secrets, more possible freedoms, and more inventions in our future than we can imagine in humanism.

Michel Foucault[1]

The story of the new world is horror, the story of America a crime.

Jodi Byrd[2]

How did Southern mercy play out in North Carolina's juvenile reformatory movement? For the Efland girls, it meant reinforced Black female invisibility in a state-obstructed reformatory and, later, neglect in a large custodial institution grounded in retribution. The Samarcand girls received sanctuary in some cases, but suffered emotional and physical attacks severe enough to inspire them to burn their dormitories to the ground. Except for one young defendant who ended her life by drinking Lysol, the Samarcand Sixteen encountered mercy in the form of long prison terms, along with protection from the electric chair. For the white boys at the Stonewall Jackson Training School, mercy involved rescue from hard labour on chain gangs, but severe institutional punishments. The Morrison Training School for Negro Boys promised merciful sanctuary for Black boys, but instead, these boys endured regular institutional mistreatment, including neglect and, occasionally, fatal beatings. North Carolina's juvenile reformatories exploited the labour of many, if not most, of the children committed to their care.

In his *Discipline and Punish* (1977), Foucault places, at the advent of modernity, a shift from coercion, punishment, and the infliction of death to pastoral benevolence, discipline, and the extension of life. Middle class reformers and state administrators governed through what they believed were merciful and "civilized" lawful methods, including extended court commitments to reform institutions for lengthy programs of normalization based on rational moral suasion rather than corporal punishment. In the late nineteenth and early decades of the twentieth century, lawfulness took precedence over vigilantism, and old-style penal practices, especially for white children, became a mark of inhumanity. Juvenile reformatory deaths resulting from beatings may have been unintended, but the persistence of severe beatings was a thorn in the side of North Carolina juvenile reform, implying irrational vengeance, and a failure to live up to ideals of moderns as an epistemologically new and "civilized" kind of people.[3]

With a merciful mandate, and seeking to restore whiteness by stemming the tide of white racial degeneracy, North Carolina's juvenile reformatory movement served as a bio-political tool of state racism, and as a means for the production of a docile working class through affective governance. Mercy also served North Carolina's regional promotion as part of a national, cross-class, white alliance.

Through acts of Southern mercy, progressive white juvenile reformers demonstrated their capacity for "civilization." Certainly liberal-humanist reformers, government officials, and much of the public expressed genuine, if selective, concern over the suffering of juvenile inmates. Yet, in some respects, these children served as pawns in a wider set of relations focused on defining white Americanism, and in negotiations for national belonging that immediately, at least, had nothing to do with them. Black and white wayward adolescents played an important role as rescued captives in Southern show trials and other spectacles of mercy, only to be abandoned to fall through the cracks once removed from the public eye. Public shame perpetuated their social invisibility long after release.

Moral reform was intrinsic to racialized nation building, and in their production of good future citizens, juvenile reformatories provide a lens through which to discern differences in racialized groups' national inclusion. Legally segregated by race and gender, and premised on "separate but equal" status for Blacks and marginal status for indigenous children, North Carolina's juvenile reform history demonstrates complicated qualities of mercy, expressed with wide variability, but consistent with non-compassionate racialization.

White reformers who supported the Morrison Training School for Negro Boys, for instance, could self-identify as more merciful than extra-legal, antimodernist Klan-based organizations, despite their shared commitment to white supremacy. Their opposition to extralegal lynch mobs largely focused on a merciful response to allegations of their own Southern barbarism, rather than on an anti-racist agenda.[4] While often spontaneous, as ritualized displays embedded in community social histories, lynchings were never isolated, random events. The formal rejection of mob murders bears meaning about the political and cultural logics of mercy in North Carolina in relation to the rest of the South, the nation, and the imperial stage.[5] In the late nineteenth and early-to-mid-twentieth centuries, New South advocates helped to secure their regional affiliation with the American empire through anti-lynching discourses, and the showcasing of mercies, variously racialized, gendered, and linked to sexuality.

In keeping with the earlier work of Balibar and Bauman, Goldberg has argued that race is a formative feature and "one of the central conceptual inventions of modernity," extending from the Enlightenment to present-day assertions that we are post-race and committed to colour-blindness. In a similar vein, Bauman has argued that "racism is a thoroughly modern weapon used in the conduct of premodern struggles"; and again, as Jean-Paul Sartre has noted, "there is nothing more consistent than a racist humanism."[6] Cynthia Nielson has observed that while historically attuned humanism has demonstrated solidarity with the oppressed, "under the banner of various 'humanisms,' so many 'others' have been exploited, enslaved, and slaughtered."[7]

Liberalism emerged in opposition to natural social hierarchy and absolutism, as an anti-feudal political philosophy grounded in individual rights and freedoms. But the shift was uneven, and attended by the re-narration of feudal absolutism incorporating gendered and racialized absolutism. Thus, under the banner of humanism, the othered have historically been exploited and eliminated. As a humanist political theory, contemporary liberalism advocates the inclusive, equitable treatment of individuals as ultimate moral equals, but this claim falters when race and gender are factored in, because the liberal individual entering into the social contract was originally conceived of as universally white and male. In the modern epoch, and at times recalling Giorgio Agamben's *homo sacer* (accursed ones who may be killed by anybody), racialized others have experienced anything but contractarianism. Rather, their experiences have included enslavement, genocide, and colonization by an imposed, rather than consensually legitimized, state.

Equality and exclusion within modern liberalism are distinctive features of modern racism. Saidiya Hartman examines the limits of emancipation and the exclusions inherent in liberalism. Emancipation, she argues, came to be little more than a "point of transition between modes of servitude and racial subjection," with the corollary that the classification of "human" is not attributed equivalently to all. "As a consequence of emancipation," she argues, "blacks were incorporated into the narrative of the rights of man and citizen; by virtue of the gift of freedom and wage labor, the formerly enslaved were granted entry into the hallowed halls of humanity, and, at the same time, the unyielding and implacable fabrication of blackness as subordination continued [in an egalitarian guise] under the aegis of formal equality."[8]

Segregated North Carolina reformatory institutions effectively renewed racism formally annulled by the Thirteenth Amendment through the pretence of neutral ascriptions of race and a façade of structural egalitarianism and universal moral equality. While intended to correct violations of Black liberty enacted in the Black Codes, the equal protection of law naturalized race by classifying and segregating "white," "negro," "mulatto," and "Indian" children, disregarding these classifications, themselves, as a violation of liberty and equality. The Republican interpretation of liberty maintained racial separation through the criminalization of interracial marriage, betraying a divided commitment to equality while reinscribing inferiority, and positioning Blacks in a liminal state within the body politic.[9] The North Carolina reformatory movement reflected what Goldberg has called the "racializing paradox at liberalism's heart"; paradoxical, because it embraced universal doctrines of equality, liberty, and fraternity while legitimizing and entrenching racial hierarchies and exclusions:

> As modernity commits itself progressively to idealized principles of liberty, equality, and fraternity, as it increasingly insists upon the moral irrelevance of race, there is a multiplication of racial identities and the sets of exclusions they prompt and rationalize, enable and sustain. Race is irrelevant, but all is race. The more abstract modernity's universal identity, the more it has to be insisted upon, the more it needs to be imposed. The more ideologically hegemonic liberal values seem and the more open to difference liberal modernity declares itself, the more dismissive of difference and the more closed it seeks to make the circle of acceptability.[10]

White privilege expands through the obscuring of political and class domination; that is, it is reinforced through its own normalized invisibility and complicity with the powers its means to dislodge. Agamben contends that a failure to question the structural foundations of hierarchical relationships essentially "maintain[s] a secret solidarity with the very powers they ought to fight."[11] George Sefa Dei, too, has noted that "one of the peculiar endowments of white privilege arises in its ability to obfuscate its relationship to the mechanisms of power, while at the same time, employing those mechanisms in language, discourse, and every other aspect of our lived reality."[12] While critiquing racism, liberal humanism presumes whiteness as the invisible standard in what it draws attention to and what it overlooks.

Racial liberalism evades all but the most superficial treatment of racial oppression. Inclusive ethnic celebrations, multicultural education, and Black History Month, in conjunction with Eurocentric history texts that minimize plantation slavery and American colonial expropriation of indigenous land effectively strengthen the white standard through a failure to take an anti-racist stance. For Hartman,

> The universality or unencumbered individuality of liberalism relies on tacit exclusions and norms that preclude substantive equality; all do not equally partake of the resplendent, plenipotent, indivisible, and steely singularity that it proffers. Abstract universality presumes particular forms of embodiment and excludes or marginalizes others ... The excluded ... variously contained ... by nature's whimsical apportionments, in fact, enable the production of universality, for the denigrated and deprecated ... are the fleshly substance that enable the universal to achieve its ethereal splendour.[13]

When we do not confront racism with a radically antiracist stance, it transmogrifies into insidious new forms that erroneously promise that we are beyond our old predilections.[14] As an illustration, conflating the demise of lynching with modern racial tolerance has enabled historical lynchings to persist in obfuscated ways into the present. Over seventy-eight incidents of lynching nooses discovered at American universities and colleges, work sites, and other public venues from 2007 to 2016 have horrified those who claim to be post-race.[15] Discourses have competed, grown obsolete, and shifted since the Jim Crow era, but the unprecedented growth of carceral control, and of police militarization has perpetuated an unremitting practice of racist police killings of Black men and boys since the antebellum period.[16]

Change is often conceptualized in a linear way, as something that ruptures with the emergence of new things, but as Foucault has argued, instead of reflecting radical historical discontinuities, discourses are reconceptualized in ever more insidious forms that revive earlier lexicons. As Stoler observes, it follows that racism seems simultaneously "new and renewed."[17]

North Carolina took the lead nationally to end formal lynchings after 1922. Southern white civic boosters and journalists disseminated the end-of-lynching discourse in the late 1920s and early 1930s, foretelling "the final" American lynching, and by the 1930s and 1940s, this end-of-lynching discourse emerged as a prevailing discourse. But as Ashraf Rushdy observes, this end-of-lynching discourse actually functioned to limit conversations about lynchings, and continues to inform the way we think about them into the present.[18]

Taking Stock

In her Memphis diary (1893), Wells wrote an anguished and prescient passage: "I have firmly believed all along that the law was on our side, and would, when we appealed to it, give us justice. I feel shorn of that belief, and utterly discouraged, and just now, if it were possible, would gather my race in my arms and fly away with them."[19] How might we assess continuity and change in race relations? Have we progressed, are we truly "post-race"? How exactly do historical practices of slavery, legal incarceration, legal executions, and vigilante lynchings resonate in the present? How are historic eugenic policies currently manifested? I turn now to a discussion of social change, and the systemic persistence of historically rooted racism in our contemporary criminal justice system, the War on Terror, and the War on Drugs.

Racial violence in the United States is marked by its genealogy as a white supremacist empire state. The literal and figurative defining of America took shape within an international crucible of empire building that persisted in new ways after the formal end of the Age of Imperialism.[20] While we may insist we are beyond lynching, racist police violence, along with the torturing of prisoners at Abu Ghraib, Guantánamo, and other American detention centres worldwide, systematically eviscerate the humanity of prisoners in ways that recall spectacle lynchings.

The notorious Abu Ghraib photographs are, for Hazel Carby, "the direct descendants," the after-images of historical lynching postcards; not just literally, but in the way they are disseminated, too. They furnish "material evidence of the wielding of power, of the performance of conquest over an enemy," and their sharing conveys a voyeuristic spectacle of white supremacy attended by warnings to the othered.[21]

In keeping with Rushdy, who argues that the War on Terror was really about subjugating the global frontier, Jodi Byrd and Roxanne Dunbar-Ortiz argue that colonizing racism has prevailed, revised to current agendas of globalization:

> That the continued colonization of American Indian nations, peoples, and lands provides the United States the economic and material resources needed to cast its imperialist gaze globally is a fact that is simultaneously obvious within – and yet continually obscured by – what is essentially a settler colony's national construction of itself as an ever more perfect multicultural, multiracial democracy … The status of American Indians as sovereign nations colonized by the United States continues to haunt and inflect its *raison d'être*.[22]

Strategically designated as "unlawful combatants" rather than prisoners of war, Guantánamo Bay detainees could be tortured by US interrogators, unprotected by the Geneva Conventions. In his egregious "Torture Memo," international law professor John C. Yoo, employing the legal category of *homo sacer*, defended the designation "unlawful combatant" with the 1873 precedent set by the US Supreme Court's opinion in *Modoc Indian Prisoners*, which expressly identified the Indian adversary as *homo sacer* to the United States.[23] In 1872, Chief Kintpuash led a group of the Modoc tribe who were fleeing from a reservation in Oregon to return home to northern California. The US Army obstructed their passage, leading to the Modoc War. Lieutenant General John M. Schofield, then commander of the US Army's Pacific Military Division, would later write of that campaign, "If the innocent could be separated from the guilty, plague, pestilence, and famine would not be an unjust punishment for the crimes committed in this country against the original occupants of the soil." Chief Kintpuash, among others, was hanged at Alcatraz, his corpse embalmed and displayed as a human zoo exhibit in circuses nationwide.[24]

At the 2001 United Nations World Conference against Racism, many argued that while it is generally presumed to be race-neutral, the expanding prison industrial complex demonstrates systematic racism in the administration of laws that result in disproportionate sentencing and overrepresentation of people of colour, especially in the United States. America currently has less than 5 per cent of the world's population, but houses over 20 per cent of the global inmate population, and the numbers have quadrupled since 1970. More than five million criminalized people are currently indentured in the criminal justice system, including those on probation, awaiting trial, or on parole. In the current US police state, more Black youth go to prison than college, two-thirds of them being arrested before reaching the age of thirty. Based on single-day counts, surveys administered in the 1990s indicated a lifetime risk of arrest at 80 to 90 per cent for young Black men living in American cities. The War on Drugs, initiated by President Nixon in the early 1970s, has renewed Jim Crow through the mass incarceration of the dispossessed, particularly the descendants of enslaved Africans, backed by white racial hostilities. Whites – especially white professionals, whose illicit drug activity is common – are more likely to avoid prison, and are criminalized at significantly lower rates than Blacks for the same offences, even when they are repeat offenders.[25]

Western criminal justice systems had been striving for centuries for what Norbert Elias has called "the civilizing process," a "refinement in sensibilities." Spectacles of pain gradually came to be rejected as uncouth. Nevertheless, as Ruth Wilson Gilmore has observed, "the laws [have] written into the penal code breathtakingly cruel twists in the meaning and practice of justice." Bureaucratically managed American prisons may no longer practise corporal punishment, but the exercise of power persists in the depersonalized, torturous conditions of confinement (especially often used solitary confinement) and the death penalty.[26]

Incarceration is tantamount to the criminalization, lucrative management, and exploitation of racialized others, who are eliminated through "a kind of waste management function." While enormously profitable for private corporations, these prisons are expensive for taxpayers, they fail to deter, and they create a publically feared, desperate population. Treated as a high-risk group, Blacks are managed for the "protection of society."[27] Barbara Hudson has argued, "The objective of the new strategies of control is identification of the different and the dangerous so as to exclude them – from the club, from the apartment building, from the estate, from the shopping mall. And even from the country."[28] This resonates with my findings on the treatment of Black boys in North Carolina's juvenile reformatory movement, who, warehoused in an isolated, "mercifully" mandated institution, were excised from national belonging through state "biologico-social racism" to ensure the security of the polity.[29]

Recalling antebellum slavery, mass incarceration prisons exploit Black labour, and felon disfranchisement laws debilitate the potential Black electorate upon release of former inmates, who must pay a fee – a new poll tax – to reinstate their voting rights.[30] "A prisoner," as the US Supreme Court stated in 1871, "is for the time being a slave of the state."[31] With the demise of formal slavery, disproportionate numbers of Blacks were criminalized and sentenced to hard labour in the lethal convict lease and, later, on chain gangs. All of this has been renewed in the contemporary American prison industrial complex.[32] As Angela Davis argues, "New leviathan prisons are being built on thousands of eerie acres of factories inside the walls ... It is clear that black bodies are considered dispensable within the 'free world' but as a major source of profit in the prison world ... In arrangements reminiscent of the postbellum convict lease system, county, state and federal governments are charged a fee by private companies for each inmate."[33] There is a resurgence of chain gangs, and a proliferation of prison factories. Three-strikes law, mandatory minimum sentences, and determinate sentencing draw huge, racialized swaths of the population into the burgeoning criminal justice system, often for minor offences.[34]

Neoliberal capitalism, characterized by deregulation, privatization, and the shrinking state, has generated massive poverty through soaring unemployment, a major cause of criminalized acts. Neoliberal capitalist discourses exhort people to reinvent themselves, and to succeed through flexibility, "right choices," and a self-regulatory "can-do" attitude, condemning them individually for failing to succeed when they reasonably find structural barriers insurmountable. Historical regulation, reconfigured, now aims to promote docility and prevent social conflict, rather than supporting resistance to diminishing institutional supports under current capitalism.[35] The prison industrial complex downplays the impact of global capitalism, neo-colonialism, and wildly inequitable wealth distribution – blaming and warehousing the racialized other.[36] Since the mid-1970s, when neoliberal capitalism took root, policies have reflected a shift from holding society accountable to amplifying the guilt of the offender. With a mandate to surveil and contain the criminalized, "correctional" facilities have abandoned even the pretence of rehabilitation.[37] Despite the "dramatic decreases in the frequency and seriousness of criminal behaviour" evident even before the expansion of the prison industrial complex, alternative restorative justice programs and rehabilitative community-based sanctions are typically bypassed as contrary to the current agenda of profit and vengeance, rather than reparation.

Mass incarceration through the War on Drugs has appealed to the insecurities of working class whites, who are encouraged to choose modern versions of the racialized opportunism extended under Jim Crow, in lieu of building interracial solidarity against capitalist exploitation. Racial hatred is not officially tolerated, but we may hate the criminal(ized). The other, stigmatized by media surveillance and spectacle, is juxtaposed with law-abiding citizens – "us" – in a binary of good vs. bad, normal vs. abnormal.[38]

Related to the criminalization inflicted through America's War on Drugs, Dorothy Roberts has examined the racist renewal of historical stereotypes of Black biological defectiveness and hypersexuality. The focus of immutable deficiencies, she argues, is now centred on in utero damage to the unborn babies of crack-addicted mothers, who allegedly pass on defective genes and deviant lifestyles to their children, as the new "bio-underclass." Assuming and anticipating their inevitable failure, state legislators cut social spending for these children. Roberts notes that policy proposals, such as Newt Gingrich's 1994 "Contract with America," recall historical eugenic sterilization schemes through their advocacy of measures to prevent pregnancies in welfare recipients. Such policies criminalize race as well as poverty, shifting interpretations of welfare fraud to welfare *as* fraud, resonating with early welfare-state priorities.[39] Ruth Hubbard has argued that the new reproductive and genetic technologies have pernicious neo-eugenic potential to jeopardize the existence of others variously identified as disabled.[40] The Anglophilic Western image of childhood innocence continues to exclude Black children.

One of Foucault's persistent interests was a suspicion of liberal humanism's ethics of the self, through which "we" construct ourselves against the other in mutually exclusive, antagonistic relationships. The conceptual framework normalizing this gendered and racialized positionality has persisted into the present, and continues to have a disquieting, ubiquitous impact. Can we be optimistic about the future, then, given that racist and other oppressive agendas are woven into the fabric of Americanism? History can take dramatic turns; nothing is natural and inevitable. But it is only when we become aware of the ways in which power produces what is held to be true that we can begin to shift public discourse in meaningful ways. An effective model for freedom obligates us to confront subjugations of the othered through a radical stance, rather than through gradualist, reformist approaches that renew old oppressions in ever more insidious ways.[41] Change is possible, and we are seeing clear signs of it in movements like Black Lives Matter. Where these resistance movements will go is not clear, but an important first step is to think about the past in different ways, as I have tried to do in this examination of Southern mercy. Change, as Bruno Latour has observed, does not obliterate the past in its wake; the present is an invention of the past, and we must come to terms with it.

Notes

Introduction

1 H.L. Mencken, "Untitled" (1921), quoted in Natalie J. Ring, *The Problem South: Region, Empire, and the New Liberal State, 1880–1930* (Athens: University of Georgia Press, 2012), 218.
2 "National Affairs: Lynching No. 12," *Time* magazine, 1 September 1930. In S. Gabbidon and H. Greene, eds, *Race, Crime and Justice: A Reader* (New York: Routledge, 2005), 30–1.
3 Quoted in Arthur Raper, *The Tragedy of Lynching* (New York: Dover Publications, 2003), 118.
4 Gonorrhoea symptoms typically appear within ten days, but can sometimes take up to thirty days to be noticeable. Raper, *The Tragedy of Lynching*, 118.
5 Ibid., 107–24, 210; Vann R. Newkirk, *Lynching in North Carolina: A History 1865–1941* (Jefferson: McFarland and Company, 2009), 112–16.
6 Tennant McWilliams, *The New South Faces the World: Foreign Affairs and the Southern Sense of Self, 1877–1950* (Baton Rouge: Louisiana State University Press, 1988), 9–10.
7 Newkirk, *Lynching in North Carolina*, 6; Ashraf Rushdy, *The End of American Lynching* (New Brunswick, NJ: Rutgers University Press, 2012), 72–3. Also see Cecilia Elizabeth O'Leary, *To Die For: The Paradox of American Patriotism* (Princeton: Princeton University Press, 1999), 4–6, 12, 49–57, 121–4; Alon Confino, *The Nation as a Local Metaphor* (Chapel Hill: University of North Carolina Press, 1997), 7; Eric Foner, *Reconstruction: America's Unfinished Revolution, 1863–1877* (New York: Harper and Row, 1984), 209; Paul V. Murphy, *The Rebuke of History: The Southern Agrarians and American Conservative Thought* (Chapel Hill: University of North Carolina Press,

2001), Introduction; David Roediger, *The Wages of Whiteness: Race and the Making of the American Working Class* (London: Verso, 1991), 170; John Fraser, *America and the Patterns of Chivalry* (London: Cambridge University Press, 1982), 35; Ring, *The Problem South*, 7.

8 Fraser, *America and the Patterns of Chivalry*, 115–18.

9 Ring, *The Problem South*, 1–2, 10, 17, 27–8, 71, 84, 143–5, 218; O'Leary, *To Die For*, 195, 433–72; Kieran Quinlan, *Strange Kin: Ireland and the American South* (Baton Rouge: Louisiana State University Press, 2005), 185. Also see V.O. Key, *Southern Politics in State and Nation* (Knoxville: University of Tennessee Press, 1977 [1949]), 206–8; Shelley Sallee, *The Whiteness of Child Labor Reform in the New South* (Athens: University of Georgia Press, 2004), 100. C. Vann Woodward, *Origins of the New South 1877–1913* (Baton Rouge: Louisiana State University Press and Littlefield Fund for Southern History of the University of Texas, 1971), 157; Fletcher Green, "Resurgent Southern Sectionalism, 1933–1955," in J. Isaac Copeland, ed., *Democracy in the Old South and Other Essays by Fletcher Melvin Green* (Nashville, TN: Vanderbilt University Press, 1969), 297–8.

10 Quoted in Ring, *The Problem South*, 143–4.

11 Walter Hines Page, "The Hookworm and Civilization," *World's Work* 24 (September 1912): 509–10.

12 C. Vann Woodward, Origins of the New South (Louisiana: Louisiana State University Press, 1971), 157. Ann Laura Stoler, "Tense and Tender Ties: The Politics of Comparison in North American History and (Post) Colonial Studies," *Journal of American History* 88 (3) (2001): 829–65, 13; Ann Laura Stoler, *Haunted by Empire* (Durham, NC: Duke University Press, 2006), 435; Ring, *The Problem South*, 17, 51. During the Age of American imperialism, from the 1890s to the end of the First World War, the United States acquired several protectorates and colonies, including Puerto Rico, the Hawaiian Islands, the Philippines, and Guam. In 1860, the United States did not have any overseas colonies, but by 1920, 120,000 American troops had moved into eight overseas territories with a combined population slightly more than that in the western third of the United States itself. See Ring, *The Problem South*, 51. See also Amy Kaplan "'Left Alone with America': The Absence of Empire in the Study of American Culture," in Amy Kaplan and Donald E. Pease, eds, *Cultures of United States Imperialism* (Durham, NC: Duke University Press, 1993); Donald Pease, "US Imperialism: Global Dominance without Colonies," in Henry Schwartz and Sangeeta Ray, eds, *A Companion to Postcolonial Studies* (Oxford: Blackwell, 2005), 203–20.

13 Ring, *The Problem South*, 61, 102; Linda Gordon, "Internal Colonialism and Gender," in Stoler, ed., *Haunted by Empire*, 435; Also see Moon-Kie Jung,

"Constituting the U.S. Empire-State and White Supremacy: The Early Years," in Moon-Kie Jung, Joao H. Costas Vargas, and Eduardo Bonilla-Silva, eds, *State of White Supremacy: Racism, Governance, and the United States* (Stanford, CA: Stanford University Press, 2011), 1–26.

14 Fox Butterfield, "Ideas & Trends: Southern Curse; Why America's Murder Rate Is So High," *New York Times*, 26 July 1998. http://www.nytimes.com/1998/07/26/weekinreview/ideas-trends-Southern-curse-why-america-s-murder-rate-is-so-high.html?pagewanted=all; Strange, *Qualities of Mercy*, 16; Michel Foucault, *Discipline and Punish: The Birth of the Prison* (New York: Vintage Books, 1995), 23.

15 Douglas Hay, *Albion's Fatal Tree: Crime and Society in Eighteenth-Century England* (London: Pantheon Books, 1975), 43.

16 Ibid., 40. In 1909, Judge Julian Mack famously proposed in the *Harvard Law Review* that a juvenile offender should be treated "as a wise and merciful father handles his own child." Julian Mack, "The Juvenile Court," *Harvard Law Review* 23 (104) (1909).

17 Donald Pease, "New Perspectives on U.S. Culture and Imperialism," in Amy Kaplan and Donald E. Pease, eds, *Cultures of United States Imperialism* (Durham, NC: Duke University Press, 1993), 22–37, 33. Interest in strengthening the nation racially was particularly strong in the 1920s given the prevalence of the Ku Klux Klan. I am grateful to Natalie Ring for this point. David Harvey, *The New Imperialism* (New York: Oxford, 2003), 26–87; Gary Gerstle, *American Crucible: Race and Nation in the Twentieth Century* (Princeton, NJ: Princeton University Press, 2001), 105. Degeneration theories warned against the consequences of racial and sexual boundary transgressions. Various groups of whites, including the institutionalized, Southern mill workers, prostitutes, were, like nineteenth century Irish "White Negroes," classified as degenerate; abject *others* – "out-groups," as Nikolas Rose has called them, or "abnormals" for Foucault. Nikolas Rose, "Authority and the Genealogy of Subjectivity," in P. Heelas, S. Lash, and P. Morris, eds, *Detraditionalization: Critical Reflections on Authority and Identity* (Oxford: Blackwell, 1996), 294–327; Anne McClintock, *Imperial Leather: Race, Gender and Sexuality in the Colonial Contest* (New York: Routledge, 1995), 47; Julia Kristeva, *Powers of Horror: An Essay on Abjection*, trans. Leon S. Roudiez (New York: Columbia University Press, 1982), 4; Michel Foucault, *"Abnormal": Lectures at the Collège de France, 1974–1975* (New York: Picador, 2003), xvii; Achille Mbembe, "Necropolitics," *Public Culture* 15 (1) (2003): 11–40, 25; McClintock, *Imperial Leather*, 46; Sander Gilman, "'I'm Down on Whores': Race and Gender in Victorian London," in David Theo Goldberg, ed., *Anatomy of Racism* (Minneapolis: University

of Minnesota Press, 1990), 240, 248; Foner, *A Short History of Reconstruction*, 82; Ring, *The Problem South*, 91, 211, 141; Ann Laura Stoler, *Race and the Education of Desire: Foucault's History of Sexuality and the Colonial Order of Things* (Durham, NC: Duke University Press, 1995), 31.

18 Foucault, *Discipline and Punish*, 24, 30.

19 Michel Foucault, *Society Must Be Defended: Lectures at the Collège de France* (New York: Picador Press, 2003), 245; also see 35–8.

20 Douglas Hay, "Foreword," in Carolyn Strange, ed., *Qualities of Mercy: Justice, Punishment, and Discretion* (Vancouver: UBC Press, 1996), vii; Carolyn Strange and Tina Loo, *Making Good: Law and Moral Regulation in Canada, 1867–1939* (Toronto: University of Toronto Press, 1997), 29, 51.

21 The exercise of sovereignty is the exercise of control over mortality "and to define life as the deployment and manifestation of power." Slavery and its aftermath involved loss of home, of rights over one's body, and of political rights. These losses generated a vanishing and social death. See Mbembe, "Necropolitics," 12, 21; Fraser, *America and the Patterns of Chivalry*, 35; Bruno Latour, *We Have Never Been Modern* (Cambridge, MA: Harvard University Press, 1993), 47–8.

22 "Mrs. Bost Finds Girls Content at Samarcand: Discipline Is Excellent and Progress of Girls Under State's Care Is Good," Raleigh *News and Observer*, 26 March 1929, North Carolina Department of Archives and History (NCDAH).

23 Nancy Maclean, *Behind the Mask of Chivalry: The Making of the Second Ku Klux Klan* (New York: Oxford University Press, 1994), 111–13.

24 Carolyn Strange, "The Undercurrents of Penal Culture: Punishment of the Body in Mid-Twentieth-Century Canada," *Law and History Review*, Summer 2001.

25 Greg Smith, "Civilized People Don't Want to See That Kind of Thing: The Decline of Public Physical Punishment in London, 1760–1840," in Strange, ed., *Qualities of* Mercy, 24.

26 Bruce Levine, "The Second American Revolution," *Jacobin*, issue 18 (Summer 2015): 36. Alex Gourevitch, "Our Forgotten Labor Revolution," *Jacobin*, issue 18 (Summer 2015): 61–9. Amy Dru Stanley, "Not Waiting for Deliverance," *Jacobin*, issue 18 (Summer 2015): 44; Roediger, *The Wages of Whiteness*, 174. While the Freedman's Bureau restored much land and power to former planters as early as 1865–6, plantation ownership no longer guaranteed wealth, and many joined the emergent middle (landlord-merchant) class. Southern agricultural statistics indicate the extent of economic ruin: while staple crops production expanded in other US regions between 1860 and

1870, acreage under cultivation plummeted in the South, and farm values declined by half. Even discounting the uncompensated loss represented by the emancipation of four million people, the real value of all property by 1870 had dropped 30 per cent below its ante-bellum figure. Allocating funds for internal improvements, the Forty-First Congress (a meeting from 1869–71 of the legislative branch of the federal government in Washington, DC) appropriated only 15 per cent for the entire South, and it was mostly in aid of railroads run by Northern capitalists. George Tindall, *The Emergence of the New South, 1913–1945* (Baton Rouge: Louisiana State University Press and Littlefield Fund for Southern History of the University of Texas, 1967), 433–72; Foner, *A Short History of Reconstruction*, 59, 72–3, 172–3, 176; Saidiya Hartman, *Scenes of Subjection: Terror, Slavery, and Self-Making in Nineteenth-Century America* (New York: Oxford, 1997), 183; Gourevitch, "Our Forgotten Labor Revolution," 61.

27 Ring, *The Problem South*, 24; Stoler, *Haunted by Empire*, 10–11.

28 Emerging from the 1870s Depression, a new, largely white middle class prospered, but by the turn of the twentieth century, only 6 per cent of the South's labourers worked in manufacturing. From 1865 to 1873, despite economic stagnation in the South, American manufacturing increased by 75 per cent, second only to Britain. Mbembe, "Necropolitics," 21; Foner, *Reconstruction*, 131, 194; Foner, *A Short History of Reconstruction*, 56, 199–202, 227, 251. Abolition had been compensated in the West Indies. See Eric Williams, *Capitalism and Slavery* (New York: Russell and Russell, 1941).

29 Ian Christian Hartman, "From Daniel Boone to the Beverly Hillbillies: Tales of a 'Fallen' Race, 1873–1968," Ph.D. diss. (University of Illinois at Urbana-Champaign, 2011), 6, 8–9, 63; Roxanne Dunbar-Ortiz, *An Indigenous Peoples' History of the United States* (Boston: Beacon Press, 2014), 94; McClintock, *Imperial Leather*, 5; Wilson, *Baptized in Blood*, 47. Also see O'Leary, *To Die For*, 4, 116, 142–6, 221; Green, "Resurgent Southern Sectionalism," 288–306. Charles Reagan Wilson, *Baptized in Blood: The Religion of the Lost Cause, 1865–1920* (Athens: University of Georgia Press, 1980), 47.

30 Also see Roxanne Dunbar-Ortiz, "North America Is a Crime Scene: The Untold History of America This Columbus Day," *Salon*, 14 October 2013. Recent historiography on US imperialism includes Kristin L. Hoganson, *Fighting for American Manhood: How Gender Politics Provoked the Spanish American and Philippine American Wars* (New Haven: Yale University Press, 2000); Amy Kaplan, *The Anarchy of Empire in the Making of U.S. Culture* (Cambridge, MA: Harvard University Press, 2002); Walter Lefeber, *The New Empire: An Interpretation of American Expansion, 1860–1898* (Ithaca: Cornell University Press, 1998); Eric T.L. Love, *Race over Empire: Racism*

and U.S. Imperialism 1865–1900 (Chapel Hill: University of North Carolina Press, 2004); Marilyn Lake and Henry Reynolds, *Drawing the Global Colour Line: White Men's Countries and the International Challenge of Racial Equality* (Cambridge: Cambridge University Press, 2008).

31 Benedict Anderson, *Imagined Communities: Reflections on the Origin and Spread of Nationalism* (London: Verso, 1991), 7; Confino, *The Nation as a Local Metaphor*, 4.

32 Gourevitch, "Our Forgotten Labor Revolution," 61. Herbert Shapiro, *White Violence and Black Response: From Reconstruction to Montgomery* (Amherst: University of Massachusetts Press, 1988), 66. By 1870, Northern financiers increasingly invested in the West rather than risking funds in the South, given its instability. Hartman, *Scenes of Subjection*, 116, 137; W.E.B. Dubois, *Black Reconstruction in America, 1860–1880* (New York: Atheneum, 1992), 166, 195–7, 256–7; Foner, *A Short History of Reconstruction*, xiv, 9, 13, 21, 98, 113–14, 142, 226–7, 247. Foner, *Reconstruction*, 131, 194, 268; Stephen J. Gould, "American Polygeny and Craniometry before Darwin," in Sandra Harding, ed., *The Racial Economy of Science* (Bloomington: Indiana University Press, 1993), 97–8; Roediger, *The Wages of Whiteness*, 167; Ring, *The Problem South*, 13, 17; Key, *Southern Politics in State and Nation*, 206–8; Green, "Resurgent Southern Sectionalism," 297–8, McWilliams, *The New South Faces the World*, 5–9, 99, 119, 141–2; Richard H. Pildes, "Democracy, Anti-Democracy, and the Canon," *Constitutional Commentary* 17 (2000): 12, 27; Michael Perman, *Struggle for Mastery: Disfranchisement in the South, 1888–1908* (Chapel Hill: University of North Carolina Press, 2001), Introduction; Glenn Feldman, *The Disfranchisement Myth: Poor Whites and Suffrage Restriction in Alabama* (Athens: University of Georgia Press, 2004), 135–6; Sydney Nathans, *The Quest for Progress: The Way We Lived in North Carolina, 1870–1920* (Chapel Hill: University of North Carolina Press, 1983), 95.

33 Bruce Levine, "The Second American Revolution," *Jacobin*, issue 18 (Summer 2015): 36, 41; Alex Gourevitch, "Our Forgotten Labor Revolution," *Jacobin*, issue 18 (Summer 2015): 63.

34 As Confino has noted, nations can simultaneously accommodate national and regional identities, but the Civil War had stirred regionalism, indelibly marking North-South identities as binary, for many. Wiebe, *The Search for Order, 1877–1920*, 92; Confino, *The Nation as a Local Metaphor*, 7; McWilliams, *The New South Faces the World*, 9–10; O'Leary, *To Die For*, 4–6, 12, 49–57, 121–4. I loosely connect Latour's discussion of "modern" with industrial capitalism and modern philosophical thought, New South progressivism, and Reconstruction era Republicanism, as described by classic historians like C. Vann Woodward and Ed Ayers. Broad, somewhat

generalizing patterns suggest that reactionary white Democrats sought
to salvage agrarianism and the wreck of the Old South through the Lost
Cause movement and vigilante lynching, whereas liberal-humanist New
South Republicans sought to promote industrialization, and rejoin the
globally and economically powerful Union. In reality, the line was blurred
between anti-modernists and modernists, New South industrialists,
and conservative agrarians, given, for instance, frequent conspiratorial
collusion between state police and lynch mobs, and lynchers' increasing
efforts to be rational and calm as they carried out their ritualistic murders.
It was contested terrain, though quite often these groups defined
themselves in opposition to each other. In keeping with Grace E. Hale's
Making Whiteness: The Culture of Segregation in the South, 1890–1940 (New
York: Oxford University Press, 1998) and Gail Bederman, *Manliness &
Civilization: A Cultural History of Gender and Race in the United States, 1880–
1917* (Chicago: University of Chicago Press, 1995). Lisa Dorr's local study
of rape in the twentieth century South, *White Women, Rape and the Power of
Race in Virginia 1900–1960* (Chapel Hill: University of North Carolina Press,
2004) argues for lynching as modern because it incorporated stylized public
spectacle and self-control rather than simple, "backward" bloodlust. But as
Foucault (*Discipline and Punish*) points out, this kind of stylized structure
also marked torture spectacles of the ancient regime. More indicative of the
move to modernist methods was the gradual turn from bodily destruction.
Archival records show, for instance, that North Carolina experimented
with death row inmates in the 1930s, giving them water to drink to ensure
that the electric chair would be quick, and would not maim. Eugenic
sterilizations supplanted more gruesome forms of population control.
I argue against progressive versus backward binaries, suggesting, in
keeping with Latour (*We Have Never Been Modern*) that we might view
lynching as a hybrid of modern and anti-modernist tendencies. While
there was often collusion between legal administrators and lynch mobs,
as Dorr points out, these actors often defined themselves as diametrically
opposed. Many racist white Southerners self-identified, and wanted to be
nationally acknowledged as "civilized." Vigilante and juridical players
commonly feared the mythical Black Rapist, each extending protection to
"white womanhood" as the National Symbolic. Also see Gail Bederman,
"'Civilization,' the Decline of Middle-Class Manliness, and Ida B. Wells's
Antilynching Campaign, 1982–94," *Radical History Review* 1992 (52): 15; A
scene from Ellen Glasgow's *The Voice of the People* (New York: Doubleday,
Page & Co., 1900), depicts a lynching wherein mob members argued about
the merits of "a lawless rage that knows control," 441–2.

35 Gourevitch, "Our Forgotten Labor Revolution," 62, 66.
36 Roediger, *The Wages of Whiteness*, 176; Hartman, *Scenes of Subjection*, 116, 133, 137; W.E.B. Dubois, *Black Reconstruction in America*, 166, 195–7, 256–7; Foner, *A Short History of Reconstruction*, 113–14, 226–7; Gourevitch, "Our Forgotten Labor Revolution," 67–9.
37 Foucault, *Discipline and Punish*, 25–7.
38 Roediger, *The Wages of Whiteness*, 176; Hartman, *Scenes of Subjection*, 116, 133, 137; W.E.B. Dubois, *Black Reconstruction in America*, 166, 195–7, 256–7; Foner, *A Short History of Reconstruction*, 113–14, 226–7.
39 Adolph Reed, Jr, "The James Brown Theory of Black Liberation," *Jacobin*, issue 18 (Summer 2015): 57; Alex Gourevitch, "Our Forgotten Labor Revolution," *Jacobin*, issue 18 (Summer 2015): 62. Mbembe, "Necropolitics," 16; Foner, *A Short History of Reconstruction*, 39, 114–16, 122, 148, 151, 155; Foner, *Reconstruction*, 204; W.E.B. Dubois, *Black Reconstruction in America*, 370–2; Hartman, *Scenes of Subjection*, 130–2; Foner, *A Short History of Reconstruction*, 75, 102–3, 110.
40 James W. Loewen, "Democracy Betrayed: The Wilmington Race Riot of 1898 and Its Legacy (review)," *Southern Cultures* 6 (3) (2000): 90–3; John DeSantis, "Wilmington Revisits a Bloody 1898 Day," *New York Times*, 4 June 2006, 1 and 33.
41 In September 1919, for instance, Black Americans unsuccessfully mounted armed resistance against white lynch mobs in seven race riots erupting in cities as regionally diverse as Omaha, Knoxville, and Washington, DC; David Krugler, "America's Forgotten Mass Lynching: When 237 People Were Murdered in Arkansas," *The Daily Beast*, 16 February 2015, http:// www.thedailybeast.com/articles/2015/02/16/america-s-forgotten-mass-lynching-when-237-people-were-murdered-in-arkansas.html; Gupta, *Justice before Reconciliation*, 14; O'Leary, *To Die For*, 114–15; Nathans, *The Quest for Progress*, 95.
42 Foner, *A Short History of Reconstruction*, 51, 124–6, 128–9, 133; Michael Perman, *Struggle for Mastery: Disfranchisement in the South, 1888–1908* (Chapel Hill: University of North Carolina Press, 2001), Introduction.
43 Tindall, *The Emergence of the New South*, 152–6; O'Leary, *To Die For*, 6–8, 111, 120, 127–8, 131–3, 239–42; Celia Applegate, *A Nation of Provincials: The German Idea of Heimat* (Berkeley: University of California Press, 1990), 5–9; Homi Bhabha, "DissemiNation: Time, Narrative and the Margins of the Modern Nation," in H.K. Bhabha, ed., *Nation and Narration* (London: Routledge, 1990). 310–11; Anderson, *Imagined Communities*, 7: Ring, *The Problem South*, 6–7.
44 Ring, *The Problem South*, 9–10.

45 Raymond Williams, *Marxism and Literature* (Oxford: Oxford University Press, 1978), 128–36.

46 Susan Iden, "N.C. Home for Delinquent Girls is Developing into Matrimonial Institution: Success of Samarcand Is Built on Faith of Miss Agnes MacNaughton, the Superintendent, in Girls, Most of Whom Want to Make Good; No Locks or Barred Gates at Sandhill Institution," Raleigh *News and Observer*, 1 October 1927.

47 Samarcand private archives, *Samarcand Manor*, Eagle Springs, NC.

48 Ann Laura Stoler, "Tense and Tender Ties: The Politics of Comparison in North American History and (Post) Colonial Studies," *Journal of American History* 88 (3) (2001): 829–65, 13; Stoler, *Haunted by Empire*, 11–16, 432–5, 443; Ring, *The Problem South*, 1–9, 17, 51. Also see Ian Hacking, "Making Up People," in T.L. Heller, M. Sosna, and D.E. Wellbery, eds, *Reconstructing Individualism: Autonomy, Individuality, and the Self in Western Thought* (Stanford: Stanford University Press, 1985), 222–36; Michel Foucault, "The Subject and Power," *Critical Inquiry* 8 (4) (1982): 777–95; Michel Foucault, *Discipline and Punish: The Birth of the Prison* (New York: Vintage Books, 1995), 170, 202–3.

49 Hartman, "From Daniel Boone to the Beverly Hillbillies," 34; Sharad Chari, "State Racism and Biopolitical Struggle: The Evasive Commons in Twentieth-Century Durban, South Africa," *Radical History Review* 2010 (108) (2010): 73–90. R. H. Wiebe, *The Search for Order, 1877–1920* (New York: Hill and Wang, 1967), 171, 181; Sallee, *The Whiteness of Child Labor Reform in the New South.*

50 Wiley Hampton Swift, Committee, National Child Labor, *Child Welfare in North Carolina* (1918), reprint (London: Forgotten Books, 2013), 6–7; Tindall, *The Emergence of the New South*, 433–72.

51 Odem, *Delinquent Daughters*, 1–2; Strange and Loo, *Making Good*, 60.

52 American social reformers were referring to the notion of "protected childhood" as early as the 1820s. Bush, *Who Gets a Childhood?* 4; Strange and Loo, *Making Good*, 79.

53 Stoler, "Tense and Tender Ties," 4, 10.

54 Nina Bernstein, *The Lost Children of Wilder: The Epic Struggle to Change Foster Care* (New York: Pantheon, 2001), 20.

55 "What Is the State Board of Public Welfare and What Are Some of the Things It Does?" *Public Welfare Progress*, Vol. 5, No. 10, October 1924. Raleigh, NC. Private Collection 255.28, Nell Battle Lewis Papers, Social Welfare 1922–38: Welfare Department, North Carolina. Discourses on interracial sex in the decades around the turn of the nineteenth century combined degeneration theories with notions of pure blood (an aristocratic

preoccupation with descent) and the American legal racial classification of the one-drop rule, which racialized those who had a great-grandparent of African descent. Stoler, *Race and the Education of Desire*, 35; Stoler, "Tense and Tender Ties"; Sallee, *The Whiteness of Child Labor*, 2; Hartman, *Scenes of Subjection*, 183–6; Foucault charts a trajectory of sexuality that emerged alongside the biopolitical state from the start of the eighteenth century to a "completely new technology of sex" by the nineteenth century in the Northeast, and later in the largely unindustrialized South, when sex became a secular state concern involving intervention in pedagogy, public health, and demography. This new organization of sexuality was tied to biopolitical state racism and to Southern national belonging. Michel Foucault, *History of Sexuality, Volume I: An Introduction* (New York: Vintage, 1980), 25, 116.

56 Stoler, *Race and the Education of Desire*, 9. Also see 50–1, 61, 68, 71–2, 84–5, 89.
57 "Civility" is defined in keeping with Norbert Elias's identification of late-eighteenth-century manifestations of politesse and *humanité*, discourses believed to have initiated the reconfiguration of penology in England. Greg Smith, "Civilized People," 27; Also see John Pratt, *Punishment and Civilization: Penal Tolerance and Intolerance in Modern Society* (London: Sage, 2002). 29. *Humanité* defined in *Webster's Revised Unabridged Dictionary*, version published 1913 by the C. & G. Merriam Co. Springfield, MA, under the direction of Noah Porter, D.D., LL.D. This version is copyrighted © 1996, 1998 by MICRA, Inc. of Plainfield, NJ. American Heritage® Dictionary of the English Language, 3rd edition Copyright © 1996, 1992 by Houghton Mifflin Company.
58 Untitled, Gertrude Weil papers, 1879–1971. Private Collections 1488, NCDAH.
59 Stoler, *Race and the Education of Desire*, 68.
60 Dipankar Gupta, *Justice before Reconciliation: Negotiating a "New Normal" in Post-riot Mumbai and Ahmedabad* (New Delhi: Routledge, 2011), 13–15, 30–1. Gupta (personal communication) argues that Agamben's state of exception overlooks the tension in "democracies" between "people" and "citizens" and has limited relevance to modern democracies, which have this tension at their base. The state of exception comes through when democracies emphasize "people," hence "nationalism" over "citizens," which is about constitutional law and liberties. Because democracy can claim both as its own, whenever leaders find it difficult to respect citizenship, for whatever reason, they pull out the concept of the people and "the nation at peril" to stay in power. This then becomes the state of exception. Also see Giorgio Agamben, *Homo Sacer: Sovereign Power and Bare Life* (Stanford: Stanford University Press, 1998), 142.

61 See Roediger, *The Wages of Whiteness*, 167–81, especially 169, 171–2; "Race
Relations in 1927," box 255.26, Nell Battle Lewis Collection, Material
for "Incidentally" (Raleigh *News and Observer* column), "The Negro,"
NCDAH; Daniel Pick, *Faces of Degeneration: A European Disorder, c. 1848–
c. 1918* (Cambridge: Cambridge University Press, 1989), 4, 39. Robert
Proctor, "Nazi Medicine and the Politics of Knowledge," in Sandra
Harding, ed., *The Racial Economy of Science: Toward a Democratic Future*
(Bloomington: Indiana University Press, 1993).

62 Arendt argues that the politics of race is linked to the politics of death. For
Mbembe, racism functions in biopower to make the murderous functions
of the state – the selection of races, prohibition of mixed marriages,
forced sterilization, and killing – acceptable. Under modernity, this
involves perceptions of the other as a national danger, whose biophysical
elimination would strengthen whites' potential to life and security. The
sovereign right to kill through mechanisms of biopower is inscribed in
the function of modern states, and is constitutive of them. The state made
the sovereign right to kill coextensive with protection, management,
and nurturing of life. For a discussion of Arendt, race, and biopower, see
Mbembe, "Necropolitics," 17–18, 23.

63 Stoler, *Race and the Education of Desire*, 143. Also see Bernard Wishy, *The
Child and the Republic: The Dawn of Child Nurture* (Philadelphia: University
of Pennsylvania Press, 1967), 181.

64 Bush, *Who Gets a Childhood?* 16. Also see Stephen J. Gould, *Ontology and
Phylogeny* (Cambridge, MA: Harvard University Press, 1977), 49–51.

65 Hartman, *Scenes of Subjection*, 183–6.

66 Kayleen Oka, "Racism 'Renewed': Nationalist Practices, Citizenship and
Fantasy Post-9/11," in Leeno Karumanchery, ed., *Engaging Equity: New
Perspectives on Anti-Racist Education* (Calgary: Detselig, 2005), 27–40.

67 Gunnar Myrdal, *An American Dilemma: The Negro Problem and Modern
Democracy* (1944) (New Brunswick, NJ: Transaction Publishers, 1996), 35–6;
Stoler, *Haunted by Empire*, 11, 20.

68 Also see Cynthia R. Nielsen, "Resistance through Re-narration: Fanon on
De-constructing Racialized Subjectivities," *African Identities* 9(4) (2011): 363–85.

69 Ewa Płonowska Ziarek, "Bare Life on Strike: Notes on the Biopolitics of
Race and Gender," *South Atlantic Quarterly* 107(1) (Winter 2008): 93; Stoler,
Race and the Education of Desire, 89.

70 Despite general commonalities of political defeat and semi-colonial
economies, North Carolina is not representative of the South, and an
analysis of the entire, diverse region is beyond the scope of this book.
Anastasia Sims, *The Power of Femininity in the New South: Women's*

Organizations and Politics in North Carolina: 1880–1930 (Columbia: University of South Carolina Press, 1997), 3–4.

71 Stoler, *Haunted by Empire*, 7.

72 Ann Laura Stoler, *Along the Archival Grain: Epistemic Anxieties and Colonial Common Sense* (Princeton: Princeton University Press, 2009), 1–5; Stoler, *Haunted by Empire*, 6, 7, 16–17, 19. Archival records are from North Carolina repositories (North Carolina State Archives, Old Records Center, the Southern Historical Collection and North Carolina Collection at the University of North Carolina at Chapel Hill, and the private archives of the Samarcand Manor, Eagle Springs).

73 Strange and Loo, *Making Good*, 11.

74 For an excellent discussion of racism and national fantasy, see Oka, "Racism 'Renewed,'" 33; on disproportionate sentencing, see Kali Gross, *Colored Amazons: Crime, Violence, and Black Women in the City of Brotherly Love, 1880–1910* (Durham, NC: Duke University Press, 2006).

75 Baker encourages the critical juxtaposition of "the consumption of a pacified and out-of-the-way Indian in Wild West shows, World Fairs and museums … with the consumption of a dangerous and in-the-way Negro in blackface minstrelsy, professionally-promoted lynchings, and buffoon-saturated advertising." While museums and world fair organizers customarily rejected requests by African American groups to set up exhibits showcasing Black contributions, spectacles of Black and white racialization abounded in extra-legal lynchings, and later in show trials promoting Southern white lawfulness, civilization, and Anglo-Saxon supremacy. See Andrew R. Valint, "Fighting for Recognition: The Role African Americans played in World Fairs," MA thesis (Buffalo State, State University of New York, 2011); Elliott Rudwick and August Meier, "Black Man in the 'White City': Negroes and the Columbian Exposition, 1893," *Clark Atlanta University Journal* 26 (4) (1965): 354–61; Nancy Parezo and Don Fowler, "Assembling the Races of Mankind," in *Anthropology Goes to the Fair: The 1904 Louisiana Purchase Exposition* (Lincoln: University of Nebraska Press, 2007), 73–99. Pascal Blanchard, et al., eds, *Human Zoos: Science and Spectacle in the Age of Colonial Empires* (Liverpool: University of Liverpool Press, 2008).

76 Bruno Latour makes a compelling case for "doing anthropology at home." Latour, *We Have Never Been Modern*, 7, 100.

1 Swamp Island

1 City of Greensboro, North Carolina Juvenile Commission letterhead, 8 February 1939. NCDAH.

2 "Mrs. Bost Finds Girls Content at Samarcand: Discipline Is Excellent and Progress of Girls Under State's Care Is Good," Raleigh *News and Observer*, 26 March 1929.
3 North Carolina State Board of Charities and Public Welfare, "Swamp Island: A Study of Conditions in an Isolated Section of North Carolina" (1921), NC Division of Social Services, Department of Health and Human Services North Carolina, State Library of North Carolina, North Carolina Digital State Documents Collection, http://worldcat.org/oclc/16894888/viewonline.
4 Ibid., 4.
5 David Roediger, *How Race Survived U.S. History: From Settlement and Slavery to the Obama Phenomenon* (London: Verso, 2008), 25, 57–9. Also see Stoler, *Haunted by Empire*, 440;
6 North Carolina State Board of Charities and Public Welfare, "Swamp Island," 5–8.
7 Ibid., 13.
8 Ibid., 14–15.
9 Ibid., 13–15; Ann Jones, *Women Who Kill* (New York: The Feminist Press at CUNY, 2009), 70, 124–5.
10 Douglas Hay, "Foreword," in Carolyn Strange, ed., *Qualities of Mercy: Justice, Punishment, and Discretion* (Vancouver: UBC Press, 1996).
11 Michel Foucault, *"Society Must Be Defended": Lectures at the Collège de France, 1975–1976* (New York: Picador, 2003), 255.
12 Foucault, *History of Sexuality*, 139.
13 Ibid., 143.
14 Strange and Loo, *Making Good.* 60.
15 "Samarcand, Moral Life-Saving Station on Highway of N.C. Progress," *Durham Morning Herald*, 26 October 1924.
16 The case of Junius Wilson is illustrative. Wilson was accused, but not convicted, of raping a white woman in 1925, at the age of seventeen. Experts declared him "feebleminded" and castrated him before committing him to North Carolina's institution for the "colored insane" at Goldsboro. A lunacy jury had found him incompetent to stand trial, but in the 1970s psychologists concluded that he had never actually been mentally ill or "feebleminded." Wilson remained at the institution until 1994. His family twice, unsuccessfully, sought his release. When North Carolina state officials released him at the age of eighty-seven, Wilson was given a cottage on the grounds of the Cherry Hospital in Goldsboro as the state's way of making amends. Shirley Steinberg, "The Dialectics of Power: Understanding the Functionality of White Supremacy," in

Leeno Karumanchery, ed., *Engaging Equity: New Perspectives on Anti-Racist Education* (Calgary: Detselig, 2005), 15–16; Martha Waggoner, "Deaf-mute jailed unjustly for 69 years," *Toronto Star*, 1 February 1996, A4.

17 Wiley Hampton Swift, Committee, National Child Labor, *Child Welfare in North Carolina* (1918), reprint (London: Forgotten Books, 2013), 6–7.

18 Mariana Valverde, *The Age of Light, Soap and Water: Moral Reform in English Canada, 1885–1925* (Toronto: McClelland & Stewart Inc., 1991), 21.

19 Garland, *Punishment and Modern Society*, 5. Strange, *Qualities of Mercy*, 5–7; Strange and Loo, *Making Good*, 91–2. A Samarcand inmate's mother wrote to Commissioner Johnson, "I have one especial request, it is. I want an American flag United States flag, for this school I want it put up where it can be seen by all … I want to come away feeling like I have not left my child in England or Ireland but that the Stars and Stripes are waving over her … I would be proud to put it there all alone. If it meant doing without the necessities of life let alone the luxuries. But oh that I could not only do that but would to God that I could do my full share to make Samarcand 100% loyal to the things that Old Glory means and stand for. I shall begin to look for a flag suitable and if my means are enough I shall get it as soon as I can … I want the school made better for my child and for other children." Mrs Bettie Watts, Parkton, NC, to Kate Burr Johnson, commissioner of public welfare, 28 March 1929, State Board of Public Welfare, Institutions and Corrections, State Charitable, Penal and Correctional Institutions, *Samarcand Manor*, box 133, NCDAH (henceforth SBPWIC-SCPCI, *Samarcand Manor*); Private Collection 255.2, Nell Battle Lewis Papers, 1862; 1920–56. Correspondence, 1931–9.

20 Author's interview with Maud Wells, 17 April 1998, Raleigh, NC; Wiley Hampton Swift, Committee, National Child Labor, *Child Welfare in North Carolina* (1918), reprint (London: Forgotten Books, 2013), 6–7; Tindall, *The Emergence of the New South*, 433–72. Ann Stoler claims that the fear of middle class white sterility, like the degeneracy discourse, was not immediately concerned with the biological survival of whites. While numbers did matter, and white middle class individuals sought only "fit" marriage partners, the discourse on race suicide was mostly about safeguarding the privilege inherent in political viability and the survival of white middle class culture. Stoler, "Making Empire Respectable," 357, 363. Also see the literature on Fitter Family Contests in the Eugenics Archive, http://www.eugenicsarchive.org/eugenics/list2.pl, Cold Spring Harbor Laboratory, New York; Rose, "Authority and the Genealogy of Subjectivity."

21 Human zoos encompassed literal enclosures of humans in zoos, as well as freak shows, African exhibits housed in zoos and museums, and American

Wild West shows. Ota Benga's 1906 exhibition at the Bronx Zoo, Saartjie
Baartman's stint as the Hottentot Venus in nineteenth century Europe,
and Wild West shows, which staged an opposition between technological
American nationhood and "Indian savagery," are all examples of human
zoos. Nineteenth century human zoos offered "exotic" human specimens
to European anthropologists for scientific study, while also providing
spectacular exhibitions for public consumption and the production of
popular knowledge. For instance, before and after Baartman's early death,
Georges Cuvier studied her body for clues to supposed African atavism,
her remains housed at La Musée de l'Homme in Paris until recently. As
precursors to modern museums, seventeenth- and eighteenth-century
cabinets of curiosities (eclectic collections of flora and fauna) preceded human
zoos, appearing as a conjunction of political, social, and economic factors. See
Anne Fausto-Sterling, "Gender, Race and Nation: The Comparative Anatomy
of 'Hottentot' Women in Europe, 1815–1817," in J. Terry and J. Urla, eds,
Deviant Bodies: Critical Perspectives on Difference in Science and Popular Culture
(Bloomington: Indiana University Press, 1995); Blanchard et al., eds, *Human
Zoos: Science and Spectacle in the Age of Colonial Empires.*

22 Ring, *The Problem South*, 84.

23 Ibid., 45.

24 The workers, he argued, were "being reduced to a state of childish
impotence where they have to be taken care of and where they produce
nothing." Ring, *The Problem South*, 148. Frank Tannenbaum, *The Darker
Phases of the South* (New York: G.P. Putnam's Sons, 1924), 40, 57.

25 Burton J. Hendrick, *The Life and Letters of Walter H. Page, Volume I* (New
York: Doubleday, Page and Co., 1923; EBook #17017, 2005, http://www.
gwpda.org/memoir/Page/PageTC.htm), 75–6.

26 Lauren Berlant, *The Queen of America Goes to Washington City* (Durham,
NC: Duke University Press, 1997), 4; Michel Foucault, *"Society Must Be
Defended,"* 61, 103; Matthew Frye Jacobson, "Barbarian Virtues: The U.S.
Encounters Foreign Peoples at Home and Abroad, 1876–1917" (New
York: Hill and Wang 2001), 223. North Carolina State Board of Charities
and Public Welfare, "Swamp Island," 4; Mbembe, "Necropolitics," 18, 23;
Stoler, *Race and the Education of Desire*, 89; Anne McClintock, "Paranoid
Empire: Specters from Guantánamo and Abu Ghraib," *Small Axe* 13 (1)
(no. 28) (March 2009): 55; Jacobson, *Barbarian Virtues*, 4; Oka, "Racism
'Renewed,'" 30.

27 McClintock, *Imperial Leather*, 46.

28 On degeneration, sexuality, and empire, see McClintock, *Imperial
Leather*, 47, 53, 56; Ella Shohat and Robert Stam, *Unthinking Eurocentrism:*

Multiculturalism and the Media (New York: Routledge, 1994); Sander
L. Gilman, *Difference and Pathology* (Ithaca: Cornell University Press,
1985), 107; Patrick Brantlinger, "Victorians and Africans: The Genealogy
of the Myth of the Dark Continent," *Critical Inquiry* 12 (1) (Autumn
1985); Gilman, "Black Bodies, White Bodies," 194; Stoler, *Race and the
Education of Desire*, 31, 41, 48; Michel Foucault, *The Order of Things: An
Archaeology of the Human Sciences* (London: Routledge, 1970), 168. Also
see Foucault, *Power/Knowledge: Selected Interviews and Other Writings,
1972–1977* (New York: Vintage, 1980), 197; Ann Laura Stoler, "Making
Empire Respectable: The Politics of Race and Sexual Morality in Twentieth
Century Colonial Cultures," in Anne McClintock, Aamir Mufti, and Ella
Shohat, eds, *Dangerous Liaisons: Gender, Nation, & Postcolonial Perspectives*
(Minneapolis: University of Minnesota Press, 1997), 346; Strange and Loo,
Making Good, 94; Gilman, "'I'm Down on Whores,'" 240, 248; Pick, *Faces of
Degeneration*,105.

29 Johanna Schoen, *Choice and Coercion: Birth Control, Sterilization, and
Abortion in Public Health and Welfare* (Chapel Hill: University of North
Carolina Press, 2005), 82–3; Foucault, *History of Sexuality*, 140–1,
143–4; Strange and Loo, Making *Good*, 63, 93; Stoler, "Making Empire
Respectable," 349; Ring, *The Problem South*, 138; McClintock, *Imperial
Leather*, 47. Nira Yuval-Davis, *Gender and Nation* (London: Sage,
1997), 23; Louis Montrose, "The Work of Gender in the Discourse
of Discovery," *Representations* 33 (1991): 1–41. Lauren Berlant, The
Anatomy of National Fantasy: Hawthorne, Utopia and Everyday Life
(Chicago: University of Chicago Press, 1991), 30–5; Yuval-Davis,
Gender and Nation, 26–37.

30 "What Is the State Board of Public Welfare?"; Stoler, "Making Empire
Respectable," 357, 363; Eugenics Archive, DNA Learning Center, Cold
Spring Harbor Laboratory, New York, http://www.eugenicsarchive.org/
eugenics/list2.pl.

31 "Information in Regard to Eugenical Sterilization in North Carolina."
Legal reference: Chapter 224, Public Laws 1933. Eugenics Board of North
Carolina, undated, untitled, p. 2. Samarcand private archives; Oka,
"Racism 'Renewed,'" 39.

32 Eugenics sterilization supporters were not concerned about the
reproduction of Blacks prior to their joining the welfare state and costing
it money. Johanna Schoen, *Choice and Coercion: Birth Control, Sterilization,
and Abortion in Public Health and Welfare* (Chapel Hill: University of
North Carolina Press, 2005), 82–3; Foucault, *History of Sexuality*, 140–1,
143–4; Strange and Loo, Making *Good*, 63, 93; Stoler, "Making Empire

Respectable," 349; Ring, *The Problem South*, 138; McClintock, *Imperial Leather*, 47. Nira Yuval-Davis, *Gender and Nation* (London: Sage, 1997), 23, 26–37; Louis Montrose, "The Work of Gender in the Discourse of Discovery," *Representations* 33 (1991): 1–41. Lauren Berlant, *The Anatomy of National Fantasy: Hawthorne, Utopia and Everyday Life* (Chicago: University of Chicago Press, 1991), 30–5.

33 North Carolina sterilization records, NCDAH.

34 Douglas Baynton, "Disability and the Justification of Inequality in American History," in Paul K. Longmore and Lauri Umansky, eds, *The New Disability History: American Perspectives* (New York: New York University Press, 2001), 33–57.

35 "What Is the State Board of Public Welfare?"

36 McClintock, *Imperial Leather*, 46–7; Stoler, "Tense and Tender Ties," 24.

37 Ring, *The Problem South*, 33, 38, 172; McClintock, *Imperial Leather*, 8, 59, 207–31.

38 Donita Summerlin, "How the Beauty of Samarcand May Affect My Life," Samarcand Scrapbook, Samarcand Private Archives. Address by Superintendent Grace M. Robson, Samarcand Manor, n.d., 2.; Strange and Loo, *Making Good*, 80.

39 "What Is the State Board of Public Welfare?"

40 W. Curtis Ezell, director, Division of Institutions and Corrections to Supt. L.L. Boyd, 21 September 1937, box 163, file: Morrison Training School, 1937–9; Strange and Loo, *Making Good*, 5, 60; Odem, *Delinquent Daughters*, 1.

41 Mary P. Ryan, *Civic Wars: Democracy and Public Life in the American City during the Nineteenth Century* (Berkeley: University of California Press, 1997), 296; Stoler, "Tense and Tender Ties," 36, 46, 48–9; Feld, *Bad Kids*, 44.

42 William S. Bush, *Who Gets a Childhood? Race and Juvenile Justice in Twentieth Century Texas* (Athens: University of Georgia Press, 2010), 13; Stoler, "Tense and Tender Ties," 841–4.

43 "Swamp Island: A study of Conditions in an Isolated Section of North Carolina," 14–15.

44 In ancient texts, Indic peoples referred to foreigners as *Mleccha*, as barbarians and "dirty ones." More recently, the term has implied those with bad hygiene. Personal hygiene was extrapolated to imperialism and Anglo-Saxon "civilization."

45 Romila Thapar, "The Image of the Barbarian in Early India," *Comparative Studies in Society and History* 13 (1971); McClintock, *Imperial Leather*, 211, 214, 226.

46 McClintock, *Imperial Leather*, 211.

47 Ibid., 214.

48 Hartman, "From Daniel Boone to the Beverly Hillbillies," 49, 70, 76. Also see Richard Louis Dugdale, *The Jukes: A Study in Crime, Pauperism, Disease and Heredity* (New York: G.P. Putnam's Sons, 1910; W.E. Barton, "Work among the American Highlanders," *The American Missionary*, December 1898; Stoler, "Tense and Tender Ties," 4, 10. Ring, The *Problem South*, 43, 53.

49 Ring, *The Problem South*, 154.

50 Feld, *Bad Kids*, 47–8; Stoler, "Tense and Tender Ties," 7, 15, 17.

51 "Samarcand, Moral Life-Saving Station on Highway of N.C. Progress," *Durham Morning Herald*, 26 October 1924.

52 Bernstein, *Lost Children of Wilder*, 20–1.

53 Neither were single professional and various other categories of women permitted to migrate, because they fell outside of the accepted criteria of respectability for European colonial women – as custodians of family welfare and as subordinate supporters of colonial men. Stoler, "Making Empire Respectable," 346, 355, 358; Robyn Wiegman, *American Anatomies: Theorizing Race and Gender* (Durham, NC: Duke University Press, 1995), 59–60; McClintock, *Imperial Leather*, 47.

54 "North Carolina Fails," *Rocky Mount Telegram*, n.d., Nell Battle Lewis Papers, Private Collection 255, box 162, NCDAH. Gilman, "I'm Down on Whores," 254–6; Stoler, "Making Empire Respectable," 362, 364; Ring, *The Problem South*, 170.

55 Sandra Gunning, *Race, Rape and Lynching* (London: Oxford University Press, 1996), 26–7; Yuval-Davis, *Gender and Nation*, 26–37; McClintock, *Imperial Leather*, 47. Louis Montrose, "The Work of Gender in the Discourse of Discovery," *Representations* 33 (1991): 1–41. Lauren Berlant, The *Anatomy of National Fantasy: Hawthorne, Utopia and Everyday Life* (Chicago: University of Chicago Press, 1991), 30–5; Strange and Loo, *Making Good*, 63. "*Samarcand Manor*," October 1918, by Mrs J.R. Chamberlain, secretary of the board of directors, in *State Journals*, clipping file through 1975, North Carolina Collection, University of Chapel Hill Library, Chapel Hill, NC.

56 Stoler, "Making Empire Respectable," 20.

57 Strange and Loo, *Making Good*, 70. Victoria Bynum, *Unruly Women: The Politics of Social and Sexual Control in the Old South* (Chapel Hill: University of North Carolina Press, 1992), 104. Also see Stoler, "Making Empire Respectable," 347; Valverde, *The Age of Light, Soap and Water*, 20.

58 Hubert L. Dreyfus and Paul Rabinow, *Michel Foucault: Beyond Structuralism and Hermeneutics* (New York: Routledge, 2013), 141.

59 Gilman, "'I'm Down on Whores,'" 248; McClintock, *Imperial Leather*, 40–1.

60 "Samarcand Manor: Its Place in State Government and the Needs of the Young Girls as They Leave the Institution," n.d., Samarcand private archives, *Samarcand Manor*, Eagle Springs, NC.

61 Although vigilante lynch mobs initially focused upon protecting white women from well-to-do families, they eventually extended regulatory protection to poor whites too. Thus, it is somewhat erroneous to assume that white middle class versions of sexual propriety held few or no benefits for poor whites because they could and did get status from being white and pure. Many poor whites were members of the second-wave Ku Klux Klan. I am grateful to Mariana Valverde for this point. Bush, *Who Gets a Childhood?* 23; "Samarcand, Moral Life-Saving Station on Highway of N.C. Progress"; Mary Odem, *Delinquent Daughters: Protecting and Policing Adolescent Female Sexuality in the United States, 1885–1920* (Chapel Hill: University of North Carolina Press, 1995), 95–6, 99, 102; Stoler, *Race and the Education of Desire*, 42, 96, 102.

62 Correspondence from Mrs Bettie Watts, Parkton, NC, to Kate Burr Johnson.

63 Gunning, *Race, Rape and Lynching*, 27.

64 G. Balfour, "Introduction: Regulating Women and Girls," in Gillian Balfour and Elizabeth Comack, eds, *Criminalizing Women: Gender and Injustice in Neo-liberal Times* (Halifax: Fernwood Publishing, 2006), 156.

65 "Mrs. Bost Finds Girls Content at Samarcand."

66 Correspondence from Mrs Bettie Watts, Parkton, NC, to Kate Burr Johnson, box; "Current Population: Girls in Institution 10 years of age and under (1–2 April 1931)," Folder "Samarcand Manor, 1931," State Board of Public Welfare, Institutions, and Correction (SBPWIC) – Samarcand, box 164, Old Records Center, North Carolina State Archives (ORC-NCSA).

67 Chap. 254, Public Laws of North Carolina, 1917. This proviso was later repealed in 1919. Strange and Loo, *Making Good*, 97.

68 J. Ehringhaus to Commissioner Bost, 13 January 1933, box 161 MTS, file 1927–34, ORC-NCSA; Strange and Loo, *Making Good*, 70.

69 "A Glimpse of Life at *Samarcand Manor*" (1920), Samarcand private archives, *Samarcand Manor*, Eagle Springs, NC.

70 Ibid.

71 Steinberg, "The Dialectics of Power," 26.

72 Bush, *Who Gets a Childhood?* 17–18; Stoler, "Tense and Tender Ties," 4; Oka, "Racism 'Renewed,'" 39; Ian Hacking, "Making up People," *London Review of Books*, 17 August 2006; Michel Foucault, "Governmentality," in G. Burchell and P. Miller, eds, *The Foucault Effect: Studies in Governmentality* (Chicago: University of Chicago Press, 1991), 87–104.

73 Nikolas Rose, *The Psychological Complex: Psychology, Politics and Society in England 1869–1939* (London: Routledge and Kegan Paul, 1985); Nikolas

Rose, *Governing the Soul: The Shaping of the Private Self* (London: Routledge, 1990).

74 "A Glimpse of Life at *Samarcand Manor*"; Kathryn Pauly Morgan, "Foucault, Ugly Ducklings and TechnoSwans: Analyzing Fat Hatred, Weight Loss Surgery and Compulsory Biomedicalized Aesthetics in America," *International Journal of Feminist Approaches to Bioethics* 4 (1), Special issue: Feminist Perspectives on Ethics in Psychiatry (Spring 2011): 188–220.

75 Even the state penitentiary appeared relatively late in North Carolina, in 1846, an event marked by enormous controversy over the centralized state power it would generate. See Edward L. Ayers, *Vengeance and Justice: Crime and Punishment in the Nineteenth-Century American South* (New York: Oxford University Press, 1984), 48–55. On local republicanism and the emergence of modern legal justice in the American South, see Ayers, *Vengeance and Justice,* 18–19, 31–2; Odem, *Delinquent Daughters,* 96, 99; Stoler, "Making Empire Respectable," 357; Foner, *A Short History of Reconstruction,* xiv, 9, 13, 21.

76 Nathans, *The Quest for Progress,* 5, 10; Pratt, *Punishment and Civilization,* 29; Garland, *Punishment and Modern Society,* 19; Strange, *Qualities of Mercy;* McWilliams, *The New South Faces the World,* 9–10; Vann Woodward, *Origins of the New South, 1877–1913,* 148, 153.

77 Grace Reeder, Stonewall Jackson Training School parole report, 12 July 1921, box 166, SBPWIC-SCPCI, State Farm for Women, Jackson Training School, Stonewall Jackson Training School (SJTS), n.d., 1917–22. Bush, *Who Gets a Childhood?* 23.

78 Mariana Valverde, "Editor's Introduction," in M. Valverde, ed., *Studies in Moral Regulation* (Toronto: Centre of Criminology, 1994); George L. Mosse, *Nationalism and Sexuality: Respectability and Abnormal Sexuality in Modern Europe* (New York: Howard Fertig, 1985). Correspondence from A. MacNaughton to the president of the board of directors of Samarcand, SBPWIC-SCPCI, *Samarcand Manor.*

79 Stoler, "Making Empire Respectable," 346, 355, 358; Stoler, *Race and the Education of Desire,* 143; also see Ring, *The Problem South,* 133, 137.

80 Stoler, "Tense and Tender Ties," 24.

81 The results were varied. Some girls would report back, sharing news of their marriages, or employment as domestics after discharge, but this was exceptional. Many young women, like Mamie King, "went to pieces immediately after final discharge and [were] now acting disgracefully in Troy." Bernstein, *Lost Children of Wilder,* 21.

82 Bush, *Who Gets a Childhood?* 15; Nell Battle Lewis, "Incidentally," Raleigh *News and Observer,* n.d.

83 Interview of resident of Carthage, North Carolina, by author, March 1995. Name withheld by request.
84 "A Glimpse of Life at Samarcand Manor."
85 Quoted in Nell Battle Lewis, "Samarcand Not Different from World of Humanity," Raleigh *News and Observer*, 20 November 1926.
86 "Samarcand Manor: Its Place in State Government and the Needs of the Young Girls as They Leave the Institution," n.d. Samarcand private archives, *Samarcand Manor*, Eagle Springs, NC.
87 Odem, *Delinquent Daughters*, 102.
88 The state also might remove unmanageable children in collusion with parents. It is important to keep the power of the state in perspective. For a discussion of this, see Strange and Loo, *Making Good*, 5; "Samarcand Manor," Samarcand private archives; Odem, *Delinquent Daughters*, 102.
89 "Samarcand Like a Well Run Boarding School," *Public Welfare Progress* (Raleigh, NC), November 1923, no. 7.2, Welfare Department, box 255.28, Nell Battle Lewis Papers.
90 David J. Rothman, "The State as Parent: Social Policy in the Progressive Era," in Willard Gaylin, Ira Glasser, Steven Marcus, and David Rothman, eds, *Doing Good: The Limits of Benevolence* (New York: Pantheon, 1978), 81–2.
91 Author interview with Maud Wells, April 1998, Raleigh, NC.
92 J. Wallace Nygard, director, to Mary Ellen Forbes, superintendent of public welfare, Tarboro, NC, box 163, file: Morrison Training School, 1937–9. Strange and Loo, *Making Good*, 96.
93 Odem, *Delinquent Daughters*, 111; Strange and Loo, *Making Good*, 96.
94 Interview of resident of Sandhill Section, NC, by author, March 1998. Name withheld by request.
95 Ibid., *Bad Kids*, 62; David Garland, *Punishment and Modern Society: A Study in Social Theory* (Chicago: University of Chicago Press, 1990), 201–2.
96 Bernstein, *Lost Children of Wilder*, 21; N.C. Code of 1921, sec. 7330, 7334.
97 Strange and Loo, *Making Good*, 96.
98 Rothman, "The State as Parent," 80.
99 Feld, *Bad Kids*, 49, 52–6, 62–4.
100 Gilman, "I'm Down on Whores," 254–6.
101 Strange and Loo, *Making Good*, 10.
102 Ibid., 25.
103 "Samarcand, an Interpretation," clipping, n.d., Samarcand Manor private archives.
104 Anne Russell and Melton McLaurin, *The Wayward Girls of Samarcand: A True Story of the American South* (Bradley Creek Press, 2012), 237.

105 I wish to thank Jo Huddleston for sharing this story with me, and for her permission to include it in this book. "There's nothing to be ashamed of in this story, and there's already been too much secrecy surrounding this situation." Correspondence from Jo Huddleston to author, 9 January 2015.

106 Ibid.

107 "Forrester Children Taken from Mother," *Durham Morning Herald*, 5 February 1922.

108 "Family Troubles Were Ironed Out," *Durham Morning Herald*, 6 December 1922.

109 Correspondence from Jo Huddleston to author.

110 Ibid.

111 Ibid.

112 "Samarcand Girls Given Chance to Prove Worth to Society," *Charlotte News*, 13 May 1946.

113 Anonymous, to Mr. Gill, October 1936, SBPWIC-SCPCI, *Samarcand Manor*, 1918–24, Restricted records, box 133, NCDAH.

114 Agnes B. MacNaughton, superintendent, "Parole Report," Samarcand Manor, Folder "Samarcand Manor, 1931."

115 "Effects of the Operation," Eugenics Record Office, Cold Spring Harbor, Long Island, NY, 21 February 1934. Folder "Samarcand Manor, 1931."

116 Feld, *Bad Kids*, 49, 52–6, 62–4.

117 Russell and McLaurin, *The Wayward Girls of Samarcand*, 237.

118 Ibid., 237.

119 Ibid., 238.

2 The Samarcand Arson Case

1 Pearl Stiles to Governor Gardner, n.d. 1931, box 162, Samarcand Arson Case, Restricted Records. Also see Nell Battle Lewis Papers, Private Collection 255, box 162, NCDAH (hereafter Lewis Papers).

2 "Says She Caused the $200,000 Blaze," *News and Observer*, 24 March 1931.

3 Measuringworth.com, http://www.measuringworth.com/calculators/ppowerus/. According to Wertheimer, the *News and Observer* estimated the damage at double this amount. John Wertheimer, Brian Luskey, et al. "'Escape of the match-strikers': Disorderly North Carolina Women, the Legal System, and the Samarcand Arson Case of 1931," *North Carolina Historical Review* 75 (1998): 444. Samarcand's total yearly appropriations were $90,000. The property was insured for less than $30,000. On Thursday, 12 March 1931, the same night as the Samarcand arson, two boys set fire to the Stonewall Jackson Training School for [white] Boys across the state,

using the same method. News of the blazes would be made public the following morning, Friday the 13th. Unlike with the Samarcand incident, reporters barely noticed the Stonewall Jackson arson attempt. Judge Walter E. Moore presided on 25 April 1931, and the court sentenced Edward Eggers to the juvenile department of the state's prison for a term of one year. The jury found John Durham not guilty on 21 April 1931. Cabarrus County Superior Court, Minute Docket, 1930–3, C. R. 016.311.18, vol. 16.

4 Lewis interview of Margaret Abernethy, age 16. "Samarcand Information Collected by Nell Battle Lewis," Lewis Papers.

5 Lewis interview of Estelle Wilson, age 16. Ibid.

6 "The Samarcand Arson Case, Carthage, N.C. May 18th 1931." Lewis Papers. Josephine French, Dolores Seawell, Margaret Pridgen, Wilma Owens, and Bertha Hall were the first to go to jail; North Carolina Code, of 1931, article 15, #4238; Lewis interview of Virginia Hayes, age 16; Lewis interview of Josephine French, age 15. Interview of Miss Ross, Matron of Chamberlain Hall, "Samarcand Information Collected by Nell Battle Lewis"; "Samarcand Girls Held Here on Arson Charge," *Moore County News*, 19 March 1931, NCDAH.

7 Samarcand documentation comes from the following sources: Lewis Papers; Records of SBPWIC, located at NCDAH and the Old Record Center, NCDAH (ORC-NCDAH); Susan Pearson, "Samarcand, Nell Battle Lewis, and the 1931 Arson Trial," Undergraduate honors essay (1989, unpublished), North Carolina Collection, University of North Carolina Library, Chapel Hill; Samarcand Manor archives, Samarkand Manor School, Eagle Springs, NC. Information, testimony, and statements by Lewis in her working notebook, "Samarcand Arson Case, Carthage, N.C. May 18th 1931," Nell Battle Lewis Papers.

8 Lewis interview of Marian Mercer, age 15. Information, testimony, and statements by Lewis in "Samarcand Arson Case."

9 "Samarcand Arson Case."

10 Ibid.

11 *News and Observer*, 17 March 1931; *Charlotte Observer*, 17 March 1931; *New York Times*, 17 March 1931; "Samarcand Information collected by NBL."

12 "Says She Caused the $200,000 Blaze," *News and Observer*, 24 March 1931; "Special Bill Passed in Samarcand Matter," *News and Observer*, 2 May 1931; "Rioting Girls Spread Terror through Prison: Feminine Inmates Attack Guards and Officers with Pieces of Broken Glass from the Windows," *The Daily Advance*, 16 April 1931; McNeill to Lewis, 30 April 1931, in "Correspondence, 1931–1939" folder, NBL, PC255, box 162, NCDAH. "Samarcand Girls," *Moore County News*, 30 April 1931.

13 Hay, "Foreword," in Strange, *Qualities of Mercy*, vii.

14 Letter to the editor, *News and Observer*, from Mrs Bettie Watts, Parkton, NC, n.d., Samarcand Arson Case. Lewis Papers, folder "Samarcand Manor, 1931," SBPWIC – Samarcand, box 164, ORC-NCSA.

15 Smith, "Civilized People Don't Want to See That Kind of Thing," 27; Norbert Elias, *The History of Manners*, vol. 1, *The Civilizing Process*, trans. Edmund Jephcott (New York: Pantheon, 1978), chap. 2.

16 Ayers, *Vengeance and Justice*, 44.

17 Guion G. Johnson, *Ante-Bellum North Carolina: A Social History* (Chapel Hill: University of North Carolina Press, 1937), 652.

18 Wiley B. Sanders, ed., *Juvenile Offenders for a Thousand Years: Selected Readings from Anglo-Saxon Times to 1900* (Chapel Hill: University of North Carolina Press, 1970), 412–13, 418.

19 Victor Streib, "Death Penalty for Female Offenders," *University of Cincinnati Law Review* 58 (1990): 848–9, 855–67. Also see Clark County Prosecuting Attorney, "The Death Penalty," http://www.clarkprosecutor. org/html/death/timeline.htm.

20 Annette Bickford, "The Merciful Executioner: Spectacles of Sexual Danger and National Reunification in the Case of George Stinney, 1944," *Southern Anthropologist* 35 (1) (2010): 41–61. Jones, *Women Who Kill*, 59; Sanders, *Juvenile Offenders for a Thousand Years*, 320–1; Streib, "Death Penalty for Female Offenders," 848–9, 855–67.

21 Jones, *Women Who Kill*, 46, 63, 76, 285, 295–7.

22 Ibid., 84–6, 285.

23 Strange, *Qualities of Mercy*, 12–13.

24 See Nell Battle Lewis, "Incidentally," "Our Official Slaughter Record," *News and Observer*, 3 February 1935, Lewis Papers. State Department of Public Welfare, "Capital Punishment in North Carolina"; Bess Davenport Thompson, "Twelve Samarcand Girls Get State Prison Terms – 18 Months to 5-Year Indeterminate Sentence Imposed," *News and Observer*, 21 May 1931, Lewis Papers; Nell Battle Lewis, "Incidentally," "North Carolina at Its Worst," *News and Observer*, 1 June 1953; Ayers, *Vengeance and Justice*, 55.

25 Susan Cahn, "Spirited Youth or Friends Incarnate: The Samarcand Arson Case and Female Adolescence in the American South," *Journal of Women's History* 94 (1998): 157, 166, 171–2. Also see Odem, *Delinquent Daughters*. Cahn and Wertheimer do not focus on race in their analyses of the Samarcand arson case.

26 Wertheimer et al., "'Escape of the match-strikers,'" 448, 452, 459.

27 Ibid., 447–8. Pearl Stiles, age 15, to Governor Gardner, n.d. 1931, box 162, NCDAH, "Samarcand Arson Case."

28 Wertheimer, "'Escape of the match-strikers,'" 447–9. "The State as Defendant," *Greensboro News*, 21 May 1931. State Board of Public Welfare, Institutions and Corrections, State Charitable Penal and Correctional Institutions, *Samarcand Manor*, 1918–24, box 133, NCDAH.

29 Smith, "Civilized People Don't Want to See That Kind of Thing," 38.

30 Douglas Linder, "Who is Clarence Darrow?" 1997. http://law2.umkc.edu/faculty/projects/ftrials/daresy.htm.

31 Thompson, "Twelve Samarcand Girls Get State Prison Terms." Also see "Defense Holds Samarcand Girls Victims of State Neglect," *News and Observer*, 20 May 1931.

32 Strange, *Qualities of Mercy*, 7; Ann Jones, *Women Who Kill*, 36.

33 Barry Wright, "The Politics of Pardons and the Upper Canada Rebellion," in Strange, *Qualities of Mercy*, 85.

34 Stuart Hall, quoted in O'Leary, *To Die For*, 4.

35 Smith, "Civilized People Don't Want to See That Kind of Thing," 24.

36 Strange, *Qualities of Mercy*, 5.

37 While no actual trial transcript survives, Anne Russell recreates it in a dramatic narrative that closely adheres to the historical record. Russell interviewed members of defendant Margaret Pridgen's family in Wilmington, offering valuable insight into the young defendant's experiences at Samarcand. Russell, *The Wayward Girls of Samarcand*. Archival records include Samarcand's *June 30, 1930–1932 Biennial Report* and its 50th anniversary pamphlet, *1918–1968, 50th Anniversary, Samarcand Manor*, in the North Carolina Collection in the University of North Carolina's Wilson Library. Scrapbooks and photographs were obtained from Samarcand's private archives, housed at the institution.

38 Jeanne Flavin, *Our Bodies, Our Crimes: The Policing of Women's Reproduction in America* (New York: New York University Press, 2008), 200 n. 32, 208 n. 51; Schoen, *Choice and Coercion*, 82; Russell, *The Wayward Girls of Samarcand*, 82–4, 87, 236, 238, 242.

39 Her column "Incidentally" began as a response contesting prevailing notions of Southern white womanhood, and ran in Raleigh's *News & Observer* from 1921 until Lewis's death in 1956. Nell Battle Lewis to Lisbeth Parrott, 2 May 1931, quoted in Susan Pearson, "Samarcand, Nell Battle Lewis, and the 1931 Arson Trial," undergraduate honors essay (unpublished, 1989), 36, 38, 42, 50–1; Lewis, "Incidentally": "Our Official Slaughter Record," *News and Observer*, 3 February 1935, Lewis Papers. State Department of Public Welfare, "Capital Punishment in North Carolina."

The year 1931 marked a juncture for Lewis, who renounced her earlier
liberal politics and became an archconservative. After the Samarcand
trial, Lewis fell ill and took a couple of years away for recuperation.
Upon her return to writing in 1933 her column reflected a marked shift in
perspective. She returned to long skirts, replacing her earlier passion for
prison reform with an interest in the supernatural. She became "militantly
negrophobic" and joined the White Citizen's Council Movement. See
Pearson, "Samarcand, Nell Battle Lewis and the 1931 Arson Case," 44–5.
When Lewis celebrated the 25th anniversary of her column in 1956, she
characterized the earlier "Battling Nell" as "a very, very callow, half-
baked liberal" who didn't know enough. "I was a South-saver," she said.
"I wanted to lift the South up in all directions and was very critical of it
in every respect." *News and Observer*, "December 29, 1991 Bicentennial
Special / Early 20th Century Raleigh 200" by Treva Jones (http://files.
usgwarchives.net/nc/wake/bicen/nell.txt); H.L. Canfield to Nell Battle
Lewis, 19 May 1931, Lewis Papers. Cahn, "Spirited Youth or Friends
Incarnate,"160.

40 Jones, *Women Who Kill*, 59–60; Gunning, *Race, Rape, and Lynching*, 26–7;
Garland, *Punishment and Modern Society*, 19. On gender policing in
the criminal justice system, see Helen Boritch, "Women in Prison,"
in John Winterdyk, ed., *Corrections in Canada: Social Reactions to Crime*
(Toronto: Prentice Hall, 2001), 213–37; Streib, "Death Penalty for
Female Offenders," 878–9. Karlene Faith and Jasmin Jiwani, "The Social
Construction of 'Dangerous' Girls and Women," in Bernard Schissel and
Carolyn Brooks, eds, *Marginality and Condemnation: An Introduction to
Critical Criminology* (Halifax: Fernwood, 2008), 135–61; Barbara Hudson,
"Punishment and Control," in Mike Maguire, Rod Morgan, and Robert
Reiner, eds, *The Oxford Handbook of Criminology*, 3rd ed. (London: Oxford
University Press, 2002), 234–62; Lisa Neve and Kim Pate, "Challenging
the Criminalization of Women Who Resist," in Julia Sudbury, ed., *Global
Lockdown: Race, Gender, and the Prison-Industrial Complex* (Routledge:
New York, 2005), 19–32; Cheryl Meyer and Michelle Oberman, *Mothers
Who Kill Their Children: Understanding the Acts of Moms from Susan Smith
to the "Prom Mom"* (New York: New York University Press, 2001), 1–18,
68–95.

41 Gunning, *Race, Rape, and Lynching*, 27.

42 Hartman, "From Daniel Boone to the Beverly Hillbillies," 42; Gilman, "'I'm
Down on Whores,'" 248.

43 "Samarcand Girls Held Here on Arson Charge," *Moore County News*, 19
March 1931, Lewis Papers; Streib, "Death Penalty for Female Offenders,"

878–9; "Samarcand Girls Not Fiends Incarnate, It Is Believed, In Spite of Recent Outbreak," *Daily Advance*, 22 April 1931. See also Kathryn Hinojosa Baker, "Delinquent Desire: Race, Sex and Ritual in Reform Schools for Girls," *Discourse* 15 (1) (Fall 1992).

44 Lewis's notebook includes a record of events pertinent to the case, calls, correspondence, mental tests results, possible defence witnesses, data collected at Samarcand, and data on each defendant organized under headings such as: age, birthplace, home, parents (including alleged morality of), brothers and sisters, diseases, education, occupation, date committed to Samarcand, reason for commitment, like Samarcand? attempts to escape, whippings, previous trouble, relations with men, knowledge of fires, confession, appearance, data in files at Samarcand, and mental condition. Lewis Papers; "Sidelights on the Samarcand Arson Case," *Moore County News*, 28 May 1931.

45 "Samarcand Girls Not Fiends Incarnate."

46 "Rebellious Girls Set Their Bunks Afire to Get Thrill," *News and Observer*, 2 May 1931.

47 "Samarcand Girls Not Fiends Incarnate."

48 Nell Battle Lewis, "Incidentally," "North Carolina at Its Worst," *News and Observer*, 1 June 1953, Lewis Papers.

49 "Samarcand Girls Not Fiends Incarnate."

50 "Sidelights on the Samarcand Arson Case."

51 "Defense Holds Samarcand Girls Victims State Neglect," *News and Observer*, 20 May 1931; "Bad Conditions at Samarcand," *Chapel Hill Weekly*, 29 May 1931; "Samarcand Girls Are Quietly Awaiting News of Their Fate," *Moore County News*, 7 May 1931; Thompson, "Twelve Samarcand Girls Get State Prison Terms"; letter to the editor of the *Fayetteville Observer*, May 4 1931, Lewis Papers; Bess Davenport Thompson, "Defense Holds Samarcand Girls Victims State Neglect," *News and Observer*, 20 May 1931.

52 Wertheimer, "'Escape of the match-strikers,'" 450; Cahn, "Spirited Youth or Friends Incarnate," 152–80; Lewis, "North Carolina at Its Worst." Also see Thompson, "Twelve Samarcand Girls Get State Prison Terms"; *Charlotte Observer*, 20 May 1931. "Sidelights on the Samarcand Arson Case"; "The Samarcand Girls," *The Prison News*, 1 July 1931; *The Charlotte Observer*, n.d., quoted in The North Carolina Court System, http://www.nccourts. org/Courts/Appellate/Supreme/Portrait/Portrait.asp?Name=Schenck. Governor Gardner appointed Schenck to a commission to amend the state constitution in 1931, and he became associate justice of the North Carolina State Supreme Court in 1934; untitled news clipping, 30 May 1931, Nell

Battle Lewis Papers, PC 255, box 162, NCDAH; Criminal Judgements, Docket "G" #4823, p. 43, Clerk of Court, Carthage, NC, before Honorable Judge Michael Schenck, 18 March1931; "Neglect of Girls," *Moore County News*, 21 May 1931, Lewis Papers; Thompson, "Defense Holds Samarcand Girls Victims State Neglect."

53 Thompson, "Defense Holds Samarcand Girls Victims State Neglect."
54 For an excellent discussion and critique of diminished criminal responsibility, see Tina Loo, "Savage Mercy: Native Culture and the Modification of Capital Punishment in Nineteenth-Century British Columbia," in Strange, ed., *Qualities of Mercy*, 104–29. Samarcand Arson Case, Carthage, NC, box "Defense Holds Samarcand Girls Victims State Neglect."
55 Lewis interview of Estelle Wilson, age 16, Lewis Papers; Thompson, "Twelve Samarcand Girls Get State Prison Terms"; "North Carolina Fails." Folder "Samarcand Manor, 1931," SBPWIC – Samarcand, box 164, ORC-NCSA; "Samarcand Girls Not Fiends Incarnate, box."
56 Many such remarks were recorded verbatim by Nell Battle Lewis in "The Samarcand Arson Case"; "The State as Defendant." SBPWIC-SCPCI, *Samarcand Manor*, 1918–24, box 133, NCDAH. Margaret Pridgen, quoted by Lewis, "The Samarcand Arson Case."
57 Statement of (Nurse) Viola Sistare, 21 March 1931, Lewis Papers.
58 Author's interview of anonymous resident of Carthage, North Carolina, 16 March 1995; "Statement Made Orally by Miss Lottie Mitchem, Former Principal of Institution's High School, in Office of State Board of Charities and Public Welfare, 27 March 1931." Inquest into conditions at Samarcand Manor, 1931, SBPWIC-SCPCI, *Samarcand Manor*, 1918–24, box 133, NCDAH.
59 "Statement Made Orally by Miss Lottie Mitchem, Former Principal of Institution's High School, in Office of State Board of Charities and Public Welfare, 27 March 1931." Inquest into conditions at Samarcand Manor, 1931, SBPWIC-SCPCI, *Samarcand Manor*.
60 Ibid.
61 Nell Battle Lewis, "A Buzzard Comes Home to Roost," Raleigh *News and Observer*, 21 October 1945, NCDAH; "Samarcand Information Collected by NBL," Lewis Papers; "Awaiting the Facts," *Greensboro News*, n.d.; "North Carolina Fails" box. See also "The State as Defendant."
62 Statement of Georgia Piland, 9 May 1931, Lewis Papers.
63 Statement of (Nurse) Viola Sistare.
64 Lewis, "The Samarcand Arson Case."
65 Statement of (Nurse) Viola Sistare.

66 Thompson, "Twelve Samarcand Girls Get State Prison Terms." Also see Thompson, "Defense Holds Samarcand Girls Victims of State Neglect."

67 Thompson, "Defense Holds Samarcand Girls Victims of State Neglect."

68 Katherine L. Boyd to Nell Battle Lewis, 25 May 1931, Lewis Papers; Thompson, "Defense Holds Samarcand Girls Victims of State Neglect." Also see "Sidelights on the Samarcand Arson Case," *Moore County News*, 28 May 1931. "The State as Defendant." Inquest into conditions at Samarcand Manor, 1931, box Nell Battle Lewis to the Rev. H.L. Canfield, 24 May 1931, Lewis Papers; Lewis, "North Carolina at Its Worst"; "Twelve Samarcand Girls Get State Prison Terms"; "Sidelights on the Samarcand Arson Case"; "The Samarcand Girls."

69 Russell, *The Wayward Girls of Samarcand*.

70 Untitled news clipping, 30 May 1931, Lewis Papers.

71 Thompson, "Defense Holds Samarcand Girls Victims of State Neglect"; "Twelve Samarcand Girls Get State Prison Terms."

72 Russell, *The Wayward Girls of Samarcand*, 211.

73 "North Carolina Fails," *Rocky Mount Telegram*, 21 May 1936, Lewis Papers.

74 "Raised a Question about Samarcand," *High Point Enterprise*, n.d., Lewis Papers.

75 "Twelve Samarcand Girls Get State Prison Terms"; "Bad Conditions at Samarcand"; "Sidelights on the Samarcand Arson Case."

76 Russell, *The Wayward Girls of Samarcand*, 240.

77 Nell Battle Lewis to Kate Burr Johnson, marked "Absolutely confidential," 26 May 1931, SBPWIC-SCPCI, *Samarcand Manor*.

78 Dr C.W. Durham to Nell Battle Lewis, 11 May 1931, Lewis Papers.

79 Statement of Georgia Piland, 9 May 1931, Lewis Papers.

80 Lottie Mitchem to Miss Tobitt, 27 February 1931, SBPWIC-SCPCI, *Samarcand Manor*.

81 Lottie Mitchem to the girls, 27 February 1931. Ibid.

82 Untitled summary of report of an investigation of Samarcand made by the State Welfare Department, SBPWIC-SCPCI, *Samarcand Manor*. "Board of Samarcand Bans Whipping Girls," *News and Observer*, 31 May 1931, Lewis Papers.

83 Statements pertaining to Viola Sistare, by Sophia McCrary and Lillian Crenshaw, 2 April 1931, Welfare board investigation notes, SBPWIC-SCPCI, *Samarcand Manor*.

84 Statement of Nora Phillips to Mr R. Eugene Brown, assistant commissioner, State Department of Public Welfare, 24 April 1931, SBPWIC-SCPCI, *Samarcand Manor*.

85 Untitled newsclipping, 30 May 1931, Lewis Papers.

86 "Misplaced Sympathies," unidentified newsclipping, n.d. (c. 1931), Lewis Papers.
87 Statement of Bessie Bishop, R.N., to Miss Mitchem, 1 April 1931, 4, SBPWIC-SCPCI, *Samarcand Manor*.
88 "Misplaced Sympathies"; "Hold Commencement Exercises at State School at Samarcand Today: Institution Given Clean Bill of Health after Investigation by Authorities," *The Pilot*, n.d., Samarcand Private Archives, Eagle Springs, NC.
89 Nell Battle Lewis, "A Buzzard Comes Home to Roost," Raleigh *News and Observer*, 21 October 1945, Lewis Papers.
90 Untitled summary of report of an investigation of Samarcand made by the State Welfare Department, SBPWIC-SCPCI, *Samarcand Manor*; "Board of Samarcand Bans Whipping Girls," *News and Observer*, 31 May 1931.
91 Kate Burr Johnson, quoted by Mrs W.T. Bost in a personal letter to Dr W.A. Stanbury, 31 August 1931, SBPWIC-SCPCI, *Samarcand Manor*.
92 "Hold Commencement Exercises at State School at Samarcand Today."
93 Untitled summary of report of an investigation of Samarcand made by the State Welfare Department, SBPWIC-SCPCI, *Samarcand Manor*.
94 Odem, *Delinquent Daughters*, 100.
95 Unidentified newsclipping, "Former *Samarcand Manor* Head Passes," Samarcand Manor Private Archives, Eagle Springs, NC. Russell, *The Wayward Girls of Samarkand*, 214; Mrs W.T. Bost, commissioner of public welfare, to Dr W.A. Stanbury, 1 August 1931, SBPWIC-SCPCI, *Samarcand Manor*. Report of Inspection of Samarcand Manor, 10 January 1934, by R. Eugene Brown, director, Division of Institutions, State Board of Public Welfare, Restricted records, box 164. Samarcand 1932–37, NCDAH; Mrs W.T. Bost, commissioner, to Col. W.A. Blair, chair, State Board of Public Welfare, Winston-Salem, NC, 1934.
96 Wolf Wolfensberger, *The Origin and Nature of Our Institutional Models* (New York: Human Polity Press, 1975), 60.
97 As noted in Strange, *Qualities of Mercy*, 7.
98 Ibid., 5.
99 Strange, *Qualities of Mercy*, 131. Also see Rothman, "The State as Parent: Social Policy in the Progressive Era," 83. With regard to the function of spectacle, it is noteworthy that an arson attempt at the Efland reform institution for girls of African descent in 1936 barely made the newspapers, there being only one brief report buried in the back pages.
100 Lewis, "North Carolina at Its Worst."
101 Russell, *The Wayward Girls of Samarcand*, 216.
102 Ibid., 218; Mrs W.T. Bost to Col. W.A. Blair.

3 The Energy of Despair

1 Considering emancipation in the American South in 1835, Tocqueville commented, "The whites of the South, even if they are abandoned to their own resources, will enter the lists with an immense superiority of knowledge and the means of warfare; but the blacks will have numerical strength and the energy of despair upon their side, and these are powerful resources to men who have taken up arms." Alexis de Tocqueville, *Democracy in America*, vol. 1 (New York: Vintage, 1945), 391.

2 Michel Foucault, *Technologies of the Self: A Seminar with Michel Foucault*, ed. Luther H. Martin, Huck Gutman and Patrick H. Hutton (Amherst: University of Massachusetts Press, 1988), 160.

3 Wade Cashion, director of institutions and corrections, "Summary," 29 April 1942, box 163, North Carolina Training School for Delinquent Girls, file 1939–41, ORC-NCDAH. Bush, *Who Gets a Childhood?* 12. Report to the Honorable J. Melville Broughton, Governor of North Carolina, Raleigh, NC, of the "commission for the purpose of studying proposals to establish a training school for delinquent Negro girls in North Carolina," 26 June 1942, box 86, SBPWIC. Correspondence concerning problems of juvenile delinquency, NCDA, North Carolina Department of Cultural Resources, Division of Archives and History, Raleigh, NC.

4 A.W. Cline, superintendent of public welfare, Forsyth County, Winston-Salem, to Mrs W.T. Bost, commissioner of public welfare, Raleigh, NC, 19 February 1941, box 163, North Carolina Training School for Delinquent Girls, file 1939–41, ORC-NCDAH.

5 This small home with a capacity for eighteen girls at Efland, NC, was founded by Dr Charlotte Hawkins Brown, as representative and president of the North Carolina Federation of Colored Women's Club from 1915–36; box 163, North Carolina Training School for Delinquent Girls, file 1939–41, ORC-NCDAH; Dorothy C. Salem, *To Better Our World: Black Women in Organized Reform, 1890–1920* (Brooklyn: Carlson Publishing Inc., 1990), 65. The reformatory movement lasted longer in the Southern Black community, eventually metamorphosing into the civil rights movement. Linda Gordon, "Black and White Visions of Welfare, Women's Welfare Activism, 1890–1945," in Darlene Clark Hine, Wilma King, and Linda Reed, eds, *"We Specialize in the Wholly Impossible": A Reader in Black Women's History* (New York: Carlson Publishing, 1995), 449–86. On Northeastern pioneering and regional analysis of the reformatory movement, see Nicole Rafter, *Partial Justice: Women, Prisons and Social Control* (London: Transaction Publishers, 1995); Odem, *Delinquent Daughters*. On the

founding of the Efland home, see Charlotte Hawkins Brown to Mrs Daniels, 27 March 1925, file "Women's Club of Raleigh, Correspondence, 1925–26," 1911–51. See also State Charitable, Correctional and Penal Institutions, n.d, box 163, North Carolina Training School for Delinquent Girls, file 1939–41, ORC-NCDAH; Hearings, n.d, box 163, North Carolina Training School for Delinquent Girls, ORC-NCDAH.

6 Charlotte Hawkins Brown Moses, president, Sedalia (NC), "An Appeal to North Carolinian Women" (1919–1934), box 163, North Carolina Training School for Delinquent Girls, file 1919–34, Old records Center, NCDAH.

7 Susan K. Cahn, *Sexual Reckonings: Southern Girls in a Troubling Age* (Cambridge: Harvard University Press, 2007), 81.

8 Correspondence from R.F. Beasley, commissioner of public welfare, to Dr Charlotte Hawkins Brown, 4 November 1919, box 163, North Carolina Training School for Delinquent Girls, file 1939–41, ORC-NCDAH. On Black women's contact with white government officials and clubwomen, see Gordon, "Black and White Visions of Welfare," 564.

9 Correspondence from Dr Charlotte Hawkins Brown to Mr R.F. Beasley, commissioner of public welfare, 12 April 1920, box 163, North Carolina Training School for Delinquent Girls, file 1939–41, ORC-NCDAH.

10 Anne McClintock, "'No Longer in a Future Heaven': Gender, Race and Nationalism," in Geoff Eley and Ronald Suny, eds, *Becoming National: A Reader* (Oxford: Oxford University Press, 1996), 104–5. Hartman, *Scenes of Subjection*, 9; Cheryl Harris, "Whiteness as Property," *Harvard Law Review* 106 (8) (1993): 1707, 1746; Linda Gordon, *Pitied but Not Entitled: Single Mothers and the History of Welfare 1890–1935* (New York: The Free Press, 1994), 112–13.

11 Lorraine Gates Schuyler, *The Weight of Their Votes: Southern Women and Political Leverage in the 1920s* (Chapel Hill: University of North Carolina Press, 2006), 94, 158. Also see Cahn, *Sexual Reckonings*, 94–5.

12 Gordon, "Black and White Visions of Welfare," 569.

13 Kate Burr Johnson, commissioner, to Charlotte Hawkins Brown,12 October 1925, box 163, North Carolina Training School for Delinquent Girls, ORC-NCDAH.

14 Gordon, "Black and White Visions of Welfare," 560–2, 565–6; Salem, *To Better Our World*, 65.

15 Dr Charlotte Hawkins Brown to Kate Burr Johnson, 1 August, 2 August, and 30 August 1930, box 163, North Carolina Training School for Delinquent Girls, ORC-NCDAH.

16 Schuyler, *The Weight of Their Votes*,157.

17 Charlotte Hawkins Brown to Kate Burr Johnson, 18 July 1921, box 163, North Carolina Training School for Delinquent Girls, ORC-NCDAH.

18 Schuyler, *The Weight of Their Votes*, 157–8, 187.
19 Cahn, *Sexual Reckonings*, 76; "Summary" 29 April 1942, box 163, 1939–41.
20 Cahn, *Sexual Reckonings*, 92.
21 "A Seductive Offer," n.d., unidentified newsclipping, box 163, North Carolina Training School for Negro Girls, 1935–8, SBPWIC-SCPCI, NCDAH.
22 Wm. R. Johnson, Report of Investigation of Industrial Home for Negro Girls, Efland, NC, 1934, Juvenile correspondence 1930–1940, box 86, SBPWIC, Correspondence concerning Problems of Juvenile Delinquency, NCDAH.
23 Correspondence from W.C. Ezell, field agent for the State Board of Public Welfare, 13 June 1935, Juvenile correspondence 1930–1940.
24 Newsclipping, *Carolina Times*, n.d., North Carolina Training School for Negro Girls, 1942–1948, J. Wallace Nygard, director, Division of Institutions and Corrections, to Mrs Minnie S. Pierson, 21 March 1938; M.S. Pearson, president, "The North Carolina Industrial Home for Colored Girls, 21 October 1939, box 163, North Carolina Training School for Delinquent Girls, file 1939–41, ORC-NCDAH.
25 "Hearings," North Carolina Training School for Negro Girls, 1939–1941, box 163. See also M.S. Pearson, president NCFCWC, 31 October 1939, Minutes of meeting of the Board of Trustees of Efland home, 15 October 1938, file: Delinquent Negro Girls: Efforts for State School, Department of Public Welfare, Work among Negroes, Public Welfare Institutes for Negro Social Workers and Child Welfare and Crime Studies, NCDAH.
26 *Winston-Salem Journal*, 30 March 1942, box 163.
27 Foner, *A Short History of Reconstruction*, 42–5, 69.
28 Newsclipping, *Carolina Times*, n.d., State North Carolina Training School for Negro Girls, 1942–1948, box 163.
29 There is little archival material that refers to education at Efland. Black clubwomen did not leave many private papers behind, but those that they did reassured whites that education would be trades oriented.
30 Minnie S. Pearson to members of the state legislature, March 1938, box 163, file 1927–1938, North Carolina Training School for Delinquent Girls, file 1939–41, ORC-NCDAH.
31 Dr Charlotte Hawkins Brown, chairman, Executive Board of Women's Federated Clubs of North Carolina, Sedalia, NC, and Minnie S. Pearson, president, NC State Federation of Women's Clubs, Durham, NC, "An Open Letter to the People of North Carolina," 22 November 1938, box 163, 1935–1938.
32 Newsclipping, *The Charlotte Observer*, n.d., 1939.

33 Author interview with Maud Wells, April 1998, Raleigh, NC.

34 Ibid. Wells described social workers' efforts as liaisons between Black clubwomen and white institutions, actively if unsuccessfully lobbying for state funding and representing Efland in correspondence with various agencies.

35 "Race Relations in 1927," box 255.26, Nell Battle Lewis Collection, material for "Incidentally," "The Negro," Minnie S. Pearson to members of the state legislature, March 1938, box 163, file 1927–1938. This letter among other documents in the file was reported missing to the state archives on 8 June 1996.

36 Kate Burr Johnson, commissioner, "Efland Training school for Girls," 4 May 1927, box 163, Efland, file 1927–1938.

37 Corinne Cannady, girls' commissioner, to Mrs W.T. Bost, state commissioner of public welfare, 4 June 1935, box 163.

38 W.R. Johnson, consultant and field agent on Negro work, to W. Curtis Ezell, director, Division of Institutions, State Board of Charities and Public Welfare, Raleigh, NC, 16 June 1937, box 163, 1935–1938.

39 George H. Lawrence, director of field work, to Dr J. Wallace Nygard, director, Division of Institutions and Corrections, State Board of Charities and Public Welfare, Raleigh, NC, 12 April 1938, box 163, folder "N. C. Industrial School for Negro Girls, 1935–1938," SBPWIC, ORC-NCSA.

40 Kali Gross and many others demonstrate that women of African descent have been disproportionally imprisoned within the current prison industrial complex. See, for example, Gross, *Colored Amazons*; Boritch, "Women in Prison"; Faith and Jiwani, "The Social Construction of 'Dangerous' Girls and Women"; Hudson, "Punishment and Control,"; Neve and Pate, "Challenging the Criminalization of Women Who Resist"; Meyer and Oberman, *Mothers Who Kill Their Children*.

41 In March 1935, E.F. Murray, superintendent of welfare for the County of Scotland, had written to Commissioner Bost requesting accommodation for a thirteen-year-old boy, convicted of breaking and entering, and "probably led into these crimes by older persons." The boy was "very much a child, but a bright and intelligent one … undoubtedly entitled to be classed as Indian." Box 86, SBPWIC, Restricted records: Racial policies, Samarcand, NCDAH.

42 Mrs Myrtle Page, *The Old Spinning Wheel*, Aberdeen, NC, 22 March 1938. Re: admitting Indian girls to Samarcand, 22 March 1938, box 86, SBPWIC.

43 J. Wallace Nygard, director, Division of Institutions and Corrections, to Grace Robson, re: Gertie Mae Oxendine (Indian) and Bessie Locklear (Indian), 18 March 1938, box 86. SBPWIC. supported, and om 1900 to 1922, and tures portrayed ere dss and Observer

44 J. Wallace Nygard, director, Division of Institutions and Corrections, to Grace Robson, re: Gertie Mae Oxendine (Indian) and Bessie Locklear (Indian), 18 March 1938, box 86. SBPWIC.

45 W.A. Stanbury of the Central Methodist Church to Miss Grace Robson, Samarcand, 19 March 1938, box 86, SBPWIC.

46 Lowery, *Lumbee Indians in the Jim Crow South*, 83–4, 166, 187.

47 Lauren Berlant, "National Brands/National Body," in Bruce Robbins ed., *The Phantom Public Sphere* (Minneapolis: University of Minnesota Press, 1993). Also see Tocqueville, *Democracy in America*, 1: 113.

48 The question of whether Jews were truly white or not was a contested one, as illustrated by the Leo Frank case. Frank was accused of raping and murdering a white girl employed in his factory. Jailed for months, he was eventually abducted by vigilantes and lynched. See Eugene Levy, "Is the Jew a White Man?: Press Reaction to the Leo Frank Case, 1913–1915," *Phylon* 35 (1974): 212–22; Harris, "Whiteness as Property," 1742; Stoler, *Race and the Education of Desire*, 52.

49 "The Efland home," *Carolina Times*, 4 February 1939, North Carolina Institution and Training School for Negro Girls, n.d., 1919–34, box 163; newspaper unrecorded, 29 January 1944, North Carolina Institution and Training School for Negro Girls, n.d., 1919–1934, box 163, file 1939–41, ORC-NCDAH; "Meeting an Acute Need," *Winston-Salem Journal*, 30 March 1942, North Carolina Institution and Training School for Negro Girls, n.d; Department of Public Welfare, Work among Negroes, Public Welfare Institutes for Negro Social Workers and Child Welfare and Crime Studies, ORC-NCDAH. See also newspaper clipping, 10 April 1944, "Reverses Action on Efland Bill: Committee Approves Gift of Negro Women; Kills License-Repeal Bill." Anna Hauser and Hattie Hughes, Committee Report of Observations Made at Morrison Training School, State Training School for Delinquent Girls, 1942–48, box 163, North Carolina Training School for Delinquent Girls. Also see "Training Needed for Negro Girls: Welfare Head Stresses Lack of Detention Homes for Delinquents," unknown newspaper, September 1927, North Carolina Institution and Training School for Negro Girls, n.d. 1919–34, box 163.

50 (Mrs) Edna B. Taylor to W.R. Johnson, State Board of Charities and Public Welfare, Raleigh, NC, 26 March 1942, North Carolina Training School for Negro Girls, State Board of Public Welfare, 1942–1948, box 163, North Carolina Training School for Delinquent Girls, ORC-NCDAH.

51 In *Abnormal: Lectures at the Collège de France, 1974–1975*, ed. Valerio Marchetti and Antonella Salomoni, trans. Graham Burchell (New York: Verso, 2003), 325.

52 On recursive patterns in the politics of punishment, see Strange, *Qualities of Mercy*, 17. Jeffrie Murphy cited in Strange, *Qualities of Mercy*, 17. Also see Mosse, *Nationalism and Sexuality*, 133–4, 182–3, 191.

53 Boritch, "Women in Prison," 214. It is also noteworthy that by the end of the Second World War racist discourses came to be questioned in unprecedented ways. The possibility of a new era of anti-racism seemed plausible as many opponents of Nazism began to radically rethink race supremacy; Nazi atrocities generated popular reference to "racism" for the first time. Additionally, the decolonizing world, along with a Soviet Cold War enemy, was watching for American "failures to live up to the American Creed," such that openly expressed racism potentially caused international embarrassment. Roediger, *How Race Survived U.S. History*, 184; Salem, *To Better Our World*, 232; Hay, "Foreword."

54 Boritch, "Women in Prison," 214. Also see Hudson, "Punishment and Control"; Faith, "The Social Construction of 'Dangerous' Girls and Women"; Bush, *Who Gets a Childhood?* 5; "Meeting and Acute Need," *Winston-Salem Journal*, 30 March 1942, North Carolina Institution and Training School for Negro Girls, n.d., 1919–1934, box 163; A.W. Cline, superintendent of public welfare, to Mrs W.T. Bost, 19 February 1941.

55 Cahn, *Sexual Reckonings*, 93–4; unidentified newsclipping, "School for Negro Girls," n.d., box 163, North Carolina Training School for Delinquent Girls, file 1939–41; newspaper unrecorded, 29 January 1944, North Carolina Institution and Training School for Negro Girls.

56 Myrdal, *An American Dilemma*, 35–6; Glenda Gilmore, *Gender and Jim Crow: Women and the Politics of White Supremacy in North Carolina, 1896–1920* (Chapel Hill: University of North Carolina Press, 1996).

57 Adolph Reed Jr., "The James Brown Theory of Black Liberation," *Jacobin*, issue 18 (Summer 2015): 49–50.

58 Foucault, *The History of Sexuality*, 100–2.

59 Hartman, *Scenes of Subjection*, 119, 134; Cahn, *Sexual Reckonings*, 85; Foucault, *History of Sexuality*, 100–2; Gordon, "Black and White Visions of Welfare," 560. Black ministers also played central roles in their communities as politicians and leaders as well as religious guides. In 1896, Winfield H. Mixon, a prominent religious leader in Alabama, wrote of "an Old testament anger, a raging fury at whites: '... Every now and then the wicked, ill-gotten, squint-eyed, blood suckers hang, lynch, shoot, burn, or flay their superiors – the ebony, pure, and most God-like in the heart Negro.'" Quoted in Ayers, *The Promise of the New South* (New York: Oxford University Press, 1992), 63. On the political space provided by Black churches, see Ayers, *The Promise of the New South*, 163–6; Foner, *A Short*

History of Reconstruction, 41. Efland's pamphlet, entitled "Save Our Girls," North Carolina Industrial Home for Colored Girls, Efland, Orange County, NC, box 163, State Board of Public Welfare, North Carolina Training School for Delinquent Girls.

60 Foucault, *History of Sexuality*, 94–6, 102.

61 Darlene Clark Hine, "'We Specialize in the Wholly Impossible': The Philanthropic Work of Black Women," in Kathleen D. McCarthy, ed., *Lady Bountiful Revisited: Women, Philanthropy and Power* (London: Rutgers University Press, 1990), 71, 82. Anne Firor Scott, "Women's Voluntary Associations: From Charity to Reform," in McCarthy, ed., *Lady Bountiful Revisited*, 38.

62 Hine, "We Specialize in the Wholly Impossible," 88.

63 Ibid.

64 Deborah Gray White, "Mining the Forgotten: Manuscript Sources for Black Women's History," *Journal of American History* 74 (June 1987): 237–42.

65 Foucault, *The History of Sexuality*, 27.

66 Aliyyah I. Abdur-Rahman, "'This Horrible Exhibition': Sexuality in Slave Narratives," in John Ernest, ed., *The Oxford Handbook of the African American Slave Narrative* (New York: Oxford University Press, 2014), 240–1.

67 Nielsen, "Resistance through Re-narration," 206. Foucault describes the elements of an apparatus in "The Confessions of the Flesh," in C. Gordon, L. Marshall, J. Mepham, and K. Soper, eds, *Power/Knowledge: Selected Interviews and Other Writings, 1972–1977* (New York: Pantheon, 1980), 194.

68 A.W. Cline to Mrs W.T. Bost, 19 February 1941. On anatomo-politics, see Foucault, *History of Sexuality*, 139.

69 Dorothy Roberts, "Killing the Black Body," in Andrea O'Reilly, *Maternal Theory: Essential Readings* (Toronto: Demeter Press, 2007), 350.

70 Dr Charlotte Hawkins Brown to R.F. Beasely, commissioner of public welfare, Raleigh, 7 November 1919. Also see Efland's pamphlet "Save Our Girls."

71 Gordon, "Black and White Visions of Welfare," 135. Also see Gerda Lerner, *Black Women in White America: A Documentary History* (New York: Vintage, 1992), 477–97.

72 Salem, *To Better Our World*, 50–51. Training in domestic science was highly morally regulatory, with the "dignity of labor" as a primary message. August Meier, *Negro Thought in America* 1880–1915 (Ann Arbor: University of Michigan Press, 1988), 86.

73 Brown and Pearson, "Open Letter to the People of North Carolina."

74 Dr Charlotte Hawkins Brown to Mr L.R. Reynolds, 31 December 1940, box 163, North Carolina Training School for Delinquent Girls, file 1939–41.

75 Mary Church Terrell, 1900, 1928, and referring to observations of Fannie Barrier William. Quoted in Linda Gordon, "Black and White Visions of Welfare," 578–9.
76 Gordon, *Pitied but Not Entitled*, 113. Gordon, "Black and White Visions of Welfare," 583.
77 Jessie Daniel Ames, quoted in Hall, *Revolt against Chivalry*, 331.
78 Barbara Welter, *Dimity Convictions: The American Woman in the Nineteenth Century* (Columbus: University of Ohio Press, 1977), 23; Barbara Welter, "The Cult of True Womanhood: 1820–1860," *American Quarterly* 18 (Summer 1966): 151–74; Rafter, *Partial Justice*, 158–9, 226.
79 Myrta Lockett Avary, quoted in Rushdy, *The End of American Lynching*, 12.
80 Roberts, "Killing the Black Body," 479–80, 488.
81 Hazel V. Carby, "'On the Threshold of Woman's Era'": Lynching, Empire and Sexuality in Black Feminist Theory," in Anne McClintock, Aamir Mufti, and Ella Shohat, eds, *Dangerous Liaisons: Gender, Nation, and Postcolonial Perspectives* (Minneapolis: University of Minnesota Press, 1997), 21, 23, 27, 33–4; Foner, *A Short History of Reconstruction*, 12, 162.
82 Carby, "'On the Threshold of Woman's Era,'" 39. In 1895 the Congress of Colored Women of the United States convened in Boston. The National Federation and the National League of Colored Women united in Washington, DC, to form the National Association of Colored Women (NACW).
83 Hine, "'We Specialize in the Wholly Impossible,'" 73, 87–8.
84 Stoler, *Race and the Education of Desire*, 83, 95. See esp. chap. 3.
85 Maude White Katz, "The Negro Woman and the Law," *Freedomways* 2 (1962): 279; Harris, "Whiteness as Property," 1707, 1719–20.
86 Roediger, *How Race Survived U.S. History*, 28–9.
87 Pascoe, *What Comes Naturally*, 30, 40, 44; Stoler, *Race and the Education of Desire*, 48.
88 Harris, "Whiteness as Property," 1707.
89 Foucault, *History of Sexuality*, 136.
90 Roediger, *How Race Survived U.S. History*, 28–9.
91 Katz, "The Negro Woman and the Law," 281.
92 Gordon, "Black and White Visions of Welfare," 464.
93 Carby, "'On the Threshold of Woman's Era,'" 38–9.
94 Claims to Black womanhood implied sexual virtue and entitlement to sexual protection under the biopolitical state. Girls' training in Black reform institutions incorporated protective anti-rape discourses, unlike white reform, which sought to "stamp out" prostitution, identifying a wide spectrum of girls' moral transgressions under that umbrella term. McClintock, *Imperial Leather*, 55; Katz, "The Negro Woman and the Law," 279.

95 Roberts "Killing the Black Body," 488.

96 Nielsen, "Resistance through Re-narration," 363–85.

97 Chris Gosden and Chantal Knowles, *Collecting Colonialism: Material Culture and Colonial Change* (New York: Berg, 2001), 243.

98 Pascoe, *What Comes Naturally*, 4.

99 Elizabeth Edwards, "Photography and the Making of the Other," in P. Blanchard et al., eds, *Human Zoos: Science and Spectacle in the Age of Colonial Empires* (New York: Oxford University Press, 2009), 240–2; Matthew Frye Jacobson, *Barbarian Virtues: The United States Encounters Foreign Peoples at Home and Abroad, 1876–1917* (New York: Hill and Wang, 2000), 141–2.

100 Gould, "American Polygeny and Craniometry before Darwin," 87.

101 Wiegman, *American Anatomies*, 7. Also see Stuart Hall, "What Is This 'Black' in Black Popular Culture?" in Gina Dent, ed., *Black Popular Culture* (Seattle: Bay Press, 1992), 31.

102 Himani Bannerji, personal communication,1996.

103 Roediger, *How Race Survived U.S. History*, 28–9.

104 McClintock, *Imperial Leather*, 55–6; Gilman, "Black Bodies, White Bodies," 231–2; Londa Schiebinger, *Nature's Body: Gender in the Making of Modern Science* (Boston: Beacon Press, 1993), 160–72.

105 Quoted in Wiegman, *American Anatomies*, 57.

106 Schiebinger, *Nature's Body*, 15.

107 Ibid., 168; Gilman, "Black Bodies, White Bodies," 232, 240, 245; Wiegman, *American Anatomies*, 56, 58; McClintock, *Imperial Leather*, 3; Schiebinger, *Nature's Body*, 168; Fausto-Sterling "Gender, Race and Nation."

108 McClintock, *Imperial Leather*, 41.

109 Wiegman, *American Anatomies*, 76.

110 The well-documented historical sexual abuse of Black females under slavery generated lasting stereotypes of Black female hypersexuality, but within an attendant genderlessness. Wiegman, *American Anatomies*, 11, 44–5; Katz, "The Negro Woman and the Law," 279.

111 Wiegman, *American Anatomies*, 4, 39.

112 Harris, "Whiteness as Property," 1737.

113 Wiegman, *American Anatomies*, 76.

114 Ibid., 60–1.

115 Howard Odum, quoted in Roberts, "Killing the Black Body," 488. Roberts critiques liberal interpretations of reproductive rights in the United States for focusing on white women's demands for individual freedom around the right to abortion, while denying Black women the reproductive freedom to procreate. As "unfit" mothers, Black women have been

assumed to pass on degenerate traits, resulting in three centuries of selectively applied birth-control policies. Roberts, "Killing the Black Body," 488. On race, single pregnancy, and the US welfare state, see Rickie Solinger, *Wake Up Little Susie: Single Pregnancy and Race before Roe v. Wade* (New York: Routledge, 1992).

116 Nielsen, "Resistance through Re-narration," 27.

117 Harris, "Whiteness as Property," 1754.

118 Stoler, *Race and the Education of Desire*, 8.

4 The Merciful Executioner

1 Ayers, *Vengeance and Justice*, 210.

2 A scene from Stephen Vincent Benet's *John Brown's Body*, quoted in Rollin Gustav Osterweiss, *The Myth of the Lost Cause, 1865–1900* (Connecticut: The Shoe String Press, 1973), 6–7.

3 Karl Marx, "On the Jewish Question" (1843), in Robert C. Tucker, ed., *The Marx-Engels Reader* (New York: W.W. Norton, 1978).

4 Georgia Cannady to Governor Clyde Hoey, 29 May 1940, Morrison Training School, box 162, NCDAH.

5 W.C. Ezell, director, Division Institutions and Corrections, "Investigation of the Drowning of Two Boys at Morrison Training School: Albert Cannady and William Brown Hoover," 6 June 1940; Ezell to Mrs Georgia Cannady, 12 June 1940.

6 Georgia Cannady to North Carolina State Board of Corrections September 1940, Morrison Training School (MTS), box 162, NCDAH.

7 Hartman, *Scenes of Subjection*, 127; A.R. Newsome, ed., *North Carolina Manual* (Raleigh: Publications of North Carolina Historical Commission, Edwards A. Broughton Co., State Printers, 1927), 267; Martha F. Taylor to R. Eugene Brown, 8 August 1935; L.L. Boyd to R. Eugene Brown, 25 July 1935.

8 Strange, *Qualities of Mercy*, 5.

9 Owen Gudger, judge of the Juvenile Court, to Mr W.C. Ezell, State Board of Charities and Public Welfare, Raleigh, NC, 5 October 1938, NCDAH.

10 Foucault, *Discipline and Punish*, 7–15, 16.

11 Wiley B. Sanders, associate professor of sociology at UNC Chapel Hill directed this study under the joint auspices of the North Carolina State Board of Charities and Public Welfare and the School of Public Welfare, University of North Carolina. *Negro Child Welfare in North Carolina* (Glen Ridge, NJ: Patterson Smith Publishing Corp., 1968), 23, 45; Strange, *Qualities of Mercy*, 12.

12 Ayers, *Vengeance and Justice*, 234.

13 Quoted in Ayers, *Vengeance and Justice*, 149.

14 Rushdy, *The End of American Lynching*, 1, 3, 8, 169.

15 Ibid., 4.

16 Tannenbaum, *The Darker Phases of the South*, 7–8; Pfeifer, *Rough Justice*, 123, 139; Newkirk, *Lynching in North Carolina*, 5, 12, 137; Rushdy, *The End of American Lynching*, 8.

17 Pfeifer, *The Roots of Rough Justice*, 83–4.

18 Ayers, *Vengeance and Justice*, 42, 54–5, 65–6.

19 Kenneth Gergen, *The Saturated Self: Dilemmas of Identity in Contemporary Life* (New York: Basic Books, 1991), 151.

20 Michelle Alexander, *The New Jim Crow: Mass Incarceration in the Age of Colorblindness* (New York: New Press, 2010), 42, 182. Also see Foucault, *Discipline and Punish*.

21 Ayers, *Vengeance and Justice*, 61–2, 150, 155, 210, 239.

22 Ibid., 246–7; Kathleen Blee, *Women of the Klan: Racism and Gender in the Nineteen Twenties* (Berkeley: University of California Press, 1991), 12.

23 Newkirk, *Lynching in North Carolina*, 137; Joel Williamson, *The Crucible of Race: Black–White Relations in the American South since Emancipation* (New York: Oxford University Press, 1984); Rushdy, *The End of American Lynching*, x, 5–6; Wiegman, *American Anatomies*, 96.

24 Ayers, *Vengeance and Justice*, 26–7.

25 Foner, *A Short History of Reconstruction*, 186–7, 190. Michael Pfeifer, *Rough Justice*, 141. John Fraser, *America and the Patterns of Chivalry*, 143–4.

26 Newkirk, *Lynching in North Carolina*, 27; Rushdy, *The End of American Lynching*, 3, 5, 32; Dora Apel and Shawn Michelle Smith, *Lynching Photographs: Defining Moments in American Photography* (Berkeley: University of California Press, 2008), 15. Also see Booker T. Washington, *Up from Slavery – An Autobiography* (Sioux Falls, ND: NuVision Publications, 2007).

27 Pfeifer, *The Roots of Rough Justice*, 67–8, 85–6; Newkirk, *Lynching in North Carolina*, 5–7, 10, 16, 97, 137. Historical essay: "Legislative Interests" / "The Negroes' Temporary Farewell: Jim Crow and the Exclusion of African Americans from Congress, 1887–1929," Black Americans in Congress, US Congress, http://history.house.gov/Exhibitions-and-Publications/BAIC/Historical-Essays/Temporary-Farewell/Introduction/.

28 Rushdy, *The End of American Lynching*, 11–12, 144.

29 Quoted in Martha Hodes, "The Sexualization of Reconstruction Politics: White Women and Black Men in the South after the Civil War," *Journal of the History of Sexuality* 3 (3) (1993): 405.

30 Bickford, "The Merciful Executioner"; Bickford, "Imperial Modernity, Regional Identity and Popular Culture in the Samarcand Arson Case,

1931"; "Civilizing Adolescence: Race, Sexuality and Nation Building in North Carolina's Reformatory Movement 1918–1944," Ph.D. diss., York University (Toronto, 2002). The merged discourse of nation, gender, and race was evident as early as the 1570s, when America was personified on maps and paintings, such as Jan van der Straet's engraving of Vespucci's discovery of America. Montrose, "The Work of Gender in the Discourse of Discovery," 3; Gunning, *Race, Rape and Lynching*, 24.

31 Rushdy, *The End of American Lynching*, 9.

32 Wilson, *Baptized in Blood*, 46–7.

33 Ayers, *Vengeance and Justice*, 240; Roediger, *How Race Survived U.S. History*, 28–9.

34 Cash, *The Mind of the South*, 115; Rushdy, *The End of American Lynching*, 9–10, 162.

35 Wilson, *Baptized in Blood*, 47; Stoler "Making Empire Respectable," 353; Gunning, *Race, Rape and Lynching*, 7; Hartman, *Scenes of Subjection*, 146; Stoler, "Making Empire Respectable," 353.

36 McClintock, *Imperial Leather*, 22–3. Liberty's sculptor, Frederic Bartholdi, stressed its unifying function thus: The statue's stability as a point of national identity depends upon her body being indivisible, like America. The iconic body provokes the translation of subjects in time and history into an unmarked plane or space of consciousness, unperforated by "gaps" or "protrusions": a whole body, indivisible although clearly divided.

37 Berlant, *The Anatomy of National Fantasy*, 30–5; McClintock, *Imperial Leather*, 24–6.

38 Ayers, *Vengeance and Justice*, 144. Southern women symbolized moral heroism through self-abnegation during wartime, a feat some actually deemed greater than that of the Confederate soldier. In his *The Women of the Confederacy* (1912) Presbyterian minister J.L. Underwood concluded: "The arm of the hero [was] nerved by his heart, and the heart of John was Mary, and Mary was the soul of the South." According to Charles Wilson, to preserve their civilization's virtue, Southern men had to stand between the Yankee invader and their women. A post-war politician and minister praised General Robert E. Lee for standing behind Southern women and "ruined innocence." His wife, Rebecca Lee, active in the church and later in politics as the first female American senator, praised the Confederates for shielding "innocence and virtue from rape and ruin" and from Yankee "soldiers that outraged Southern women." Wilson, *Baptized in Blood*, 47.

39 Rushdy, *The End of American Lynching*, 100.

40 Kathy A. Perkins and Judith Louise Stephens, *Strange Fruit: Plays on Lynching by American Women* (Bloomington: Indiana University Press, 1998), 313.

41 Linda O. McMurry, *To Keep the Waters Troubled: The Life of Ida B. Wells* (New York: Oxford University Press, 2000), 212.

42 Hall, *Revolt against Chivalry*, 337–8, 340; Jacquelyn Dowd Hall, "'The Mind That Burns in Each Body': Women, Rape and Racial Violence," in A. Snitow, C. Stansell, and S. Thompson, eds, *Powers of Desire: The Politics of Sexuality* (New York: Monthly Review Press, 1983); Ring, *The Problem South*, 7.

43 Michel Foucault, *"Society Must Be Defended": Lectures at the Collège de France, 1975–1976* (New York: St Martin's Press, 2003), 242; Hartman, *Scenes of Subjection*, 10.

44 Rushdy, *The End of American Lynching*, 4, 6, 160–1.

45 Waldrep, *African Americans Confront Lynching*, 47; Newkirk, *Lynching in North Carolina*, 12, 29; Cash, *The Mind of the South*, 115; Pfeifer, *Rough Justice*, 144.

46 Gould, "American Polygeny and Craniometry before Darwin," 98.

47 Newkirk, *Lynching in North Carolina*, 12, 138–40; Rushdy, *The End of American Lynching*, 71; Michael Pfeifer, *Rough Justice: Lynching and American Society, 1874–1947* (Chicago: University of Illinois Press, 2004), 123, 139, 144–7.

48 Ayers, *Vengeance and Justice*, 246–7.

49 Maclean, *Behind the Mask of Chivalry*.

50 Greg Smith, "Civilized People Don't Want to See That Kind of Thing: The Decline of Public Physical Punishment in London, 1760–1840," in Strange, *Qualities of Mercy*, 19. Also see Carolyn Strange, "The Undercurrents of Penal Culture: Punishment of the Body in Mid-Twentieth-Century Canada," *Law and History Review*, Summer 2001.

51 Pratt, *Punishment and Civilization*, 18, 23–7.

52 Stoler, *Race and the Education of Desire*, 76.

53 Commissioner Bost to R. Eugene Brown, 5 June 1937, Morrison Training School, box 163, file 1937–9.

54 Newkirk, *Lynching in North Carolina*, 139–40; Rushdy, *The End of American Lynching*, 52–3; "Race Relations in 1927," box 255.26, Nell Battle Lewis Collection, Material for "Incidentally," "The Negro," NCDAH.

55 Sanders, *Negro Child Welfare in North Carolina*, 5.

56 Foner, *A Short History of Reconstruction*, 65–6.

57 Karlos K. Hill, "Lynching and the Making of Modern America," *Reviews in American History* 39 (4) (December 2011): 652–9.

58 Waldrep, *African Americans Confront Lynching*, 49, 57, 59, 64, 67–8, 70–1, 74, 77, 79–80, 83–4, 146; Rushdy, *The End of American Lynching*, 11; Pfeifer, *Rough Justice*, 139, 146.

59 Gail Bederman, *Manliness & Civilization: A Cultural History of Gender and Race in the United States, 1880–1917* (Chicago: University of Chicago Press, 1995), 19, 68–9.

60 Ibid., 68.

61 Waldrep, *African Americans Confront Lynching*, 47, 49.

62 Newkirk, *Lynching in North Carolina*, 138.

63 Foucault, *Discipline and Punish*, 14.

64 Quoted in *The Literary Digest: A Repository of Contemporaneous Thought and Research*, vol. 9 (New York: Funk and Wagnalls, 1894), 5.

65 Bederman, *Manliness & Civilization*, 67.

66 Bederman, "'Civilization,'" 18; Ida B. Wells, *Southern Horrors: Lynch Law in All Its Phases*, reprinted in Trudier Harris, *Selected Works of Ida B. Wells-Barnett* (New York: Oxford University Press, 1991); McMurry, *To Keep the Waters Troubled*.

67 North Carolina Conference for Social Service, program of the Fifth Annual Session, Raleigh, NC, 1916. Private collection 1488.71, Gertrude Weil Papers, Goldsboro Bureau for Social Service, Miscellaneous. North Carolina Federation of Women's Clubs, Goldsboro Women's Club, NCDAH.d

68 Rushdy, *The End of American Lynching*, 11, 67, 71, 171.

69 Printed in a pamphlet issued by the Association of Southern Women for the Prevention of Lynching, February 1937, Organizations Committed to a Program of Education to Prevent Lynching in the South, General Federation of Women's Clubs, Federation of Women's Clubs, NC, Gertrude Weil Papers, NCDAH.

70 Pfeifer, *Rough Justice*, 122–4, 126, 128–9, 141, 144, 146.

71 Legal lynchings, Ames complained, "rocked the foundations of American democracy." Quoted in Hall, *Revolt against Chivalry*, 200.

72 Foucault, *Discipline and Punish*, 8–12.

73 Bickford,"The Merciful Executioner." Also see David Bruck, "Executing Teen-Age Killers Again: The 14 Year-Old, Who in Many Ways, Was Too Small for the Chair," *Washington Post*, 15 September 1985; David Bruck, "Executing Juveniles for Crime," *New York Times*, 16 June 1984; Joy James, *States of Confinement: Policing, Detention and Prisons* (New York: Palgrave, 2002).

74 Newkirk, *Lynching in North Carolina*, 5–6.

75 Pratt, *Punishment and Civilization*, 29.

76 R.F. Beasley to a governor-appointed committee to propose legislation to the legislature. The commission was appointed "under resolution of the Special Session of the Legislature for consideration of certain measures for the benefit of negro race in North Carolina" (24 November 1920).

G.V. Cowper to R.F. Beasley, 1 December 1920, State Board of Charities and Public Welfare, MTS, box 162, NCDAH.

77 R.F. Beasley, commissioner of public welfare, Raleigh, NC, to A.M. Moore, 10 June 1920, ibid.

78 A.M. Moore to R.F. Beasley, 13 December 1919, ibid.

79 Trustees and Advisory Board to the Honorable Senators and Representatives of the General Assembly of North Carolina, Session 1919, 22 January 1919, Public Laws 1911 Chapter 122; Beasley to Moore, 10 June 1920, ibid.

80 H.H. Hart, director, Department of Child-Helping, Russell Sage Foundation, New York, to Mrs Clarence A. Johnson, commissioner, State Board of Charities and Public Welfare, Raleigh, NC, 6 February 1922. T.J. Edwards, principal, Virginia Manual Labor School for Colored Boys, to Mrs Clarence A. Johnson, 8 June 1922. Rhoda Kaufman, director, Division Children's Institutions, Department of Public Welfare, Atlanta, GA, to Mrs C.A. Johnson, 31 May 1922. In a letter describing the institution to the commissioner of public welfare, in Raleigh, Lemuel B. Green penned at the bottom of the page: "The State has no such institution for negro girls. But a private one – the Girls' Rescue Home has recently been opened for 40 girls by the Alabama Federation of Colored Women's Clubs; L.B. Green, State of Alabama Child Welfare Department, to Mrs C.A. Johnson. Mrs Johnson to W.H. Everett, 3 June 1922.

81 Commissioner Johnson to W.P. Hawfield, county superintendent of public welfare, Raeford, NC.

82 C.A. Johnson, to Thad L. Tate, trustee, State Training School for Negro Boys, Charlotte, NC, 1 February 1922.

83 W.N. Everett to Mrs C.A. Johnson, 26 and 31 May 1922; Samuel E. Leonard, superintendent of public welfare, to Kate Burr Johnson, commissioner of public welfare, 6 October 1922.

84 Newsome, *North Carolina Manual*, 267.

85 Ibid.

86 "A Study of the Adjustment of Negro Boys Discharged from State Training School," 1 July 1940–30 June 1943. Unit of Work among Negroes, State Board of Public Welfare, Raleigh, NC.

87 Thad L. Tate to C.A. Johnson, 14 February 1922.

88 Sanders, *Negro Child Welfare in North Carolina*.

89 Kevin Gaines, "Black Americans' Racial Uplift Ideology as 'Civilizing Mission': Pauline E. Hopkins on Race and Imperialism," in Amy Kaplan and Donald E. Pease, eds, *Cultures of United States Imperialism* (Durham, NC: Duke University Press, 1993), 442; W.E.B. Dubois, *The Souls of Black Folk* (New York: Signet, 1969), 126; Foner, *A Short History of Reconstruction*, 65–6.

90 N.C. Newbold, director, Division of Negro Education, Department of Public Instruction, to W.H. Everett, 21 March 1923; Kate Burr Johnson, commissioner of public welfare, to Thad L. Tate, 15 September 1923. Washington argued that African Americans who "went through the school of American slavery were materially, intellectually, morally and religiously the most advanced black people in any other portion of the globe." Gaines, "Black Americans' Racial Uplift Ideology," 441. Also see Ruth Wilson Gilmore, *Golden Gulag: Prisons, Surplus, Crisis, and Opposition in Globalizing California* (Berkeley: University of California Press, 2007), 190.

91 Rev. L.L. Boyd to T.L. Tate, 20 November 1923.

92 W.N. Everett, secretary of state, to Mary Shotwell, School of Public Welfare, NC, 9 July 1924; Mrs C.A. Johnson to T.L. Tate, 1 February 1922; Kate Burr Johnson to T.L. Tate, 15 September 1924.

93 Rev. L.L. Boyd to Kate Burr Johnson, 15 October 1924.

94 Kate Burr Johnson to Fay Davenport, superintendent of public welfare, Gastonia, NC, 10 December 1923.

95 N.C. Newbold, Department of Public Instruction, to Senator L.R. Varser, 19, 24 December 1924.

96 Bush, *Who Gets a Childhood?* 16.

97 Newsome, *North Carolina Manual.* 267; C. C. Spaulding, Board member, to L. A. Oxley, Director, Bureau of Work Among Negroes, State Board of Charities, Raleigh, N.C. 24 February, 1926; Inspection of State Institutions. Regular Form Prepared by the North Carolina State Board of Heath. Raleigh, N.C. n.d.

98 C.C. Spaulding, board member, to L.A. Oxley, director, Bureau of Work among Negroes, State Board of Charities, Raleigh, 24 February 1926.

99 Rev. S.N. Griffith to Kate Burr Johnson, 22 July 1926.

100 W.C. Ezell, director, Division of Institutions and Corrections, State Board of Charities and Public Welfare, to K.W. Davis, boys' commissioner, Winston Salem, 6 March 1933; L.L. Boyd to R. Eugene Brown, 3 February 1933; Commissioner Kate Burr Johnson to Rev. S.N. Griffith, 28 July 1926; Commissioner Johnson to Boyd, 27 November 1929; Edward Boshart to Kate Burr Johnson, 11 October 1929; Boyd to Commissioner Johnson, 18 February 1929; Martha F. Taylor to R. Eugene Brown, 8 August 1935; L.L. Boyd to R. Eugene Brown, 25 July 1935; Commissioner Johnson to Boyd, 14 December 1928.

101 Rev. L.L. Boyd to W.C. Ezell, 16 November 1932; Ezell to Boyd, 21 November 1932.

102 W.C. Ezell, "Report of Visit to Morrison Training School," 27 April 1934, Morrison Training School, boxes 161 and 162, file 1927–34.

103 Ibid.

104 Morrison Training School, box 162, file 1935–6, State Board of Charities and Public Welfare, MTS, box 162, NCDAH.

105 S.B. Simmons, itinerant teacher-trainer, "Report on visit to Morrison Training School, Hoffman, North Carolina," Morrison Training School, box 162, file 1935–6, State Board of Charities and Public Welfare, MTS, box 162, NCDAH.

106 Mrs Hattie J. Hughes and Mrs M. Anna Hauser, North Carolina Federation of Negro Women's Clubs "Committee Report of Observations Made at Morrison Training School." Submitted to Mrs. W.T. Bost, Superintendent of Public Welfare, State Board of Charities and Public Welfare, MTS, box 162, 1935.

107 National Negro Health Week Observance at Morrison Training School, 3–12 April 1936.

108 Morrison Training School hearing with superintendent and board of trustees, 30 October 1936; "Questionnaire on estimates for 1937–1939 as required under budget memorandum No. 229." W.R. Johnson to Commissioner Bost, 9 November 1935; J. Wallace Nygard to L.L. Boyd, 9 August 1938; J. Wallace Nygard to Dr J. Wilton Black, 26 May 1938; W. Johnson to R. Eugene Brown, 30 August 1935; S.B. Simmons, "Report on visit to Morrison Training School"; Thad Tate to F.L. Dunlap, assistant director, Budget Bureau, 25 October 1935, box 162; J.R. Raper, caseworker, to W.C. Ezell, 25 October 1937, box 163, NADCH. Harry Bice to Dr Ambrose Caliver, specialist in the education of negroes, Office of Education, Department of the Interior, 24 May 1937, MTS, box 163, file 1937–9.

109 Rev. L.L. Boyd to members of the staff, 1 September 1933, "1933–34 Schedule," MTS, boxes 161 and 162, file 1927–34.

110 L.L. Boyd to R. Eugene Brown, 21 September 1934.

111 E. Farrell White to R. Eugene Brown, 18 September 1934; L.L. Boyd to Brown, 21 September 1934, MTS, box 161, file 1927–34.

112 Anonymous to Mrs Bost, 5 March 1935, MTS, box 161.

113 W.R. Johnson to R. Eugene Brown, 30 August 1935; R. Eugene Brown, "Investigation of Complaint Re: Confinement Quarters and Other Matters at Morrison Training School," 23 March 1935. MTS, box 162.

114 W.R. Johnson to Brown, 5 March 1936; K.T. Futrell to Brown, 22 May 1936; Brown to Futrell, 21 May 1936; Mrs J.R. Nunn, superintendent, to Brown, 9 May 1935; Belle Hester to Mr Graham, 23 August 1936. SBPWIC-SCPCI, MTS, box 162, file "Investigation of deaths, complaints of mistreatment, etc., 1935–41."

115 W.C. Ezell, "An evaluation of the child welfare worker at Morrison Training School," 22 April 1939. MTS, box 162.

116 "Morrison Training School hearing with Superintendent and Board of
    Trustees," 30 October 1936; "Questionnaire on estimates for 1937–1939
    as required under budget memorandum No. 229"; Wm. R. Johnson to
    Commissioner Bost, 9 November 1935; J. Wallace Nygard to L.L. Boyd, 9
    August 1938; J. Wallace Nygard to Dr J. Wilton Black, 26 May 1938; Wm
    Johnson to R. Eugene Brown, 30 August 1935; S.B. Simmons, "Report on
    visit to Morrison Training School,"; Thad Tate to F.L. Dunlap, 25 October
    1935; J.R. Raper to W.C. Ezell, 25 October 1937; Harry Bice to Dr Ambrose
    Caliver, 24 May 1937.

117 "A Case in Court," *Charlotte Observer*, 16 March 1940.

118 "Report of Superintendent," Morrison Training School, *Reports of North
    Carolina Juvenile Correction Institutions for the Years Ended June 30, 1942*.

119 "Evaluation of the child welfare worker at Morrison Training School."

120 "Report of Superintendent," Morrison Training School; "The Morrison
    Training School Stench," *Carolina Times*, 12 February 1944.

121 "Auditors Report Another Mix-Up," news clipping, 25 March 1944.

122 Ibid.

123 "Paul R. Brown Chosen Morrison School Head," news clipping, untitled,
    3 March 1944.

124 Stoler, *Race and the Education of Desire*, 84–5.

125 Orlando Patterson, *Rituals of Blood: Consequences of Slavery in Two American
    Centuries* (Washington: Civitas/Counterpoint, 1998), 220; McClintock,
    Imperial Leather, 47; Julia Kristeva, *Powers of Horror: An Essay on Abjection*,
    trans. Leon S. Roudiez (New York: Columbia University Press, 1982), 4.

126 Foucault, *Discipline and Punish*, 17–19; quoted in Sanders, *Negro Child
    Welfare in North Carolina*, 185.

127 Sanders, *Negro Child Welfare in North Carolina*, x.

128 Wiley Sanders and William Ezell, *Juvenile Court Cases in North Carolina
    1929–1934* (Raleigh: State Board of Charities and Public Welfare, 1937),
    31–2.

129 Douglas A. Blackmon, *Slavery by Another Name: The Re-Enslavement of Black
    Americans from the Civil War to World War II* (New York: Anchor, 2009), 4.

130 Ayers, *Vengeance and Justice*, 61–2, 198–201, 210, 212.

131 Stoler, *Race and the Education of Desire*, 72, 79; Lisa Lindquist Dorr, *White
    Women, Rape and the Power of Race in Virginia 1900–1960* (Chapel Hill:
    University of North Carolina Press, 2004).

132 Foucault, *Discipline and Punish*. Also see Pratt, *Punishment and Civilization*,
    15–34, 81–96.

133 Stoler, *Race and the Education of Desire*, 9, 68, 71, 203.

134 Frederickson, *The Black Image in the White Mind*, 255.

135 Rising numbers of Black commitments in 1928 demonstrate over-representation in juvenile court cases. People of African descent represented 5 per cent of the nation's juvenile population, and 16 per cent of reported juvenile court cases. See Bush, *Who Gets a Childhood?* 20–1; Hartman, *Scenes of Subjection*, 130, 145. The right over life and death was one of the central attributes of sovereign rule. See Foucault, *Discipline and Punish.*

136 Pascoe, *What Comes Naturally*, 9.

137 J. Wallace Nygard to Mrs Mary Ellen Forbes, superintendent of public welfare, Tarboro, NC, 30 October 1937, MTS, box 162, 1935–6, NCDAH. Strange, *Making Good*, 96; Foucault, *"Society Must Be Defended,"* 103; Jacobson, *Barbarian Virtues*; Stoler, *Race and the Education of Desire*, 10, 50–1, 61, 64, 68, 71–2, 81; Ring, *The Problem South*, 88.

138 Stoler, *Race and the Education of Desire*, 72, 119. Roberts, "Killing the Black Body," 482–500.

139 J. Morgan Kousser and Larry J. Griffin, "Forum: Revisiting a Festival of Violence," *Historical Methods* 31 (4) (Fall 1998): 172.

140 Stoler, *Race and the Education of Desire*, 68–74.

141 Foucault, *"Society Must Be Defended,"* 54.

5 The Prodigal Son

1 Kontakion hymn.

2 Stow, quoted in Rose, "Authority and the Genealogy of Subjectivity," 219.

3 Letter to Chas. E. Boger, superintendent, Stonewall Jackson Training School, 4 November 1919, box 166, SBPWIC-SCPCI, State Farm for Women, Jackson Training School, SJTS, n.d., 1917–22.

4 "Where a life began and what happened," 15 January 1921, vol. 9, Biennial report ending 1 December 1920, 4.

5 Jackson Training School, n.d., "Along Concord's Rialto," scrapbook.

6 Letter to C.E. Boger, 4 Nov. 1919.

7 "Where a life began and what happened."

8 Editorial, "A Reformatory Department," 12 January 1891.

9 J.P. Caldwell, quoted in *The Charlotte Observer*, n.d. The Democratic Party was in power in 1891, but unprecedented Populist-Republican solidarity would lead to its defeat in 1896. James Beeby, *Revolt of the Tar Heels: The North Carolina Populist Movement, 1890–1901* (Jackson: University Press of Mississippi, 2008).

10 Ayers, *Vengeance and Justice*, 198–201, 212. *Concord Daily Standard*, 9 January 1891. Memorandum: J.P. Cook, editor of *Concord Daily and Weekly Standard*,

P.C. 221.1, James P. Cook, Scrapbook, 1891–1956. Foucault, *Discipline and Punish*, 26–7; Lisa Downing, *Cambridge introduction to Michel Foucault*, 18.

11   Foucault, *The Order of Things*, 168; Foucault, *Power/Knowledge*, 197.

12   Stoler, *Race and the Education of Desire*, 89.

13   Barbara Hudson, "Punishment and Control," 235–6; Émile Durkheim, "Two Laws of Penal Evolution," in S. Lukes and A. Scull, eds, *Durkheim and the Law* (Oxford: Basil Blackwell, 1986).

14   Foucault, "What Is Enlightenment?" 313–15; "*Society Must Be Defended,*" 242.

15   David J. Rothman, "The State as Parent: Social Policy in the Progressive Era," in W. Gaylin, I. Glasser, S. Marcus, and D. Rothman, eds, *Doing Good: The Limits of Benevolence* (New York: Pantheon. 1978), 74–8.

16   Chas. Boger, superintendent, to Hon. R.F. Beasley, 31 October 1919, SBPWIC-SCPCI, State Farm for Women, Jackson Training School, SJTS, n.d., 1917–1922, box 166, Jackson Training School; Yuval-Davis, *Gender and Nation*, 26–37. Paul Johnson observes that Christian self-control was the "moral imperative around which the Northern middle class became a class." P.E. Johnson, *A Shopkeeper's Millennium: Society and Revivals in Rochester, New York, 1815–1837* (New York: Hill and Wang, 1978), 7.

17   Stoler, *Race and the Education of Desire*, 83; Rothman, "The State as Parent," 74–8; Odem, *Delinquent Daughters*, 100.

18   Foucault, *Discipline and Punish*, 216.

19   David J. Rothman, "The State as Parent: Social Policy in the Progressive Era," in W. Gaylin, I. Glasser, S. Marcus, and D. Rothman, eds, *Doing Good: The Limits of Benevolence* (New York: Pantheon. 1978), 74–8.

20   *The Uplift*, vol. 17, published by the printing class of the Stonewall Jackson Manual Training and Industrial School, 30 March 1929, 7.

21   See Foucault's discussion of the art of distributions. *Discipline and Punish*, 141.

22   Stoler, "Tense and Tender Ties," 4, 10; Strange, *Making Good*, 79.

23   Mbembe, "Necropolitics," 18. Mitchell Dean, *Critical and Effective Histories: Foucault's Methods and Historical Sociology* (London: Routledge, 1994), 171.

24   On biopower and capitalism, see Michael Hardt and Antonio Negri, *Empire* (Cambridge: Harvard University Press, 2001), 23–5, 33.

25   Downing, *Cambridge Introduction to Michel Foucault*, 77, 293, 298–9. Stoler, *Race and the Education of Desire*, 33–4

26   Foucault, *Discipline and Punish*, 136

27   Ibid., 136, 138, 293, 298–9. Stoler, *Race and the Education of Desire*, 33–4.

28   Foucault, *Discipline and Punish*, 293, 298–9. Stoler, *Race and the Education of Desire*, 33–4.

29   C. Boger to Governor J. Ehringhaus, 21 August 1936, SBPWIC-SCPCI, State Farm for Women – Jackson Training School, box 166, 1935–1952.

30 Stoler, "Making Empire Respectable," 362, 364.

31 Ring, *The Problem South*, 160–1.

32 Sally E. Hadden, *Slave Patrols: Law and Violence in Virginia and the Carolinas* (Cambridge: Harvard University Press, 2001). 205

33 Ring, *The Problem South*, 163.

34 Ibid., 162; "Race Relations in 1927," box 255.26, Nell Battle Lewis Collection, Material for "Incidentally," "The Negro," NCDAH.

35 Stoler, "Tense and Tender Ties."

36 Newkirk, *Lynching in North Carolina*, 12, 138; Beeby, *Revolt of the Tar Heels*.

37 Hubert Smith to J.P. Cook, 29 March 1892, P.C. 221.1, James P. Cook, Scrapbook, 1891–1956.

38 Letter to C.E. Boger, 4 Nov. 1919.

39 "The Governor and the Reformatory," *Concord Daily Standard*, 9 January 1891.

40 Ibid.

41 Tom MacCaulty, "After a Lifetime Crusade for Youths, ANC Network of Training Schools," *Durham Morning Herald*, 9 December 1956.

42 *The Uplift*, vol. 17, 7.

43 *The Uplift*, vol. 17, 26 January 1929, 11; SJTS, "Along Concord's Rialto"; J. Klutz, chair, to Mrs W.T. Bost, welfare commissioner, 17 April 1933, SBPWIC-SCPCI, State Farm for Women – Jackson Training School, box 166, 1923–1934.

44 Mary E. Shotwell, Division of Child-Caring Institutions; Stonewall Jackson Manual Training and Industrial School, visited 9 October 1924, 2. Stonewall Jackson Manual and Industrial School, Report for the Fiscal Year ending 30 November 1920, SBPWIC-SCPCI, State Farm for Women – Jackson Training School, box 166, 1923–1934.

45 Refers to section 7322. In re-Watson, 157–340. See sec. 5047. Unnamed, Bureau of Child Welfare, to Mrs H.K. Holcott, Norfolk, VA, 2 January 1923, SBPWIC-SCPCI, State Farm for Women – Jackson Training School, box 166, 1923–1934.

46 M.E. Shotwell, visited 9 October 1924, 1.

47 "Along Concord's Rialto."

48 Beasley to R.K. Davenport, chair, Board of County Commissioners, 2 January 1920. Beasley to J.P. Cook, 27 August 1920.

49 Jackson Training School – Statement of Assets, 29 July 1946.

50 C.E. Boger to R. Eugene Brown, director, Division of Institutions, State Board of Charities and Public Welfare, 11 August 1931.

51 Stonewall Jackson Manual and Industrial School, Report for the Fiscal Year ending 30 November 1920.

52 Jackson Training School – Statement of Assets, 29 July 1946.

53 Ibid.

54 Unnamed to Mrs H.K. Holcott, 2 January 1923.
55 Ibid.
56 Jackson Training School Celebrates Its 40th Year, n.d.; C.E. Boger to R. Eugene Brown, 15 January 1936. M.E. Shotwell, visited 9 October 1924, 1. Correspondence from Chairman to Mr B.N. Duke, New York, 26 October 1925. R. Eugene Brown to Chas Boger, superintendent, Query about institutional population statistics, 14 August 1930.
57 Correspondence from chairman to Mr B.N. Duke. Stonewall Jackson Training School parole report, Grace Reeder, 1921, box 166, SBPWIC-SCPCI, State Farm for Women, Jackson Training School, SJTS n.d., 1917–22.
58 Mr King, *Concord Tribune*, Mooresville, NC, n.d.
59 Correspondence from chairman to Mr B.N. Duke, 26 October 1925.
60 Stoler, *Race and the Education of Desire*, 38.
61 Anonymous, "Public Pulse," *Greensboro Daily News*, 8 October 1930.
62 C. Boger to anonymous, Sanford, NC, 10 January 1939; "Judge Criticizes Jackson School," *News and Observer*, 1 May 1946, SBPWIC-SCPCI, State Farm for Women – Jackson Training School, box 166, 1935–1952.
63 Strange, *Making Good*, 70.
64 Wade Cashion, director of institutions and corrections, to Agnes Thomas, superintendent of public welfare, in Gastonia, 4 March 1942, SBPWIC-SCPCI, State Farm for Women – Jackson Training School, box 166, 1935–1952.
65 Christopher Castiglia, "Abolition's Racial Interiors and the Making of White Civic Depth," *American Literary History* 14(1) (Spring 2002): 33.
66 Marshall Berman, "Why Modernism Still Matters," in Scott Lash and J. Friedman, eds, *Modernity and Identity* (Cambridge: Blackwell, 1992), 49; Marshall Berman, *All That Is Sold Melts into Air: The Experience of Modernity* (New York: Simon & Schuster, 1982), 113, 145; Gergen, *The Saturated Self*, 247, 253, 257; Odem, *Delinquent Daughters*, 96, 99; Stoler, "Making Empire Respectable," 357.
67 Superintendent Boger to Kate Burr Johnson, commissioner, 8 May 1924, SBPWIC-SCPCI, State Farm for Women – Jackson Training School, box 166, 1923–1934.
68 Rose, *Governing the Soul*; Rose, *The Psychological Complex*.
69 Foucault, *Discipline and Punish*, 82. Hudson, "Punishment and Control," 241.
70 Minnie Brown to Col. W.A. Blair, Chairman, State Board of Public Welfare, Winston-Salem, NC, 26 July 1934. SBPWIC-SCPCI, State Farm for Women – Jackson Training School, box 166, 1923–1934.
71 Latour, *We Have Never Been Modern*, 34, 36–8, 53, 87, 89.
72 Ibid., 36–7.

73 Hartman, "From Daniel Boone to the Beverly Hillbillies," 77; Ethel Speas to J. Frank Scott, superintendent, Stonewall Jackson Manual Training and Industrial School, 15 July 1952. Strange, *Making Good*, 93.

74 Secretary to C.E. Boger, superintendent, Jackson Training School, 26 October 1934.

75 Gould, "American Polygeny and Craniometry before Darwin," 90–2.

76 Gilman, "Black Bodies, White Bodies," 192.

77 Gould, "American Polygeny and Craniometry before Darwin," 90–2.

78 Stoler, *Race and the Education of Desire*, 141.

79 Michel Foucault, *Foucault Live: Collected Interviews, 1961–1984* (New York: Semiotext(e), 1989), 216.

80 Superintendent, Stonewall Jackson Training School, to Staff, "Instructions regarding Training and Discipline," 25 February 1943.

81 Ibid.

82 [Unknown] to Col. W.A. Blair, Winston-Salem, 26 July 1934, SBPWIC-SCPCI, State Industrial Farm Colony for Women (Dobb's Farms) – Stonewall Jackson Training School, box 166, Old Records Center.

83 Mariana Valverde, *The Age of Light, Soap and Water*, 20.

84 SBPWIC-SCPCI, State Farm for Women, Jackson Training School, SJTS, n.d., 1917–1922, box 166, Jackson Training School – Statement of Assets, 29 July 1946.

85 David Rothman, *Conscience and Convenience: The Asylum and Its Alternatives in Progressive America* (New York: Transaction Publishers, 2002), 219.

86 Samuel E. Leonard to S.G. Hawfield, superintendent, Jackson Training School, 14 April 1947, SBPWIC-SCPCI, State Farm for Women – Jackson Training School, box 166, 1935–1952.

87 Maclean, *Behind the Mask of Chivalry*, 112–13.

88 Hadden, *Slave Patrols*, 214.

89 W.B. Sanders to C.E. Boger, superintendent, Jackson Training School, 16 April 1923.

90 Superintendent Boger to W.B. Sanders, 21 April 1923.

91 M.E. Shotwell, visited, 9 October 1924, 15–16.

92 Mrs M.E. Braswell, Charlotte, NC, to Mrs Kate Burr Johnson, 26 October 1929.

93 Ibid.

94 Mrs Kate Burr Johnson to Mrs M.E. Braswell, 4 November 1929.

95 R. Eugene Brown and L.G. Whitley, report on visit to Jackson Training School, 15 January 1930.

96 Mrs Kate Burr Johnson to Mrs M.E. Braswell, 7 February 1930.

97 Stoler, *Along the Archival Grain*, 4.

98 R.F. Beasley, commissioner, to Charles Boger, superintendent, 3 December 1919.

99 Memorandum made from stenographic notes of conversation between Mrs Johnson and Dr Klein by Mrs C.D. Powell, 12 December 1919.

100 Ibid.

101 Commissioner Johnson to W.A. Blair, Winston-Salem, 15 June 1922.

102 Ibid.

103 Commissioner Johnson to Dr C. Banks McNairy, superintendent, Caswell Training School, 12 December 1922.

104 Commissioner Johnson to J.P. Cook, 12 June 1922.

105 Rothman, *Conscience and Convenience*, 80–1.

106 C.A. Johnson to W.A. Blair, Winston-Salem, NC 31 May 1922.

107 Ibid.

108 Commissioner Johnson to Chas Boger, superintendent, 13 March 1922.

109 C.A. Johnson W.A. Blair, Winston- Salem, NC, 31 May 1922.

110 Chair J.P. Cook to State Welfare Commissioner Mrs Clarence A. Johnson, 27 May 1922.

111 Commissioner Johnson to J.P. Cook, 12 June 1922.

112 C.A. Johnson W.A. Blair, Winston- Salem, NC, 31 May 1922.

113 Foucault, *History of Sexuality*, 25, 82, 116, 139.

114 R. Eugene Brown to C. Boger, Query about institutional population statistics.

115 Commissioner Johnson to Dr C. Banks McNairy, 12 December 1922.

116 Superintendent Boger to Mrs A.E. Howell, 10 March 1922.

117 Commissioner C.A. Johnson to Blanche Carr Sterne, county superintendent of public welfare, 8 April 1922.

118 Kate Burr Johnson, Commissioner, to Governor McLean, 16 October 1926

119 R. Eugene Brown to C. Boger, 14 August 1930.

120 C. Boger to R. Eugene Brown, n.d. August 1930.

121 J. Wallace Nygard, director, Division of Institutions and Corrections, to Grace Robson, re: Gertie Mae Oxendine (Indian) and Bessie Locklear (Indian), 18 March 1938. Nygard also states: "The Prison Division of course is required by law to accept Indians and it has been their practice to house them in the white prison camps. In cases of friction some are kept in Central Prison and not in intimate contact with either whites or Negroes." SBPWIC. Restricted records box 86: Racial Policies, Samarcand, NCDAH. Ethel Speas, Jackson Training School, n.d.; E.F. Murray, superintendent, County of Scotland, to Mrs W.T. Bost, commissioner of public welfare, Raleigh, 25 March 1935; S.G. Hawfield, superintendent,

Jackson Training School, to Kate S. MacLeod, superintendent of public welfare, Lumberton, NC, 24 November 1944.

122 R. Eugene Brown to Chas Boger, 20 July 1931; Brown to Boger, 29 July 1931.

123 R. Eugene Brown to Chas Boger, 24 March 1932.

124 Director of Institutions and Corrections to Charles E. Boger, 21 September 1937.

125 Ethel Speas to Mrs W.T. Bost, account of visit to Jackson Training School, 25 October 1937.

126 Ezell to Boger, 16 September 1939.

127 Mrs E.M. Land, Superintendent of Public Welfare, Iredell County, to Mrs Bost, "Personal," 19 September 1933.

128 A.T. Clifford, supervisor, field social work, to Mr R. Eugene Brown, assistant commissioner, Weekly report for week ending 11 September 1937, Mecklenburg County, 15 September 1937.

129 Commissioner to J.P. Cook, president, board of trustees.

130 "Investigation of treatment of George White Goodman, 16 July 1934," "Investigation of Death, 1934," SBPWIC-SCPCI, State Industrial Farm Colony for Women (Dobb's Farms) – Stonewall Jackson Training School, box 166 ORC.

131 "Investigation of Treatment of George White Goodman." C.E. Boger, Supt, to R. Eugene Brown, director, Division of Institutions, State Board of Public Welfare, SBPWIC-SCPCI, no date. State Industrial Farm Colony for Women (Dobb's Farms) – Stonewall Jackson Training School, "Investigation of Death" folder, box 166 ORC, NCSA.

132 Stonewall Jackson Training School parole report, Grace Reeder, 12 July 1921, box 166, SBPWIC-SCPCI, State Farm for Women, Jackson Training School, SJTS, n.d.,1917–1922.

133 "Investigation of Treatment of George White Goodman, Stonewall Jackson Training School, 16 July 1934. To R. Eugene Brown, director, Division of Institutions, State Board of Public Welfare, SBPWIC-SCPCI. State Industrial Farm Colony for Women (Dobb's Farms) – Stonewall Jackson Training School, "Investigation of Death" folder, box 166 ORC, NCSA. Stonewall Jackson Training School parole report, Grace Reeder, 12 July 1921, box 166. SBPWIC-SCPCI, State Farm for Women, Jackson Training School, SJTS, n.d.,1917–1922.

134 Mrs W.T. Bost to Colonel W.A. Blair, chairman, State Board of Public Welfare, Winston-Salem, NC, 1934.

135 Report on Progress Made Toward Reorganization of Jackson Training School. 23 August 1934.

136 Chas Boger to R. Eugene Brown, 24 January 1935.

137 Minnie Brown to Col. W. A. Blair, Chmn., State Board of Public Welfare, Winston-Salem, NC, 26 July 1934.
138 Mrs W.T. Bost to Col. Blair, n.d. 1934.
139 "Investigation of Treatment of George White Goodman." C.E. Boger, Supt, to R. Eugene Brown, director, Division of Institutions, State Board of Public Welfare, SBPWIC-SCPCI, no date. State Industrial Farm Colony for Women (Dobb's Farms) – Stonewall Jackson Training School, "Investigation of Death" folder, box 166 ORC, NCSA.
140 Anonymous inmate to John C.B. Ehringhaus, governor of North Carolina, 20 February 1935. Handwritten on institutional letterhead.
141 Governor John Ehringhaus to Mrs Bost, Commissioner of Public Welfare, 23 February 1935.
142 W.C. Ezell, field agent, Report re: complaint, Jackson Training School, 13 June 1935.
143 Superintendent, Stonewall Jackson Training School, "Instructions regarding Training and Discipline."

Epilogue

1 Foucault, *Technologies of the Self*, ed. Martin, Gutman, and Hutton, 15.
2 Jodi Byrd, quoted in Roxanne Dunbar-Ortiz, "North America Is a Crime Scene: The Untold History of America This Columbus Day," *Salon*, 14 October 2013.
3 The spanking of children has, until recently, been widely regarded as an acceptable disciplinary measure; but the flogging of prisoners in North Carolina had been banned at the turn of the twentieth century.
4 Stoler, *Race and the Education of Desire*, 50–1, 61, 68, 71–2, 84–5, 89.
5 Garland, *Punishment and Modern Society*, 19; Strange, *Qualities of Mercy*, 10; Rushdy, *The End of American Lynching*, 19; Anderson, *Imagined Communities*.
6 David Theo Goldberg, *Racist Culture: Philosophy and the Politics of Meaning* (Oxford: Wiley-Blackwell, 1993), 3, 6–7; Sartre, Preface to Frantz Fanon, *The Wretched of the Earth* (New York: Grove Press, 1963); Zygmunt Bauman, *Modernity and the Holocaust* (Oxford: Polity Press, 1989), 61–2. Susan Searls Giroux "On the State of Race Theory: A Conversation with David Theo Goldberg," *JAC: A Journal of Rhetoric, Culture & Politics* 26 (1–2) (2006): 23–4. Also see Stoler, *Race and the Education of Desire*, 9, 37.
7 Nielsen, "Resistance through Re-narration," 382 n. 36.

8 Hartman, *Scenes of Subjection*, 8–10, 119, 129, 139; Foner, *A Short History of Reconstruction*, 12–13, 21, 23; Foner, *Reconstruction: America's Unfinished Revolution*, 210–12, 219, 235.

9 Hartman, *Scenes of Subjection*, 183–6, 192; Kristina DuRocher, *Raising Racists: The Socialization of White Children in the Jim Crow South* (Lexington: University Press of Kentucky, 2011), 114–15; Foner, *A Short History of Reconstruction*, 93; Peggy Pascoe, *What Comes Naturally: Miscegenation Law and the Making of Race in America* (New York: Oxford, 2009), 3, 5.

10 Goldberg, *Racist Culture*, 6–7.

11 Agamben, *Homo Sacer*, 133.

12 G.J.S. Dei, L.L. Karumanchery, and N. Karumanchery-Luik, *Playing the Race Card: Exposing White Power and Privilege* (New York: Peter Laing Publishing, 2004), 49.

13 Hartman, *Scenes of Subjection*, 122–3.

14 Stoler, *Race and the Education of Desire*, 50–1, 61, 68, 71–2, 84–5, 89.

15 Hill, "Lynching and the Making of Modern America"; Rushdy, *The End of American Lynching*, 174.

16 Rushdy, *The End of American Lynching*," 19, 163–4, 167; Taylor Lewis, "Angela Davis Talks 'Racist Police Killings' at MLK Convocation," *Essence*, 4 February 2015.

17 Stoler, *Race and the Education of Desire*, 68, 89, 200.

18 Rushdy, *The End of American Lynching*, 16–18, 100, 137.

19 Ida B. Wells, *Crusade for Justice: The Autobiography of Ida B. Wells*, ed. Alfreda M. Duster (Chicago: University of Chicago Press, 2013), xvii. Christopher Waldrep, *African Americans Confront Lynching: Strategies of Resistance from the Civil War to the Civil Rights Era* (New York: Rowman & Littlefield Publishers, Inc., 2009), 45. Mia Bay, *To Tell the Truth Freely: The Life of Ida B. Wells* (New York: Hill and Wang, 2009), 55.

20 See Harvey, *The New Imperialism*; Strange, "The Undercurrents of Penal Culture."

21 Apel, *Lynching Photographs*, 77; Rushdy, *The End of American Lynching*, 163–5.

22 Byrd, quoted in Dunbar-Ortiz, "North America Is a Crime Scene."

23 A *homo sacer* is one who can be killed without this being designated as homicide, one subject to sovereign power, but lacking legal protection. Giorgio Agamben, Matthew Calarco, and Steven Di Caroli, eds, *Sovereignty and Life* (Stanford: Stanford University Press, 2007), 52; Dunbar-Ortiz, "North America Is a Crime Scene."

24 Dunbar-Ortiz, "North America Is a Crime Scene."

25 Nils Christie, *Crime Control as Industry: Towards Gulags, Western Style*, 3rd ed. (London: Routledge, 2000), 12; David Cayley, *The Expanding Prison* (New York: Anansi Press, 1998), 4, 21–2, 24–6; Angela Davis, *Are Prisons Obsolete?* (New York: Seven Stories Press, 2003), 85–6, 92; Michelle Alexander, *The New Jim Crow: Mass Incarceration in the Age of Colorblindness* (New York: New Press, 2010), 184–6, 192, 197, 200; Paul Butler, "Racially Based Jury Nullification: Black Power in the Criminal Justice System," *Yale Law Journal* 105 (1995): 705; Hartman, *Scenes of Subjection*, 189.
26 Ruth Wilson Gilmore, *Golden Gulag: Prisons, Surplus, Crisis, and Opposition in Globalizing California* (Berkeley: University of California Press, 2007), 6, 11.
27 Cayley, *The Expanding Prison*, 3, 30; Feeley, "The New Penology," 467–70.
28 Hudson, "Punishment and Control," 246–7.
29 Stoler, *Race and the Education of Desire*, 68–74.
30 Alexander, *The New Jim Crow*, 185, 187; Davis, *Are Prisons Obsolete?* 85; Cayley, *The Expanding Prison*, 10–11; Feeley, "The New Penology," 467.
31 Cayley, *The Expanding Prison*, 6.
32 Gilmore, *Golden Gulag*, 7; Davis, *Are Prisons Obsolete?* 94–5
33 Davis, *Are Prisons Obsolete?* 84, 95.
34 Faizal Mirza, "Mandatory Minimum Prison Sentencing and Systematic Racism," in *Osgoode Hall Law Journal* 39 (2/3) (2001): 492–3.
35 Review of *Keywords in Youth Studies: Tracing Affects, Movements, Knowledges*, by Nancy Lesko, and Susan Talburt, eds (New York: Routledge, 2012).
36 Foucault, *Discipline and Punish*, 265; Gilmore, *Golden Gulag*, 15; Cayley, *The Expanding Prison*, 6, 8, 21–2, 30; Malcolm Feeley and Jonathan Simon, "The New Penology: Notes on the Emerging Strategy of Corrections and Its Implications," *Criminology* 30(4) (1992): 449–74.
37 Cayley, *The Expanding Prison*, 41–2; Feeley, "The New Penology," 469.
38 Cayley, *The Expanding Prison*, 8, 29–30; Alexander, *The New Jim Crow*, 186, 194, 197. Also see Edward Said, *Orientalism* (New York: Vintage, 1979).
39 Ruth Hubbard, "Abortion and Disability: Who Should and Who Should Not Inhabit the World?" in Lennard J. Davis, ed., *The Disability Studies Reader* (London: Routledge, 2006), 93–103; Dorothy Chunn and Shelley Gavigan, "From Welfare Fraud to Welfare as Fraud: The Criminalization of Poverty," in Balfour and Comack, eds, *Criminalizing Women*, 217–32. Elias, *The History of Manners*, chap. 2.
40 Roberts, "Killing the Black Body," 499; Ruth Hubbard, "Abortion and Disability: Who Should and Who Should Not Inhabit the World?" in Lennard J. Davis, ed., *The Disability Studies Reader* (London: Routledge, 2006), 93–103; Dorothy Chunn and Shelley Gavigan, "From Welfare Fraud to

Welfare as Fraud: The Criminalization of Poverty," in Balfour and Comack, eds, *Criminalizing Women*, 217–32. Elias, *The History of Manners*, chap. 2.

41 Moon-Kie Jung, "Constituting the U.S. Empire-State and White Supremacy: The Early Years," in Moon-Kie Jung, Joao H. Costas Vargas, Eduardo Bonilla-Silva, eds, *State of White Supremacy: Racism, Governance, and the United States* (Stanford: Stanford University Press, 2011), 27–8, 30, 32, 38–9, 42; 71–2. Nielsen, "Resistance through Re-narration," 382 n. 36; Foucault, *Technologies of the Self*, ed. Martin, Gutman, and Hutton, 15, 15; Dunbar-Ortiz, "North America Is a Crime Scene."

Bibliography

Abdur-Rahman, Aliyyah I. "'This Horrible Exhibition': Sexuality in Slave Narratives." In *The Oxford Handbook of the African American Slave Narrative*, edited by John Ernest, 235–47. New York: Oxford University Press, 2014.

Adelman, Jeremy, and Stephen Aron. "From Borderlands to Borders: Empires, Nation-States, and the Peoples in Between in North American History." *American Historical Review* 104, no. 3 (1999): 814–41.

Agamben, Giorgio. *Homo Sacer: Sovereign Power and Bare Life*. Stanford: Stanford University Press, 1998.

Agamben, Giorgio, Matthew Calarco, and Steven Di Caroli, eds. *Sovereignty and Life*. Stanford: Stanford University Press, 2007.

Alexander, Michelle. *The New Jim Crow: Mass Incarceration in the Age of Colorblindness*. New York: New Press, 2010.

Anderson, Benedict. *Imagined Communities: Reflections on the Origin and Spread of Nationalism*. London: Verso, 1991.

Apel, Dora, and Shawn Michelle Smith. *Lynching Photographs: Defining Moments in American Photography*. Berkeley: University of California Press, 2008.

Applegate, Celia. *A Nation of Provincials: The German Idea of Heimat*. Berkeley: University of California Press, 1990.

Ayers, Edward. *The Promise of the New South: Life after Reconstruction*. New York: Oxford University Press, 1992.

– *Vengeance and Justice: Crime and Punishment in the Nineteenth-Century American South*. New York: Oxford University Press, 1984.

Baker, Kathryn Hinojosa. "Delinquent Desire: Race, Sex and Ritual in Reform Schools for Girls." *Discourse* 15, no. 1 (1992): 49–68.

Baker, Lee. *Anthropology and the Racial Politics of Culture*. Durham, NC: Duke University Press, 2010.

Baldwin, Sidney. *Poverty and Politics: The Rise and Decline of the Farm Security Administration.* Chapel Hill: University of North Carolina Press, 1968.

Balfour, G. "Introduction: Regulating Women and Girls." In *Criminalizing Women: Gender and (In)justice in Neo-liberal Times,* edited by Gillian Balfour and Elizabeth Comack. Halifax: Fernwood Publishing, 2006.

Bannerji, Himani. "Popular Images of South Asian Women." In *Returning the Gaze,* edited by Himani Bannerji, 144–52. Toronto: Sister Vision Press, 1993.

Barton, W.E. "Work among the American Highlanders." *The American Missionary,* December1898.

Bauman, Zygmunt. *Modernity and the Holocaust.* Oxford: Polity Press, 1989.

Bay, Mia. *To Tell the Truth Freely: The Life of Ida B. Wells.* New York: Hill and Wang, 2009.

Baynton, Douglas, "Disability and the Justification of Inequality in American History." In *The New Disability History: American Perspectives,* edited by Paul K. Longmore and Lauri Umansky, 33–57. New York: New York University Press, 2001.

Bederman, Gail. "'Civilization,' the Decline of Middle-Class Manliness, and Ida B. Wells's Antilynching Campaign, 1982–94." *Radical History Review* 52 (1992): 5–30.

– *Manliness & Civilization: A Cultural History of Gender and Race in the United States, 1880–1917.* Chicago: University of Chicago Press, 1995.

Beeby, James. *Revolt of the Tar Heels: The North Carolina Populist Movement, 1890–1901.* Jackson: University Press of Mississippi, 2008.

Berlant, Lauren. *The Anatomy of National Fantasy: Hawthorne, Utopia and Everyday Life.* Chicago: University of Chicago Press, 1991.

– "National Brands / National Body: Imitation of Life." In *The Phantom Public Sphere,* edited by Bruce Robbins, 173–208. Minneapolis: Minnesota University Press, 1993.

– *The Queen of America Goes to Washington City.* Durham, NC: Duke University Press, 1997.

Berman, Marshall. *All That Is Sold Melts into Air: The Experience of Modernity.* New York: Simon & Schuster, 1982.

– "Why Modernism Still Matters." In *Modernity and Identity,* edited by Scott Lash and J. Friedman, 33–58. Cambridge: Blackwell, 1992.

Bernstein, Nina. *The Lost Children of Wilder: The Epic Struggle to Change Foster Care.* New York: Pantheon, 2001.

Bhabha, Homi. "DissemiNation: Time, Narrative and the Margins of the Modern Nation." In H.K. Bhabha, *Nation and Narration.* London: Routledge, 1990.

Bickford, Annette L. "Civilizing Adolescence: Race, Sexuality and Nation Building in North Carolina's Reformatory Movement 1918–1944." PhD diss., York University, 2002.

– "Imperial Modernity, Regional Identity and Popular Culture in the Samarcand Arson Case, 1931." *Nations and Nationalism: Journal of the Association for the Study of Ethnicity and Nationalism* 13, no. 2 (2007): 437–60.

– "The Merciful Executioner: Spectacles of Sexual Danger and National Reunification in the Case of George Stinney, 1944." *Southern Anthropologist* 35, no. 1 (2010): 41–61.

Blackmon, Douglas A. *Slavery by Another Name: The Re-Enslavement of Black Americans from the Civil War to World War II.* New York: Anchor, 2009.

Blanchard, Pascal, Nicolas Bancel, Eric Deroo, and Sandrine Lemaire, eds. *Human Zoos: Science and Spectacle in the Age of Colonial Empires.* Liverpool: University of Liverpool Press, 2008.

Blee, Kathleen M. *Women of the Klan: Racism and Gender in the 1920s.* Berkeley: University of California Press, 1991.

Boritch, Helen. "Women in Prison." In *Corrections in Canada: Social Reactions to Crime*, edited by John Winterdyk, 213–37. Toronto: Prentice Hall, 2001.

Brantlinger, Patrick. "Victorians and Africans: The Genealogy of the Myth of the Dark Continent." *Critical Inquiry* 12, no. 1 (1985): 166–203.

Bruck, David. "Executing Juveniles for Crime." *New York Times*, 16 June 1984.

– "Executing Teen-Age Killers Again: The 14 Year-Old, Who in Many Ways, Was Too Small for the Chair." *Washington Post*, 15 September 1985.

Bush, William S. *Who Gets a Childhood? Race and Juvenile Justice in Twentieth Century Texas.* Athens: University of Georgia Press, 2010.

Butler, Judith. "Endangerer/Endangering: Schematic Racism and White Paranoia." In *Reading Rodney King / Reading Urban Uprising*, edited by Robert Gooding Williams, 15–22. New York: Routledge, 1993.

Butler, Paul. "Racially Based Jury Nullification: Black Power in the Criminal Justice System." *Yale Law Journal* 105, no. 3 (1995): 677–725.

Bynum, Victoria. *Unruly Women: The Politics of Social and Sexual Control in the Old South.* Chapel Hill: University of North Carolina Press, 1992.

Cahn, Susan K. *Sexual Reckonings: Southern Girls in a Troubling Age.* Cambridge, MA: Harvard University Press, 2007.

– "Spirited Youth or Friends Incarnate: The Samarcand Arson Case and Female Adolescence in the American South." *Journal of Women's History* 9, no. 4 (1998): 152–80.

Carby, Hazel V. "'On the Threshold of Woman's Era': Lynching, Empire and Sexuality in Black Feminist Theory." In *Dangerous Liaisons: Gender, Nation, and Postcolonial Perspectives*, edited by Anne McClintock, Aamir Mufti, and Ella Shohat, 330–43. Minneapolis: University of Minnesota Press, 1997.

Cash, W.J. *The Mind of the South*. New York: Alfred A. Knopf, 1941.

Castiglia, Christopher. "Abolition's Racial Interiors and the Making of White Civic Depth." *American Literary History* 14, no. 1 (2002): 33–59.

Cayley, David. *The Expanding Prison*. New York: Anasi Press, 1998.

Chari, Sharad. "State Racism and Biopolitical Struggle: The Evasive Commons in Twentieth-Century Durban, South Africa." *Radical History Review* 2010, no. 108 (2010): 73–90.

Charsley, S. "Sanskritization: The Career of an Anthropological Theory." *Contributions to Indian Sociology* 32, no. 2 (1998): 527–49.

Christie, Nils. *Crime Control as Industry: Towards Gulags, Western Style*. 3rd ed. London: Routledge, 2000.

Chunn, Dorothy, and Shelley Gavigan. "From Welfare Fraud to Welfare as Fraud: The Criminalization of Poverty." In *Criminalizing Women: Gender and (In)Justice in Neo-liberal Times*, edited by Gillian Balfour and E. Comack, 217–32. Halifax: Fernwood Publishing, 2006.

Confino, Alon. *The Nation as a Local Metaphor*. Chapel Hill: University of North Carolina Press, 1997.

Davis, Angela. *Are Prisons Obsolete?* New York: Seven Stories Press, 2003.

Dean, Mitchell. *Critical and Effective Histories: Foucault's Methods and Historical Sociology*. London: Routledge, 1994.

Dei, G.J.S., L.L. Karumanchery, and N. Karumanchery-Luik. *Playing the Race Card: Exposing White Power and Privilege*. New York: Peter Laing, 2004.

DeSantis, John. "Wilmington Revisits a Bloody 1898 Day." *New York Times*, 4 June 2006, 1 and 33.

Dorr, Lisa Lindquist. *White Women, Rape and the Power of Race in Virginia 1900–1960*. Chapel Hill: University of North Carolina Press, 2004.

Downing, Lisa. *The Cambridge Introduction to Michel Foucault*. Cambridge: Cambridge University Press, 2008.

Dreyfus, Hubert L., and Paul Rabinow. *Michel Foucault: Beyond Structuralism and Hermeneutics*. New York: Routledge, 2013.

Du Bois, W.E.B. *Black Reconstruction in America, 1860–1880*. New York: Atheneum, 1992.

– *The Souls of Black Folk*. New York: Signet, 1969.

Dugdale, Richard Louis. *The Jukes: A Study in Crime, Pauperism, Disease and Heredity*. New York: G.P. Putnam's Sons, 1910.

Dunbar-Ortiz, Roxanne. *An Indigenous Peoples' History of the United States*. Boston: Beacon Press, 2014.

- "North America Is a Crime Scene: The Untold History of America This Columbus Day." *Salon*, 14 October 2013.

Durkheim, E. "Two Laws of Penal Evolution." In *Durkheim and the Law*, edited by S. Lukes and A. Scull. Oxford: Basil Blackwell, 1986.

DuRocher, Kristina. *Raising Racists: The Socialization of White Children in the Jim Crow South*. Lexington: University Press of Kentucky, 2011.

Edwards, Elizabeth. "Photography and the Making of the Other." In *Human Zoos: Science and Spectacle in the Age of Colonial Empires*, edited by Pascal Blanchard, Nicolas Bancel, Eric Deroo, and Sandrine Lemaire, 239–46. New York: Oxford University Press, 2009.

Elias, Norbert. *The Civilising Process: The History of Manners and State Formation and Civilisation*. Translated by Edmund Jephcott. Oxford: Blackwell, 1994.

Faith, Karlene, and Jasmin Jiwani. "The Social Construction of 'Dangerous' Girls and Women." In *Marginality and Condemnation: An Introduction to Critical Criminology*, edited by Bernard Schissel and Carolyn Brooks, 135–61. Halifax: Fernwood, 2008.

Fausto-Sterling, Anne. "Gender, Race and Nation: The Comparative Anatomy of 'Hottentot' Women in Europe, 1815–1817." In *Deviant Bodies: Critical Perspectives on Difference in Science and Popular Culture*, edited by J. Terry and J. Urla, 19–48. Bloomington: Indiana University Press, 1995.

Feeley, Malcolm, and Jonathan Simon. "The New Penology: Notes on the Emerging Strategy of Corrections and Its Implications." *Criminology* 30, no. 4 (1992): 449–74.

Feld, Barry C. *Bad Kids: Race and the Transformation of the Juvenile Court*. New York: Oxford University Press, 1999.

Feldman, Glenn. *The Disfranchisement Myth: Poor Whites and Suffrage Restriction in Alabama*. Athens: University of Georgia Press, 2004.

Flavin, Jeanne. *Our Bodies, Our Crimes: The Policing of Women's Reproduction in America*. New York: New York University Press, 2008.

Foner, Eric. *Reconstruction: America's Unfinished Revolution, 1863–1877*. New York: Harper and Row, 1984.

- *A Short History of Reconstruction 1863–1877*. New York: Harper and Row, 1990.

Foucault, Michel. *"Abnormal": Lectures at the Collège de France, 1974–1975*. New York: Picador, 2003.

- "The Confessions of the Flesh." In *Power/Knowledge: Selected Interviews and Other Writings, 1972–1977*, edited by C. Gordon, L. Marshall, J. Mepham, and K. Soper, 194–228. New York: Vintage, 1980.

- "The Subject and Power" *Critical Inquiry*, 8:4 (1982): 777–95

- *Discipline and Punish: The Birth of the Prison*. New York: Vintage Books, 1995.

– *Foucault Live: Collected Interviews, 1961–1984*. New York: Semiotext(e), 1989.
– "Governmentality." In *The Foucault Effect, Studies in Governmentality*, edited by G. Burchell and P. Miller, 87–104. Chicago: University of Chicago Press, 1991.
– *History of Sexuality: An Introduction*. Vol. 1. New York: Vintage, 1978.
– *The Order of Things: An Archaeology of the Human Sciences*. London: Routledge, 1970.
– *"Society Must Be Defended": Lectures at the Collège de France, 1975–1976*. New York: Picador, 2003.
– "What Is Enlightenment?" In *Ethics: Subjectivity, and Truth*, vol.1 of *The Essential Works of Foucault, 1954–1984*, edited by Paul Rabinow, 303–19. New York: New Press, 2001.
Foucault, Michel, Luther H. Martin, Huck Gutman, and Patrick H. Hutton, eds. *Technologies of the Self: A Seminar with Michel Foucault*. Amherst: University of Massachusetts Press, 1988.
Foucault, Michel, and Paul Rabinow. *The Foucault Reader*. New York: Pantheon Books, 1984.
Fraser, John. *America and the Patterns of Chivalry*. London: Cambridge University Press, 1982.
Fredrickson, George. *The Black Image in the White Mind*. Middleton, CT: Wesleyan University Press, 1971.
Freedman, Estelle B. *Their Sisters' Keepers: Women's Prison Reform in America, 1830–1930*. Ann Arbor: University of Michigan Press, 1984.
Gabbidon, S., and H. Greene, eds. *Race, Crime and Justice: A Reader*. New York: Routledge, 2005.
Gaines, Kevin. "Black Americans' Racial Uplift Ideology as 'Civilising Mission': Pauline E. Hopkins on Race and Imperialism." In *Cultures of United States Imperialism*, edited by Amy Kaplan and Donald E. Pease, 433–55. Durham, NC: Duke University Press, 1993.
Garland, David. *Punishment and Modern Society: A Study in Social Theory*. Chicago: University of Chicago Press, 1990.
Gergen, Kenneth. *The Saturated Self: Dilemmas of Identity in Contemporary Life*. New York: Basic Books, 1991.
Gerstle, Gary. *American Crucible: Race and Nation in the Twentieth Century*. Princeton: Princeton University Press, 2001.
Gilman, Sander. "Black Bodies, White Bodies: Toward an Iconography of Female Sexuality in Late Nineteenth Century Art, Medicine, and Literature." *Critical Inquiry* 12, no. 1 (1985): 204–42.
– *Difference and Pathology*. Ithaca: Cornell University Press, 1985.

– "'I'm Down on Whores': Race and Gender in Victorian London." In *Anatomy of Racism*, edited by David Theo Goldberg, 146–70. Minneapolis: University of Minnesota Press, 1990.

Gilmore, Glenda. *Gender and Jim Crow: Women and the Politics of White Supremacy in North Carolina, 1896–1920.* Chapel Hill: University of North Carolina Press, 1996.

Gilmore, Ruth Wilson. *Golden Gulag: Prisons, Surplus, Crisis, and Opposition in Globalizing California.* Berkeley: University of California Press, 2007.

Glasgow, Ellen. *The Voice of the People.* New York: Doubleday, Page & Co., 1900.

Goldberg, David Theo. *Racist Culture: Philosophy and the Politics of Meaning.* Oxford: Wiley-Blackwell, 1993.

Gordon, Linda. "Black and White Visions of Welfare, Women's Welfare Activism, 1890–1945." In *"We Specialize in the Wholly Impossible": A Reader in Black Women's History*, edited by Darlene Clark Hine, Wilma King, and Linda Reed, 449–86. New York: Carlson Publishing, 1995.

– "Internal Colonialism and Gender." In *Haunted by Empire: Geographies of Intimacy in North American History*, edited by Ann Laura Stoler, 427–51. Durham, NC: Duke University Press, 2006.

– *Pitied but Not Entitled: Single Mothers and the History of Welfare 1890–1935.* New York: The Free Press, 1994.

Gosden, Chris, and Chantal Knowles. *Collecting Colonialism: Material Culture and Colonial Change.* New York: Berg, 2001.

Gould, Stephen J. "American Polygeny and Craniometry before Darwin." In *The Racial Economy of Science*, edited by Sandra Harding, 84–115. Bloomington: Indiana University Press, 1993.

– *The Mismeasure of Man.* New York: W.W. Norton, 2006.

– *Ontology and Phylogeny.* Cambridge, MA: Harvard University Press, 1977.

Gourevitch, Alex. "Our Forgotten Labor Revolution." *Jacobin*, issue 18 (Summer 2015): 61–9.

Green, Fletcher. "Resurgent Southern Sectionalism, 1933–1955." In *Democracy in the Old South and Other Essays by Fletcher Melvin Green*, edited by J. Isaac Copeland, 288–306. Nashville: Vanderbilt University Press, 1969.

Gross, Kali. *Colored Amazons: Crime, Violence, and Black Women in the City of Brotherly Love, 1880–1910.* Durham, NC: Duke University Press, 2006.

Gunning, Sandra. *Race, Rape and Lynching.* London: Oxford University Press, 1996.

Gupta, Dipankar. *Justice before Reconciliation: Negotiating a "New Normal" in Post-riot Mumbai and Ahmedabad.* New Delhi: Routledge, 2011.

Hacking, Ian. "Making up People." *London Review of Books* 28, no. 16 (2006): 23–6.

Hadden, Sally E. *Slave Patrols: Law and Violence in Virginia and the Carolinas.* Cambridge, MA: Harvard University Press, 2001.

Hale, Grace Elizabeth. *Making Whiteness: The Culture of Segregation in the South, 1890–1940.* New York: Oxford University Press, 1998.

Hall, Jacquelyn Dowd. "'The Mind That Burns in Each Body': Women, Rape and Racial Violence." In *Powers of Desire: The Politics of Sexuality,* edited by A. Snitow, C. Stansell, and S. Thompson. New York: Monthly Review Press, 1983.

– *Revolt against Chivalry: Jesse Daniel Ames and the Women's Campaign against Lynching.* New York: Columbia University Press, 1993.

Hall, Stuart. "What Is This 'Black' in Black Popular Culture?" In *Black Popular Culture,* edited by Gina Dent, 21–33. Seattle: Bay Press, 1992.

Hardt, Michael, and Antonio Negri. *Empire.* Cambridge, MA: Harvard University Press, 2001.

Harris, Cheryl. "Whiteness as Property." *Harvard Law Review* 106, no. 8 (1993): 1707–91.

Harris, Trudier. *Exorcising Blackness: Historical and Literary Lynching and Burning Rituals.* Bloomington: Indiana University Press, 1984.

Hartman, Ian Christian. "From Daniel Boone to the Beverly Hillbillies: Tales of a 'Fallen' Race, 1873–1968." Ph.D. diss., University of Illinois at Urbana-Champaign, 2011.

Hartman, Saidiya. *Scenes of Subjection: Terror, Slavery, and Self-Making in Nineteenth-Century America.* New York: Oxford, 1997.

Harvey, David. *The New Imperialism.* New York: Oxford, 2003.

Hay, Douglas. *Albion's Fatal Tree: Crime and Society in Eighteenth-Century England.* London: Pantheon Books, 1975.

– Foreword to *Qualities of Mercy: Justice, Punishment, and Discretion,* by Carolyn Strange, vii–x. Vancouver: UBC Press, 1996.

Hill, Karlos K. "Lynching and the Making of Modern America." *Reviews in American History* 39, no. 4 (2011): 652–9.

Hine, Darlene Clark. "'We Specialize in the Wholly Impossible': The Philanthropic Work of Black Women." In *Lady Bountiful Revisited: Women, Philanthropy and Power,* edited by Kathleen D. McCarthy. London: Rutgers University Press, 1990.

Hodes, Martha. "The Sexualization of Reconstruction Politics: White Women and Black Men in the South after the Civil War." *Journal of the History of Sexuality* 3, no. 3 (1993): 402–17.

Hoganson, Kristin L. *Fighting for American Manhood: How Gender Politics Provoked the Spanish American and Philippine American Wars.* New Haven: Yale University Press, 2000.

Hubbard, Ruth. "Abortion and Disability: Who Should and Who Should Not Inhabit the World?" *The Disability Studies Reader*, edited by Lennard J. Davis, 93–103. London: Routledge, 2006.

Hudson, Barbara. "Punishment and Control." In *The Oxford Handbook of Criminology*, 3rd ed., edited by Mike Maguire, Rod Morgan, and Robert Reiner, 234–62. London: Oxford University Press, 2002.

Iden, Susan. "N.C. Home for Delinquent Girls Is Developing into Matrimonial Institution: Success of Samarcand Is Built on Faith of Miss Agnes MacNaughton, the Superintendent, IN Girls, Most of Whom Want to Make Good; No Locks or Barred Gates at Sandhill Institution." *News and Observer* (Raleigh, NC), 1 October 1927.

Jacobson, Matthew Frye. *Barbarian Virtues: The U.S. Encounters Foreign Peoples at Home and Abroad, 1876–1917*. New York: Hill and Wang, 2001.

James, Joy. *States of Confinement: Policing, Detention and Prisons*. New York: Palgrave, 2002.

Johnson, Guion G. *Ante-Bellum North Carolina: A Social History*. Chapel Hill: University of North Carolina Press, 1937.

Johnson, Paul E. *A Shopkeeper's Millennium: Society and Revivals in Rochester, New York, 1815–1837*. New York: Hill and Wang, 1978.

Jones, Ann. *Women Who Kill*. New York: The Feminist Press at CUNY, 2009.

Jung, Moon-Kie. "Constituting the U.S. Empire-State and White Supremacy: The Early Years." In *State of White Supremacy: Racism, Governance, and the United States*, edited by Moon-Kie Jung, Joao H. Costas Vargas, and Eduardo Bonilla-Silva. Stanford: Stanford University Press, 2011.

Kaplan, Amy. *The Anarchy of Empire in the Making of U.S. Culture*. Cambridge, MA: Harvard University Press, 2002.

– "'Left Alone with America': The Absence of Empire in the Study of American Culture." In *Cultures of United States Imperialism*, edited by Amy Kaplan and Donald E. Pease, 3–21. Durham, NC: Duke University Press, 1993.

Katz, Maude White. "The Negro Woman and the Law." *Freedomways* 2 (1962): 278–86.

Key, V.O. *Southern Politics in State and Nation*. Knoxville: University of Tennessee Press, 1977.

Kousser, J. Morgan, and Larry J. Griffin. "Forum: Revisiting a Festival of Violence." *Historical Methods* 31, no. 4 (1998): 171–80.

Kristeva, Julia. *Powers of Horror: An Essay on Abjection*. Translated by Leon S. Roudiez. New York: Columbia University Press, 1982.

Krugler, David, "America's Forgotten Mass Lynching: When 237 People Were Murdered in Arkansas." *The Daily Beast*, 16 February 2015.

http://www.thedailybeast.com/articles/2015/02/16/america-s-forgotten-mass-lynching-when-237-people-were-murdered-in-arkansas.html.

Lake, Marilyn, and Henry Reynolds. *Drawing the Global Colour Line: White Men's Countries and the International Challenge of Racial Equality*. Cambridge: Cambridge University Press, 2008).

Latour, Bruno. *We Have Never Been Modern*. Cambridge, MA: Harvard University Press, 1993.

Lefeber, Walter. *The New Empire: An Interpretation of American Expansion, 1860–1898*. Ithaca: Cornell University Press, 1998.

Lerner, Gerda. *Black Women in White America: A Documentary History*. New York: Vintage, 1992.

Levy, Eugene. "Is the Jew a White Man? Press Reaction to the Leo Frank Case, 1913–1915." *Phylon* 35, no. 2 (1974): 212–22.

Lewis, Taylor. "Angela Davis Talks 'Racist Police Killings' at MLK Convocation." *Essence*, 4 February 2015.

The Literary Digest: A Repository of Contemporaneous Thought and Research, volume 9. New York: Funk and Wagnalls, 1894.

Loewen, James W. "*Democracy Betrayed the Wilmington Race Riot of 1898 and Its Legacy* (review)." *Southern Cultures* 6, no. 3 (2000): 90–3.

Loo, Tina. "Savage Mercy: Native Culture and the Modification of Capital Punishment in Nineteenth-Century British Columbia." In *Qualities of Mercy: Justice, Punishment, and Discretion*, edited by Carolyn Strange, 104–29. Vancouver: UBC Press, 1996.

Love, Eric T.L. *Race over Empire: Racism and U.S. Imperialism 1865–1900*. Chapel Hill: University of North Carolina Press, 2004.

Lowery, Malinda Maynor. *Lumbee Indians in the Jim Crow South: Race, Identity, and the Making of a Nation*. Chapel Hill: University of North Carolina Press, 2010.

Mack, Julian. "The Juvenile Court." *Harvard Law Review* 23, no. 2 (1909): 104–22.

Maclean, Nancy. *Behind the Mask of Chivalry: The Making of the Second Ku Klux Klan*. New York: Oxford University Press, 1994.

Martin, Luther H., Huck Gutman, and Patrick H. Hutton, eds. *Technologies of the Self: A Seminar with Michel Foucault*. Amherst: University of Massachusetts Press, 1988.

Marx, Karl. "On the Jewish Question." In *The Marx-Engels Reader*, edited by Robert C. Tucker. New York: W.W. Norton, 1978.

Mbembe, Achille. "Necropolitics." *Public Culture* 15, no. 1 (2003): 11–40.

McClintock, Anne. *Imperial Leather: Race, Gender and Sexuality in the Colonial Contest*. New York: Routledge, 1995.

McClintock, Anne. "'No Longer in a Future Heaven': Gender, Race and Nationalism." In Geoff Eley and Ronald Suny, eds, *Becoming National: A Reader*, 104–23. New York: Oxford University Press, 1996.

– "Paranoid Empire: Specters from Guantánamo and Abu Ghraib." *Small Axe* 13, no. 1 (2009): 50–74.

McMurry, Linda O. *To Keep the Waters Troubled: The Life of Ida B. Wells*. New York: Oxford University Press, 2000.

McWilliams, Tennant. *The New South Faces the World: Foreign Affairs and the Southern Sense of Self, 1877–1950*. Baton Rouge: Louisiana State Press, 1988.

Meier, August. *Negro Thought in America 1880–1915*. Ann Arbor: University of Michigan Press, 1988.

Meyer, Cheryl, and Michelle Oberman. *Mothers Who Kill Their Children: Understanding the Acts of Moms from Susan Smith to the "Prom Mom."* New York: New York University Press, 2001.

Mirza, Faizal. "Mandatory Minimum Prison Sentencing and Systematic Racism." *Osgoode Hall Law Journal* 39, no. 2/3 (2001): 491–512.

Montrose, Louis. "The Work of Gender in the Discourse of Discovery." *Representations* 33 (1991): 1–41.

Morgan, Kathryn Pauly. "Foucault, Ugly Ducklings and TechnoSwans: Analyzing Fat Hatred, Weight Loss Surgery and Compulsory Biomedicalized Aesthetics in America." *International Journal of Feminist Approaches to Bioethics* 4, no. 1 (2011): 188–220.

Mosse, George. *Nationalism and Sexuality: Respectability and Abnormal Sexuality in Modern Europe*. New York: Howard Fertig, 1985.

Murphy, Paul V. *The Rebuke of History: The Southern Agrarians and American Conservative Thought*. Chapel Hill: University of North Carolina Press, 2001.

Myrdal, Gunnar. *An American Dilemma: The Negro Problem and Modern Democracy*. New Brunswick, NJ: Transaction Publishers, 1996.

Nathans, Sydney. *The Quest for Progress: The Way We Lived in North Carolina, 1870–1920*. Chapel Hill: University of North Carolina Press, 1983.

Neve, Lisa, and Kim Pate. "Challenging the Criminalization of Women Who Resist." In *Global Lockdown: Race, Gender, and the Prison-Industrial Complex*, edited by Julia Sudbury. Routledge: New York, 2005.

Newkirk, Vann R. *Lynching in North Carolina: A History 1865–1941*. Jefferson: McFarland and Company, 2009.

Newsome, A.R., ed. *North Carolina Manual*. Raleigh: Publications of the North Carolina Historical Commission, Edwards A. Broughton Co., State Printers, 1927.

Nielsen, Cynthia R. "Resistance through Re-narration: Fanon on Deconstructing Racialized Subjectivities." *African Identities* 9, no. 4 (2011): 363–85.

Odem, Mary. *Delinquent Daughters: Protecting and Policing Adolescent Female Sexuality in the United States, 1885–1920*. Chapel Hill: University of North Carolina Press, 1995.

Oka, Kayleen. "Racism 'Renewed': Nationalist Practices, Citizenship and Fantasy Post-9/11." In *Engaging Equity: New Perspectives on Anti-Racist Education*, edited by Leeno Karumanchery. Calgary: Detselig, 2005.

O'Leary, Cecilia Elizabeth. *To Die For: The Paradox of American Patriotism*. Princeton: Princeton University Press, 1999.

Osterweiss, Rollin Gustav. *The Myth of the Lost Cause, 1865–1900*. Hamden, CT: The Shoe String Press, 1973.

Page, Walter Hines. "The Hookworm and Civilisation." *World's Work* 24 (1912): 504–18.

Parezo, Nancy, and Don Fowler. "Assembling the Races of Mankind." In *Anthropology Goes to the Fair: The 1904 Louisiana Purchase Exposition*, 73–99. Lincoln: University of Nebraska Press, 2007.

Pascoe, Peggy. *What Comes Naturally: Miscegenation Law and the Making of Race in America*. New York: Oxford, 2009.

Patterson, Orlando. *Rituals of Blood: Consequences of Slavery in Two American Centuries*. Washington: Civitas/Counterpoint, 1998.

Pearson, Susan. "Samarcand, Nell Battle Lewis, and the 1931 Arson Trial." Unpublished undergraduate honours essay, NCC-UNC,1989.

Pease, Donald. "New Perspectives on U.S. Culture and Imperialism." In *Cultures of United States Imperialism*, edited by Amy Kaplan and Donald E. Pease, 22–37. Durham, NC: Duke University Press, 1993.

– "US Imperialism: Global Dominance without Colonies." In *A Companion to Postcolonial Studies*, edited by Henry Schwartz and Sangeeta Ray, 203–20. Oxford: Blackwell, 2005.

Perkins, Kathy A., and Judith Louise Stephens. *Strange Fruit: Plays on Lynching by American Women*. Bloomington: Indiana University Press, 1998.

Perman, Michael. *Struggle for Mastery: Disfranchisement in the South, 1888–1908*. Chapel Hill: University of North Carolina Press, 2001.

Pfeifer, Michael. *Rough Justice: Lynching and American Society, 1874–1947*. Chicago: University of Illinois Press, 2004.

Pick, Daniel. *Faces of Degeneration: A European Disorder, c. 1848–c. 1918*. Cambridge: Cambridge University Press, 1989.

Pildes, Richard H. "Democracy, Anti-Democracy, and the Canon." *Constitutional Commentary* 17, no. 2 (2000): 295–320.

Pratt, John. *Punishment and Civilization: Penal Tolerance and Intolerance in Modern Society*. London: Sage, 2002.

Proctor, Robert. "Nazi Medicine and the Politics of Knowledge." In *The Racial Economy of Science*, edited by Sandra Harding. Bloomington: Indiana University Press, 1993.

Quinlan, Kieran. *Strange Kin: Ireland and the American South*. Baton Rouge: Louisiana State University Press, 2005.

Rafter, Nicole Hahn. *Partial Justice: Women, Prisons and Social Control*. London: Transaction Publishers, 1995.

Raper, Arthur. *The Tragedy of Lynching*. New York: Dover Publications, 2003.

Razack, Sherene H. "Gendered Racial Violence and Spatialized Justice: The Murder of Pamela George." *Canadian Journal of Law and Society* 15, no. 2 (2000): 91–130.

– "Race, Space and Prostitution: The Making of the Bourgeois Subject." *Canadian Journal of Women and the Law* 10, no. 2 (1998): 338–76.

Ring, Natalie J. *The Problem South: Region, Empire, and the New Liberal State, 1880–1930*. Athens: University of Georgia Press, 2012.

Roberts, Dorothy. "Killing the Black Body." In *Maternal Theory: Essential Readings*, edited by Andrea O'Reilly, 482–99. Toronto: Demeter Press. 2007.

Roediger David. *How Race Survived U.S. History: From Settlement and Slavery to the Obama Phenomenon*. London: Verso, 2008.

– *The Wages of Whiteness: Race and the Making of the American Working Class*. London: Verso, 1991.

Rose, Nikolas. "Authority and the Genealogy of Subjectivity." In *Detraditionalization: Critical Reflections on Authority and Identity*, edited by P. Heelas, S. Lash, and P. Morris, 294–327. Oxford: Blackwell, 1996.

– *Governing the Soul: The Shaping of the Private Self*. London: Routledge, 1990.

– *The Psychological Complex: Psychology, Politics and Society in England 1869–1939*. London: Routledge and Kegan Paul, 1985.

Rothman, David. *Conscience and Convenience: The Asylum and Its Alternatives in Progressive America*. New York: Transaction Publishers, 2002.

Rothman, David J. "The State as Parent: Social Policy in the Progressive Era." In Willard Gaylin, Ira Glasser, Steven Marcus, and David Rothman, *Doing Good: The Limits of Benevolence*. New York: Pantheon, 1978.

Rudwick, Elliott, and August Meier. "Black Man in the 'White City': Negroes and the Columbian Exposition, 1893." *Clark Atlanta University Journal* 26, no. 4 (1965): 354–61.

Rushdy, Ashraf. *The End of American Lynching*. New Brunswick, NJ: Rutgers University Press, 2012.

Russell, Anne, and Melton McLaurin. *The Wayward Girls of Samarcand: A True Story of the American South*. Wilmington, NC: Bradley Creek Press, 2012.

Ryan, Mary P. *Civic Wars: Democracy and Public Life in the American City during the Nineteenth Century*. Berkeley: University of California Press, 1997.

Said, Edward. *Orientalism*. New York: Vintage, 1979.

Salem, Dorothy C. *To Better Our World: Black Women in Organised Reform, 1890–1920*. Brooklyn: Carlson Publishing, 1990.

Sallee, Shelley. *The Whiteness of Child Labor Reform in the New South*. Athens: University of Georgia Press, 2004.

Sanders, Wiley B., ed. *Juvenile Offenders for a Thousand Years: Selected Readings from Anglo-Saxon Times to 1900*. Chapel Hill: University of North Carolina Press, 1970.

– *Negro Child Welfare in North Carolina*. Glen Ridge, NJ: Patterson Smith Publishing Corporation, 1968.

Sanders, Wiley, and William Ezell. *Juvenile Court Cases in North Carolina 1929–1934*. Raleigh: State Board of Charities and Public Welfare, 1937.

Sartre, Jean-Paul. Preface to Frantz Fanon, *The Wretched of the Earth*. New York: Grove Press, 1963.

Schiebinger, Londa. *Nature's Body: Gender in the Making of Modern Science*. Boston: Beacon Press, 1993.

Schoen, Johanna. *Choice and Coercion: Birth Control, Sterilization, and Abortion in Public Health and Welfare*. Chapel Hill: University of North Carolina Press, 2005.

Schuyler, Lorraine Gates. *The Weight of Their Votes: Southern Women and Political Leverage in the 1920s*. Chapel Hill: University of North Carolina Press, 2006.

Scott, Anne Firor. "Women's Voluntary Associations: From Charity to Reform." In *Lady Bountiful Revisited: Women, Philanthropy and Power*, edited by Kathleen D. McCarthy. London: Rutgers University Press, 1990.

Segrest, Mab. "The Milledgeville Asylum and the Georgia Surreal." *Southern Quarterly* 48, no. 3 (Spring 2011): 114–50.

Shapiro, Herbert. *White Violence and Black Response: From Reconstruction to Montgomery*. Amherst: University of Massachusetts Press, 1988.

Shohat, Ella, and Robert Stam. *Unthinking Eurocentrism: Multiculturalism and the Media*. New York: Routledge, 1994.

Sims, Anastasia. *The Power of Femininity in the New South: Women's Organizations and Politics in North Carolina: 1880–1930*. Columbia: University of South Carolina Press, 1997.

Smith, Greg. "Civilized People Don't Want to See That Kind of Thing: The Decline of Public Physical Punishment in London, 1760–1840." In *Qualities of Mercy: Justice, Punishment, and Discretion*, edited by Carolyn Strange, 21–51. Vancouver: UBC Press, 1996.

Solinger, Rickie. *Wake Up Little Susie: Single Pregnancy and Race before Roe v. Wade*. New York: Routledge, 1992.

Sommerville, Diane Miller. *Rape and Race in the Nineteenth-Century South*. Chapel Hill: University of North Carolina Press, 2004.

Steinberg, Shirley. "The Dialectics of Power: Understanding the Functionality of White Supremacy." In *Engaging Equity: New Perspectives on Anti-Racist Education*, edited by Leeno Karumanchery, 13–26. Calgary: Detselig, 2005.

Srinivas, M.N. *Religion and Society amongst the Coorgs of South India*. Oxford: Clarendon Press, 1952.

Stanley, Amy Dru. "Not Waiting for Deliverance." *Jacobin*, issue 18 (Summer 2015): 43–7.

Stoler, Ann Laura. *Along the Archival Grain: Epistemic Anxieties and Colonial Common Sense*. Princeton: Princeton University Press, 2009.

– *Haunted by Empire*. Durham, NC: Duke University Press, 2006.

– "Making Empire Respectable: The Politics of Race and Sexual Morality in Twentieth-Century Colonial Cultures." In *Dangerous Liaisons: Gender, Nation, and Postcolonial Perspectives*, edited by Anne McClintock, Aamir Mufti, and Ella Shohat. Minneapolis: University of Minnesota Press, 1997.

– *Race and the Education of Desire: Foucault's History of Sexuality and the Colonial Order of Things*. Durham, NC: Duke University Press, 1995.

– "Tense and Tender Ties: The Politics of Comparison in North American History and (Post) Colonial Studies." *Journal of American History* 88, no. 3 (2001): 829–65.

Strange, Carolyn. "The Undercurrents of Penal Culture: Punishment of the Body in Mid-Twentieth-Century Canada." *Law and History Review* 19, no. 2 (2001): 343–85.

Strange, Carolyn, ed. *Qualities of Mercy: Justice, Punishment, and Discretion*. Vancouver: UBC Press, 1996.

Strange, Carolyn, and Tina Loo. *Making Good: Law and Moral Regulation in Canada, 1867–1939*. Toronto: University of Toronto Press, 1997.

Streib, Victor L. "Death Penalty for Female Offenders." *University of Cincinnati Law Review* 58, no. 3 (1990): 845–80.

Swift, Wiley Hampton Committee, National Child Labor. *Child Welfare in North Carolina*. 1918. Reprint London: Forgotten Books, 2013.

Tannenbaum, Frank. *The Darker Phases of the South*. New York: G.P. Putnam's Sons, 1924.

Thapar, Romila. "The Image of the Barbarian in Early India." *Comparative Studies in Society and History* 13, no. 4 (1971): 408–36.

Tindall, George. *The Emergence of the New South, 1913–1945*. Baton Rouge: Louisiana State University Press and the Littlefield Fund for Southern History of the University of Texas, 1967.

Tocqueville, Alexis de. *Democracy in America*. Vol. 1. New York: Vintage, 1945.

Trost, Jennifer. *Gateway to Justice: The Juvenile Court and Progressive Child Welfare in a Southern City*. Athens: University of Georgia Press, 2005.

Valint, Andrew R. "Fighting for Recognition: The Role African Americans Played in World Fairs." MA thesis, Buffalo State, State University of New York, 2011. http://digitalcommons.buffalostate.edu/history_theses/3/

Valverde, Mariana. *The Age of Light, Soap and Water: Moral Reform in English Canada, 1885–1925*. Toronto: McClelland & Stewart, 1991.

– Editor's introduction to *Studies in Moral Regulation*, edited by M. Valverde. Toronto: Centre of Criminology, 1994.

Vann Woodward, C. *Origins of the New South 1877–1913*. Baton Rouge: Louisiana State University Press and the Littlefield Fund for Southern History of the University of Texas, 1971.

Waggoner, Martha. "Deaf-Mute Jailed Unjustly for 69 Years." *Toronto Star*, 1 February 1996, A4.

Waldrep, Christopher. *African Americans Confront Lynching: Strategies of Resistance from the Civil War to the Civil Rights Era*. New York: Rowman & Littlefield, 2009.

Washington, Booker T. *Up from Slavery – An Autobiography*. Sioux Falls, SD: NuVision Publications, 2007.

Wells, Ida B. *Crusade for Justice: The Autobiography of Ida B. Wells*. Edited by Alfreda M. Duster. Chicago: University of Chicago Press, 2013.

– *Selected Works of Ida B. Wells-Barnett*. Edited by Trudier Harris. New York: Oxford University Press, 1991.

– "Southern Horrors: Lynch Law in All Its Phases." In *Selected Works of Ida B. Wells-Barnett*, edited by Trudier Harris. New York: Oxford University Press, 1991.

Welter, Barbara. "The Cult of True Womanhood: 1820–1860." *American Quarterly* 18 (1966): 151–74.

– *Dimity Convictions: The American Woman in the Nineteenth Century*. Columbus: University of Ohio Press, 1977.

Wertheimer, John, Brian Luskey, et al. "'Escape of the match-strikers': Disorderly North Carolina Women, the Legal System, and the Samarcand Arson Case of 1931." *North Carolina Historical Review* 75 (1998): 435–60.

White, Deborah Gray. "Mining the Forgotten: Manuscript Sources for Black Women's History." *Journal of American History* 74 (1987): 237–42.

Wiebe, R.H. *The Search for Order, 1877–1920*. New York: Hill and Wang, 1967.

Wiegman, Robyn. *American Anatomies: Theorizing Race and Gender*. Durham, NC: Duke University Press, 1995.

Williams, Eric. *Capitalism and Slavery*. New York: Russell and Russell, 1941.

Williams, Raymond. *Marxism and Literature*. Oxford: Oxford University Press, 1978.

Williamson, Joel. *The Crucible of Race*. New York: Oxford University Press, 1984.

Wilson, Charles Reagan. *Baptized in Blood: The Religion of the Lost Cause, 1865–1920*. Athens: University of Georgia Press, 1980.

Wishy, Bernard. *The Child and the Republic: The Dawn of Child Nurture*. Philadelphia: University of Pennsylvania Press, 1967.

Wolfensberger, Wolf. *The Origin and Nature of Our Institutional Models*. New York: Human Polity Press, 1975.

Wright, Barry. "The Politics of Pardons and the Upper Canada Rebellion." In *Qualities of Mercy: Justice, Punishment, and Discretion*, edited by Carolyn Strange, 77–103. Vancouver: UBC Press, 1996.

Yuval-Davis, Nira. *Gender and Nation*. London: Sage, 1997.

Ziarek, Ewa Płonowska. "Bare Life on Strike: Notes on the Biopolitics of Race and Gender." *South Atlantic Quarterly* 107, no. 1 (2008): 89–105.

Websites and Web Articles

Historical essay: "Legislative Interests" / "The Negroes' Temporary Farewell: Jim Crow and the Exclusion of African Americans from Congress, 1887–1929." Black Americans in Congress, US Congress. http://history.house.gov/Exhibitions-and-Publications/BAIC/Historical-Essays/Temporary-Farewell/Introduction/.

Butterfield, Fox. "Ideas & Trends: Southern Curse; Why America's Murder Rate Is So High," *New York Times*, 26 July 1998. http://www.nytimes.com/1998/07/26/weekinreview/ideas-trends-southern-curse-why-america-s-murder-rate-is-so-high.html?pagewanted=all

Clephane, Elizabeth C. "The Ninety and Nine." *Timeless Truths: Free Online Library*. 1868. http://library.timelesstruths.org/music/The_Ninety_and_Nine/

Eugenics Archive, DNA Learning Center, Cold Spring Harbor Laboratory. http://www.eugenicsarchive.org/eugenics/

Linder, Douglas. "Who Is Clarence Darrow?" http://law2.umkc.edu/faculty/projects/ftrials/daresy.htm

North Carolina State Board of Charities and Public Welfare. "Swamp Island: A Study of Conditions in an Isolated Section of North Carolina." Raleigh, NC: NC Division of Social Services, Dept. of Health and Human Services North Carolina, 1921. http://worldcat.org/oclc/16894888/viewonline

Wikipedia contributors. "Parable of the Prodigal Son." *Wikipedia, The Free Encyclopedia*. Last modified 8 February 2015. http://en.wikipedia.org/wiki/Parable_of_the_Prodigal_Son

Index

capital punishment, 64, 67–8; Civil
War, 7, 10–11; concept of racial
purity, 121; criminal justice system,
197–8; discourses on interracial
sex, 209–10n55; domestic politics
during Great Depression, 168;
economy in post–Civil War,
204–5n26, 205n28; emancipation
in the South, 231n1; execution
of children, 68; expansionism,
11–12; federal census of
institutionalized children,
161; Fifteenth Amendment of
Constitution, 132; Fourteenth
Amendment of Constitution,
12; free labour, 12, 14; historical
memory of emancipation,
15–16; imprisonment of women
of African descent, 234n40;
inmate population, 197; internal
colonialism, 18; juvenile
population, 249n135; legal
execution of women and children,
65–8; Modoc War, 197; national
amnesia, 14, 16; national identity,
12–13; prison industrial complex,
198, 199; racial politics of culture,
25–6; racism, 176, 196, 197, 200;
recognition of African Americans
as citizens, 132; reformatory
institutions, 143; reproductive
rights, 239–40n115; rights of
prisoners, 198–9; slavery, 204n21,
246n90; violence against prisoners,
196–7; War on Drugs, 199–200;
War on Terror, 197; women
convicts, 67

vagrancy, 53
Valverde, Mariana, 30, 50

Vanzetti, Bartolomeo, 66
Varner, L.R., 146

Washington, Booker T., 14, 130, 145
Watson, G.W., 187
Watts, Bettie, 86
Watts, Mildred, 43–4
wayward children, 50–1
Wells, Ida B., 117, 131, 138, 196, 234n34
Wells, Maude, 31, 52, 104
Wertheimer, John, 68, 69, 70, 71
White, Benjamin, 131
White, Deborah Gray, 113
White, George, 132
White, Walter, 139
white middle class, 36–7, 49, 214n20
whiteness, racial concept of, 118, 121
white virgin, iconography of, 133
white women and girls:
    criminalization of, 74–5;
    glorification of, 118–19, 242n38;
    political representation of, 99, 189–90
Wiegman, Robyn, 119, 120, 121
Wilkes, Annie, 29
Wilkes, Jane, 39
Willard, Francis, 134
Williams, Alfred, 139
Williams, Fannie Barrier, 117
Williamson, Joel, 131
Wilmington Coup d'État, 14–16
Wilson, Charles, 242n38
Wilson, Estelle, 60, 61, 84, 88
Wilson, Junius, 213n16
Winston, Ellen, 101
Winston-Salem Journal, 103, 110
Wolfensberger, Wolf, 93
Women's migration restrictions, 218n53
Woodward, C. Vann, 5, 206n34

Yoo, John C., 197